SURVIVAL
HOLOCAUST SURVIVORS TELL THEIR STORY

... Although some survivors of the Holocaust published their memoirs soon after the war, they failed to attract wide attention as they were written mainly in languages unfamiliar to readers in the western world. The majority of the survivors found it difficult to describe what had happened to them. It was still too early to face the past. Only the passage of time and the insistence of their children and grandchildren made it possible for them to talk about their experiences and to write their memoirs.

In recent years, many survivor memoirs have been published in England... In this excellent compendium, the editor, Wendy Whitworth, has done well to select wide-ranging material so as to highlight different aspects of the Holocaust experience. She has achieved this by gathering together glimpses from survivors originating from Poland, Hungary, former Czechoslovakia, France, Germany, Holland, Belgium, Austria, and even from former Palestine. The accounts of the survivors do not have the searing emotional impact of Elie Wiesel or the profound reflection of the human condition of Primo Levi. The importance of these stories rests not on what they have to say about this or that unsolved problem of the Holocaust. It lies rather in the unforgettable image of young boys and girls living in a time of unparalleled cruelty and horror, struggling to survive, displaying remarkable courage, never giving up hope. It should be of interest to the average reader and of great help to teachers and their pupils.

Ben Helfgott
Chairman of the '45 Aid Society Holocaust Survivors.

SURVIVAL

HOLOCAUST
SURVIVORS
TELL THEIR
STORY

SURVIVAL

HOLOCAUST
SURVIVORS
TELL THEIR
STORY

FOREWORD BY SIR MARTIN GILBERT

EDITED BY WENDY WHITWORTH

Quill

in association with

THE
HOLOCAUST
CENTRE

SURVIVAL
HOLOCAUST SURVIVORS TELL
THEIR STORY

EDITED BY WENDY WHITWORTH

Published in Great Britain by
Quill Press in association with The Holocaust Centre
Laxton, Newark, Nottinghamshire
NG22 0PA

© 2003 Quill Press
Second Edition, April 2004

First published in Great Britain by
Quill Press in association with The Aegis Institute
Lound Hall, Bothamsall, Retford,
Nottinghamshire. DN22 8DF

British Library Catalogue in Publication Data
A catalogue record for this book is available from the British
Library

ISBN 0-9543001-1-4

Printed and bound by Jellyfish Print Solutions, Swanmore

To all the people whose stories were never told

CONTENTS

CONTENTS

CONTENTS

Sir Martin Gilbert

Foreword

Many peoples have suffered through history, and been the victims of persecution and mass murder. Few have left such copious testimonies as the survivors of the Holocaust. Throughout their history, the Jews have been adept at recording their experiences. The Bible is a sustained and often dramatic historical narrative, replete with individual stories, conversations, confrontations and debate. At Passover, Jews recite a vivid narrative of the exodus from Egypt. At Purim, the averted destruction of the Jews of Persia is given graphic representation in the reading of the Book of Esther.

During the Holocaust, many Jews kept diaries, or were encouraged to record their experiences while the destruction was at its height. The great Jewish historian Simon Dubnov is said to have cried out, as he was shot down in the streets of Riga in December 1941, *"Schreibt – und farschreibt"* ("Write – and record!") Even in Auschwitz-Birkenau, members of the *Sonderkommando*, Jewish slave labourers forced to work in and around the gas chambers before being themselves murdered, kept notes and buried them in the earth for posterity to learn what had taken place at the very centre of mass murder.

From the first days of the post-war world, when so much of what had happened was still unknown, survivors began to write, and to publish their memoirs. Most of the early ones were in Yiddish. The number who wrote their memoirs was small. In the first decade after the war fewer than a hundred Holocaust memoirs had been published. Even today the number is certainly no larger than four or five thousand, including those privately printed and with a limited distribution. That means that only five per cent of survivors have published their memoirs in book form. Perhaps another five per cent have written manuscripts but never published them.

Finding publishers is often hard. There is a limit to the number of memoirs that can be published even by a publishing house to which Holocaust memoirs are a priority – such as Vallentine Mitchell, whose Library of Holocaust Testimonies, begun in 1982, now numbers more than 40 titles. A new venture, the Holocaust Memoir Digest, provides teachers and students with a detailed summary and quotations from individual memoirs: and is about to publish the first of its annual volumes; it will include a number of memoirs in each volume.

It is at this point that the Holocaust Centre at Beth Shalom makes a significant contribution to Holocaust literature and Holocaust memory. Like the Library of Holocaust Testimonies and the Holocaust Memoir Digest – both mentioned above – the task of this Holocaust Centre book, *Survival: Holocaust Survivors Tell Their Story*, is to make the stories of the Holocaust more widely known to both teachers – who need the highest quality material, which is also easy to use – and to students. Beth Shalom, under whose auspices this book is published, is a leading contributor to Holocaust education.

The needs of students include accessibility, clarity, detail, and a human voice. It was Elie Wiesel who wrote: "Memory is transformed into study, and study into memory," and this is nowhere more true than in the work being done to provide survivor testimonies in a highly readable and usable form. In this book, brevity is used as the road to understanding. Each of the survivors whose recollections are included in this volume has been able to convey aspects of the Holocaust in a short, powerful and direct manner: in no more than a few pages, through which shine suffering and hope, grim experiences and, above all, the will to live. Each account casts yet more light on some aspect of the dark story.

The fact that each recollection is short adds to the impact of this book. It is a moving, strong, wide-ranging, informative, passionate and personal portrayal of an era that must never be forgotten, and from which future generations will learn that, alongside the torment and evil-doing, stands the strength and nobility of the human spirit. One voice in this book concludes with what so many of the voices express; it is that of Josef Perl, who went through horrors as terrible as those of any survivor, and who writes: "My experiences have not destroyed my belief in humanity's goodness."

Martin Gilbert
Merton College
Oxford
12 March 2003

Marina H. Smith

Introduction

Every life is different. Every story is different too. This may seem like stating the obvious, but this book came about precisely because the more I worked with survivors, the more deeply touched I was, not by the similarity of the form of brutality they shared, but the variation of their struggle to live.

When we created the Holocaust Centre at Beth Shalom, in the mid-1990s, we made it an objective to create a place where survivors would feel at home. We hoped they would feel that it went some small way to providing a place of respect for the loved ones they had had snatched away from them. We wanted to reassure them that memory would be permanent and dignified, that not only would their stories be told, but they would be embedded in the fabric of the centre and its life. As such, Beth Shalom was never solely a place of documentary history, but one where personal histories were woven into a rich texture of narrative and reflection, where the lives of those who endured the worst excesses of the Holocaust would be heard and respected. Most of all we wanted survivors to feel at home there, to feel comfortable bringing their children and grandchildren to a place where they could speak to a new generation of young people.

Beth Shalom has found a place in the minds and hearts of many survivors who saw it as their memorial, their education centre, their statement to the world. The result of this has been an inspiring friendship and sense of purpose shared with members of the survivor community. Every one of the 500 children who visits the centre each week has listened intently to personal testimony and shared questions like "Can you forgive?"; "Have you been back?"; "Can you believe in God?" Survivors have written books and poems, created works of art, contributed to educational resources, and shared with professionals from many walks of life. The dialogue has been rich, the questions endless.

From all these experiences it seemed time to invite our friends and colleagues to contribute to a single volume of short testimonies. All the people in this book have worked at the centre in a voluntary capacity at some point. Most have shared their testimonies; all have shared their lives. We did not realise how large and significant this contribution had been, and still is. We looked at the list, to discover almost 50 people; all with a story to tell.

The result is this volume. All of the survivors have condensed the largest chapter of their lives into just a short chapter for this book. None of them are more than a single frame of a movie that could run for hours. But nevertheless they are vivid, poignant and deeply personal, for those who have written and for those who will read them too. They are not intended as comprehensive life histories, but as vignettes of the most significant reflections these individuals have 60 years on. They have all been authored individually and edited and compiled by Wendy Whitworth. They are presented in alphabetical order and cover the gamut of refugee and Kindertransport experience, ghetto, labour camp, death camp and experiences in hiding. There is flight, rescue and resistance, denial and collaboration. Every one of them is a story of families shattered by the most hideous of all human actions – the act of genocide. In these 400 pages one family after the next is torn apart, whose faint and ever-fading memories fill the gaps between the lines.

I know personally all of the people in this volume. I have shared many long hours with most, more fleeting times with a few. But from everything I have learned and shared with each of them, I know that I have only ever heard a fraction – and understand a mere sliver of that. But I do know how much it has meant for these authors to encapsulate a few pages of their lives and place them alongside those who have shared that similar painful journey. And so when this volume sits on my shelf, it will be more than a collection of short testimonies; it will be an indelible insight into their lives, a reflection of their dedication and a memorial to all those whom they loved and lost.

For that, every word carries its message and its silence.

Marina H. Smith
Founder, Beth Shalom

ACKNOWLEDGEMENTS

This book could not have been compiled and published without the constant help and guidance of the Smith family, founders of Beth Shalom Holocaust Centre, and above all the inspiring leadership and invaluable guidance of Marina Smith. Not only did she create the original concept for the book, but she nurtured and developed the project from its earliest beginnings and was key to the gathering of such a wide range of authors. Deep-felt thanks go to Marina for the warmth of her support and encouragement at all stages of the publication, and her guidance and suggestions throughout.

I am most grateful to Sir Martin Gilbert for his thoughtful Foreword to the book, and to Jane Cocker, both for the compilation of the Notes for Teachers and for helpful suggestions throughout from an educational point of view. Special thanks also go to another teacher, Fiona Assersohn, who read the texts and gave me the benefit of her advice and ideas.

I would also like to thank the Design team at Beth Shalom, especially Glen Powell, for their important contribution to the production of the volume.

Last, but most important of all, my sincere thanks and admiration go to all the survivors who have co-operated so effectively and efficiently with me. It has been a pleasure to work with them all, and I have learned so much from their courage and resilience.

Wendy Whitworth
Cambridge
March 2003

Map showing the locations of the main Nazi concentration and death camps

Victoria, Milan, 1939

VICTORIA ANCONA-VINCENT

Beyond Imagination

I was born in Jerusalem on 26 June 1923, the youngest of nine children. My mother died when she was 39 years old, shortly after my birth. My father, Saul Mordecai Ancona, was a banker and stockbroker and had moved to Jerusalem from Syria, where he was born. I have many happy memories of that time in Jerusalem although I was only six years old when we left for Brussels.

My father remarried a kind French woman, Esther Bijio, whom we called Aunt Esther, and decided in 1930 to transfer his business to Brussels. His financial situation was good and we lived surrounded by luxury. We continued to celebrate the Jewish festivals as we had done in Jerusalem. At school I never felt the need to hide the fact that I was Jewish. Antisemitism was never a problem to us there. My brothers and sisters studied, married and moved away and by 1935 there were only three of us living with our father and stepmother – my sisters Olga, Rachel and myself.

In 1936 my father transferred his business to Alexandria, Egypt and we joined him in July 1937. I do not remember much about our short stay there, but the business was not a success, and so in December 1937 my father returned to Europe via Italy. Two months later, we rejoined him in Milan. He immediately applied for the family to be included in the USA Italian Immigration Quota, intending to take us to New York, but by the summer of 1938 we had not received any notification for our names to be included, and we never did. When we tried to renew our passports, they were confiscated by the authorities and we were forced to remain in Italy.

I went to a French school in Milan until July 1938 when Italy proclaimed racial laws forbidding Jews from attending non-Jewish schools. Then I went to a Jewish school until June 1939, when the Italian fascist government closed all Jewish schools. The racial laws in Italy closed around us like a net.

My father had not been permitted to start any new business and Jews could only find employment as 'undeclared employees', paid much less than the normal rate. My father was unable to find any employment. In

1

June 1939 he tried to arrange for me to go to Israel as I had been born there. But the regulation was that I required two years' subsistence money and this was out of the question. In a couple of years, we had gone from being comfortably off to being without any means of supporting ourselves.

To earn some money, I gave some private French lessons to children and adults. Individually the Italians were sympathetic towards the Jews, even though they were at risk with the authorities for employing them. But new restrictions were brought in against Jews in September 1939: identity cards now had to carry the word 'Jew' and the owner's thumbprint. Since we were law-abiding citizens, we dutifully complied with every restriction.

Our father's financial situation continued to deteriorate and he was forced to sell jewellery, furniture and carpets. By March 1940 when I was not yet 17, I was so angry at not finding work and always being hungry that without telling anyone, I wrote a letter to the Italian fascist leader, Benito Mussolini,

> Dear Sir,
> Perhaps you do not realize that because Jews are not allowed to work, they are going hungry. Jews are also made of flesh and blood. I am sure you will find it in the kindness of your heart to revoke the racial laws. I thank you in advance. [My translation]

As a result of my letter, I was asked to report in person on 3 May 1940 to the Police Headquarters in Milan. I waited for over two hours and was then called into the office of the Chief of Police. I was informed that Mussolini had received my letter and replied that there was nothing he could do to help the Jews.

At the beginning of 1940, the Italian government set up Labour legions for all foreign-born Jews. Accordingly, in June 1940, my sisters and I had to report to a box-making factory, where about 20 Jewish girls were working. We were paid less than the regular Italian workers and by comparison to them, were considered too slow and unsuitable. As a result, we were dismissed after only six weeks. At the end of July 1940 I found work in a typing agency, then I worked in a bookshop from December 1940. In October 1941, I took a day off to look for a better job and I enquired at Cappelli Publishers in Via Francesco Sforza. I was interviewed by a man named Franco Maisano. He was pleased that I had experience working in a bookshop and that I could speak English and French. He said he did not have a vacancy but he thought he might be able to help me. In giving me back my identity card, which was stamped with the word 'Jewish,' he said, "It's all right, do not worry." He quickly wrote a quick note and gave it to

me, addressed to Miss Giovanna Fogagnolo, 40 Corso Venezia. The following day I went to the bookshop and I met Miss Fogaglono and gave her the
envelope from Mr Maisano. After a little while, he came into the shop and
they both went into a back room. They soon came out and offered me
undeclared employment to start work on 15 October 1941. They seemed
very pleased I could speak English.

From the end of 1941, Milan was regularly bombed and we spent many
nights seeking shelter in the cellars. Often we would have to walk to work
because the trains were out of action. Sometimes Miss Fogagnolo, my
employer at the bookshop, would give me sealed envelopes to deliver and I
noticed that there were occasionally large sums of money in the cash box.
Throughout that winter, I became ever more curious about these parcels,
the money and visits from unfamiliar men to the shop. Eventually Miss
Fogagnolo told me that she and her fiancé were helping certain people to
avoid arrest. They knew I was Jewish and told me that they were in the
Resistance and were helping Jews. The parcels contained hidden messages
for the Resistance. Although I was then 18, I still looked only 15 and
perhaps I had the right innocent appearance for a Resistance messenger.

By this time, our financial situation at home was getting desperate and
we really had a problem whenever the rent was due. There was nothing
more my father could sell and he was forced to ask the Jewish community
for help. This was very painful for him because before he had always given
large donations to the Jewish communities. Italian monthly food rationing
was minimal, and my stepmother was reduced to collecting discarded
vegetables on her daily visits to the market. These were terrible and humiliating times for Jews.

With the fall of Italy's fascist government, Mussolini was arrested on
25 July 1943 and imprisoned. To most Italians, and above all to the Jews, it
was as if a dark cloud had been lifted from over our heads. All of a sudden,
there were no fascist Black Shirts to be seen and people started smiling and
talking to each other, without any fear of being overheard. But on 10
September 1943, Mussolini was rescued by the Germans, who were now
occupying the northern half of Italy. They then put him in charge of a
puppet government.

From the time of Mussolini's arrest, the bookshop where I worked had
been used by the Italian resistance to give overnight shelter, food and clothing to Allied prisoners of war, and to help them reach Switzerland. At
9 a.m. on 9 November 1943, two Germans in civilian clothing, whom I
suspected were Gestapo, entered the bookshop and asked for Miss
Fogagnolo. She had not yet arrived, but I was unable to warn her. When
they returned, they took our identity cards and without any questioning,

arrested us both and took us to San Vittore prison, Milan. We were put in the political section and locked in cells.

I was very worried about my family who knew nothing abut my work with the Italian Resistance. After the war, I learned that on the day of my arrest, the Gestapo searched our flat, looking for anything connecting me to the Resistance. My family were not arrested, but decided to go into hiding immediately with friends of my sister Rachel. These non-Jewish friends sheltered my father, stepmother and Rachel until the end of the war.

In San Vittore prison, a British prisoner of war was being used by the Germans as an interpreter. He was very kind and said he would try to hide my papers and delay my interrogation. I was not interrogated by the Gestapo for six months, but at the end of April 1944, my turn eventually came. Unnecessary and irrelevant questions were repeated over and over again, as were the slaps and beatings. I do not know what they sought to achieve as my fate had already been decided simply by virtue of my racial status.

After the brutal interrogation, I was moved from the political to the Jewish section of the prison on 3 May 1944. On the evening of 15 May, I was transported with all the Jews in the section to Fossoli transit camp near Modena. The next evening about 575 men, women and children were marched to the railway siding at the edge of Fossoli camp and loaded into cattle wagons by SS guards. We were given a small piece of bread and a bucket of water to be shared among 100 of us. Nothing else. The wagon doors were sealed and the trains set off. We had no idea where we were going. We were so cramped that we had to take it in turns to sit with our legs stretched out. All that was provided was a metal drum for us to relieve ourselves in front of each other. It was humiliating in the extreme.

At least three people died during the journey in our carriage. We nearly suffocated from the stench and the lack of air. We had to take it in turns to breathe fresh air from the small grilles, near the top of the wagon, climbing over each other's legs. Our train was destined for Auschwitz-Birkenau and during that terrible, six-day journey, the doors were only opened once for us to empty the latrine drums. We were give another bucket of water, but no food. The SS did not take the dead out of the wagons.

We arrived in the evening of 22 May 1944, but were left in the sealed wagons until the morning of 23 May. The doors were opened by men in striped clothing, and SS guards with barking dogs herded us out of the wagons shouting "'*Raus!* '*Raus! Schnell! Schnell!*'" (Out! Quickly!) I did not know where we were, nor what was really going on there. As we had been waiting in the wagon, we had been aware of the very strong odour of burning flesh, but could not understand what it was. We certainly did not even consider that they might be burning people. What we were about to encounter was beyond imagination.

After climbing out of the wagon, we were separated from the men and arranged in rows of five. Slowly the column moved forward until I found myself standing before a small wooden desk. I was later to discover that the SS officer conducting the selection that day was the notorious Dr Mengele, who with the move of his finger indicated left towards death, and right to live a little while longer. He calmly sent the old, the infirm, the sick, the women with children, the pregnant women, the young women who would not leave their mothers or older relations, all to the left side. The few of us who remained were marched away. Of the 575 on the transport, only 57 were not sent straight to the gas chambers.

We were taken to a low brick building, ordered to undress and our bodies were searched by male deportees. Every piece of jewellery was taken from us. We were then pushed into the shower room and when we came out, our belongings and clothing were gone. Next, other male deportees shaved our heads, armpits and between our legs. I felt very ashamed. After waiting what seemed to be hours, we were given our 'new' clothes. I was given ill-fitting wooden clogs and a dirty-looking, rough dress. We were then ordered to go into another room where female deportees were sitting at small tables. When my turn came, the girl asked my name, age and where I came from. She then tattooed my left forearm with the number A-5346, my new identity.

We were marched in ranks of five to the quarantine section of the camp where I was to spend the next two months. As we walked, we saw flames coming out of a very tall chimney. It was not long before we knew the horrifying truth: Jews were being gassed and burned here.

In our block, there were three-tier bunks, each covered with a thin straw mattress and a blanket. We were given a reddish-brown tin bowl which we kept tied round our waist, day and night. Without it, we would not be given soup or the brownish, watery liquid they called coffee.

Our daily routine was one of hunger, exhaustion and fear. We were awakened at three or four in the morning for roll-call and had to stand outside in silence, whatever the weather, in rows of five, for over three hours until the SS had counted everyone in the camp. After that, we were given weak, tepid liquid which was called coffee. Nothing else. For most of the day, we had to wait at the back of the block, to be detailed for work in the camp. In the middle of the day, we were given soup, in which there were potato peelings and the occasional cabbage leaf or small piece of swede. After afternoon roll-call, we were given a small chunk of nearly black, very dry bread with a tiny piece of rancid margarine, a blob of sugar beet jam or a small slice of something resembling salami. Nothing to drink. Thirst and dehydration were a constant agony.

On 15 June 1944, some girls from our block were waiting to go for our first shower in the camp. As we waited, I saw a group of women deportees approaching with SS guards. They were talking and I thought I heard my sister Olga's voice. I waited until the group came nearer and shouted her name in disbelief. I was shocked when she actually turned round and looked at me. We recognised each other, difficult as it was in such circumstances. We did not have time to touch hands and only managed to say a few words. Occasionally, when my sister's group returned in the evening from their work in the *Schuhkommando* (Shoe work group) she would try to see and speak to me. One day, she gave me a clove of garlic which she had 'organised' – it was my 21st birthday.

In August 1944 I joined my sister at the *Schuhkommando*. I later learned that Olga had given several of her bread rations so that I could be with her. After morning roll-call, we left the camp for work, which was about 60 minutes walking distance away. We had to line up in columns of five per row and anyone out of line would be beaten, punished or threatened with being sent to the crematorium. Near the camp gate, an orchestra of women deportees was forced to play marches. At the *Schuhkommando* we had to strip the shoes and boots of the deportees with a small sharp tool. Whenever we came across a child's shoes, we were saddened beyond words because we knew what happened to everyone here.

Throughout the months we were in Birkenau, the selections for the gas chambers were carried out at any time. We were forced to stand naked outside and wait for hours for Dr Mengele and other SS. When our turn came, we tried to stop shivering, stand very straight and look strong. It was beyond any human understanding why some of us were deemed fit for work and others to die.

Being together was a great comfort for my sister and me, but we also had constant worry for each other. In addition to the selections, there were many deaths from typhus, cholera, dysentery, beatings and starvation. We were also at great risk of being chosen for 'medical' experiments by Dr Mengele and his staff. From the day we arrived to the day we left Auschwitz-Birkenau, trainloads of deportees continued to arrive night and day, from many countries in Europe.

On 29 September 1944 we were transferred from Auschwitz-Birkenau to the main Auschwitz camp. There we were housed in brick buildings, but otherwise the treatment was the same. When work at the *Schuhkommando* was finished, we were made to move paving stones, broken stones or heavy planks of wood. The following day we had to move them back again. This useless task was one of the ways in which the SS tried to dehumanise us.

As the months went by, it became bitterly cold with icy winds. Some of us were clothed in only a thin dress and had no cover on our shaven heads. But our group of friends had managed to stay together and we never allowed ourselves to feel nostalgic. We never cried. We never said *if* we get back home, but *when*. We spoke of composers and authors and tried to remember bars of music and titles of books.

Very early in the morning of 18 January 1945, the SS hastily evacuated Auschwitz camp because of the Russian advance. We were told to take a blanket, but were given no food or drink. It was freezing cold. The death march had begun.

Deportees who stepped out of line, stopped or did not keep up were shot dead. The second day, 19 January, was still bitterly cold and it continued snowing. We were very thirsty but were given nothing to drink. We tried to collect clean snow to quench our thirst. We had been walking since early morning and we passed through some villages. At one of them, some women came out of their houses and gave us jugs of water. The SS kept pushing them back with rife butts. We walked all day with short halts, without any food or drink. At intervals, we heard rifle or revolver shots and we knew that more deportees were being shot dead.

On the third day, 20 January, the death march started at dawn. By now the rifle shots had increased so much that each one sounded like an echo of the previous one. We were very tired and so weak that we slept as we marched like automatons.

On the fourth day, 21 January, we were taken to a train and pushed into open wagons. There were about 70 deportees in each wagon and one SS armed guard. It snowed most of the time and the wind was icy cold. We were very cramped. We spent the rest of the day, the night and part of the fifth day, 22 January, travelling in the wagons.

On the evening of the fifth day, we were ordered off the train and the death march resumed. At 2 a.m. on the sixth day, 23 January, we arrived at Ravensbrück camp. We had to sleep outside in the snow, one blanket underneath two of us and one blanket covering us. It was bitterly cold and we could not stop shivering. When dawn came, we were marched to a reception area and given new numbers. A large group of us were put in the washrooms and all the time we were in Ravensbrück camp, we had to sleep there on the bare floor. Our food ration was as bad as in Auschwitz-Birkenau and sometimes worse.

On 11 February 1945, we were transferred to Malchow, north-east of Ravensbrück, and put in a huge, single-storey building. We slept on thin pallets. Our clothing was nothing but rags and full of lice, which caused a continuous itching. By now we were very much weaker. The bread ration had been getting smaller and many deportees fainted at roll-calls. We thought and spoke of nothing but food.

On 2 April 1945 we were transferred to Leipzig camp. There was no change in our small ration of food, nor in the brutal treatment of the SS. Eleven days later, the SS evacuated the camp and our second death march lasted nine nights and eight days. During that time, we were only once given food – a handful of raw rice. We spent every night in the open and walked all day. We were in a terrible physical state. To get some moisture we chewed grass and spat it out, we ate dandelions and when we could get them the tops of swedes. We had to be careful for the SS shot anyone who went near the fields, stopped or lagged behind. We heard distant heavy gunfire. We hoped it was the Russians advancing from the east or the Allies from the west.

The SS seemed to be in confused disarray and were marching us in circles. More than once we saw the same signposts. On 22 April 1945 we finally arrived at the River Elbe. We continued to hear heavy gunfire and knew the battle was getting closer. We sensed that the SS themselves were now becoming afraid.

My five remaining friends and I decided to take advantage of the dark night and escape. We quickly crossed the road and carried on walking until we came to a hut where some Italians in soldiers' uniforms were actually boiling potatoes. They gave us some food and sheltered us for the night. We then spent the rest of the day hiding and before nightfall found refuge in a wooden shed. Throughout the night we could hear the sound of gunfire.

At dawn on 24 April, there was a lull in the battle and the five of us decided to go out and see what was happening. At some distance away, we saw a soldier on horseback coming towards us. To our great relief, it was a Russian officer, who on seeing our starved appearance, pointed to some suitcases containing food, which had been left on the roadside by fleeing German civilians. He made us understand that we should take the road towards the east, through a thickly wooded area. By this time my sister Olga had developed a painful and swollen knee. She had great difficulty walking without my help. The two of us trailed behind the others and as we rested, our thoughts went back to our sufferings in the camps and on the death marches. I knew it was only our love for each other that had given us the strength to survive.

We could hear gunfire once again, and the Russian soldiers who passed us told us we must hurry as there was a German counter-attack. We finally came to the end of the wooded area, to a deserted village. We were exhausted and Olga could walk no further. We entered one of the deserted houses and slept on a bed for the first time in over 12 months.

From 24 April to 5 May 1945, we walked from village to village, eating wherever we found food and sleeping in deserted houses. After 12 days of walking, we finally reached Cottbus on 5 May. The camp there was run by the Russians for Italian military ex-internees and we were the only women. We stayed there for 76 days and during the first five weeks were terribly weak and ill with diarrhoea and sickness. There were no doctors or medicines. The Italian soldiers did what they could to help us. Slowly we were able to take some food and get a little stronger.

On 15 July 1945 the whole camp left for Spremberg, another camp run by the Russians. We stayed there until 2 September when the Russians took us all by train to Mittenwald on the Austrian border, a camp run by the Americans. There we were given food and a place to sleep while we awaited our return journey to Milan.

We eventually arrived in Milan on 12 September 1945. Olga and I were worried because we had no idea what had happened to our family. I telephoned the bookshop where I used to work and was relieved to hear Miss Fogagnolo tell me that as far as she knew, the family was safe and living in Via Glavani school. We went there and found our father, stepmother and our sister Rachel. It was a very emotional reunion. They did not know what had happened to Olga and me after our arrests – not even if we were alive or dead.

After the war, I hoped to try and continue my education because I had always wanted to study medicine. But our financial circumstances were such that Rachel and I had to find employment. My father and stepmother were old and in poor health. We found jobs with the British military as interpreters/clerks. Even then our troubles were far from over. We were given so little help. I felt that survivors from the concentration camps needed professional help for them to accept that they had survived – when six million Jewish men, women and children had been murdered – to remove the guilt for having survived and to learn to live once again. There was so little help and virtually no understanding of our situation. I had to rely on myself and the love of my family.

I went about my daily life, living it on the surface only; inside I was still in Birkenau and on the death marches. I felt I was surrounded by an electric wire fence which I could not break through. The nights were worse. My nightmares were so clear and vivid as I relived the horrors of the concentration camps.

At the end of March 1946 I met a British soldier, Alfred Vincent, who befriended me. He was gentle, kind and very patient. With his help, I gradually regained my self confidence. Alfred and I became engaged, and in December 1946 we were married. In the summer of 1947 we moved to Nottingham in the UK with our new son David. I settled into my life in England quite quickly and have happy memories of my first years here.

David our son is married to Jill. We have a lovely granddaughter, Sarah Rachel Victoria, and a grandson, Jonathan Alexander James. My father would have been very proud to know that after living through the racial laws against Jews, living in hiding and surviving the concentration camps and death marches, Olga, Rachel and I remained as close together as we had always been.

Victoria died on 5 August 1996 and her story has been adapted from her book, *Beyond Imagination*, (Witness Collection, Beth Shalom, 1995).

This story is dedicated to Victoria's two sisters: to Olga who understands everything; and to Rachel who shares it all.

Victoria and her father, Milan, 1938

Toby, 2003 (By kind permission of Richard Kolker)

TOBY BIBER

Life Would Never Be The Same Again

When the Germans invaded Poland on 1 September 1939, I was 14 years old, but neither my grandparents, parents, my four sisters and two brothers nor all our aunts, uncles and cousins (of whom there were many), realized that our lives would never be the same again.

I was born Toby Trompeter, into a happy, middle-class Orthodox Jewish family in the town of Mielec in southern Poland and our home was at 13 Sandomierska Street. My father was a grain merchant and my mother ran her own business, a general store. As I truly remember, it was a close, comfortable and very happy existence.

For Jews in Poland, however, life was never really comfortable; the Poles were and are antisemitic; educational opportunities were limited because Orthodox Jews would not send their children to compulsory Saturday school (because of *Shabbat*, the Sabbath), and for young men like my eldest brother, there was the possibility of conscription into the Polish army.

I became aware that something might happen in the months leading up to the invasion. There were a lot of rumours, but often not real news; too few people had radios. However, we were concerned, and when the war started, our town, which had an aeroplane factory, was bombed on that first day.

The Germans marched into the town on the eve of Rosh Hashanah (the Jewish New Year) and atrocities began. The Poles were willing collaborators and showed the Germans where the better-off Jews lived and which were the Jewish-owned shops. They were looted.

It took no time for the Germans to carry out their first act of genocide. When the Germans learnt that there were Jews in the *mikveh* (ritual bath house), they herded them, 60 or 70 people, into the square outside and with the help of Poles who brought barrels of oil, burned those 60 or so people alive. The screams of the dying are still a horrible memory. The flames

13

spread to the three synagogues that were just across a square from our home and they burned for days.

After the Russians occupied part of Poland, my mother helped my eldest brother, a *yeshiva* (theological school) student, to escape to the Soviet zone. My other brother was caught by the Germans and sent to a concentration camp. An uncle managed to get to the Russian-occupied zone, but he took the risk of returning for his family. He was caught by the Germans and executed.

We remained in Mielec where life was difficult and dangerous. First, there was the curfew that meant you could only go out at certain times, and then having to wear the yellow Star of David. If a Jew was caught out of doors during the curfew, the result was instant – death by shooting. At other times, one could be rounded up for forced labour tasks. My family for one lived behind drawn curtains, which gave us some sense of security, but not much.

On 9 March 1942, it was a grey and cold day I remember, the Germans rounded up every Jew and drove us to the town square. From there, we were marched to the nearby forest where there were aeroplane hangars, and there we remained for five days without food or water. Not everyone made it. Those unable to walk were shot. The hangars were cold and damp and we had nowhere to sleep but on the damp ground.

From the forest we were moved to a small town called Dubienko. If you were lucky enough, you could obtain forged papers and my father obtained documents for my sister Sarah and myself, so that we could rejoin our relatives. We left our immediate family and never saw them again.

Sarah and I moved from place to place, never staying anywhere for more than a few days at a time. Eventually we reached Krakow, where we remained until the autumn of 1942, when the ghetto was liquidated and we moved into the camp at Plaszow. I say a camp, but there was nothing there except for an old Jewish cemetery. We were made to use the tombstones as material for footpaths and had to build our own huts. As for food, there was something liquid that I still cannot describe and some bread. Those Jews who worked on the outside in Krakow often tried to smuggle in food, an offence punishable by death. On one occasion, a group of maybe 50 or 60 were searched on their return, found to have food and they were executed on the spot.

Some mothers tried to smuggle their children into the camp, but if they were found, they were taken away and never seen again. Children, wherever they were, had no rights.

We worked long hours in a shoe factory and the camp commandant would visit factories to satisfy himself that we were working. He had two vicious dogs which he would sometimes let loose on anyone he may have thought was not working hard enough. They were torn to pieces by those animals.

Then there was the roll-call during which the guards counted us meticulously. If anyone was missing, we had to stand, whatever the weather, until that person was accounted for.

I developed fluid on the lungs and was given a few days off to see if I could recover. The German doctor insisted that I was well enough to work and a Polish-Jewish lady doctor urged me to go back to work as she could then protect me. Her advice was not to get my feet wet.

In the summer of 1943, Sarah and I were deported to Auschwitz-Birkenau. There I was given my number, A 17537, which was tattooed onto my left arm. The most terrifying thing was the selection process. It was cruel and sadistic; if you were sent in one direction, it meant death, in the other it was survival.

In Plaszow we had been able to wear our own clothes; in Auschwitz, all our hair was shaved off, we were given striped dresses and wooden clogs. The tallest people seemed to be given the shortest dresses and the shortest the longest. We looked as if we had escaped from a lunatic asylum.

I was given the job of cleaning the barracks in which we lived. It is hard to describe the conditions. One thousand women to each barracks, in which there was just one latrine and no items for personal hygiene. The death rate was high and each morning bodies had to be removed.

There was no work in Auschwitz and all that we could do was talk or hope silently that it would end. We cheered when the Russians bombed the camp in the hope that the end might come quickly.

One night in the summer of 1943, we were lined up for roll-call and we saw flames coming from the chimneys of the camp's four crematoria rather than the customary smoke. It was a terrible sight and we knew that the ovens were working on overtime. We were given a blanket and some bread and then, quite suddenly, loaded onto cattle trucks – for where, we knew not.

That journey was to the camp at Bergen-Belsen. In our camp uniforms, we were marched through the town, but that seemed to attract no attention from the people going about their daily lives. It seems impossible that after the war they could deny any knowledge of what the camp was at Bergen-Belsen.

When we reached a clearing in the forest, we found tents with straw on the ground inside. It was cold and damp, and then a storm blew up and our tent collapsed on top of us. We crawled out and, just covered with our blankets, could do nothing but let the rain pour down on us.

Conditions in Bergen-Belsen were worse than in Auschwitz. It seems to me that Bergen-Belsen was nothing more than a starvation camp. We were there about eight months and the mix of inmates was quite large. There were Hungarians, non-Jewish Poles interned for their political views, and Dutch Jews who seemed to have some privileges, including having children with them. I recall that after the war I met some of those who had been in Bergen-Belsen as children.

We did not get on well with the non-Jewish Poles, though some of them may have felt that we shared a common adversity. The mood in the camp was one of even greater despair than at Auschwitz and you only talked if you felt like it. The death rate among inmates was incredibly high, mainly from typhus, which accounted for the piles of bodies that greeted the British troops when they liberated Belsen on 15 April 1945.

My sister, Sarah, died eight days after the liberation and on that same day I was taken away on a stretcher suffering from typhus. There was a temporary hospital, but little medical care and conditions in the camp were still appalling. Gradually, I started to recover and was moved to an army barracks where we lived five people to a room.

Later that year, I met my husband-to-be. Max, who came from the town of Zamosc in Poland, was serving in Germany with the Polish Army under British command. We were married in Belsen on 7 August 1946. However, I had to remain in Belsen as a displaced person for two years, and was not allowed into Britain until September 1947 when I joined Max at an army camp in Wiltshire.

At the end of the war, I had lost all my immediate family except my two brothers: that was my parents, grandparents and my four dear sisters.

I often question how and why I survived. Maybe the reason was that I was young and had the physical endurance to survive? But deep down, I think it was destiny. I cannot explain it or find any other word that will do.

I dedicate this chapter to the memory of my parents, Jakob Izak and Gitla, my four sisters, Sahra, Miriam, Risha and Ester, and numerous uncles, aunts and cousins who all perished in the concentration camps.

Toby Biber's family in Mielec, 1939. Toby is the girl on the right, her mother and father Jacob and Gitla Issac are in the centre of the picture. Her four sisters all perished in the Holocaust. Her two brothers survived.

Growing up in England, aged 14 in 1944

MARTHA BLEND

A Child Alone

When, in 1938, the Germans invaded Austria, my parents knew that as Jews, we were in for a hard time. They had read about Hitler's harassment of the Jews of Germany in the newspaper, but had thought – wrongly – that he wouldn't invade our country. As an eight-year-old child I had already picked up vibes of fear when the grown-ups mentioned names like "Hitler", "Gestapo" (the Nazi secret police), "SS" (Hitler's Storm Troopers) and "Dachau" (a notorious concentration camp). I also became aware of the vicious propaganda put out against the Jews in the newspapers and on the radio, as Hitler used us as scapegoats for all the problems of the world. My parents, realising our danger, tried to emigrate to another country, but all the countries that could have taken us in only allowed a trickle of refugees to enter, and it would have been years before our turn came.

I have described what life was like for me as a Jewish child in Austria, and what happened later, in a book called *A Child Alone*. Here is an extract from it:

> Now in the street, wherever you went, there were uniformed men in brown or black shirts with swastika armbands stepping out aggressively in their jackboots. Every week we were importuned by people shaking their collection-boxes in our faces for this or that Nazi cause. Army lorries packed with fierce-looking blackshirts sent out threatening signals as they swept past. At other times the snarl would turn into a smile: the lorries would be laden with gifts to the Austrian people from a beneficent Führer. A burly SS-man would stand astride the tailboard smirking ingratiatingly as he held out bananas for the taking. I knew instinctively that these goodies were not intended for me and kept my hands tightly clenched as I crept away from the happy throng.
>
> On my way home, I wondered how it was that neighbours who had until recently been friendly now kept their distance, and acquaintances who a short while ago had trumpeted their

devotion to Austria now seemed comfortable with the new order.
One day I could hardly believe my ears: from the flat below came
the unmistakable sounds of *Heute haben wir Deutschland* – today
we have Germany, tomorrow the world – the proud boast of the
Nazi Party. My friend Karl was thumping out the tune on his
piano with gusto...

About this time a measure was introduced which affected me
personally: a decree that Jewish children were not fit to be educated with Aryan children and must be taught in separate classes.
Up to now my beloved teacher had regarded me as a prize pupil,
always ready to throw herself into any activity with enthusiasm.
How did this square with the official view? I knew I hadn't
changed, so this blanket condemnation was all the harder to bear.
Suddenly I was cut off from the place which had been a safe haven,
the teacher I loved and the children I had known, among them my
friend Grete. I now had to enter the school building by a different door and found myself in a different classroom with a new
teacher who was said to be Jewish. She was nice enough, but no
substitute for my beloved Leopoldine Hanner. For the first time
I was in a class with boys as well as girls. There was an air of
impermanence about this arrangement – everybody was trying to
get somewhere else – Switzerland, France, Sweden – anywhere out
of the clutches of the Nazis. Our teacher, Fräulein Steckler, went
through the motions of teaching us, but I don't remember learning much in that class, though I still have the exercise book I used.
It contains little more than the words of the Lorelei song.

In the autumn of 1938 a young Jewish man named Grynszpan, after he
had heard that his parents had been horribly ill-treated by the Germans,
shot a German diplomat called Von Rath. The revenge that followed,
known as *Kristallnacht* (Night of the Broken Glass) was out of all proportion
to the crime. In every town in Germany and Austria synagogues were
burned, shops owned by Jews smashed up and looted, homes broken into.
Worst of all, thousands of Jewish men were arrested and sent to concentration camps like Buchenwald and Dachau. My father was one of those
arrested and I can never forget the sound of the Nazi jackboots stomping up
our stairs and battering on the door. My mother's pleas were ignored as he
was taken away, an unarmed man with no power to resist the heavily-armed
SS guards.

He was released that time after some weeks of detention. In their
now desperate search for a safe place to go to, my parents heard of an

organisation called the *Kindertransport* that had been set up to allow unaccompanied Jewish children from Germany and Austria to come to England as temporary refugees. When our GP told my parents of a couple he was in touch with in England who were willing to foster a child, they put me down on the list of children, as the prospects for their own immigration were poor.

When my parents broke this news to me, I was devastated: an only child who had never been away from home, to travel to a strange country and to strange people with a different language! It seemed more than my now nine-year-old self could be expected to cope with. But gradually, as the harassment by the Nazis grew worse, I realized that I had no choice but to go. I have described my departure for England in my book:

> It was now June and a letter arrived, giving the date of my departure for England: we were to assemble at a Viennese railway station late on the night of 20 June. We were to bring a small suitcase packed with our belongings, and there were to be no emotional farewells. Jews, it seemed, were not even to be allowed the luxury of expressing their grief at parting from their loved ones.
>
> Preparations for the journey now began in earnest. My mother found a small attaché case which in due course was packed with a few belongings: some underwear, a skirt and blouse, a dress and my most treasured possessions – the blonde doll that had been a present from my aunt in Belgium, some pictures of my parents, my autograph book and some of my favourite reading-books such as the *Arabian Nights* in German, printed in Gothic script. (I have it still.) My mother bought me an air-cushion to put under my head to sleep on, as the journey was likely to be a long one. Each stage of these preparations seemed like another little death, but by then I was too numb and shocked to put up any serious resistance.
>
> My father was apparently still in the same police-prison in Vienna, and the day before I was due to leave my mother took me to see him. We waited in a small office and eventually my father was brought in, flanked by two guards. He looked sad and unshaven, very different from the debonair man I had known as a little child. I don't remember much of what he said to me. What could he say? And what could I do? Scream, curse at this outrage? Throw my arms around him and refuse to leave? I did none of those things. He embraced me tenderly and wished me a safe journey. Then I saw my mother press some money into his

hand as she kissed him goodbye before he was led away. That was my last sight of my father.

I lived through the next day as though in a trance – nothing seemed real any more. My case was packed, I said goodbye to my aunt and cousins and promised to write to them. My mother made me some ham sandwiches – a strange choice considering the Jewish taboo against pig-meat. I expect by then she had given up on the Jewish God and no longer thought it worth appeasing him. Or perhaps she had simply decided this was a practical way to stave off hunger on the journey.

That evening, my mother took me to the station. When we arrived, there were already large numbers of children and their parents there. I was surprised to see, despite our strict orders not to be emotional, a mother and daughter with their arms round each other's necks, both crying bitterly. But my mother and I kept to the rules: not a tear was shed. Suddenly, before the expected time, the great doors at the end of the waiting-room were swung back to reveal a platform with a train ready to be boarded. I embraced my mother for the last time. Then with a light suitcase, a heavy heart and a silly red hat that kept flopping into my face, I climbed into a compartment. It had several children of varying ages in it. Wearily I found a seat. Suddenly there was an outcry and a rush to the windows. Parents had been told that they must on no account follow their children on to the platform, but some, disobeying orders, had surged out of the waiting-room and on to the platform. Their children, spotting them joyfully, were able to wave a last goodbye. I scanned the sea of faces anxiously, hoping to have a last glimpse of my mother, but she wasn't there.

The train took us through Germany along the river Rhine and into Holland. There we boarded a ship bound for Harwich on the English east coast, and then another train to Liverpool Street station, London, where we waited in a big room till our names were called out and we met the person who was to look after us. In my case it was my foster mother who took me to her home in Bow in east London.

The day after I arrived in England, waking up in a strange bed in an unfamiliar room made me feel very homesick. However, when you're young it's hard to be miserable all the time and my foster mother did her best to comfort me. I had learned a little English before leaving Austria, but not enough to fully grasp what people were saying, and this led to some funny misunderstandings:

Two days after my arrival, my foster mother decided I needed to be with children of my own age. Never one to let the grass grow under her feet, she marched me up to the houses of two neighbours and, in obedience to her command, two girls trooped out to play with me in the street. We played bouncing games against the air raid shelter that was already in place at the top of the street; then more ball-games on the pavement (there was no traffic in sidestreets apart from the occasional horse and cart, so playing was safe). Then one of the girls produced a skipping-rope and we had a few turns at this. There was little I could say to them, so we smiled and nodded at each other.

Finally one of them asked: 'Are you tired?'

I had no idea what this meant, so I must have looked blank. Now there followed a series of mimes: they let their heads droop and closed their eyes and put their hands to the side of their heads. Thinking that this was like the game of 'statues' I had played in Vienna, I imitated everything they did and was surprised by their look of exasperation. In the end one of the girls took me to her mother who said to me in Yiddish (a German dialect): *'Di bist mid?'*

Light dawned and I replied: *'Ja, ich bin müde'* (Yes, I'm tired) much to everyone's relief.

Later that year came the order for all London schoolchildren to be evacuated to the country, as war was imminent and London was sure to be a target for German bombers. My foster mother evacuated herself and me to Paignton in Devon. After we had settled in, I was enrolled in the local primary school, and again I describe what happened next:

The local primary school was housed in a bright modern building in the shape of a square. Along three of its sides were classrooms, and inside the square ran a corridor supported by pillars. This was open on one side to the prevailing winds and weather, since it was considered healthy for the children to have plenty of fresh Devon air in all seasons. In the middle of the building was a grassy space, and at the top end of it were the hall and the headmistress's room, into which we were shown by the school secretary.

The headmistress was a tall, formidable-looking lady. Sensing trouble, she cast a wary eye over me. After this inspection she handed me a piece of paper and a pencil and commanded: 'Write "I like living in Paignton!"'

I was not sure that I did, but thought I had better do as I was asked. By now my English was improved and I was able to write the sentence out correctly, taking particular care with the spelling of 'Paignton'. The headmistress noted my effort with some surprise. She had evidently been told that the new pupil had little or no English. 'That's very good!' she said. This must have prompted her to put me in a class with children of my own age.

In the weeks to come lessons floated by me in a fog of incomprehension. I was absorbing words and phrases, but contributing nothing myself. One day when the fog cleared a little, I heard the teacher say:

'Today we're going to learn about area. Now does anyone know what I mean by that?'

This rang an immediate bell with me, for hadn't I heard the grown-ups at home repeatedly saying: 'Must have an aerial – no good without an aerial'?

Triumphantly, I put up my hand. The teacher, a tall, red-haired Welshman, flushed with pleasure at this unexpected intervention from the foreign pupil.

'Yes, Martha,' he smiled encouragingly, 'what do we mean by area?'

'It's for wireless', I replied eagerly.

And the class fell about laughing.

I came to England as a nine-year-old child, but when the war ended, I was fifteen. I had had no word from my parents for five years and was dreading the discovery of what had happened to them. Rumours about the fate of the Jews in Europe did not make me feel optimistic. Soon I learned the sad fact that my parents, along with grandmothers, aunts, uncles and cousins, all had shared the fate of the millions of Jews who were exterminated in Hitler's concentration camps and gas chambers.

There was nothing to go back to Austria for, so I made my home in this country and have lived in England ever since as a naturalised British citizen. After I had gone to school and university, I spent 25 years as a teacher of (strangely enough) English, my second language. Since my retirement I have written the book about my experiences. I have also told my story to the pupils of many schools: not for its own sake, but to show how hate-propaganda can lead to terrible consequences of murder and mayhem. That is a lesson we dare not forget today.

Martha's story is told in full in *A Child Alone* (Vallentine Mitchell, London, 1995).

With my foster mother at the seaside,
August 1939

Martha Blend, 1990

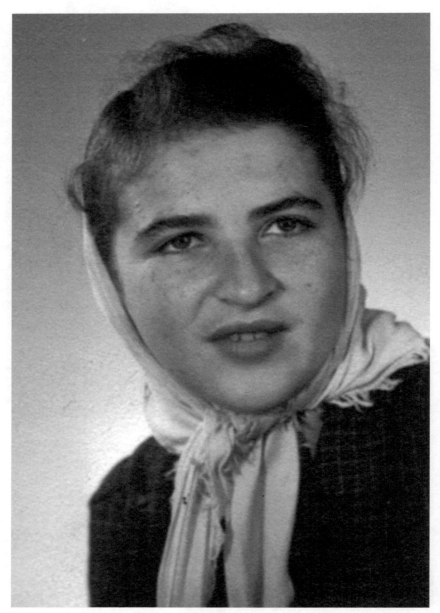

First photo after Liberation, Malmö, Sweden, 1945

ESTHER BRUNSTEIN

But Not Without Scars

More than half a century has passed since the events I am going to describe took place, but for me not a single day has gone by without me reliving at some point the pain and the trauma. It just comes and haunts me. I still cannot come to terms with – let alone comprehend – the total, calculated destruction of the world I knew, and the life I was born into.

I was born in Lodz, Poland, in 1928 into a very closely-knit and enlightened working-class family. My parents were active members of the *Bund* (Jewish Socialist Organisation). Father was also very actively involved in the Trade Union movements and a one-time official. I had two older brothers, David, 18, and Peretz, 15 years old, at the outbreak of war. Peretz is the only other survivor, apart from myself, of my entire family, immediate and extended.

Life in pre-war Poland was difficult, and even as a child I was acutely aware of antisemitism and personally experienced many jibes in my direction. But my memories of childhood are happy, because I grew up in a home where there was love and understanding. I was fortunate to attend an excellent secular Jewish school which imbued me with a love of humanity, a strong sense of Jewish identity, security and belonging. I treasure those memories and drew strength from my background in the darkest moments of my life.

My whole world started falling apart in September 1939. Just a week after the outbreak of hostilities, the Germans marched into Lodz. Immediately, life became chaotic and disorientated, and the Jewish population was threatened and deprived of every status which protects citizens under the law. Wearing the yellow star, identifying us as Jews, became compulsory. I remember so vividly feeling outrage, anger, humiliation and even shame. As a child, I bitterly resented being made to look different and shed many tears over it. But one day, I discussed it with a few school friends and we all agreed that we must walk with our heads held high because we had done nothing wrong.

We were afraid to go into town. Jews were beaten up in the streets, thrown out of their homes, forced to abandon all possessions and move to the poorest, most overcrowded part of the city, which was designated as the future ghetto as early as November 1939. The German soldiers used to amuse themselves by rounding up a few bearded Jews in a courtyard; then they would ask the Polish tenants for a pair of scissors and gleefully proceed to cut off the Jews' beards (or force them to cut off each other's). They made sure that many Jews were present to watch the spectacle. I was unfortunate in being forced to witness many such scenes. What still hurts so much to this day is the many pairs of scissors made available to the German soldiers by our Polish neighbours.

Before 1939 came to a close, we as a family had had our share of misfortune. My young uncle, my father's brother, who was correspondent for a Bundist Yiddish daily newspaper, was arrested by the Gestapo. He was tortured for many months and then shot in a prison near Lodz. My brother David, like many other young men, left for the Russian-occupied territory. Many years later, here in England, I learned of his fate. He was on the point of going further into Russia to escape the rapidly advancing German army, but apparently missed his chance of escape by one day. On entering the city, the German army rounded up the entire Jewish population in the market place and shot everyone. He was 20 years old.

Many political arrests were taking place, and my father was advised to leave town because his name was well known and his safety was threatened. So on 31 December 1939, he left for a small town near Warsaw. This was the last I saw of my wonderful dad. To this very day, New Year's Eve has always been overshadowed by this painful memory.

On 1 May 1940, some 180,000 men, women and children were herded into the barbed wire enclosure which was the Lodz ghetto. It was officially closed and sealed off. It was like a maximum security prison surrounded by barbed wire instead of walls, with armed German posts at regular intervals. All contact with the outside world ceased for us on that day and escape was physically impossible. I lived through the Lodz ghetto until its liquidation in August 1944. Compared with what followed later, this was a lesser hell.

Despite unimaginable starvation, disease and constant fear, we did not give up hope and did our utmost not to become totally demoralised. In the ghetto, political parties functioned, schools re-opened for a while, meetings were held, lectures took place on all possible subjects, music recitals were held, choirs formed, theatrical performances given. Even demonstrations took place, with demands for more food and fuel, and I myself marched in some of them. By the skin of our teeth, we held onto some semblance of human dignity, trying hard not to succumb to the depths of despair where nothing mattered any more. And all the time deportations were taking place. Many of my friends died or disappeared.

Food rations were getting smaller and smaller and the gnawing pain of constant hunger had a devastating effect on all ghetto dwellers. Potato peelings could only be obtained from the public kitchens on producing a doctor's certificate. People at work received some watery soup once a day, but if you could not work because of illness, you were deprived of it. Mother became very ill in the summer of 1942 and so Peretz and I would bring home some of our soup ration for her every evening. I worked in a factory weaving carpets from second-hand clothing. (We learned later that the clothes belonged to deportees.) Peretz worked in a carpentry workshop and would occasionally bring home a few pieces of firewood – a great luxury. One day, he was caught and severely punished by being forced to work for two weeks clearing excrement. However, at the end of each day he was given an extra piece of bread. We often wondered, in those far-off days, whether the outside world knew of our plight and the heinous crimes being committed against mankind.

1942 was the darkest period in the Lodz ghetto. Deportations had been taking place since the beginning of the year. Mother was so ill that she had to go into hospital at the beginning of August. I saw her face, full of anguish and sorrow, and yet I could still discern a loving smile in her sad eyes. And I, not so long before, a happy and mischievous girl, was by then so timid and frightened – and so old at 14 with the pain and burden of my generation.

Then on 1 September 1942, the Germans arrived in the ghetto with trucks and loaded patients from all the hospitals onto them. Mother miraculously escaped, but my brother was taken hostage in her stead. Luckily, he too managed to escape in a most ingenious way. Had he failed, I would be the sole survivor of my entire family.

A strict curfew was enforced soon after, for a week or maybe ten days, during which time the Germans came into the ghetto with trucks and dogs and dragged away 15,000-20,000 people – mainly children and the elderly. No child under 10 or person over 65 was seen again in the ghetto streets. Some old and young who escaped deportation had connections within the *Judenrat*, the governing body of the ghetto.

We dreaded those round-ups. My brother Peretz and I might have stood a chance of not being taken, but there was no hope whatever for mother because of her outward appearance. Although she was only 42 then, she looked old and was very ill at the time. We did our best to avoid selection. As one courtyard led onto another and we knew all the secret paths and passages, we would run from place to place, hiding in houses that had already undergone selection. But very early one morning, the SS caught up with us. They arrived in trucks in front of our block of flats and immediately posted guards in every part of the courtyard. We were quite convinced that the end had come.

We lived on the top floor of the building and there was a big loft above, with access through a trapdoor, reached by a ladder. All of us – all the neighbours on that floor – decided in a flash to climb up the ladder and hide in the loft. We left the trapdoor open, hoping it would make it less obvious that anyone was up there. One young couple, whose gorgeous little girl of three was asleep in a wicker basket in their flat, thought it safer to leave her there, rather than risk her cries if she was woken up. They piled lots of bedding and clothes in the basket and hoped that the flat would not be thoroughly searched.

In dead silence, we huddled together. We heard the SS go from floor to floor and the screams of people as they were brutally beaten and dragged out of their rooms. They were our neighbours and we knew them all; most of them were too ill to leave their beds. They reached the top floor and we heard them ordering the Jewish policeman to search each room. We held our breath, praying for little Danusia, asleep in the wicker basket. Alas, in vain. We heard a big thump, something being kicked over and Danusia's cry of "Mummy, Mummy!" Can anyone imagine what it was like for her parents and all of us in the loft not to let a sound escape our lips while Danusia was dragged away?

After they had searched all the rooms, we heard the SS order a Jewish policeman to climb up the ladder and search the loft. I was pressing closely to my mother and I remember vividly bidding silently goodbye to my mother, my brother, my young life and all that was dear to me. The policeman climbed up, looked around and saw us, but we heard him say as he climbed down, "No one up there." It was a chance in a million that his word would be taken – but he took that chance, risking his life. The policeman's name was Jakubowicz. He survived the war but his wife and young daughter did not. It is probably thanks to his display of great courage – not an isolated case – that I am alive today and not fully shattered in my belief in mankind. It also afforded me the great fortune of being with my mother for two more years.

Still not abandoning all hope, with our will to survive so strong, those of us left in the decimated ghetto carried on and cultural activities resumed. It was our mental, spiritual and intellectual resistance against tyranny. At the risk of death, a few people in the ghetto surreptitiously listened to the BBC World Service and in April 1943 news reached us about the uprising in the Warsaw ghetto. How we rejoiced and how proud we were of them!

How we longed to have the opportunity to do the same! But alas, in the Lodz ghetto nothing could be done because of our total isolation from the outside world, although there was talk of it.

In March 1944, my brother Peretz was deported to a munitions factory in Czestochva. I then became very ill and had to go into hospital, but came out in August 1944 in time to join my mother for what was to be our last journey together. I did not know then that our destination was Auschwitz. We were herded into closed-in cattle trucks, as many as would go into each one. There was barely enough air for us to breathe, with just a glimmer of daylight from a vent at the very top. There were two buckets in the centre; one with water, and one for our bodily functions. I huddled close to my mother; we talked so much, recalling happy pre-war years and telling our-selves that maybe at the end of the journey, there would be a nice place waiting for us. To this day, I really don't know how long that nightmare lasted. We seemed to be going back and forth and back again in semi- or total darkness.

When the train finally came to a halt, the iron bars were removed and the doors were thrown open. Many of our number were dead on arrival. We were pushed out – women to the left and men to the right – and told to form rows of five. Looking around, I saw barbed wire in the distance, and creatures with shaven heads behind the fence. (I learnt later that the wire was electrified and then understood why a woman, whom I saw touch it, dropped dead.) We looked at each other in fear and disbelief and were convinced that this was a lunatic asylum, that it was not for us, that it was only a stopover on the way to our real place of resettlement. What followed is the hardest memory to verbalise; for my mother, although only 44 at the time, did not pass selection for life.

To this day, I cannot fully recall the details of Auschwitz. All I know is that the experience has left me with a feeling of total madness, as if the whole world had fallen into an abyss of apocalyptic proportions.

By some miracle, I found myself selected for a transport to a labour camp situated on the outskirts of Hanover. Conditions were appalling; we were subjected to hard labour, but at least we each had a bunk to sleep on at night and a daily food ration. But in mid-January 1945, our labour camp was disbanded and we were forced to march to Bergen-Belsen. On the way we saw nice, neat little houses, people peering out of their windows and even some civilians. So why is it that most Germans say they did not know what was going on?

We marched to Belsen quite unaware of the place and what might greet us there. My memory of my arrival there is hazy. There were 400 of us and we were herded into different barracks, which were already overcrowded with living and decaying corpses. Total chaos and the stench of dead bodies everywhere: that is how I remember Belsen, a living 'inferno'. I see myself – a skinny, bewildered 16-year-old – running from hut to hut, looking, searching, hoping to find a friend, a cousin or maybe an aunt still among the living. Everything seemed so unreal.

One day a friend told me to go very early next day to a certain point where a few women would be chosen to work in the kitchen, peeling potatoes and vegetables. I got very excited at the mere thought of perhaps having a little extra food. Luck was with me. I was chosen. I worked in that kitchen barrack for a few days and it was there, one day, sitting with my cold feet deep in mud that I felt a fever taking possession of my body. I was quite aware that it was probably the end of the road for me.

Typhus and dysentery were rampant in the camp and I recognised the symptoms. Two friends helped me by holding me up to march back to our section of the camp and somehow got me inside a so-called Isolation Block. I remember slipping slowly into an unconscious state of mind with occasional moments of lucidity. I knew that I was lying on the lowest bunk next to the bucket, the only receptacle for our bodily needs. There were four women to each two-foot wide bunk. The three women who shared my bunk were in the last throes of death and would soon join the heap of corpses just outside the barrack. Indeed, that lower bunk which I occupied was meant for those for whom there was no hope of survival.

When moments of consciousness returned, I vividly remember feeling hollow and devoid of emotion. To experience emotion requires some physical effort, of which I was no longer capable. I was resigned to my fate, but felt deep regret that after so much suffering and the struggle I had put up, I would not make it after all. I recalled the images of all those who were dear to me.

When I awoke from a dreadful nightmare, there were friendly, smiling faces around me telling me it was all over. I was too numb and too confused to make sense of what they were saying. I was liberated on 15 April, but have no memory of it as I lay unconscious. When I regained consciousness, I found four portions of black bread and four tins of Nestlé's condensed milk beside my bunk. I looked at the bread and burst out crying. I had so longed for, and dreamed of the day when I could just eat and eat, but I was too ill even to taste the food.

The first few days after liberation were joyous and yet sad, confusing and bewildering. I did not know how to cope with freedom after years of painful imprisonment. Looking out of the window, I could see German soldiers being made to clear the mountain of corpses. The inmates had to be restrained from attacking them.

I was taken to Sweden where I gradually regained some physical strength. One would have thought that after surviving this unparalleled tragedy, there would have been ample help and support to unite the remnants of families. Not so. Strict rules were in operation and no visas were issued to anyone without visible means of support. I waited two more long and lonely years before I was able to come to England in 1947 on a special permit as a domestic worker, a maid to an elderly couple. I was then able to join my brother, Peretz, who had been liberated from Theresienstadt by the Russians. At the time, England had offered to take in 1,000 youngsters under the age of sixteen: in the event only 732 could be found. My brother Peretz had to lie about his age in order to qualify for entry into England.

When Belsen was liberated, *The Times* correspondent began his story with the words, "It is my duty to describe something which is beyond the imagination of mankind." There was murder in all of us who were liberated there, and it scared me. I remember praying silently, more fervently than I had ever prayed in all my life. I prayed that I would not forever be consumed nor destroyed by hatred. I would say that against all the odds, I have succeeded. But not without scars.

In memory of my parents, Sarah Rifka and Ephraim Fishel Zylberberg,
my brother David and all members of my family
who perished under the Nazis.

Some of my mother's family taken in 1925, three years before I was born, showing my parents, grandparents, aunts, uncles and cousin. My father is on the back row, far right; my mother, holding my brother Peretz, is on the far right; and my brother David is in the middle at the front between my grandparents.

John Chillag, 2003

JOHN CHILLAG

Memories of a Lost Youth

Although Hungary, the country where I spent my childhood, was an ally of Germany, Jews fared relatively better there than in Germany and the other countries overrun by the Nazis. That is – until the Germans occupied Hungary on 19 March 1944, when I was just 17 years old.

Before that, between 1938 and 1941, three so-called "Jewish Laws" came into force, each harassing and curtailing the lives of Jews in Hungary more and more. As early as 1922, the *numerus clausus* law had limited the number of Jewish students in Hungarian universities to 6 per cent of the total intake. It was the first twentieth-century anti-Jewish law in Europe and preceded similar legislation by Germany's Third Reich by 12 years! By 1943, thousands of Jewish men had lost their lives in Labour Battalions on the Russian front, and many "non-resident" Jews were deported to Kamenets-Podolsky in the Ukraine, and massacred there.

Within a fortnight of the occupation of Hungary, all the anti-Jewish Nuremberg laws implemented in the Third Reich and the countries occupied by the Nazis became fully operational. We had to wear a yellow star; all valuables, radios and bicycles had to be handed in; Jews could no longer practise their profession or trade; our movements and shopping were curtailed, our telephones disconnected. I could no longer attend school.

But back to my origins: my parents, grandparents and their ancestors – and I can trace the family back to 1706 – came mainly from various parts of the Habsburg Empire. After World War I, my father went into political exile from Hungary to Vienna, where he met my mother. They got married and I was born there in 1927. In 1934, shortly after a failed Nazi attempt to overthrow the government in Austria, we moved to Györ in Hungary, where my father's family had a contracting and building materials business. Most the family worked in the firm, and my father became their accountant.

In 1938, immediately after Austria was annexed into Germany, the first influx of battered Jewish and political refugees flooded into our town, which was close to the Austrian border. It was an ominous beginning to times to come. 1938 also saw the introduction of the first "Jewish Law" in Hungary. Later that year, political circumstances required the army to be called up, and military-age Jews, including my father, were mobilised. But under the new "Jewish Law", they were put into separate Labour Battalions and had to dig trenches, load lorries, and so on. By luck, my father was stationed in the village where my maternal grandparents lived, so he could go there for an extra meal, a shower and to meet us.

War broke out in September 1939 and many countries were overrun, but at that stage Hungary was not involved, and many refugees sought sanctuary there. When the Germans attacked the Soviet Union in the summer of 1941, the Hungarian army got involved on that front, but war with the Western allies only began after the Japanese attack on Pearl Harbour. When the Soviet forces began their counter-attacks in 1943, the Hungarian army and some 50,000 Labour Battalion Jews, who were mainly on mine-clearing duties, were wiped out. The fortunes of war had changed on all fronts and preparations for the "invasion" were progressing. No one in Hungary thought that the Germans would occupy Hungary at that stage. But on 19 March, 1944, they did.

From that moment on, the SS reiterated daily to the Jewish population that they would be moved "somewhere to the East", along with their families, to work for "German victory". In the isolation in which we were living in Hungary (before TV, e-mail, etc.), we were completely ignorant of what was happening to Jews throughout Europe. This was 1944, with the war slowly, but surely, coming to an end. The country's Jewish population, unaware of the realities of the Final Solution, moved to the ghettos resigned to a disagreeable, but hopefully short, period of a difficult fate.

In April 1944, one district of Győr was evacuated of its population and designated as the ghetto area for the 5,000 Jews of the town (10 per cent of the population). The 35 members of my family managed to move into the small house of one of our tradesmen. However crowded we were, at least the family managed to stay together. But this was very temporary. One day in May, we were brutally driven by the SS, the local gendarmerie and police with their dogs into the central square of the ghetto. We were strip-searched, everything was taken away from us and we were moved off into a regional ghetto on the outskirts of Győr. There we were crammed in extremely crowded conditions, without water, gas, electricity or sanitation in dilapidated, leaky barracks, with scarcely any food. The SS told us that we would be moved shortly.

On 11 June 1944, we were marched, with the "encouragement" of the

SS, their pickaxe handles and dogs, to the local railway marshalling yards. A train with about 40 cattle wagons was waiting there. Some 80 people were forced into each truck; a bucket with water was put in, and another one for sanitation, then the doors were sealed. The trucks were extremely crowded, with just a small air-hole with barbed wire over it. It was suffocating in the summer heat of June. From Györ the train proceeded via Budapest and north-east Hungary through the Carpathian mountains. Three days later, it stopped in a siding at a place no one had ever heard of before. We had reached our destination: Auschwitz-Birkenau.

The doors were swung open and we had to get off the train onto the platform. A number of people died on the journey, many others were very sick and weak; the people on the train included many infants and old people. We had to line up on the platform in lines of five, and then pass in front of a group of SS officers, including the infamous Dr Mengele. They were selecting and directing people in two different directions. There was a smaller group of more working-age people, which included me, my father and one of my uncles. All the other people in the transport – older people and women with children – were directed into a second, much larger group. We were told that this group, which included over 30 members of my family, was being moved to the "family accommodation" and we would meet up with them later.

Our group was marched off to the shower block of Birkenau camp. After a cold, drips-only shower, our head and body hair was shaved and we were smeared with a stinking and stinging disinfectant. We were issued with ill-fitting, blue-grey striped prison garb, a cap and wooden clogs, but virtually no underwear. We were then marched off to the part of the compound called the gypsy camp, one side of which was earmarked for Hungarian Jews. In the period April-June of 1944, over a quarter of a million Hungarian Jews arrived on 137 deportation trains. Why a gypsy camp? Jews were not the only people persecuted and deported by the Nazis. Other groups included gypsies, Slavs, political, criminal and anti-social prisoners, homosexuals, "race defilers", conscientious objectors, Jehovah's Witnesses and other religious groups.

The compound was surrounded by two electrified wire fences, with fierce dogs running between them and the SS in their watchtowers training machine guns at us. Each of the "barracks" (they were originally stables for horses) became "home" to about 1,000 prisoners. It was so crammed that even sitting down was difficult. By the time we got to the barracks, we had already learnt from others in the camp that our families had not gone to any "family accommodation", but to the gas chambers, killed and burnt. I lost my mother and 30 members of my family that day. We were in shock and incredulous at first, but the smoke from the crematoria and the smell of burning flesh soon convinced us.

Most of our day in the camp was taken up by repeated roll-calls. Our daily food was a slice of bread, a sliver of margarine, a small ladleful of very watery cabbage soup, and a cup of dark liquid (allegedly tea) laced with a sedative. There was no drinking water in the camp and sanitation was atrocious.

After 3-4 weeks of this, a group of SS officers and civilian Nazis came to the barracks to pick slave-labourers for war production plants in Germany. With my father and 270 others, I was "selected" to work in the steel plant of the *Bochumer Verein* in Bochum (Westphalia), the largest armament works of the Third Reich.

There were about 30,000 slave-labourers in Bochum, some 3,000 in my part of the plant. I had to work a 12-hour shift in atrocious conditions at a steel-forging press operating at 1,000 degrees centigrade, and with no protective clothing. Many of my fellow prisoners were killed or injured there. We were fed better than in Auschwitz, but we still used up far more calories than we got. In such conditions, people got very weak and succumbed to illnesses, including my father who died there in December 1944. Life then became very difficult for me. We relied so much on each other, and now I was alone. I had lost all my family in Auschwitz, and now my father had gone as well. But I still had the will to live. I knew (or I was hoping at least) that the war would end soon.

When the Allied forces reached the Rhine, I was evacuated with 1,500 other prisoners to Buchenwald concentration camp, one of the earliest and largest camps set up by the Nazis in 1937, mainly for political prisoners. Bochum and hundreds of other camps were all so-called "external" camps (*Aussenlager*) of Buchenwald. By this time, I was extremely weak and my survival was doubtful. On arrival in Buchenwald, I was taken to the camp infirmary – which was not a hospital, but a "sound" Nazi logistical exercise! It was adjacent to the crematorium, and was almost always just a "one-way street". My fellow prisoners in the crowded bunks there included Elie Wiesel, later a Nobel prizewinner, and Max Perkal, now an American writer.

On 11 April 1945, the American forces liberated Buchenwald. By that time I was extremely weak, unable to move from my bunk. Within a day or so, field hospitals were established in the old SS barracks and I was moved there. At the time I weighed just 56 lbs (25 kg). After numerous blood transfusions and treatment with sulpha drugs, by some miracle, I survived and was nursed back to some kind of health.

As Buchenwald was to become part of the Soviet occupation zone, the

Americans had to leave the area. The US forces were removing equipment and industrial documentation in war reparation and I supervised the loading of some patent and work-process documentation. Almost unbelievably, I was reunited with some of that same material 18 years later, when I joined the (now) British Library in 1963.

And what else happened in the intervening 18 years? When the Americans left Buchenwald, I returned to Hungary, hoping that someone from my family might have survived the Holocaust. Alas, no one else did. I restarted the family business, but it was nationalised in 1949 by the then Communist regime. I then escaped from Hungary, became a refugee in Austria and was accepted as a migrant to Australia, where I worked first in the world-renowned Snowy Mountains Hydro-Electric scheme, and later at the Australian Atomic Energy Commission. I got married in Australia and my wife and I had our children there.

Then we came to England and from 1963-1991 I worked at the British Library in Yorkshire, then a few more years at Leeds Metropolitan University. Parallel with my working life, I was, and still am, involved in voluntary work with disability issues, nationally and internationally. For many years I served not only on the national council of Mencap, but also on a similar world governing body on intellectual handicap. In the last few

years, I have given many talks about my Holocaust experiences in schools, at the Beth Shalom Centre and in Germany, in the hope that younger generations may learn from events and work for a better future.

In memory of my parents and the 57 other members of my family who lost their lives in the Holocaust – in Auschwitz and other camps, as slave labourers or in Labour Battalions.

Young John Chillag, aged 5, 1932

Eva aged about four months with her mother in 1945

EVA CLARKE

A Baby in Mauthausen

Prague: March 1939-November 1941

In March 1939 the Germans invaded Czechoslovakia and one of their first acts was to close the universities. My mother, Anka Kaudrova, had been studying law and now tried to find some other, more immediately practical occupation. It was a sensible decision at that time, and she became a trainee milliner.

My father, Bernd Nathan, had left Hamburg in Germany for Prague in 1933 following the rise of Hitler. He thought he was going far enough away from danger. He wasn't, but if he hadn't gone to Prague he wouldn't have met my mother and I wouldn't exist!

In Prague he set up a small practice as an architect/interior designer and had some success designing restaurants and night-clubs – for the Germans! On a superficial level he felt quite at home dealing with German officers. He was a German first and foremost and up to that time had scarcely thought about the fact that he was Jewish.

Bernd and Anka were married on 15 May 1940 and for just under one and a half years, they lived a relatively normal life in a flat in Prague but with an increasing number of restrictions. One of these was wearing the yellow star to indicate they were Jewish.

Another restriction was the curfew: Jews had to be back in their homes by 6 p.m. and so were not allowed to go to concerts, cinemas, theatres or to visit friends. One evening my father decided that he, my mother and a non-Jewish friend, Otto Artner from Germany, would go for a walk. My mother said she was frightened they would be stopped and arrested for breaking the curfew. My father's response was to tell Anka to keep silent if they were stopped and questioned because although she spoke fluent German, she had a Czech accent. He reasoned that as both he and Otto were Germans and spoke *hoch Deutsch* (high German, the equivalent of BBC English), they would be able to convince the soldiers of their right to be out at that time of day. Fortunately, they were not put to the test and returned home unscathed.

Another time my mother, who was an avid cinema fan, was desperate to see a particular film and so went to the cinema. However, she deeply regretted her rash impulse when the Gestapo entered the cinema and, row by row, started demanding that the audience show their identity papers. She was in real danger but the Germans ceased their search for Jews just one row in front of her. Anka was so relieved that she never took such a risk again and has completely forgotten what the film was!

On another occasion in September 1941, Anka went to her home village of Trebechovice near Hradec Kralove to visit her parents as her older brother, Tonda (Antonin), had died of a brain tumour on 19 June of that year. Jews were not allowed to travel and while she was in her parents' house, a group of Gestapo came in demanding identity papers etc. My grandmother, Ida, had great presence of mind and offered the Gestapo coffee and cake and while the rest of the family, including my mother, were making polite conversation, my grandmother went to find all the money in the house and hid it in her ample bosom. Soon after, the Gestapo left. They were very polite but warned my mother she definitely should not have travelled from Prague and should not do so again.

At the end of November 1941, my parents received notification by letter from the Jewish Council to come to an empty warehouse, about 500 yards from Holesovice Station in Prague. Bernd was required to leave a few days before my mother. Anka spent three days and three nights in this warehouse, along with hundreds of others, but without sufficient food or washing facilities. Some time later, one of her friends remarked that during those three days and nights Anka continued to maintain appearances despite getting grubbier and grubbier and was seen brushing her hair, doing her make-up and even curling her eyelashes!

On the third day the prisoners were marched to Holesovice Station. Anka was not only carrying the small suitcase that was allowed but also a large, square and unwieldy cardboard box which contained two or three dozen doughnuts she was taking to my father, as she had no idea where the next meal was coming from. The Gestapo marched the prisoners off and one of the Nazis, an 18-20 year-old young man, spoke to my mother and said: *"Es ist scheiss egal ob die Schachtel mitkommt"* (I couldn't give a shit whether the box goes along), implying that it wouldn't be needed where she was going.

Theresienstadt December 1941–October 1944

In December 1941 my parents were sent to Theresienstadt, a barracks town which normally housed about 10,000 Czech soldiers. The soldiers were sent away and the whole place was turned into a ghetto for Jews (at one time more than 100,000) from all parts of Europe. It was a transit stop before the prisoners were sent East to the extermination camps.

My parents were part of a group of so-called 'pioneers' who were made to help set up the camp. The Gestapo 'promised' this group of young, able-bodied men and women that they would not be sent East and certainly, they remained in Theresienstadt for three years – much longer than most – because they were young, capable of work and luck had a lot to do with it. The old, the sick, the disabled and families with children were 'sent East' after a few months.

It was advisable to try to get some sort of job and my mother worked in the provisions store. This helped her a lot, as at one time she was respon-sible for feeding 15 members of her family, including my maternal grand-parents, Stanislav (31.3.1870–21.1.1944) and Ida (18.10.1882–10.7.1944) Kauder. Anka had contacts in the kitchens from which the very meagre provisions were allocated and when all else failed, she would resort to steal-ing a potato, a carrot or a swede to supplement a thin and watery soup.

During her time in Theresienstadt my mother met her parents-in-law for the first time. My paternal grandfather, Louis Nathan (1878–1956), was the only one of my grandparents to survive the war. This is one of the many ironies in my story: in World War I, my grandfather had been in the German Army; he had been blinded by the gas and decorated with the Iron Cross, First Class (the highest military honour the Germans bestow on their soldiers). My mother believes that this fact saved his life in World War II. He remained in Theresienstadt and in 1945 was reunited with his younger son, my uncle Rolf.

My parents believed they would survive the war in Theresienstadt and decided to have a baby even though the sexes were segregated! In such dire circumstances people found comfort where they could and thought 'to hell with the consequences'. However, when the Gestapo discovered that my mother and four other women were pregnant, they made them all sign a paper agreeing to hand over the babies at birth – to be killed. This was the first time my mother had heard the word 'euthanasia' (so-called mercy killing).

In the event, this did not happen – my brother Jiri/George (or Dan, the Jewish name the Gestapo insisted on) was not taken away from my mother. He was born on 11 February 1944 and died from pneumonia two months later on 10 April 1944. *His death meant my life* because if my mother had arrived in Auschwitz with a baby, she would have been sent straight to the gas chambers and although she arrived there knowing she was pregnant, no one else was aware of the fact and it didn't show.

Auschwitz-Birkenau: 1–10 October 1944

My father was sent to Auschwitz on 28 September 1944 and from there to a satellite camp, Bismarckhutte. He was evacuated from there in mid-January 1945 and was shot in the cattle wagon in which they were travelling on 18 January 1945. My mother learned this in July 1945 from a friend of his who had witnessed the shooting.

Anka *volunteered* to follow him the next day, but she never saw my father again and he had no idea she was pregnant. She had no idea what Auschwitz was and presumed it would be a camp similar to Theresienstadt where they had survived for three years and once again, she thought they would survive. Anka was in Auschwitz from 1-10 October 1944 and says it was indescribable – hell on earth. After a horrendous, terrifying journey in a packed railway wagon without any food or water, when the prisoners were herded off the trains at Auschwitz-Birkenau, they were confronted with Gestapo screaming orders, dogs barking viciously, a general sense of panic, flames billowing from chimneys and above all, a very strange and unforgettable smell.

They then experienced their first 'selection' although they didn't realize the implications of where the old, the sick and families with babies and young children were being sent. When my mother was eventually sent into one of the wooden huts, she asked those prisoners already there what was happening. When she was told, she just couldn't believe what they said – that everyone would literally go up in smoke.

The ten days my mother was in Auschwitz were absolutely terrifying. Roll-calls occurred twice a day, at 4.00 a.m. and 6.00 p.m. and lasted 3-4 hours at a time, regardless of weather conditions. Anka fainted several times during these roll-calls and when she came round, was always relieved to find that friends had been holding her up to prevent her falling and thereby attracting the Gestapo's attention.

The prisoners also had to endure 'selections' which meant life or death. During one 'selection' she heard the notorious Dr Mengele say: *"Diesmal sehr gutes Material"* (This time very good material)... not human beings but units of slave labour.

When my aunt Zdena was first sent to Auschwitz, she was made to write a postcard to another cousin in Prague. The text had to be in German so the content could be heavily censored. It almost reads: "Having a wonderful time, wish you were here!" My aunt was desperate to send some sort of coded message and she succeeded – in the address. Instead of writing Frau Olga Sronkova (her cousin's name), she wrote Frau *Lechem* Sronkova. *Lechem* is the Hebrew word for bread. Zdena was trying to tell Olga they were starving and her codeword was understood. Her cousin got the message, sent a parcel, but of course it didn't do Zdena any good. She had been killed three weeks before the card was sent.

Freiberg: October 1944–April 1945

Following my mother's final 'selection' at Auschwitz, she still appeared capable of physical labour despite being severely malnourished and was sent with a group of women as slave labour to an armaments factory in Freiberg, near Dresden in Germany. On arrival there, the prisoners were confronted by bedbugs, hundreds of bedbugs – on the floor, the walls, the ceiling – and they were pleased because the presence of bedbugs meant food and warmth! And they also ascertained quite quickly that there were no gas chambers.

The prisoners were put to work on the V-I, the unmanned flying bomb, nicknamed the Doodlebug. At the time, none of them knew what they were working on and my mother only discovered the truth after the war. Added to this, she also had to sweep the factory floors for several hours a day and suspects that this rigorous daily exercise, while pregnant, helped her experience a relatively easy birth (mine) within seven months' time.

The Dresden air raids occurred during Anka's time in Freiberg and for her, they were the most wonderful spectacle. During the raids the Gestapo would lock the prisoners in the factory while they found shelter. Even though the prisoners knew that the next bomb could kill the lot of them, they were delighted. They knew it was the Allies and help was coming – visibly. After the war, there was considerable controversy about the morality of the Dresden raids, but when anyone raised the subject with my mother, she said, "What about Liverpool, Coventry and the London Blitz?"

Here the story moves to my father-in-law, Kenneth Clarke (2.6.1910–31.12.1973), an RAF navigator in Bomber Command who was on the Dresden raids. After the war he suffered something akin to a nervous breakdown, possibly as a result of these raids: he had had no idea that they were bombing civilian targets. When Kenneth met Anka and heard her story, he was devastated at the thought that he could easily have killed her. Her response to his genuine anguish was: "But, Kenneth, you *didn't* kill me."

Mauthausen: 29 April 1945

At the beginning of April 1945, the SS evacuated the Freiberg factory. Under "normal circumstances", they would have sent the prisoners back to Auschwitz to be killed, but this was no longer possible because Auschwitz had been liberated by the Russians on 27 January 1945. So they were put onto another train, but this time in open coal trucks and travelled round and round the countryside for three weeks without any food and hardly any water. They kept trying to work out where they were being sent, but quite soon realized that the Germans didn't know what to do with them. It's a blessing that they weren't just shot.

Every day or so the train would halt in the middle of the countryside, to avoid any witnesses, in order to throw out the dead and empty the bucket which was the only toilet. On one such occasion, Anka was standing by the open door when a farmer walked by. He was stunned by the spectre of this scarcely living, pregnant skeleton and brought her a glass of milk. As she was about to accept it, the SS officer standing nearby raised his whip to above shoulder height as if to beat her if she accepted the milk. However, he did not hit her – why, she has no idea. Anka gratefully drank it even though she loathed milk and reckoned that drink saved our lives.

The train moved on and arrived in Mauthausen in Austria on Sunday 29 April. Mauthausen is a beautiful village on the banks of the Danube, close to Braunau (near Linz), Hitler's birthplace. Ironically, Anka also shared her birthday, 20 April, with Hitler and invariably, flags were flying in the camps on that day. This time she did know what the name Mauthausen meant and was so shocked at the prospect of this notorious concentration camp that her labour pains began.

The prisoners had to walk up the hill from the station to the camp and those who couldn't had to climb onto a high wooden cart and were pulled up. My mother was one of these. Another inexplicable thing happened at this point: an SS soldier walking alongside the cart could see my mother was in labour and said: *"Du kannst weiter schreien"* (You can continue screaming). Obviously, she had been screaming as labour is painful but Anka had no idea whether he was being sarcastic or compassionate.

Another reason for our survival on the day of my birth was that the Nazis had blown up the gas chamber the day before. A prisoner-doctor was found to cut the umbilical cord. The Germans then proceeded, almost literally, to kill my mother with food in the form of a bowl of the greasiest noodles. By this time she weighed about 5 st/35 kg and this food really could have killed her. Her body was so unused to any form of nourishment that she couldn't digest any food, let alone such unsuitable food, and she developed instant diarrhoea. But even this she withstood.

I weighed about 3 lb/1.5 kg, like a bag of sugar. I had a full head of dark brown hair, was wrapped in paper – obviously there were no baby clothes – and my mother just held me for three days. Incredibly, even in that poor physical condition, she was able to breastfeed me.

The main reason we both survived was that three days later, the Americans liberated the camp. Anka maintains that she wouldn't have survived much longer without help. Three weeks later, once we were strong enough, we were sent back to Prague.

Prague: May 1945–August 1948

We arrived on a dark and dismal night at Prague station, Anka still in her prison garb, but by then I had been given some baby clothes. Anka was given the tram fare and we made our way to my aunt Olga's flat. My mother's innate sense of optimism had never left her and, contrary to all logic, she was sure that her cousin would be in her own home. As invariably happens, the grapevine had worked very effectively and the Sronek family knew that my mother was the only family member to have survived and that she had a baby.

We arrived on their doorstep to be welcomed by bread and salt, the traditional form of welcome, i.e. the basics of life. My mother rang the bell and all four members of the family answered it. Anka's first, very practical words were: "We haven't got lice." In fact, we were riddled with lice and scabies but she didn't realize it at the time. We were welcomed into the small flat and much more importantly, we became part of a very close family – our own personal support group. My mother asked if we could stay for a few days to recover and we stayed for three years!

On 20 February 1948, Anka married Karel Bergman (2.9.1902-14.9.1983). My stepfather had left Czechoslovakia in 1939, came to England and joined the RAF as an interpreter in Fighter Command. After the war, Karel returned to Prague to pick up the pieces of his family, most of whom had perished in Auschwitz. He met Anka whom he had known as a family friend before the war.

Cardiff: September 1948

With the arrival of the Communists in Czechoslovakia in 1948, my stepfather decided that he would emigrate again. We travelled by train and arrived in London and eventually settled in Cardiff in September 1948 to start a new life.

To my mother

Eva and Anka, Cardiff 1950

Anka and Eva at Beth Shalom, 21 April 2002 (the day after Anka's 85th birthday)

Batsheva Dagan, 2000

BATSHEVA DAGAN

Imagination: Blessed Be, Cursed Be

Batsheva Dagan was born in Lodz, Poland, and at the outbreak of World War II, she was a student in high school. When Jews were ordered into the ghettos, her elder brothers and one sister escaped to Soviet Russia. She, her parents and two sisters went to live in the town of Radom.

In 1941, a ghetto was imposed on Radom. Batsheva became active in the Zionist movement, "Hashomer Hatzair", and served as a messenger to the Warsaw ghetto, where she met the leaders of the movement. She carried the newspaper *Against the Stream* on her back from Warsaw to Radom. In August 1942, the Radom ghetto was liquidated. Batsheva's parents and her older sister were sent to Treblinka. Having obtained forged Aryan papers, she escaped to Germany and worked as a housemaid in a Nazi home. She was denounced after several months in Germany.

On her way to Auschwitz-Birkenau, she was kept in six German prisons. Reaching Auschwitz in May 1943, she was an inmate for twenty months, until 18 January 1945. As the Soviet army neared Auschwitz, the Germans transported the prisoners to other camps, and Batsheva was sent to Ravensbrück and later to Malchow.

In May 1945, Batsheva was liberated by US forces and went to Belgium. Four months later, she moved to Palestine. She is the only one of her family who survived German-occupied Poland.

Today she works as a psychologist and lecturer, and has developed a psycho-educational approach towards introducing the subject of the Holocaust to young children.

When she is in England, Batsheva speaks regularly to student groups at Beth Shalom.

Batsheva's poems depict the experiences of camp inmates during the Holocaust. She memorised and internalised the poems and songs of other inmates while in the camp, and wrote them from memory afterwards. Her own poems were inspired by her feelings, thoughts and experiences while there, and composed later. Batsheva writes in the Introduction to *Imagination: Blessed Be, Cursed Be:*

Though I didn't write all the poems when I was in the concentration camp, I felt they were part of me, belonged to me. I heard, I remembered, I recorded in my mind. The words were transmitted from one to another, restoring our spirits and uniting us. Day after day, Nazi boots, polished and shining, accompanied the march of clogs on their way to work. The rhythm of marching, *"Links, Zwei, Drei, Vier,"* imposed itself on tortured masses of human beings. This rhythm, drummed into my mind, demanded another rhythm, a personal, intimate rhythm, my very own. Most of the other poems came to me naturally, in moments of inspiration, at different times in the years after the Holocaust.

WITH THE NUMBER ON MY ARM

The number on my arm
tattooed on my skin
cannot be erased
without or within.
It's a constant reminder,
and to those who don't believe,
I'll tell them all about it
and pull up my sleeve.

    To some it is strange,
    but it is no shame.
    They gave me a number
    instead of my name.
    The number meant one thing,
    'freedom was not mine',
    an unjust verdict,
    I'd committed no crime.

The ultimate fear
was the chimney's black smoke,
the grim bitter fate
of so many folk.
But I have survived
with dignity,
reclaimed my own name
and my own I.D.

But the number remains
clear and straight.
We are both free,
I survived my fate.

THE SENTENCE

Getting a number
instead of a name
that was a source
of deep painful shame.
But what was harder
still to bear
was when they shaved off
all my hair.
My head was covered
in stubbly thorn,
I was almost bald
completely shorn.
My hair, my crown,
my femininity,
my hair, my own
that belonged to me.

I looked in the window
to see my reflection.
What stared back at me
was complete rejection.
Who was that stranger
strange as could be?
Could that weird image
really be me?

They shaved us
to ward off
lice from our heads,
and then took the hair
for mattresses, beds.

At last my hair
began to grow
as in nature's way.
A sign of hope,
I might survive
this living hell one day.

By force and against our will
heads were shaved
to humiliate more,
we were truly enslaved.

EIGHT TO A BUNK

In a wooden barrack, really a stable
On bunks, three tiers high,
we all lay together, each on her side,
somewhere in the middle was I.

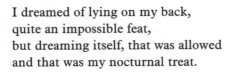

    Straw palliasses were our beds
    for two or three, we were eight.
    No one could turn unless we all did,
    together at the same rate.

I dreamed of lying on my back,
quite an impossible feat,
but dreaming itself, that was allowed
and that was my nocturnal treat.

    For no one can take away that right,
    and squashed in my bunk, I dreamed every night.

LIVING WITH BUGS

Bugs and lice
flies and fleas
lived on my body
with perfect ease.
Without any soap,
an item not seen,
I fought them from habit
and tried to keep clean.

    We lived as a team,
    the bugs and I,
    our lives had no value,
    we all would die.
    To my life
    that couldn't be any worse,
    they only added
    another curse.

HOW WE ATE OUR DAILY BREAD

Lena ate hers all in one go,
that was the safest way.
Piri divided hers in two,
two tiny portions each day.

Sala ate hers, a morsel each bite,
that way it lasted much longer.
It was like a drug, like tiny pills,
that was her way to keep stronger.

Each way I tried
to make the bread last,
nothing succeeded
each way was a fast.

Once a rat gnawed at my ration
right beside my head,
leaving me a crumb or two
of my piece of bread.

THE BIRTHDAY PRESENT
(a poem about a poem composed in Auschwitz-Birkenau)

It was a special present,
a birthday gift for me,
given in a place
where no one was free.

The place a concentration camp,
a place of fear and shame,
where humanity lost its way,
Auschwitz was its name.

Time was measured not by clocks
but by daily roll call lines,
we were counted every day,
not once but many times.

A present like this deserves description,
all done without a fuss,
a drawing, a precious slice of bread,
my friend was one of us.

It was a gift
for my eighteenth year
from Zosia, my friend,
a friend so dear.

Together we dreamed
one day we'd be free,
we'd live once again
without fear, in liberty.

What can be given
in a place like hell?
There's nothing to be found,
not to buy, or sell.

Zosia could write
and she wrote lots of rhymes,
she could cheer us up
in those difficult times.

In her heart she kept
songs and tales, a store
in times of war, of peace,
she'd sing songs galore.

For me she made a drawing
a birthday song she wrote.
She sacrificed her bread,
a sacrifice of note.

The drawing showed a table
laden with tasty food,
roast chicken, soup and borsht,
it looked so real, so good!

Our mouths watered just to see
fruit juice and sweet red wine.
Apples and honey – what a feast,
the drawing was divine.

The tasty meal that Zosia drew
was only in imagination,
though the bread was real, the sausage too,
a cause for celebration.

The slice of bread, swallowed and gone
the drawing like dust faded away,
but in my heart it still remains
from then – until today.

Biding its time, the poem remained,
hidden, out of sight,
hoping that one day
it could be brought to light.

With thanks and gratitude
for my dear friend
who encouraged us all
that one day it would end.

One day we'd be out
we'd leave hell behind
for a world that is free,
that's what we'd find.

And her special poem
in my memory is saved.
A precious gift
on my heart engraved.

A sign of love, a sign of hope,
my battle will be won.
Though Zosia perished on the last march
her memory lingers on.

Selected Poems from *Imagination: Blessed Be, Cursed Be*
Translated by Anna Sotto
Memoir Publications, Newark, Notts, 2001

Illustrations by Yaakov Guterman, a child survivor.

Go on asking questions; go on looking for answers;
go on trying to distinguish between good and evil.
Instead of hating, learn how to respect and love.

Nicole aged three, 1939

NICOLE DAVID

Growing up in Hiding

I was born in Antwerp in September 1936, the only daughter of Chawa Matzner and Munisch Schneider, my parents having moved to Belgium from Poland in the 1920s. When Belgium was invaded on 10 May 1940, the same day as Holland, we joined the long line of refugees, Jews and non-Jews, in the flight to France, in the belief that the French army could protect us. We found ourselves on the road to Dunkirk, amidst intense bombing during the British army's retreat to England. My father decided to go inland, and we stayed for a few weeks in a small village near Dunkirk.

My first language was German, as my parents were born near Cracow in the part of Poland that belonged to the Austro-Hungarian empire, and schooling there was in German. Shortly after our arrival in the village in France, German soldiers arrived. They were delighted to hear me speaking German when I was playing with another child. They came over to talk and bring us chocolate. The next day, they came with a doll. My father started talking with them, and they told him that their Führer, Adolf Hitler, would lead them to a quick victory over Europe because their army was the strongest. Their discipline was such that if they received orders to shoot us children, to whom they had just brought chocolate and dolls, they would do so. My father called me in, and told me that from then on I was not allowed to speak German. Though I was only three years old, I was made aware of the danger we were in. The memory of that incident remained with me for the rest of the war.

We soon went back to Antwerp and moved to Profondeville near Namur in the Walloon part of Belgium at the end of 1940. For the first two years, there were various laws restricting the freedom and movement of Jews. We were not allowed to run our own businesses, to be treated by non-Jewish doctors, attend non-Jewish schools. Cinemas, theatres or parks were out of bounds. Antisemitic decrees were in place and getting tougher. I wasn't even supposed to go to school, but a nun agreed to let me attend Kindergarten. One day, we were told, "Christ is everywhere." I was a bright, inquisitive child. I asked, "How do we know that if we can't see him?" That afternoon the nun called my mother and said, "You'd better take her out of here, she doesn't sound anything like a Catholic child."

In May 1942, Jews had to wear the yellow star which they had to buy. Although I was exempt from this regulation as I was not six years old, I do remember coming home from a walk to find my mother very agitated. Two German soldiers were inspecting my parents' overcoats and jackets to ensure that the star was correctly sewn on them.

The trains taking Jews to death camps (generally Auschwitz in the case of Belgium) started on 4 August 1942. The last train left Mechelen on 31 July 1944. Less than one month before the liberation of Belgium, the Germans were still making detailed plans to deport Jews. Of the 25,124 Jews and 351 Gypsies taken to the camps, only five per cent of adults and one per cent of children survived.

At the end of August 1942, my parents decided to go into hiding. Having failed to find a place that would take all three of us, my mother placed me in a Catholic orphanage, run by nuns, while they hid in an attic, protected by a Belgian family. I was very unhappy, as this was the first time I had been separated from my parents. I had constant tonsillitis, and the orphanage could not keep me. Antibiotics were not available then. I needed a tonsillectomy.

As the hospital would not take me, we returned – against my father's will – to the house where we had lived before going into hiding. There was a very good paediatrician there. We planned to stay one week so that I could have the operation, and my mother found a family willing to take me in when my health was restored.

I was so happy to be home, not only to be with my parents, but also to play with the nine-month-old baby of the other Jewish family living in the house. They had not gone into hiding because it was difficult to find someone willing to take a family with a baby and an elderly grandmother.

The day before the operation, 7 October 1942, I went out for a walk with my father, while my mother was preparing lunch. It was a beautiful day and we stopped on the terrace of a café on the river Meuse. When my father and I returned home, we saw three German lorries in front of the house. I never saw my mother again.

Someone from the Resistance was waiting for us and took us to a safe house, belonging to an Italian family. We spent the rest of the day there while the Germans were searching for us. In the evening, members of the Resistance took my father back to the attic where he had been hiding, and I was taken to stay with Monsieur and Madame Gaston Champagne, the Catholic parents of a neighbour whom my mother had befriended. They had ten children, five of whom were still at home, the youngest being 15.

The family took me in, knowing full well that they did so at the risk of their own lives and the lives of their children.

I lived with them for one and a half years, treated as one of the family. They never took any money for keeping me. My only outing was going to church with the family, and for me this was a great treat.

My mother had asked them to remind me to say my Jewish prayers, and so every evening Paulette (the daughter in whose room I slept, who later became a nun) would remind me not to forget to say my prayers. I did not go to school, as questions from other children might have been dangerous. Paulette was my teacher. Most of the time I was by myself and quite lonely. Every day I spent hours and hours making up fantasy stories which always involved an imaginary friend called Mickey. I had not been a loner by nature. I loved company and loved to talk. But I developed into a very self-sufficient person.

Exceptionally, on my seventh birthday, I was allowed to go for a walk with Ilse, now called Yvonne, the German Jewish girl who had been with us since 1938. She had blond hair and blue eyes, and was working locally on false papers. While waiting, I decided to walk out on my own, and before I realized it, found myself at the home of the Champagne's married daughter, at the other end of the village. By that time the whole family was looking for me, and as a punishment, I had to write out 250 times "I am not allowed to go out alone."

After about one and a half years, I was separated from the Champagne family and moved to another village to escape the bombing of a nearby ammunition dump. I was moved to Besinne-Arbre, the same village as my father, and we were briefly reunited.

Very soon after my arrival, the Germans drove up to the farm where I was staying. As soon as I saw the car approaching, I ran to my room, got into bed and pretended to be ill. Fortunately they were not interested in me, but were looking for the farmer's two sons, whom they wanted for work in Germany. I was moved on and hidden again, as it was too dangerous for me to stay in this village.

By then, there were rumours that the Americans were coming. The rumours were true and I was liberated by the Americans on 6 September 1944. An American soldier jumped from his lorry to give me a bar of chocolate. I was so frightened by his uniform that I ran away. When the family I was with and the soldier caught up with me, they explained that this was a friendly uniform.

The surrounding woods were still full of German soldiers and shooting continued for a while. In fact two young men were killed by Germans while they were hoisting the Belgian flag on the Town Hall.

It was some time before it was safe to travel along the country roads. Finally I was reunited with my father, but soon we had to flee again. We were in the midst of the heavy fighting of the Battle of the Bulge, and there was a genuine fear of a German victory against the Americans. We had intended going to France. Luckily before we got to the border, we were told that the Germans had been defeated, and so we went to Brussels, where we stayed until the end of the war.

My father did not want to return to Antwerp, which was being bombarded by V-1 and V-2 missiles. Because he was homeless, we were separated once again and I was placed in a convent in Brussels until the end of the war. Although he came to see me almost daily, this last separation was very difficult for me, coming so quickly after we had been reunited, and I had been assured that the Germans had fled.

When we returned to Antwerp after the liberation in May 1945, my father and I lived as lodgers in separate families for more than a year, until he could start earning again and find a flat, as Antwerp had been so badly bombed. Owing to illness, I started school a few months later, when I was nearly ten years old. After all the chaos, normal life resumed, unfortunately without many of our loved ones. But it was a period that was as difficult as everything that had gone before.

It was not until 1982, when the Belgian Memorial Book was published, that I had any indication of what had happened to my mother after she had been bundled into the lorry on 7 October 1942. After her arrest, she was put on a train three days later. According to the list, 1,679 people, including 487 children, were put on that train which arrived at Auschwitz on 12 October. Only 54 people from that convoy survived the war. The book was a copy of the detailed lists, methodically prepared by the Germans at Mechelen, the Belgian transit camp for all the people arrested and subsequently deported to the death camps. The lists had been found and handed to the Belgian authorities by the British soldiers who liberated the camp in 1944. They were produced in 1980-81 at the trial in Germany of Kurt Asche, the Gestapo man in charge of the "Final Solution" for Jews in Belgium. After an eight-month trial, he was given seven years' imprisonment.

My mother was one of seven brothers and sisters. All were married and had children. Only two survived.

Some six years ago, I returned for the first time to the café where I had stopped for a drink with my father on the day of my mother's arrest by the Germans. When I explained to the owner who I was, he went to fetch the daughter of the previous owners of the café, who was living next door. She told me she remembered 7 October 1942. It was a day she would never forget. It was indeed a beautiful day, and she was doing some shopping at the greengrocer's opposite our house. Screams were heard, and when she and the other customers came outside, they saw two women and a man being taken to the lorries in front of our house. The mother of the nine-month-old baby was begging for her baby, but she was brutally thrown into one of the lorries. The woman who was speaking to me added, "The other woman was your mother." The baby was taken in and looked after for the rest of the war by the two elderly sisters from whom we had rented the house.

There are thousands of individual stories like mine of separation, terror, physical and emotional hardship. But I think it is important to remember that there was goodness amongst all the evil. People who put their lives and those of their family at risk, in order to save us, my father and me. In Belgium during the war, some rail-workers tried to sabotage the trains, some postmen steamed open letters if they suspected denunciation, and warned people of impending

Nicole aged 3, with her mother aged 36 in Antwerp Park, winter 1939

arrest before forwarding the letters. Social workers helped Resistance movements to save children. Many priests and convents took in Jewish children and adults. This happened not only in Belgium, but also in France, Italy and other countries, thereby saving many who otherwise would have been sent to a certain death.

It helps us to remember that individuals in society can make a difference.

This story of my survival is dedicated to my mother, paternal grandmother, uncles, aunts and cousins on both sides of our family who did not survive.
They were brutally murdered not for anything they had done, but for being Jewish, by people who had always nurtured a deep-rooted antisemitism, and who had been conditioned to demonise and vilify Jews until they were considered sub-human beings that could be killed at will.

Victor, Manfred, Regina and Joe, Leipzig 1927

MANFRED DESSAU

It Could So Easily Have Been Me

My name is Manfred Dessau. I was born early in the morning of 9 August 1926 in Leipzig, Germany. Many years later, my mother told me that I was actually due on the previous day, 8 August, the date of my parents' wedding anniversary. To the best of my knowledge, I haven't been late once since that day!

My story begins many years before 1926 with the birth of my father Victor (named Izaac Leib by his parents) on 11 November 1896 in Pietrikav, Poland. Victor left Poland for Germany in the first decade of the twentieth century and seems to have adopted, or was given, the first name Wicus. He kept this name until late 1934 when a friend in England decided that henceforth he would be known as Victor. It was a very appropriate name for a man who became a victor over all adversities.

My mother was born Rifka Ruchela Rotenstein in Lodz, Poland on 23 October 1900, and was called Regina after her family's move to Germany. After her marriage to Victor on 8 August 1922, she was one of three family members called Regina Dessau and gladly accepted the shortened version of the name – Gina – by which she was happily and affectionately known until her death.

I should also add that my brother, born in 1923, was given the name Joachim, which he changed to Joe the day after we arrived in England, 2 November 1935.

I was and am Manfred. I never liked the shortened versions Manny or Fred.

History has shown that antisemitism was rife in Eastern European countries, especially Russia and Poland, long before the majority of the German people knew the word. It is not surprising that Victor (whose family had moved to Lodz in the early 1900s) made the brave decision to escape from military conscription for Jewish teenagers in Poland. Conscription was associated with diabolically cruel treatment, sometimes worse than slavery, and suicide was not unknown among the conscripts. This was why he went to live in Germany.

Victor was the only one of his family who made his escape in this way. His mother and father remained in Lodz with his two brothers and two sisters. My paternal grandparents both died natural deaths. Of his four siblings, one brother passed away in 1925; his other brother, Jacob, was a Holocaust survivor, but, tragically, his two sisters and their entire families were amongst the six million Jews who perished in that gruesome period of history. Despite many efforts, Victor was never able to find any trace of where or how his other brother and two sisters had died.

Regina was more fortunate. With her mother, father and one sister, she left Poland for Germany in the early years of the twentieth century, where her mother passed away peacefully at a very early age. Her father married again and was blessed with one son and three daughters from this marriage. And there was more good fortune for the family because they all escaped the Holocaust at various times during 1938 and 1939. Two found refuge in Israel and the rest in England.

Many of my memories of the early years in Leipzig are fairly clear in my mind even if I cannot always remember names. I do recall that we lived first at 33 Breitenfelder Strasse and in fact I went to school in the same street. Later we moved to Lindenauer Markt and finally, before Regina, Joe and I departed for England, we moved in with my grandfather's family at 8 Kreutz Strasse, also in Leipzig.

By the time of this last move, my father had already left Germany rather hurriedly in 1934. He had little choice as he was scheduled for a court appearance because of a motoring offence – for a Jew this would undoubtedly have meant being sent to a prison, and later to a concentration camp. With hindsight we can attribute this rapid departure to my father's fear of what might happen in Germany with the rapid rise of the Nazi Party.

At the time, these fears were not shared by all of Germany's Jews. Many thousands of them were sure that they would not be included in the horrors happening every day, in the streets of every town and city throughout the land. They were the Jews whose families had lived for many generations in Germany, who considered themselves to be a cultural part of that community. They were quite sure that the antisemitism spreading like a plague throughout Germany was directed at Eastern European Jews who had arrived in Germany in more recent years. They were known by other Jews as the *Yeckes* because they wore the same clothes as the rest of the German people, they talked and looked like them, and felt sure they had been integrated with the majority of the population. How wrong they were! By the mid-1930s, they learnt very quickly that they were simply Jews, just the same as the rest of us.

So my father left Germany in great haste in July 1934 and could only do so because he was able to obtain a Polish passport – which I still have. But he had to leave behind his wife and two sons. It was only some years later that I fully understood the difficulty this caused Victor and Gina. In order to gain entry to the United Kingdom, Victor had to have a guarantor, someone who would offer him a job and assure the authorities that he would not be a cost to the state. This man, one of many Jews in the UK who offered paid jobs to Jewish immigrants in the 1930s, was Jacob Prevezer, the owner of Derby and Midland Mills in Derby. He was also the grandfather of Ronald, who many years later was to become one of my closest friends.

Meanwhile, my mother, brother and I were experiencing a most difficult time during those months when we were left in Germany without a husband and father to take care of us. Like all Jewish children after 1933, Joe and I were forced to leave the school in Breitenfelder Strasse and transfer to the Jewish Carlebach School, named after a distinguished rabbi.

I also recall quite clearly the parades of the Black Shirts (*SS Schutzstaffel*: elite troops of the Nazi party). They did not hesitate to use their batons to beat anyone who got in the way of those marches, but at the time I did not associate these awful acts only with the Jewish people. Those memories are clear enough for me to say that to this day I have never been able to wear a black shirt.

As I write, I remember the day Adolf Hitler visited Leipzig and the huge crowds that lined the streets as he stood in his car, accompanied by his entourage. Those crowds hysterically raised their arms and screamed "*Heil Hitler*" loudly non-stop. And I am not at all sure that I wasn't amongst them – such was the power of mass hysteria.

Finally mother, Joe and I made it to England – and again it was because Gina was able to obtain a Polish passport with our names included in it. We left Leipzig on 1 November 1935, travelling by train to the Hook of Holland and then by boat to Harwich. We arrived there on 2 November and then went by train to London, where we were met at the railway station by our cousins Zonia and Helen Dessau.

I remember little or nothing of those first 24 hours in London, but certainly cannot forget the eager anticipation of our next train journey from St. Pancras, London, to Nottingham's Victoria Station. The carriage had hardly stopped before I jumped out straight into my father's arms. I clearly recall that both Victor and Regina were crying on that station platform, but they were tears of joy and relief. Waiting with Victor was our cousin Heinz Dessau. His father (for whom Victor was working at that time) had kindly lent his car to take us to a rented house, our first home in Great Britain – Number 2A, Burnham Street, Sherwood, Nottingham.

Our first meal there was prepared by Heinz and it was actually beans on toast! I reminded him about that many years later and he laughed, telling me that he actually hated beans, but it was the only thing that he knew how to cook and, in any case, everybody in England ate baked beans.

Our second day in Nottingham was 5 November. Our house at Number 2A was next to an open piece of land belonging to the Sherwood and Carrington Working Men's Club, and I was to play and make several friends there in the months ahead. But on that day, it was the site for an enormous bonfire and large numbers of fireworks. It is difficult to describe how Joe and I reacted to that wonderful display. Believe it or not, at the time we really thought it was a welcoming celebration for the Dessau family!

Soon after that memorable day, Victor talked to Regina, Joe and me about our future in our new country. I remember his words with great clarity and have repeated them many times since 1935: "We are in England now, so we will speak English and we will be English." It did not mean, of course, that we would not be Jewish, or that we could not go to synagogue. But it did mean that we should mix and integrate with the people of Sherwood who were our neighbours and would become our friends.

Victor already had a good command of English and it did not prove to be a great problem for Joe and myself. For Gina, who went neither to work nor to school, it was a gargantuan task which she overcame with difficulty – and over a much longer period of time. Just imagine her having to go shopping on Mansfield Road, Sherwood, and finding the only way she could spend the few shillings and pennies her husband had given her was by pointing to this and that and, maybe, the other.

I do remember clearly that for one of the first meals we had as a family in Burnham Street, there was butter on the table – remarkable because Jews in Germany, even in 1935, were only allowed to buy margarine. And in case you should wonder how the German shopkeepers knew that we were Jews, I remind you that we had to wear a yellow Star of David on our outer garment.

And then for Joe and Manfred it was off to Haydn Road Primary School, just a few hundred yards away from our home, knowing that we were not only immigrants but also refugees from another country. But we were determined to brave all that was ahead of us – bearing in mind that neither of us could speak one word of English! As it turned out, everyone was very friendly – there was more curiosity than the animosity I had suffered in my last days at German state school in Leipzig. Of course, our school contemporaries in 1935 had no idea why we were there, and they probably wouldn't have understood if we had been able to explain it to them

– which we were not. I was wearing knickerbockers (knee-length trousers) and a round hat with a pompom in the middle. How I wish that I had a photograph of me in that outfit!

There was one teacher at school who had served in the trenches in the First World War and he was able to recall a few words of German which he used with some success. Going to school so very promptly was the great blessing that enabled us to learn the English language quickly and with a good old Nottingham accent. I think it would be quite fair to say that within a very few months Joe and I were quite fluent, and we had no difficulty with our lessons at Haydn Road School.

We both made great efforts to integrate with our new-found schoolfriends, wanting to assure them that we were not really different. It was not too long before we were no longer a curiosity, but happily settled in that new environment. Interestingly enough, there were no other Jewish boys at Haydn Road.

Within 18 months, Joe had left Haydn Road for the Claremont School on Hucknall Road and I had even made it to form monitor before taking an entrance exam that would lead to a place at High Pavement Grammar School in 1937. That was quite a different school and I was definitely looked upon as "the foreigner", but not with any obvious anti-Jewish bias. My scholastic achievements there were not brilliant but – more important for me – I became a member of the Junior School Rugby team and joined the Dramatic Society. Rather than being bullied myself, I am ashamed to admit that for a while I was one of the school bullies. Very soon my Housemaster, a Mr Crossland, had me in his office and reminded me why I was in England and at this school. It was a very sobering 15 minutes but, I am glad to say, my bullying days were over.

Apart from my being at the Grammar School, 1937 was also a very important year for our family, particularly for Victor, although I didn't appreciate this fully at the time. Having left the job with Henry Dessau, he was offered an opportunity by a Mr Frank Johnson to start a factory making men's dressing gowns – an opportunity that came with a loan of £500. Victor was really thrilled, and when Frank said we would have to think of a name for this new company, he didn't hesitate: "We'll call it Burnham Manufacturing" (after our street) and the name was registered on 27 September 1937.

In the midst of all that activity, I also started attendance at the *Cheder* School – that's Sunday School if you like – and started lessons for my Barmitzvah or confirmation classes. But before I leave 1937, I must tell you that our sister Faye was born in November of that year, bringing much joy to Gina and Victor.

While I was at my *Cheder* Class on Sunday 3 September 1939, I heard the announcement on the wireless, "This country is now at war with Germany." It was to strike fear into the hearts of so many people like my mother and father, a fear not only fuelled by the thought of war, but also by the frightening prospect of what might happen in the event of a German victory.

Only two weeks after the outbreak of the war – I was then just 13 – all the pupils of High Pavement School were evacuated to Mansfield, a town just 15 miles away from Nottingham. My first "hosts" there were a coal-mining family living in Chesterfield Road and I must confess that I was not too happy there. I shared a room with their son of similar age and he seemed to resent my presence as much as I did his. One memory of that stay was that I ate egg and chips for supper every evening. They knew that I was Jewish and I am sure that they simply didn't want to offend my eating customs.

I reported my unhappiness to the person in charge of the evacuees and was moved shortly afterwards to another home, again in Chesterfield Road, the home of Dr Stronach. I had a much happier stay there. Dr Stronach's wife, daughter and son had moved to Canada, presumably to get away from the war, and I had a lovely room all to myself. He was a good host and, with other "guests," we had regular sing-songs to his piano accompaniment. His favourite song was "Run Rabbit, Run Rabbit, Run Run Run."

Many years later, around 1995, I visited Mansfield General Hospital and met another Dr Stronach, obviously the son of my former host. "I slept in your bed once," I told him and to his utter amazement, I was able to tell him the story of my stay at 317 Chesterfield Road in 1939 and 1940.

My evacuation to Mansfield lasted only about 18 months and early in 1941, I was living back at home, in Ramsdale Crescent where we had moved early in 1939.

"And what did you do in the war, Dad?" is a familiar question children asked their fathers in the 1950s and 60s. Well, unlike Joe, I didn't get into the army, although I did try. Somewhere I have a letter signed by Captain H. A. Brown advising me – incorrectly as it happens – that if I wished to enlist, it would have to be in the Polish Army or the Pioneer Corps. In any case I was too young.

I did, I suppose, do my bit. Whilst in Mansfield, and also when back at home, all the students were "conscripted" to work on farms during the summer holidays. I worked at a nice farm near Farnsfield, Notts, in the first year and on a farm quite near to Sherwood Forest the year after. I was in the Boy Scouts and also joined the "Civil Defence Cadet Corps", a kind of junior ARP (Air Raid Precautions). It meant that if we had bicycles, we could run errands and messages for the Air Raid Wardens. I served until the end of the war and finished up as the Sergeant Major at the age of 18.

One interesting sideline to the Cadet Corps job happened when somebody found out that I could speak German. Very soon I was being called on to interpret for the German prisoners of war as they arrived at Nottingham's Eastcroft Station. It wasn't really interrogation – more practical questions about personal needs. One evening the POW train arrived just after an announcement that there had been an unsuccessful attempt on Hitler's life. I told the news to the group of some 15 prisoners and clearly remember one of them saying *"Gott sei Dank"* (Thank God!) but I couldn't tell if he meant thank God for the attempt, or that it had failed

Reflecting on those dark days and the suffering of those left behind in much of Europe, I have often thought about my feelings towards the German people and, indeed, have been asked several times to express those feelings. I have no problem to this day with those born after the late 1930s, but those older than me were almost all enthusiastic supporters of the Nazi regime and I am still not totally comfortable with them. In fairness to them, it is perhaps not surprising considering the political and media support for Adolf Hitler.

I left High Pavement School in 1942 at the age of 16 with quite poor School Certificate results and then got a job as an electrician's mate with Thomas Danks & Co. Ltd., a then very well known Nottingham company. Why an electrician's mate? Victor had very strong views about careers for his sons. We had to have jobs that could be done anywhere in the world. Having been forced twice in his youth to flee to a new life in a different country, he was convinced that as an electrician, plumber or mechanic of any sort, you would get a job wherever you were. As a doctor or lawyer, you would arrive in a new country and have to start all over again before you could practise your profession.

My job was quite good fun and very good for me, but the first thing I had to learn from the electrician was the answer to the daily question, "Ay yer mashed?" (Have you made the tea?) One of my first jobs as mate was at The Ransom Sanatorium, near to Mansfield. For days – indeed weeks – I had to prepare holes in concrete walls to which porcelain cable supports would be attached, into which the wiring was fed. The only problem was that this was long before the days of electric drills and the holes had to be made manually with a hammer. Many years later, in 1996, I paid a return visit to Ransom (it was now called a Hospital), but this time as representative of the Secretary of State for Health to officially open a new wing. I spent quite a long time looking for those wiring cable supports but couldn't find them anywhere!

I served as an apprentice for only 18 months or so before Danks called me in to work on the electrical counter in their retail shop in Thurland Street, selling whatever in those difficult days might be available. I actually did quite well there and as the end of the war came, with a shortage of skilled men, I was appointed manager of the whole electrical department. Strangely enough, it was at Danks that I had my first experience of antisemitic attitudes – attitudes born out of resentment by others who thought that they should have been offered this great opportunity.

In 1949 my father asked me if I would like to join him at his company and it wasn't hard to say "Yes please" when he offered me a starting wage of £2,000 per year – when I had only been paid £25 per week at Danks. I joined him as soon as I had worked my notice. So began a career that was to last 40 years until my retirement from the garment industry in 1989. And it ends this part of my life story – the first 24 years of my life.

In between that career ending and the stories that follow I married Mirelle in 1956. We have three children: Caroline, named after one of Victor's sisters; Vicky, named after Victor; and Nigel, named after Mirelle's father Nathan. We now have five grandchildren.

In 1991, the year after the Berlin Wall came down, I decided to make a return journey to Leipzig, the city of my birth, in the company of Mirelle, my cousin Bob Kutner, also born in Leipzig, and his wife Barbara.

The journey there was in itself quite an event but I will concentrate on our arrival in Leipzig, where we had been told to find *Das Judische Amt*, the Jewish Bureau. We went in the afternoon after our arrival, but were asked to come back the following morning as they could not see visitors in the afternoon. We duly arrived at 9 o'clock and the very friendly people, who spoke good English, gave us a sheet of paper and asked us to write down everything we could remember – names of parents and grandparents, addresses where we lived, schools and so forth. We did that, handed over those pieces of paper and they gave us a cup of coffee while we waited. In not much more than ten minutes, they came back with my whole family history, including mention of the names of my father, mother, Joe and myself. Not only did they give me photocopies of the information, which I will always treasure, but they then asked us if we would like a driver to take us round to the places we had listed. It was an opportunity we simply couldn't refuse.

Before we left home I had drawn some not very artistic sketches of all my homes and schools. I cannot begin to express my emotions and joy at seeing them all – except for Lindenauer Markt which no longer existed. The sketches turned out to be quite accurate, showing that our long-term memories are often better than the short-term. I will never forget that visit and the emotions and tears it brought to me. We even visited Kreutz Strasse, the very street where in the latter part of 1935 I had seen the Black Shirts beat the hell out of anyone getting in their way.

Then, some ten years later at the age of 75, I made the decision that for the first time in my life, I must visit Poland, the birthplace of my parents. I was accompanied by my wife Mirelle and our friends Margaret and Alan Abrams. The visit started in Warsaw, a wondrous city to see, and not only from the Jewish historical point of view. The city was completely destroyed by the departing German army and has since been rebuilt as near as possible to its original state. There are 26 Jewish historical sites to be seen, including everything from the ghetto walls to the *Umschlagplatz*, the assembly point from which ghetto Jews were transported to the concentration camps from July 1942 at the rate of 5,000-6,000 each day. It is now a memorial site, and the following inscription is engraved on the wall, "Along this path of suffering and death over 300,000 Jews were driven in 1942-43 from the Warsaw ghetto to the gas chambers of the Nazi extermination camps." I sat at the foot of this memorial for a full ten minutes, talking to no one – except to myself.

And then by hired car we travelled to Pietrikav, the birthplace of my father, not knowing what we would find, nor indeed where we would find it. With luck we found the synagogue, which was now a library and student hall. I crossed the road to take a photograph and our friends immediately called me back to look at a plaque on the wall outside the main door. It was engraved with names and Dessau appeared three times, although I didn't recognise any of the first names.

The building was closed, but with more luck we found the local Memorial Museum which we were invited to look round. There I found one member of staff who could speak enough German to tell us that the Jewish Cemetery was in Jerusalem Road, which we found without difficulty. The cemetery was closed as well, but to our utter amazement we found a plaque by the gate with those same names inscribed on it. As we were looking at it, a lady came out waving her arms to indicate that the cemetery was closed. I took a brave step forward and pointing to myself said "Dessau – me Dessau", whereupon she immediately invited us to go in. She escorted us to the largest gravestone with that same name on it, not three but six times. She also showed me a memorial book with all the names of the people buried here. I cannot find words to describe my feelings at the time.

Our next stop was Krakow, and from here we went on a guided bus tour to Auschwitz-Birkenau, perhaps the most well known place of genocide in the world. From the moment I saw the *Arbeit Macht Frei* sign over the entrance gate, I knew that this was not going to be my best day, but it was a day I had to experience. We saw everything, the storage areas filled with hair, shoes, suitcases, glasses and so on. Most of the time my companions left me to myself and I was grateful for that.

In one glass-topped table with lots of papers inside, I saw one very formal document with the name Dessau on it. As no one could interpret the words for me, I took a photograph and after getting a translation, I wish perhaps that I had not done so. Dessau is the name of a town in the eastern part of Germany, some 70 miles at the time from the Polish border. This is what the paper said, "Permission for vehicles leaving for Dessau to collect Zyklon B, the poison needed for 'Special Action' or for 'Resettlement of Jews'." (The inverted commas are not mine – they are a part of the notice.)

I also learnt later that the town of Dessau was one of two places to which trains from all over Europe came with their cargoes of Jews – before they were shipped on to Auschwitz and Birkenau.

Please believe me when I tell you that so many times that day I had to say thank you to Regina and Victor. "It could so easily have been me." And I have been able to express my feelings by planting a rose in the Memorial Gardens at Beth Shalom, together with a plaque inscribed with the words, "You brought me out in time."

There is one final sentence. Having talked to our families about the visit and shown them the many photographs, our two oldest grand-daughters, Juliette and Debra, aged 17 and 15 at the time, asked us to take them on this same historical journey, and this we did one year later in July 2002. It was important for them and for me for the memories and lessons to be passed on.

This story is dedicated to Juliette, Debra, Gina, Kelly and David.

Manfred Dessau, at his desk, 1996

Daniel, dressed up for a photograph, about 1918-19

Daniel Falkner

Surviving the Warsaw Ghetto

I was born in Poland in 1912. I lost my father very early in life and have no recollection of him. My mother married again and we moved to Rzeszow, a town with a thriving Jewish community. Poverty among Jews was great, but this did not prevent youngsters from taking part in all sorts of cultural activities. We had a dramatic society, a sports club where we played football, tennis, took part in swimming and skating. We even had an orchestra where more experienced players instructed younger ones. It was a real community.

I grew up in Rzeszow and went to school there. I wanted to study medicine but there were very restricted entries for Jews into medical schools and I lost my first academic year just trying to get in. I was approaching the age of compulsory military service and was sent to a school for officers in reserve. There were about 700-800 cadets in the school and among them only six Jews. Of those six, only two of us passed out as officers in reserve. After military service, I had an offer of a job in an export-import firm in Warsaw and moved there in 1936.

Anti-Jewish propaganda was increasing with every day. Radio from Germany was broadcasting stories about the 'evil' Jews and this propaganda fell on eager ears in Poland. Then in 1938, the propaganda barrage turned against Poland itself. In 1939, ominous troop movements took place in Germany and threats made against Poland were obvious signs that war would not be far off.

Because of tension on the borders, the Polish Government decided to call for a small mobilisation and among many thousands of reservists, I was called up and sent to the very border of Poland and East Prussia. We came under artillery fire even before war officially broke out. We were forced to withdraw and were constantly under tremendous pressure from the overwhelming power of the German war machine. We were withdrawing all the time, almost to the Rumanian border in the south. Here our division surrendered to the Germans.

We were all taken to a temporary prisoner of war camp. The local people told us that there had been other Polish troops in this camp before and that Jews were separated from the rest and marched off in a different direction. There and then, I decided to escape, which I managed to do. I decided to make my way to my parents to let them know that I was alive. I walked most of the way back to my home town.

I was such a sight that my own mother almost could not recognise me. I had already decided to hitch-hike back to Warsaw, where I knew a young girl, and the following day, I got up very early and said goodbye to my parents. It was a long and dangerous journey, particularly as Jews were not allowed to travel by train, but I succeeded.

Life was continuing in Warsaw with all sorts of harassment, shootings and arbitrary arrests. In the autumn of 1940, the Germans ordered all Jews who lived scattered throughout Warsaw to move to a small dilapidated area previously occupied by about 50,000 people. At the same time, all non-Jews were to move out of that area. You cannot imagine the desperation and utter confusion of half a million Jews being squeezed into a small area, trying to find accommodation.

Soon, a ten-foot brick wall was erected and we found ourselves in the ghetto. The food situation was deteriorating with every month. While the Polish population was issued with 1,000 calories per day, the Jews received only 500-600. In spite of the daily danger and deprivation, cultural life still continued. There were musical performances, small theatre shows, private tuition for children, both religious and secular. At the same time, there were nightly raids on intellectuals and others, and people just disappeared without trace. As time went on, the density of the population and the meagre food ration caused an outbreak of typhus in the ghetto and hundreds of people were dying every day.

This went on until the summer of 1942 when the Germans announced that people who wanted to improve their situation would be taken to the "East" for work. At the beginning, there were many volunteers and every day, about 6,000 people were evacuated to the "East". Soon, however, suspicion was aroused when the Germans started to round up people in the streets, young and old, strong and weak. People noticed that the train taking Jews to the "East" was always the same; it travelled only a short distance and had some writing inside the wagons, indicating that the travellers had suffered greatly. Then one young man managed to escape and return to the ghetto to warn us that the people were being taken to the concentration camp at Treblinka, and systematically killed. From then on, people stopped believing the Germans and did everything possible to hide; they were burying themselves underground to try and escape the daily raids.

In the meantime, young people conspired in order to put up resistance, although they realized it was against impossible odds. Nevertheless, the Jewish underground organisation came into existence. The first attack was waged against the Jewish police chief in Warsaw as a representative of collaboration with the Germans. He was shot in the street. It was a sign that the resistance movement was gathering strength.

On 5 January 1943, a young man who lived in the same block as us came down to our flat with his younger sister. He said that he wanted to say goodbye, and to warn us that something terrible was going to happen that very night. With this sort of news we could not even think of going to bed.

I was pacing up and down the room contemplating what to do. Finally, I decided to risk my life and try to inform people of the impending danger. I went down to the main gate, then ran from doorway to doorway until I came to the Jewish hospital. I knew there were many Jewish personalities working there. The hospital director was a good friend of mine. I knocked at the gate and after a long while, a little window opened and I asked to speak to the director. The doorkeeper hesitated. I assured him that it was very important. After a while, the director came and I told him that something awful was going to happen that night. Of course, he could not believe it, as for the past three months everything had been quiet. I finally managed to convince him to take some precautionary measures.

I made my way back to the flat via Mila Street, where I left a similar message. We did not go to bed that night but were hanging about behind the curtained windows to see what was going to happen. Everything was quiet until about 5.00 a.m. when in the distance we heard the regular clatter of marching feet approaching the ghetto wall. Finally, we saw a column of German soldiers approaching the gates. As they marched through, they divided into two columns: one going towards Mila Street, where they were shot at from various directions and suffered many casualties.

The sense of elation at seeing German casualties caused by Jewish fighters was indescribable. At the same time, the other column turned right and headed straight for the Jewish hospital. As they gained entrance to the ward, the Germans started shooting without any provocation at everybody alive. Then they withdrew. When things quietened down, I went to the hospital. The scene was bizarre. Men and women were in their sick beds all shot dead, some still bleeding, the staff attending them also dead.

In the meantime, the Jewish fighters had taken away the guns and ammunition from the dead Germans. The Germans now realized that there was an armed resistance movement in the ghetto and in order to overcome it, they would have to reorganise and plan properly. Another period of intense quiet descended – until April 1943.

At the beginning of February 1943, I managed to escape from the ghetto to the other part of Warsaw, risking being discovered by the Poles. Discovery could mean being faced with threats of denunciation, unless a substantial bribe was paid. I must, however, stress that there were cases where Poles helped Jews to survive and this was true in my own case. With great danger to herself, Margaret, my wife's old nurse, undertook to keep a few of us in complete secrecy, and without any fee. My wife had escaped there a few weeks earlier.

We settled in Margaret's ground-floor flat and immediately adopted a strict regime, talking amongst ourselves in whispers and walking in socks or slippers so as not to raise suspicions with the neighbours. We also started to dig a hiding place in case of emergency. We practised how to collect all our clothing and bedding in an emergency and slip through a secret hole into our hiding place, making the flat look as if only one person lived there.

Our resources for sustenance were small and diminishing every day. There was no question of going out to work or earning anything. We had one friend, a solicitor called Romek, the only person who knew our hideout and visited us from time to time. Through him we sold our engagement ring, the only valuable thing we had and although we bought only very plain and staple food, we could see our money running out soon.

By the time of the Polish uprising, there were already seven people hiding from the Germans in our place. When shooting started in the streets, we all went out and offered to give a hand in defeating the common enemy. We built barricades in the streets – it was long and exhausting work.

Soon the Germans brought in a new SS division who systematically set alight house after house, occupying street after street, killing the inhabitants in cold blood. The same night, the Germans came to our district and set alight the fourth and second floors of our block, calling through loudspeakers that everybody must go down to the courtyard. As our flat was on the ground floor, we could hear shots being fired at the inhabitants gathering in the courtyard. The fires were burning fiercely and we could hear ceilings collapsing above us, and finally the ceiling in our living room gave way. Luckily, we were all gathered in the kitchen where the ceiling still held. Just then, one of our party of Jews decided to get out of the burning trap and ask for mercy for himself and his wife. I had very little time for a decision. I knew that if I allowed him to go, his fate would be sealed with a bullet, and he might lead the Germans to our hiding place. I decided not to let him go and pointed my pistol at him, saying we would either all perish or hold out some while longer.

Soon after that, the main gate of our block caught fire and the Germans withdrew. I waited a little longer to hear if they had all left. Then I opened the door and led all the people into the courtyard. There was a store of sacks and cement at the end, and I arranged a temporary shelter, behind which we all took cover. It was about 1-2 a.m. and everywhere was brightly illuminated by fires. We did not know where to go and decided to stay in this shelter until daytime. When finally daybreak came, I went back to our house to explore the possibilities of returning. But it was completely burned out except for the skeleton of the walls and chimneys.

I noticed that the cellar had not collapsed and by shovelling away a passage through the little window at ground level, you could slide into it. I thought that the Germans would not waste time looking for survivors in a burned-out building, particularly since fighting still continued in other districts of Warsaw and the Russian armies were approaching. Especially at night, we could hear the booming of distant artillery. I thought it was a question of surviving another few days and salvation would be at hand. I explained the possibility of hiding in the cellar to the others and we made our way past the heaps of smouldering debris through a small window into the darkness of an unknown cellar.

There was some light coming through near the entrance, but further on it was complete darkness. We had nothing with us except the clothing we had on, no food or drinks. When our eyes became accustomed to the darkness, we started to explore and found a whole system of underground corridors underneath the building. Luckily we found water, a small sack of flour and some tins of jam, and we lived on this for a few weeks. We established a rota of guard duty and once or twice we heard Germans in the yard above, ordering people to collect up the corpses.

There was a lot of activity in the yard during the days, particularly after our third week hiding in the cellars. We heard strange screeching noises, followed by explosions in the distance. To us, buried alive in the heat of the cellars, hungry, dehydrated and in constant semi-darkness, it meant only doom. Once, the wind blew in some leaflets in Polish, calling for endurance and proclaiming the Red Army was near. Of course, this gave us new strength and determination to hold out. Unfortunately, days and weeks passed and nothing changed – except that we grew weaker.

After the fourth week of hiding, a party of soldiers arrived one day at the cellar's main entrance. They began digging away at the heaps of rubble. I happened to be on watch with my friend Bolek; the rest of the people were hidden deeper in the cellar. After some energetic digging, an opening was made and bright light penetrated into the cellar, revealing myself and Bolek. It was too late to escape. A figure in German uniform and jackboots appeared in the entrance, pointing a rifle at us. I still do not know why he did not pull the trigger. More soldiers arrived, including a sergeant who ordered us to come out, hands raised. They led us to their temporary headquarters which happened to be nearby.

Fighting was still going on in other parts of Warsaw and the soldiers were surprised to have found us at the back of their headquarters. We were half-naked and had a month's growth of beard, our bodies were shrunken and our eyes wild. We were then taken under escort to Gestapo Headquarters.

We walked through the deserted streets of Warsaw with its empty skeletons of burned-out houses. Heavy fighting was still going on in other districts and in the distance we could see German planes dive-bombing parts of the city. We arrived at a house near the Vistula river. I was the last one of our party and as I stepped in, heavy blows began to fall on my face and body. For a split second, I raised my eyes and saw an enormous figure of a man in a German SS uniform. I was then led into a big room where the other members of my party were waiting, all battered in one way or another. I learned later that this was only the softening up process.

After some waiting, the Germans started to call us in, one after another, for investigation, but my friends never came back into the room again. It seemed very ominous to me. My turn finally came. I was led into a large room with closed shutters. It was semi-dark, but sitting at the table I saw a middle-aged SS sergeant, with documents and a leather riding stick on the table in front of him. As I approached, my heart was pounding with apprehension. He told me in German to sit down, then asked me how we came to be there, in their compound. I tried to explain that we were only hiding in the place where we used to live. He then addressed me in English and demanded an answer.

Apparently Bolek, who was interrogated before me, had a notebook on him in which there were cryptic entries on various dates and some entries in English. A few nights earlier there had been air raids and parachute drops by the RAF. Obviously the sergeant suspected that we might have had something to do with it. He repeated the question in English, grabbed the riding stick from the table and hit me on the back of the head with such force that I passed out. The interrogation was then broken off and I was taken to another room, where I met Bolek. We had no chance to exchange any information.

We were issued with bread and tinned meat and could not believe our eyes, but soon dark thoughts began to cloud our horizon. Perhaps they were giving us the last supper before our execution? A few minutes later, an SS man took out his automatic pistol and urged us to go out into the courtyard. I was quite convinced that we were marching to a place of execution. I felt no remorse and tried to visualise my mother's smiling face, my wife and my friends. I was ready to face what was to come.

We were led into a dark, damp dungeon. Perhaps the execution would be early next morning? So the night passed, and we thought that every minute could be the last. In the morning, we were led out of the dungeon and sent under escort for further interrogation to another Gestapo branch. Warsaw by that time was already a town in agony. Fighting was still going on and in some parts we had to duck to avoid snipers' bullets. Fires and explosions had turned the city into a heap of rubble and although I had lived there for many years, I could not recognise some of the streets. Our escort found it difficult to find a coherent way through the streets.

As we came near to a T-junction, we saw an enormous column of Polish civilians, old men, women and children, walking under escort. I heard our escort ask the other guard for directions. He probably did not understand the question and replied that we should join him. I realized that we had a chance to get lost in that column of people, and Bolek and I managed to vanish into the crowd. After a few hours walking, we arrived at a churchyard in Wola, a western district of Warsaw, and from there we were all transported by train to Pruszkow, a small town about 30 kilometres away.

Pruszkow was now an enormous temporary camp, from which train-loads of people were sent to various concentration camps in Germany. I stayed there for three days and did not go out during the day for fear of being recognised as a Jew among the Poles. Then one day, Bolek and I found ourselves on a cattle train, loaded with thousands of innocent people, travelling to the unknown. After two days of travelling, the train stopped in a field and the guards opened the doors.

The women and children were formed up on one side of the train and the men on the other, then we were marched off in the direction of a wood. Through a clearing, we saw a sight which has imprinted itself on my mind. It was my first contact with concentration camp life. In a field, we saw a troop of six slender figures in striped pyjama uniforms, pulling a huge peasant cart loaded with beetroots.

We were herded on the way with more shouts and kicks. In front of us was an enormous gate announcing the camp "Sachsenhausen – *Arbeit macht frei*" (Work brings freedom). We were formed up six abreast into a long column and they counted and counted again. Finally, we were marched through the gates.

We stopped at a big square and were ordered to drop any bundles we had with us. Then we were told to queue up before the registration desk, after which we had to undress, have all our hair shaved and go through a medical examination. Then we were given our new clothes – striped pyjama suits. I became an inmate of Sachsenhausen.

It was already autumn and the first few days were spent in inactivity. After morning roll-call, we were sent out into the open and the cold autumn wind blew through our flimsy clothing. At night, we were allowed to go inside, but after midnight, we were woken by wailing sirens because of an RAF raid. We had to run out of the hangar and into the bushes within the camp perimeter. This repeated itself for several more nights until one day, we were lined up and sent under guard to Oranienburg, another camp near Berlin. There the same thing happened and every night, we were exposed to air raids. Finally, they decided to send us to Dachau.

We were put on cattle trains and for several days and nights, we were shunted backwards and forwards. Finally we arrived in the middle of nowhere, at a labour camp which I later learned was an outpost of Buchenwald. Not far away was a mountain range and our task was to quarry the rock and build halls under the mountains for underground air-craft factories.

The regime in the camp was harsh, with very little food and heavy labour. We worked a 12-hour shift, day and night. Life expectancy was at most 2-3 months. I was put in charge of a pneumatic drill to make deep holes in the face of the rock. Then a German professional miner packed the holes with explosives, we withdrew 10 or 15 metres and the explosion took place. The accident rate was tremendous.

We were gradually growing weaker and I found it difficult to lift my legs over the smallest obstacle like a stone or twig. Yet our spirit grew stronger with every day. From snippets of conversation with our foreman, we deduced that the Allied forces were coming nearer. Then one day in broad daylight, we saw hundreds of American bombers coming quite low over our camp. With each explosion we heard, our hearts were filled with more hope. We felt that the end could not be far off.

One day in April 1945, we were told that we were to assemble for evac-uation. I was determined not to trust the Germans and looked for a place to hide. When everybody had gone, I loosened a floorboard, squeezed below and waited. I stayed there until darkness fell and came out when I could hear no movement. A few others had had similar ideas and slowly came out of their hiding places.

The Germans had assembled several thousand camp inmates and marched them into the unknown. They left behind those who were too ill to move and those like me who had managed to hide. For three days and nights, we were without guards, and without food or drink. We were too weak to venture out of the camp. Then suddenly we saw American tanks passing, and two ventured into the camp. When they saw that hell on earth, they ordered local Germans to clear the corpses and bury them in one mass grave. Then a fleet of American ambulances arrived and the sick were loaded onto stretchers and taken to an American hospital. Although we were fed and nursed magnificently, many of the people hospitalised died of various complications.

In retrospect, I would like to sum up in a few words the Nazi approach to solving the Jewish problem in Europe. In the first place, they humiliated you, then they robbed you, then they took away your name and gave you a number instead, then they worked you to the last breath in your lungs and finally they killed you.

Slowly I showed signs of recovery and after six weeks' stay in hospital, I was strong enough to be discharged and placed in a Polish Displaced Persons camp in the British Military Zone. Germany at that time was like a melting pot. People of various nationalities from all over Europe were moving in all directions. People incarcerated for so many years suddenly felt the warmth of freedom.

Because I could speak English, German, Polish and Russian, the British military soon used me to help with translation whenever there was a problem. One day, the Captain asked me if I would like to join the British Army as an interpreter. I agreed of course and after that life became much easier. I also submitted a search letter to the International Red Cross with all the particulars of my wife. I had no idea if she was alive or where she might be. Many months passed and I received no reply. I began to doubt if my wife was alive.

In the autumn of 1946, rumours began to circulate that my unit was going to be returned to the UK. I was very excited and looked forward to being able to start a new life in England. One day in late autumn, a young lady in military uniform entered the guard room and asked to see me. I began to see some familiar features and then suddenly recognised my wife. We fell into each other's arms and after a few emotional tears, started to tell each other how we had managed to survive. She told me that after the war ended, she had worked for the Polish Red Cross and one day accidentally came across my letter.

In the meantime my unit was already getting ready to move back to the UK and it was too late to include my wife on the same transport. We lived in Germany for another few weeks and then we had to part. I arrived in the UK early in February 1947, and my wife joined me few months later.

I arrived in this country without a penny, but with hard work and perseverance, in a climate of tolerance and liberty, I earned a living and became a respectable member of society. I retired from business at the age of 68 and decided to pay back to society some of the benefits I had gained. Since then I have been able to help Israeli High School students come to the UK every year to take part in London's International Youth Science Fortnight. This gives an opportunity for youngsters from over 60 countries to attend lectures, exchange ideas and develop friendships. I also help support some PhD students in this country and abroad, and with two of my friends, I have established an annual prize in Israel for applying biotechnology in medicine. I was always interested in science. Although I could not achieve any degrees myself because of the circumstances of war, I have at least been able to help others.

Daniel in High School uniform, one year before matriculation

Gisela on the St. Louis, 1939

GISELA FELDMAN

Boat to Nowhere

I was born in Berlin on 18 September 1923. My father, Leo Knepel, was born in 1885 in a little town near Rzeszow, which was then part of the Austro-Hungarian Empire, but became Poland after the First World War. His parents owned land, grew grain and ran a small business there, but I never met them. My father had two sisters and five brothers. He left home at the age of 15 to join an older brother in Berlin. Another brother joined them later. The eldest brother had emigrated to England at the turn of the century. The others stayed in Poland and had 11 children between them. None of these families survived the Holocaust.

My mother, Chaja Hella Wurzel, was born in 1894 in Tarnow, a slightly bigger town in Galicia, Poland. She went to Berlin to find employment in 1910. Her parents, two sisters and two brothers joined her after the end of the First World War. My mother's family settled in Berlin and opened a grocery store. One sister married and moved to Rumania. She was the only one who died of natural causes; the others perished in the concentration and death camps.

My parents met in Berlin and were married in 1920. In spite of a severe housing shortage, they were lucky to find a flat to rent. I was born three years later, in 1923, and my own memory goes back to my mother coming home from the hospital with my baby sister, Sonja, wrapped in a big feather pillow. I was two years and nine months old. I remember having a doll's pram exactly the same colour as my sister's pram. I walked proudly next to my mother, each pushing 'our baby'.

My mother worked with my father in our grocery shop and as I grew older, I loved to help, weighing and grinding coffee, patting butter from a big barrel and checking eggs for freshness by holding them against an electric light bulb.

For the first ten years of my life, I had a normal childhood. Most of our leisure time was spent with the family. We visited our grandparents regularly, particularly on the Jewish holidays. With my father's two brothers and their families, we were a very close-knit family and would spend birthdays and all family celebrations together. Every Sunday morning as soon as the fine weather started, they would phone each other to arrange a picnic in the countryside. Sonja and I were roughly the same age as our cousins Salo James and his brother Harry, and we had a wonderful time together. Salo James managed to get to England before the war and worked in a warehouse doing all sorts of menial jobs. Being a young idealist, he felt he needed to do his duty and joined the Polish Army when war broke out. He was killed in battle in France. All the other family in Berlin ended up in the gas chambers.

My sister and I went to the local primary school. It was usual to start school at the age of six and on the first day you were met by your mother with a *Schultüte*, a container shaped like a witch's hat filled with sweets.

In the early 1930s, my parents were lucky enough to get a much better flat, nearer to our shop and school. It had belonged to a Jewish family who had obviously seen the writing on the wall and decided to emigrate before the borders were closed. We enjoyed playing in the street with the other children and life still felt normal. But this feeling of security was shaken by the Mayday parade in 1932 or 1933. There were clashes between the Communists and the Brown Shirts (Nazi Storm Troopers). Someone in our block of flats was shot and I watched the body being carried out. I remember feeling that life would never be the same again.

Once Hitler came to power, open antisemitism started. My class teacher was very kind and of a different political persuasion. He very bravely told the other children that I was no different from anybody else and was to be treated no differently. He even wanted to make me secretary for the weekly collection for the Hitler Youth. Perhaps the fact that I was a blue-eyed blonde helped.

But things gradually got worse. My father was beaten up once or twice, our shop was daubed, telling people not to buy from Jews. Wholesalers did not always deliver goods to Jews and my mother often went to the whole-sale market in the early hours of the morning to buy things for us to sell in the shop. Most of our customers were very loyal and still bought from us – even when a Brown Shirt stood outside trying to frighten them.

More people started to leave Germany. It was an easier decision for either the rich or the poor. The rich managed to get enough money out to make a new start. The poor had nothing to lose. Of course you needed a visa from the country you wanted to go to. But things were much easier at the beginning. The middle classes, however, were very reluctant to give up their security and take their families into the unknown. Anyway, most people thought such madness could not last in a cultured, civilized society.

I left my primary school at the age of 11 when it was time to go to grammar school, with strict instruction from the teacher to my mother that I should eventually go to university. Alas, even the teacher did not realize that higher education would very quickly become an impossibility for us. My parents sent me to a Jewish school, which was just as well because shortly afterwards Jewish children were no longer tolerated in the state system. My sister had to leave her school.

At school we were beginning to hear rumours of some fathers being picked up and disappearing, or spending nights away from home to avoid being arrested. Our own parents had Polish passports and so we felt a little safer. German Jews were the first target despite the fact that many had fought side by side with the German soldiers for the 'Fatherland' in the First World War. Indeed, many had been awarded the Iron Cross military decoration.

I think our parents protected us from many of their worries and so we carried on with our school lives. My school, the Grosse Hamburgerstrasse, was the first Jewish grammar school to be re-opened in Germany after the war. It was closed in 1942 by the Nazis and most of the students sent to camps. On one of my visits after the war, I was told that another former student had visited and burst into tears when she saw the piano. Her music teacher had pushed her into learning to play, and that had saved her life in the camp as she was able to entertain the guards.

I enjoyed my schooling. I learnt English from the age of 11 and started French at 14. Little did I know how important my knowledge of English would be. My favourite subject was PE and I played for the school in the netball team.

We still continued our annual holidays at the seaside, and in 1936 and 1937 my mother

My first day at school, I am on the right

took us to Poland to meet my father's family. On our return I noticed that our parents were getting more and more worried. It started to affect my father's health and a lot of responsibility fell on my mother's shoulders. There was a shortage of food. Hitler was arming and the slogan was "Guns before butter". In the summer of 1938, my parents finally decided to close the business.

All efforts to get a visa to anywhere in the world proved fruitless. People were getting desperate and were quite prepared to send their children away to save them, not knowing if they would ever see them again. In Germany you took the nationality of your parents, so my sister and I had Polish passports even though we were born in Germany. Most countries issued visas on a quota basis and the Polish quota was always full – unless you could find someone to guarantee that you would not be a burden on the country. In those days the world was either not aware of the evil Hitler represented, or not willing to burden itself with other people's problems, even though their lives really were threatened.

In 1938, when I was 15, my parents decided that I should leave school to learn a trade. It was considered important to learn a trade because it would enable you to earn a living in another country, even if you could not speak the language. I took a crash course in a dressmaking school and did some practical work with a gentlemen's tailor. For years I felt cheated that I had not been able to complete my education and was determined to do something about it one day.

Suddenly, in the middle of the night on 28 October 1938, our flat was raided. Two SS men came and told my father to get dressed and take his passport. My mother was shocked, my sister started shouting at them in her anxiety and my mother was told that Sonja would be taken as well if she was not quiet. I really don't know what made me go into the kitchen and make sandwiches for my father. I felt that was all I could do for him. I also crept out to a public telephone box to warn my uncle, but it was too late – a stranger answered the phone.

It appears that the Polish government had threatened to withdraw Polish nationality from those who had not visited Poland in recent years. The Germans did not want to be left with all these people and decided to deport them across the Polish border. There was great confusion and as soon as daylight broke, lots of families went to the various railway stations to catch a last glimpse of their loved ones and find out where they were going. But the operation was so efficient that they had already left. Neither side wanted them and they were being shunted to and fro until the Poles finally set up a camp for them. My father and his brothers still had family in their home town and were lucky to be able to go there.

Shortly after our father's deportation, *Kristallnacht*, the Night of the Broken Glass, happened in November 1938. I walked to my aunt's house next morning to see if she was alright. I did walk on broken glass! Jewish shops had been smashed, synagogues set alight, people arrested. It was a frightening experience.

After our father had been taken away, we really had to do something. But which country would have us? My mother had managed to get some money out of Germany illegally and convert it into the magic currency – dollars. Visas often had to be paid for in foreign currency. Eventually my mother heard that the Cuban Embassy was selling visas and she managed to get them for the whole family, including our father. It was hoped that in time this would be the gateway to the USA. Meanwhile, the most important thing was to get out of Germany.

For emigration purposes, my father would be allowed to come back to Germany in transit. Once the visas were promised, we had to find a passage. Eventually we got four berths on a luxury liner, the S.S. St. Louis, due to leave Hamburg on 13 May 1939. My father applied for permission to pass through Germany on our way out.

In the meantime, we had to give up our flat to a German family, although luckily a German judge gave us a two months' extension. We crated up the few things we were allowed to take with us and moved in with our aunt, whose husband had also been deported. One of our former customers at the shop, Mr Riemer, worked for the Customs and Excise department. He felt a sense of guilt and shame at the direction Germany had taken and was prepared to take enormous risks to help us. He helped several of our friends by stamping their crates to prevent them being searched, thus enabling them to pack some valuables. Arranging this was a real cloak and dagger situation. He could not come to us, we could not go to him, so we had to arrange a secret meeting. He took his chance when he saw my sister or me playing in the street, and walked past, whispering, "Tonight at 8.30 p.m. behind the phone box." My mother and I then ventured out in the dark, looking all around us as we went to the meeting place. Mr Riemer survived the war. We later sent him food parcels and, at his request, signed papers saying that he had not been a Nazi.

Our emigration plans did not go smoothly. Although our visas had been purchased with dollars. my mother had to go to the Cuban Embassy time after time. We only received them finally the day before we were due to sail. In fact my mother had already set off to cancel our passage when the papers arrived. I followed her and then we had to phone my sister, who was only 12, to start packing in a hurry!

Our greatest problem was that father had not received his transit visa. There was a mix-up with the paperwork and the wrong brother was sent back to Germany. My father phoned constantly, pleading with my mother not to leave without him. How hard it must have been for her to make this decision, but she was determined that her children had to be saved. Finally, she was offered a berth for father on a boat leaving two weeks later, and she hoped that his papers would be sorted out by then.

Mother, Sonja and I took a train to Hamburg and although it was Friday night, family and friends came to see us off. We knew in our hearts that it was goodbye for ever. Even now, more than 60 years later, I cannot see anybody off at the station without feeling choked.

We left Hamburg on 13 May 1939, with over 900 mostly Jewish refugees on board. We were only allowed to take ten Marks with us – I don't think it was more than £1. The Captain, Gustav Schroeder, gave strict instructions to the crew to make the journey as enjoyable as possible for us. We learnt later that he was not a Nazi Party member, although there were Gestapo members among the crew.

Once we were on the St. Louis, we children felt some excitement at sailing on a luxury liner. The meals were wonderful, there was a cinema, a sports deck with swimming pool, dances, shows and so on. There were also two rooms to be used for religious services. Hitler's portrait hung there, but the Captain allowed us to remove it for the duration of the services. Like most women, mother had brought candlesticks to light on Friday nights, which created a wonderful family-like atmosphere.

When we reached the rough seas of the Bay of Biscay, many passengers were seasick and stayed in their cabins. I was the only one at our table. With so many passengers on board and quite a lot of teenagers, our social life flourished. We knew we had two weeks to relax and then we would have to face the unknown. My mother did not take part in many things. I am sure the responsibility of what the future would hold must have been a heavy burden, along with the worry of having to leave her husband behind.

On 25 May, our last night aboard (as we thought), we had a fancy dress party because it was the Jewish festival of Shavuot. Our landing cards were also handed out. On the next day, we saw land – beautiful white buildings, blue skies, palm trees, a very welcoming sight. We started packing and preparing for our disembarkation in the early hours of the morning. I don't think anybody slept. We had to report for breakfast at 4.30 a.m.

We were surprised when the boat anchored a fair distance from the shore, but assumed the harbour was too shallow for a big liner. We all waited eagerly with our suitcases, but as time went by and nothing happened, we began to wonder... Was there a reason why we had to pay for our return journey? Did they already suspect problems? Later on, patrol boats started to surround us and the Cuban police came on board. They were very friendly and tried to joke with us. It was always *mañana*, it will be OK tomorrow. The rumours started – our passports were not in order, the visas were not in order, they were preparing a camp for us. We still thought it was only a question of time.

Passengers whose families had emigrated to Cuba earlier were visited by them in little boats. They called out names as they sailed around the St.

Louis. Fathers who had hoped to be reunited with their families felt so near – and yet so far. It was such a sad situation. I remember one man shouting to his wife, "Throw my son down, at least I'll have him."

A few people were allowed to leave the St. Louis as it appears they had official visas and ours were called 'landing permits'. We now know that it was all a question of money. With the desperate situation in Germany, a Cuban official had seen a way of becoming rich. He set up a chain of officials across Europe to sell landing permits 'wholesale', for a fixed sum of money. He is said to have made $100,000 dollars. However, the president of Cuba felt he should have a share of this, and when he didn't get it, decided to take his revenge on the unfortunate passengers.

After a few days, the beautiful view didn't seem so beautiful. Our morale was sinking lower and lower. The Captain tried to keep our hopes up and told us that someone from the American Refugee Association was negotiating with the Cuban authorities and offering money as a guarantee for the passengers.

Eventually one of the American negotiators came on board and told us that they were trying to prevent our return to Germany. That possibility had never been mentioned, but now this fear passed through everybody's mind. Some passengers had been allowed out of concentration camps in order to emigrate and had signed papers saying that they would never return to Germany. They felt trapped and feared for their lives.

We were supposed to leave the harbour after three days to make room for other boats, but the Captain went ashore and managed to get two extensions. One day, I was standing by the railings deep in thought when I saw a man walking towards the rail with blood dripping from his wrists. Before I could comprehend what was happening, he had jumped overboard. In no time a sailor jumped after him and managed to get him into a rescue boat in spite of the man's desperate struggle. He had been in a concentration camp and did not want to be saved. He was taken to hospital where he made another attempt to kill himself. His wife and children were not allowed to visit him. However, he did survive and eventually joined his family in England.

There were other suicide attempts and the Committee which had been formed arranged for patrols to check the gangways and cabins, day and night. Suddenly everything had become so sinister. We all felt so helpless and so hopeless. My mother never talked about her fears but we were of course aware, and sensed the atmosphere. Captain Schroeder tried very hard to keep our spirits up by making optimistic progress reports and posting encouraging messages on the bulletin board.

On 2 June we left Havana harbour. We were told it was simply to make room for other shipping and we would be circling around while negotiations continued. They were still discussing how many dollars per person were required to make this 'human cargo' acceptable to the Cuban President.

Back in Germany by this time, the next boat had left Hamburg with 200 passengers, including my father. But when news of our plight reached the Captain, he turned the boat back to Germany without telling the refugees on board. They were not aware of this until they entered Hamburg harbour. We never saw our father again.

Between 2 and 6 June, we were steaming between Havana and Miami. Whenever we got too near the American coast, a gunboat was sent out in case anyone tried to swim ashore. About three quarters of the passengers had quota numbers for eventual entry into the USA. They certainly felt they would be allowed to go to the USA ahead of time rather than risk going back to certain death in Germany. But no amount of pleading on their behalf helped.

On 7 June, we set sail towards Europe. By then we were running out of food and water. On the way back, a group of young people became so desperate that they considered scuttling the ship. Captain Schroeder tried to calm a volatile situation by announcing that whatever happened, he would not take us back to Germany.

On 10 June, four weeks after our departure, we were informed that our cause had been taken up by the Refugee Committee in Paris, led by the American who had worked on our behalf in Cuba. We were finally told that Belgium, Holland, France and Britain had agreed to divide the refugees between them.

Back in Germany, my father seemed to be fully informed of our plight because he sent us a telegram saying, "Choose England". We found out later that Joseph Goebbels, Hitler's Minister of Propaganda, had used the St. Louis as a propaganda exercise by saying, "You see, nobody else wants them either, at least we are building camps for them!"

At this point in the story, the English I had learnt at school proved useful. Although I was only 15, my mother pushed me forward to talk to immigration officials. She thought that was all that was needed to get us into Britain, where most of the refugees wanted to go.

We had docked in Antwerp on 17 June after five and a half weeks at sea and the officials of the four countries came on board. I stood in the queue for Britain. The Foreign Office representative, Mr Brister, was very sympathetic and of great help later on. Mother, Sonja and I were lucky to be allowed into England – the refugees who went to the other three countries were very soon overrun by the Germans.

The St. Louis had to be rushed back to Hamburg as she was due to go on a cruise to New York. We still had to be transported across the Channel. A cargo ship was found and very quickly transformed to accommodate around 300 people. We slept in bunk beds in the hold, women and children in one part and men in another. Washing and toilet facilities were inadequate. But what did it matter when freedom was so close? We arrived in Southampton on 21 June to a spectacular display of fireworks. Surely not to welcome us? It turned out to be a rehearsal for the return of King George and Queen Elizabeth, due to arrive from America the next day.

A train was waiting to take us to London. On our arrival at Waterloo station, members of the Refugee Committee welcomed us and took us to small hotels in the Russell Square area. We were given some money for food. On our first Friday, my mother sent me out to buy candles. I had a hard time because I kept asking for 'lights', but eventually I found the right word.

After a few days we had to report to Bloomsbury House where all refugee matters were dealt with. The only work we were allowed to do was domestic work. I was sent as a cleaner to a convalescent home in Broadstairs, along with my friend Rosie Guttman, who was also from the St. Louis. The matron was not very kind and we were often hungry. My pay there was two shillings and sixpence a week.

My mother and sister were given a small weekly allowance for a short time and found a furnished room. My mother found a cleaning job in order to buy food and keep a roof over their heads. I stayed in Broadstairs until September 1939. By then we had been issued with gas masks as war seemed inevitable.

Our entry visas stated that leave to land was granted on condition that the holder would emigrate from the United Kingdom and not take any employment in the UK (other than domestic work). Of course, the war changed all that and by the time it was over in 1945, we had been here long enough to qualify for British nationality. A great day in my life!

I carried on working in the convalescent home until September 1939. One day, I met a Jewish family on the beach. They had two children of eleven and six, and offered me an au pair's job at ten shillings a week. What riches! I accepted and went back to London with them, and of course was able to see my mother and sister again.

I was treated like a member of the family. The parents went to work and at the age of sixteen, I had the responsibility of the children, the cooking and the cleaning. I was even left to write sick notes when the children were absent from school. I wonder what the teachers made of them! When the Blitz started, we slept in cellars and sometimes in Marble Arch underground station.

My sister meanwhile had been evacuated with her school and my mother had found accommodation with the parents of the lady I worked for. My mother's life must have been very hard. She never complained, but she had no husband, no money and the responsibility of two daughters. The only work she could do legally was cleaning.

After our arrival in London, we went to see Mr Brister at the Foreign Office to ask if we could do anything to get my father out of Germany. He told us that if we could find somebody to guarantee him, he would help us get a visa. My mother walked the streets of London's East End, hardly speaking any English, and found a grocer who was willing to give a written guarantee. Mr Brister immediately set things in motion. Unfortunately the staff at Bloomsbury House did not have the same dedication. When Mr Brister saw my mother a little later, he was annoyed that the matter had not been dealt with and tried to speed things up. Unfortunately, it was too late: war had broken out.

With the outbreak of war, we were allowed to do 'war work'. I left 'my family' and rented a room with my mother. My first job was making gunpowder bags. After that I made soldiers' uniforms.

One day in 1942, I met my future husband, Oscar Feldman, at a Czech garden party. We were married in 1943 and that was the beginning of another chapter in my life... I did eventually manage to continue my education and took an Open University degree at the age of 50. It is never too late! I then worked as a teacher of English as a Foreign Language in the further education sector. I was fortunate to have a happy marriage and three children, Frances, David (who died in 1970) and Adrian. Oscar died in 1993, but I am lucky in my children and their spouses.

I am still in touch with other survivors of the St. Louis. Some of us were invited to Miami to take part in a documentary, "The Voyage of the St. Louis" shown on Channel 4 television. The survivors were later invited to Canada, Florida and Israel by various Church leaders who wanted to apologise for their governments' lack of compassion and understanding when only 900 people needed sanctuary, instead of allowing a possible return to Hitler's Germany and certain death. How many lives could have been saved!

The planned reunion in Cuba in 2003 will now take place in 2004. I wonder if we will finally set foot on Cuban soil?

I would like to dedicate this to my children and grandchildren,
so that the members of my family who were murdered by the Nazis
are not forgotten,
and the younger generation will hopefully play its part
in building a more tolerant world.

My mother Chaja (third left), my sister Sonja (first right) and myself (first left) on the St. Louis, 1939

Nine survivors of the St. Louis who took part in the documentary, The Voyage of the St. Louis, made in 1994, meeting at the Miami Holocaust Museum to say a prayer for those who did not survive.

Dorli Oppenheimer (now Fleming), aged 9, on holiday in the Austrian Tyrol, summer 1937. With parents, Erich and Hanna and sister Lisi, aged 3. All wearing Austrian national costume – Dirndl and Lederhosen.

DOROTHY FLEMING

All of a Sudden the Atmosphere Changed

I was one of the lucky ones. Let me tell you my story.

After the *Anschluss*, when Austria had been annexed by Germany in 1938, the persecution of the Jews became more awful by the day. People were thrown out of their schools and universities; most lost their jobs and businesses and, even if they wanted to leave, that was made hard for them too. But I was one of the lucky ones...

I was Dorli Oppenheimer then, born in Vienna in 1928, so I was ten years old when Hitler arrived in Austria. My family was Jewish and consisted of my father, Erich; my mother, Hanna and my grandmother, Marie Oppenheimer. In 1934 my little sister, Lisi, arrived, to everybody's great delight. We were consciously Jewish but not Orthodox and that meant that we kept the High Holidays but did not go to the synagogue regularly. This was what the majority of Vienna's Jews were also like. Our family had been in Vienna for three generations and, before that, had lived in other parts of the Austro-Hungarian Empire. We were well established and my father owned two optician's shops. Both were on the Kärntnerstrasse, one opposite the Vienna Opera House and the other one near St. Stephen's cathedral.

We lived in a big flat in the 5th district; it needed to be big because there had to be room for my parents, my grandmother, my sister and me, our cook/housekeeper and a nanny. This does not mean that we were very wealthy; it's how people like us lived at that time. It was no different from the way middle-class families lived in the rest of Europe, including England.

At the age of five I went to a Kindergarten (nursery school) for a year, before starting school at six. This was the norm in Austria and on the continent in general. Primary school in Vienna in the early 1930s was dramatically different from how things were here in England. School was only in the morning, from 8.00 a.m. to 1.00 p.m., with just a short break at mid-morning. Teaching was very formal and we were only taught the traditional academic subjects. I never knew my teacher's name; she had to be addressed as *"Frau Lehrerin"* (Mrs. Teacher) and she never used my first name – I was *die Oppenheimer* (the Oppenheimer girl) when I was spoken to at all.

What did I do in the afternoons? Apart from doing my homework, I had piano lessons, gymnastic and dancing lessons, I learnt to swim and to skate and, perhaps most important of all, I had English lessons. I was one of the lucky ones; most of the children who came here on *Kindertransports* had no English when they arrived, which must have made settling in even harder than it would be anyway.

The usual thing was for children to be taught French as the extra foreign language, but somehow my mother thought that English might turn out to be more useful for me – and how right she was! How lucky for me that this was my parents' choice.

In March 1938, when Hitler marched into Austria, I had already started at the High School, where I was supposed to study until I went to university. I had made a good start and, judging by entries in my autograph book of that time, I had already made some friends. The first thing that happened after the *Anschluss* was that the teacher told those of us in class who were Jewish to go and sit at the back of the room, facing the wall. Then she told the other girls not to speak to us or play with us because we were Jewish, and therefore bad and to be left alone. Up until then, no particular attention had been paid to people's religion and this sudden separation was not only hurtful but also hard to understand.

Gradually the Aryan girls were joining their equivalent of the Hitler Youth – the *Bund Deutscher Mädchen* (League of German Girls) – and appeared in school in their new uniforms of navy blue skirts, white blouses, dark ties and white knee-length socks. One day, quite soon after the *Anschluss*, the teacher spoke very seriously to the girls. "You will know that we have a new regime now; new people are in charge. You will want to be as helpful as possible in these new circumstances, so I'm going to tell you what you have to do. At home I want you to keep your eyes and ears open and listen carefully to what your parents, their friends and your brothers and sisters are saying. If you hear them saying anything nasty or critical about our new system, you are to report it to me. I'm sure you understand what I mean and that you will do your best to be very attentive at all times."

Of course she was encouraging her pupils to spy on their families and report to her. This shocked me so much that I have always remembered it and the memory was even strengthened when it turned out that other people had had similar experiences. This was one of the many surprises that emerged at the Reunion of *Kindertransports* when 1,000 of us who had come here as children met for two amazing days in London in June 1989 – 50 years after we had left our parents behind and travelled alone to England. The government at that time had given permission for 10,000 unaccompanied children to come to this country, away from their homes in Nazi-occupied Europe, to be looked after here until their parents could join them. Again, I was one of the lucky ones; 95 per cent of the children who came here never saw their parents again. Mine came out four months after me, though we were not able to be together as a family for another two years.

After summer 1938, Jewish children could no longer go to ordinary schools so my education stopped. I did take the entrance exam for the only Jewish high school in Vienna, where the Orthodox children went, and I passed, but by then I think it was too risky to travel across town so, sadly, I never went to a wholly Jewish school.

Now it was November 1938. The *Kristallnacht* (Night of the Broken Glass) had already taken place and the changes I had been noticing at home were becoming more marked. These changes were in the atmosphere as much as anything else. Where there had been smiles, there were now grim faces. Where there had been noise and laughter, there was now silence. And where there had been talk of all kinds of exciting and interesting events, there was now only talk of permits and visas, who had got away, and what desperate measures people were taking. I can clearly recall talk of people committing suicide in their total failure to find anywhere to escape to.

One of the topics that was discussed all the time was what to do now that the Nazis had taken over both Daddy's shops. Shortly after the *Kristallnacht,* two men in black leather coats had come to the shop by the opera and told my father to go home, they were taking over the business now as well as the branch by the cathedral. There was nothing he could do but to go home – and that was the end of his livelihood!

It was actually surprising that nothing had happened to father's shops until November, as all the other dreadful events started so quickly following the *Anschluss*. This delay was explained by my mother only quite recently. It seems that very soon after the annexation of Austria, one of father's suppliers had come to the shop and made an astonishing offer. He told my father that he had joined the Nazi party and was employed in their office. He said he had seen the list and, of course, father's two shops were on it. When father asked, "What list?" he was told that it was the list of all the Jewish businesses that were to be taken over. The man offered to put the relevant sheet at the bottom of the pile – but it would cost 200 Schillings (about £10). Father asked for time to think it over, as it could of course have been a trap. He asked advice from my uncle and they decided together that it was worth the risk. So the offer was accepted and that explains why our shops were not touched until seven months after the Nazis took over. When it happened, however, he was left, as so many others, with no income at all.

So it was at this time, when everything was looking black and hopeless, that my parents got to hear about the possibilities offered by the *Kindertransport*. Endless discussions must have gone on before they made the decision to apply for me to be included on one of the transports. As they phrased it on the original application, in answer to the question, "Why do you want to send this child to England?", they replied, "To continue her education" because it seemed altogether too dramatic to say "To save her life". The result of their brave decision was, of course, that my life was saved, but my parents always steadfastly maintained that they were neither courageous nor brave to send me away because they "knew" that it would all be all right in the end. Of course they could not have known that, but they must have had to believe it in order to take this vital step.

We still have the application form for the *Kindertransport* to England which my parents completed. Strangely, however, at the bottom of the form it says, "CANCEL". How could that be? The answer came from the late Tilly Hall, the wonderful lady who became my foster mother.

Tilly explained how she was at a meeting at her mother's house in Chapeltown, Leeds, where a Mrs. Ross was telling the assembled group about the situation for Jewish families in Nazi-occupied Europe. She then told them all about the *Kindertransport* scheme and showed them the photographs and application forms from families like mine; and she asked whether any of them could offer a home to one or more of these children. This would be until the parents could come out and join their children again. (No one understood or could believe at that time that most parents would not be able to join their children. We know now that six million Jews perished in the Holocaust, 1.5 million of them children.)

Tilly said, "If you have a girl of about ten who can speak a bit of English, we'll be glad to give her a home." Immediately Mrs. Ross showed her my picture and the form my parents had sent. So it was agreed that Tilly and Theo Hall's details and offer would go to my parents with all speed.

Just as she was leaving the room at the end of the meeting, Tilly turned round once more to look at the table full of photographs. One picture caught her eye and she said, "Who is that beautiful child?" Mrs. Ross looked startled and replied that this was Lisi, the four-year-old sister of the girl Tilly had just picked. Tilly hesitated for just a moment and then said,

"Well, I don't know how we'll do it, but I really can't bear the idea that these two girls should have to be separated from their parents as well as from each other... we'll take them both." And that is how the first application was cancelled. When my parents heard of the Hall family's generous offer, they immediately completed a second form with both our names on it (we have it, too) and it was agreed that we should both travel to England as soon as a place could be found for us on a transport.

The next thing that happened must have been when we were taken to say our goodbyes to family and friends. I know that this happened on 28 December 1938, for two reasons. One is that my autograph book suddenly has a whole batch of entries in German on that date. The other proof comes from photographs taken by my father at that time, showing my mother with Lisi and me, standing on pavements full of snow and, in one picture, in front of a shop door which displayed the swastika – the Nazi emblem.

My parents were careful to explain to me that we were going to a kind family in Leeds where I would have a chance to practise my English and also have the longed-for opportunity to take care of Lisi, my little sister. And, of course, they would be seeing us again soon.

I was looking forward to all this. I'd been away from home on a number of occasions before; I was very independent and old for my age, and I was really anxious to see England, the country I'd been learning about. In all of this I was very lucky again; few of the children who were going on the transports knew any English, and hardly any had left home before. Also, I was fortunate in having parents who explained carefully to me what was going to happen and I had some understanding of the reason for it. Many of the other children neither knew what was to happen to them, nor could grasp the reasons for it. It is no wonder that, for many of them, the whole experience was traumatic.

So, on 10 January 1939, with our one permitted piece of luggage each, Lisi and I went to the Western railway station in Vienna with our parents, to set off for England. I remember that there were lots of families on the platform and lots of noise. Again, we were lucky in that our parents were able to be with us on the platform. It seems that later on, because of all the distressful scenes there had been, parents had to leave their children outside the station and say their farewells there; that must have made it even worse. Our parents saw us into the compartment and said, "Bye bye, we'll see you soon; be good girls and we'll soon be together again." Then they very sensibly left. Some of the departures we saw were agonising, some parents even snatched their little ones back at the last moment, they just could not bear to part with them.

As soon as the parents had gone, those of us who were older began to try to organise ourselves. There were two little ones among us: my sister, Lisi, and one other. We decided to put them both up into the netting luggage rack – we thought they might be able to sleep there. As soon as Lisi was up there, she was promptly and massively sick. That kept me occupied for the next half hour and it was probably a good thing. I have no recollection of the train actually leaving; lucky again.

As the train moved on, messages started to come from other compartments warning us to be careful when we got to the frontier. We were not supposed to have anything of value with us, and if anything forbidden was found, or our papers were not in order, there could be big trouble. One of the boys in our compartment had been given his father's gold watch and he grew very agitated as we neared the frontier. In desperation, he dropped the watch into a slit in the ventilation grille and, to everyone's relief, it was not discovered when the frontier inspection came. Nothing awful happened to us during the inspection; I learned much later that this was not always the case. Often children were very badly treated at this time and frequently articles were stolen from them. So we cheered as we left "enemy territory" and our friend tried to recover his watch from its hiding place. He struggled and struggled, but could not get it out. It was awful to see how upset he was and I remember trying to comfort him by saying that it was only a watch and his father would not be angry; he would just be pleased that his son was safe.

We all remember arriving in Holland. There were lots of ladies dressed in black standing on the platform as the train drew in. They were all smiling and welcoming us and they offered us orange juice or hot chocolate drinks and sweet buns. Their smiles were the best; it had been a long time since we had seen smiles.

Crossing the channel was quite a "moving" experience and I heard that many children were sick. My sister had nothing left to be sick with, and I turned out to be quite a good sailor, so the two Oppenheimer girls were all right. I have little recollection of arriving in London, but fortunately my mother had kept a letter she received just a few days after our arrival. This came from a refugee friend, Mrs. Lerski, who had come to meet us and described in great detail what she had seen. She told of the great noise and confusion on the station and how distressed some of the children were, particularly if no one was there to meet them. Also she told how composed we were and the trouble she had claiming us. Mrs. Ross, the organiser from Leeds, had not been able to come and Mrs. Lerski had some difficulty proving that she knew us and would be entitled to take us away. In the end, she was recognised and vouched for by a member of the Refugee Committee and was able to take us to an aunt's house for the night.

The letter describes how devotedly I took care of Lisi, who was so tired that she slept standing up, while we undressed her and put her to bed. After that, Mrs. Lerski writes, I managed to enjoy a good meal, a warm bath and a good night's sleep. She then took us to the station next morning, but was worried about letting us travel on to Leeds alone. I apparently reassured her that I could manage very well; that I had a list of all necessary names and addresses and that I had already been interpreting for the others on the journey. Mrs Lerski put us into a carriage and asked a Salvation Army officer to keep an eye on us, which he did. Her last glimpse of us, she says, was as Lisi was happily sliding back and forth on the plush-covered seat in our third-class compartment. This would have been a special treat, as on the continent, only first-class had such elegant upholstery.

What a relief it must have been for my parents to receive this letter! Written on 14 January, two days after our arrival in England, it must have been reassuring to know that, so far at least, their little girls were all right and had completed their journey with no terrible mishaps.

My first memory of Leeds was arriving at Theo and Tilly's house, 3 Garmont Road, in Chapeltown. Uncle Theo and Auntie Tilly were lovely people; young, smiley and loving and, what was more, they had a dog! A golden retriever called Buster who became my friend straight away. All my dreams were coming true. After living in a flat in Vienna, I'd always hankered to live in a house; because of the flat, we had never had a dog and now there was one; what more could anyone wish for? The only problem was Lisi, my unhappy little sister. She had never been away from our parents before and, speaking no English, she couldn't understand what was being said to her. She cried and clung to me and would not be comforted. She even went back to wetting her bed – a sore trial for all of us. It took her a very long time to settle, but eventually she did. In the process, she forgot all her German and had to relearn it later.

For me, being in Leeds was great. Theo and Tilly were the kindest and most thoughtful foster parents one could possibly want. I enjoyed going to school in Cowper Street and all the different things we did there, especially all the "fun" things I'd never had at school in Vienna. For example: we acted the Mad Hatter's Tea Party from *Alice in Wonderland* and we had gym or games almost every day; we learnt folk songs to sing and sometimes listened to music and there was quite a lot of art and craft. The only subject that was hard for me was arithmetic. I'd been brought up on the decimal system, but here I had to learn inches, feet, yards, rods, poles and perches, and – even worse – ounces, pounds, stones and hundredweights! Those endless, long sums! But I must have managed it in the end as I later took and passed the notorious 11+ exam to go to grammar school.

No one made me feel bad about being a foreigner or a Jew at this school. That's my luck again in having very good teachers, especially my class teacher, Miss Bland, who was particularly kind and understanding. I think she even invited me to her home now and again; such a thing would have been unheard of in Vienna. Sometimes a fellow pupil would ask me to say something in German; I never minded that and was always happy to oblige.

There were, of course, many reasons why I was happy with the Hall family in Leeds. They made sure we had company by inviting similarly aged young nieces over to play with us; they arranged a whole series of enjoyable outings for us and, perhaps most importantly, they helped us to maintain contact with our parents and never tried to make us forget them. I was so lucky to be with a young, kind and Jewish couple, but I had to grow up a lot before I could really understand just how fortunate I was.

My sister went to a nursery school and eventually settled down. Everything changed, however, when my parents arrived. They could only come to us briefly, but it was a wonderful reunion. They had to travel on quickly to Newcastle where the optician who had saved their lives by offering father a job was awaiting them. Seeing them and then having them disappear so quickly quite devastated Lisi; she went back to her difficult behaviour, and when it turned out that our parents could not stay in Newcastle, she joined them when they eventually made their way to London. In London she went to school briefly, but was soon caught up in the rush to evacuate all children, owing to fears about war and bombing. In all, she was evacuated to four different locations and this must have contributed to all the personal and emotional troubles she had in later life.

I stayed with Theo and Tilly in Leeds until July 1939. Then, as it looked as if Theo might be evacuated with the school where he taught, it was thought best that I join my parents in London. For various reasons, this turned out not to be possible and I was sent to stay with my Uncle Paul and Auntie Pipi in Whitchurch, near Cardiff. There I went to school and was again lucky with my teachers.

At home it was not so good. I loved looking after my baby cousin, Helly, but got into fearful trouble for staying out too late when I took her for a walk in her pram. It took many years for my aunt and uncle to forgive me, and I'm not sure whether they ever did completely. The other problem there was my long hair. Washing and drying it presented huge difficulties and the upshot was that my plaits were cut off. This was what I could not forgive and it caused me to start making plans to run away to join my mother in London. By then, my father had been interned as an "enemy alien" and was behind barbed wire on the Isle of Man. Also, the Blitz had started and I was genuinely worried about my mother.

So I started saving up my pocket money and eventually got enough together to buy a single ticket to London. (I had no intention of ever coming back.) As I was so young and ignorant – all of 11 years old – I made the big mistake of confiding my plans to my schoolfriend. She, of course, went straight to the headmaster with the story, he contacted my uncle and, as I stood waiting on the platform at Cardiff station, the two men furiously descended upon me. "How could you be so thoughtless and ungrateful? How could you even think such an escapade would please your mother? How could you let your teachers down?" and so it went on. Of course I was taken back to my uncle's house and to school, but not so many weeks later, I got my way and travelled to London to join my mother officially. I started school there, but only days later the whole school was evacuated to Wiltshire. So then I found myself in tiny Westbury, at the foot of the Westbury White Horse.

After Westbury, my sister and I were reunited for one night in London on our way to Cardiff, where the whole family were to be together again at long last. That night in London was 10 May 1941 and it was the night of the biggest air raid on the docks up to then. We could see the fires blazing in the East End from where we spent the night with friends in Hampstead. But being together again in Cardiff was a great relief and I could at last get on with being a normal teenager. At age 16, I too became an "enemy alien", which meant I had to report regularly to the police, especially if I had to travel anywhere. I was hurt by this because by then I felt completely English, and nobody, meeting me for the first time, ever guessed that I had come from abroad.

Eventually I studied to become a teacher and met and married my husband, a doctor, who was also from Vienna but had escaped from Hitler in a very different way.

If it had not been for the *Kindertransport* Reunion, I doubt if I would have been able to put this story together. It has been important for me to remember the past and to write quite a bit of it down; I hope it might be important for my six grandchildren too, and perhaps for some others as well.

Dorothy's poem, "Changes" (overleaf), also describes these experiences in her young life.

CHANGES

All of a sudden the atmosphere changed;
At home it was quiet – the laughter all gone.
At school we were outcasts –
"Don't talk to them – they're Jewish!"
The teacher said; she who'd liked me before
The friends who wrote in my autograph book
Were no longer friends, wore uniforms now;
Bund Deutscher Mädchen, Hitler Youth,
In my school, my town, strangers to me.

All of a sudden the atmosphere changed;
No longer talk of music, of plays and of fun.
Now it was permits and visas and death;
Friends going missing, lucky ones left,
Less lucky those who were taken away –
Who could know where and for what?
Streets full of danger, new banners and flags
Frightening because no one explained
What it all meant, what would come next.

All of a sudden the atmosphere changed;
"There are people in England who'll give you a home
Until we get out and join you again –
You'll get chance to practise your English
And live with an uncle and auntie in Leeds
And take care of your little sister
Until we get out and join you again."
Train journey of fears and surprises
We remember the smiling and kindly Dutch
And arriving in smoky London; for some it was all too much.

All of a sudden the atmosphere changed;
In Yorkshire now, long way from home.
Strange names and bedrooms and breakfasts;
Phone calls from Vienna to Chapeltown, Leeds:
"Are you sure you're looking after your sister?
Behaving yourselves and learning at school?
Is Lisi still crying, still wetting her bed?
We'll come to you soon, just wait a bit more
And thank Uncle Theo and give Tilly a kiss!"

All of a sudden the atmosphere changed.
Settled in Leeds now, the plaits an attraction;
Sister has calmed down and school can be fun,
Dancing round maypole, learning some folk songs –
But arithmetic's agony, all those long sums!
Parents are coming! Longed-for reunion
Big hugs and kisses – and then they are gone! And
All of a sudden the atmosphere changed.

War comes and evacuation – travelling all over
This surprising new country of ours.
Where can we settle? Father's interned.
Now he's an enemy alien – who loves this country so much!
At last we're all together in Wales
War work for Daddy and new schools for us;
No longer refugees, evacuees or any -ees,
Just two girls growing up and seeing that
All of a sudden the atmosphere changed.

Many years later we suddenly found out
That *Kindertransport* had been what saved us.
We'd been the lucky ones, our parents survived –
Most of the children were orphaned.
Terrible memories suddenly stirred –
Some could hardly believe it;
Friendships renewed, experiences shared
With families now and emotions bared – and
All of a sudden the atmosphere changed.

Page 1 of Dorli Oppenheimer's autograph book where her father, Erich, illustrated a 'This is Your Life' of her ten years in Vienna before she left on a Kindertransport for England. The dedication reads: 'To the child who obeys and loves her parents, everything in life that's beautiful, sunny and good.' Daddy 1938

1936 entry in Dorli Oppenheimer's autograph book from Vera, a friend she lost after the Anschluss of 1938. It says: You kindly found a place for me in your friendship book; I should like to be remembered in your heart's secluded nook! Remember me, later too. Your friend Vera.

I dedicate this chapter to my grandchildren: Roland, Gabrielle, Anat, Yuval, Neta and Madeleine, as well as to the memory of my grandmother, Clara Schönmann, who perished in the Lodz ghetto.

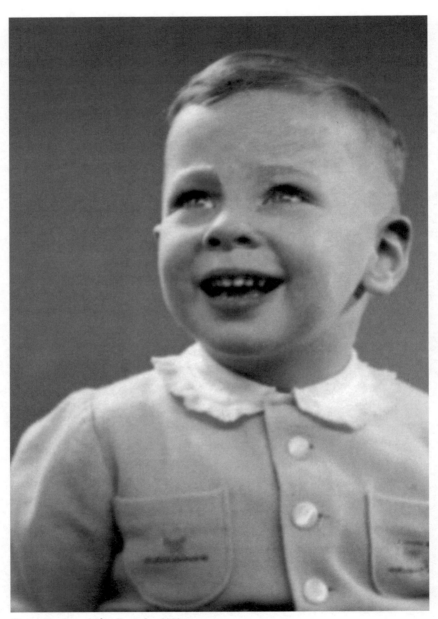

Steven Frank aged 3^1/$_2$, December 1938

STEVEN FRANK

A Second Chance to Live

I was nearly five years old when I witnessed the march of German jackboots upon the cobbled streets of Amsterdam.

My father came from Zwolle, a town north-east of Amsterdam, where his father was the director of the local hospital and a pioneer of the appendix operation. My father was the youngest of four with three elder sisters. He was very clever and went to Leiden University where he read law and represented the university in several sports, and completed a doctorate there. During this period he was co-author of a book outlining the history of the students' union.

My mother was born in Eastbourne, Sussex, and was the middle child of three daughters. Her parents came to England in 1899 to seek work. They were both successful professional musicians. After a normal education, her parents sent her to a "finishing" school in Amsterdam and that was where she met my father, married and had three sons, of whom I am the middle one.

At the outbreak of war, my father was a well known and very successful lawyer. He was on the boards of several non-political organisations. He was particularly interested in mental health. With the threat of German invasion, he was certainly aware of what might happen to the Jews of Holland. We had a good escape route to England, but my father was the legal board member of a famous mental hospital called *Het Apeldoornse Bos*, which was very forward-thinking in mental heath treatment and had a large Jewish contingent. He felt it was unacceptable to escape to the safety of England, whilst leaving these poor people behind at the mercy of Nazi fanatics. He felt he needed to speak for them. So we stayed.

With increasing restrictions placed on the Jewish community, my father joined the Dutch resistance and was responsible for issuing false papers to get desperate Jews out of Holland through Belgium and France, to the safety of Switzerland. One early morning in January 1943, he kissed us all goodbye and walked to his office in the centre of Amsterdam – the use of public transport or bicycles was forbidden – and I never saw him again.

From eyewitness accounts, we know that he had been betrayed, and was arrested at his office by the Gestapo, taken to a prison in Amersfoort, tortured and sent to Westerbork transit camp. He arrived there in very poor physical condition and shortly afterwards was deported to Auschwitz, where he was murdered in the gas chambers with many others on about the 21 January 1943.

My mother did manage to see him briefly by pretending to be a cleaner in the prison where he first went. We went into hiding for a short while, but nothing happened to our house so we returned. With no income coming in, my mother opened a school for Jewish children, and cut Jewish men's hair as by now Jews were barred everywhere.

Three of my father's non-Jewish friends bravely petitioned the Nazi authorities for clemency for him, citing all the wonderful and important things he had done in his short life. Although the Germans would not do anything for my father, they allowed his wife and three sons to be placed on a priority list. There were several of these lists around and we hoped it would exempt us from being deported east to "work for the German Reich". We were placed on the Barneveld list and in retrospect, this delayed our almost certain departure to the gas chambers of Auschwitz sufficiently long enough for us to be eventually liberated.

In March 1943, we were summoned to report to the railway station to be sent to Barneveld, a small town in mid-southern Holland. The place was a castle and its inmates were mostly Dutch Jews from the upper echelons of the professions in Holland. There were no fences or guards, but nobody attempted to escape. We had been promised that we would be allowed to remain in Holland, and if you escaped and were caught, then deportation was a certainty. Food was adequate but the camp was very overcrowded. We children had little schooling, and being taught arithmetic by an eminent professor of mathematics was not that interesting! But in September 1943, the German army suddenly entered the camp and gave us all about 20 minutes to pack for transport to Westerbork. This caused panic and fear, as most people knew that from Westerbork you went east into the unknown.

Westerbork was a totally different place: after the war it was described as "the Auschwitz made of wood". The railway line went into the centre of the camp. The perimeter was surrounded by a moat and barbed wire fence about six feet high, with sentry boxes on stilts containing guards with machine guns, and searchlights. The camp was situated on sandy heath-land in an isolated part of north-east Holland, near the town of Assen. When it was dry, sand flew in all directions. It was in your clothes, your food and everywhere. When it rained, you wallowed in sandy mud as there was no concrete or paving in the camp. Conditions were severe and sanitation appalling. The camp was rife with scarlet fever, polio, yellow jaundice, dysentery and lice which were everywhere. The whole of the Barneveld group were placed in one single storey barrack, number 85, with men on the left, and women and children on the right. At each end of the barrack, there were washing facilities consisting of a central pipe with taps at varying intervals, draining into a central gutter. No hot water was available.

In our barrack, there were trestle tables in front of each window. These seated about 14 people, who formed a sub-group of the whole Barneveld group, and we got to know each other quite well. On our table we had an old couple in their sixties who were great Anglophiles and would talk at length with my mother in English about holidays spent in England in the past. There was a great deal of reminiscence about the "good old times gone by". We children "adopted" this couple as our surrogate grandparents. They were so sweet and kind to us. Between the tables, there were metal bunk beds two tiers high. The centre of the barrack contained three-tier bunk beds which fitted just under the apex of the wooden roof. Our clothes hung from the sides of the bunks, or were suspended from the metal beams in the roof. The whole barrack was terribly overcrowded, but we got used to that.

The toilets were situated in a separate barrack. A large pit was dug into the sand, over which were placed planks of wood with holes cut into them to serve as toilet seats. There were two rows of about 35 seats – the largest loo I have ever seen – with no segregation of the sexes, everybody in together. It was particularly hard for the women to cope with. As everyone had dysentery at one time or another due to the filthy conditions, these toilets were nearly always pretty full of people. I remember my mother making us "toilet seat covers" out of paper so that we wouldn't "catch anything".

We had no schooling and were always wary of the camp police inmates (called OD's), and we kept well away from them. I remember one instance when I was alone, running past the side of a barrack somewhere near the perimeter wire, when I was suddenly confronted by two German guards with an alsatian guard dog. I froze and we looked at one another. The guard unleashed the dog and it came bounding over, barking and snarling. I covered up my face, but was left bleeding on my arms and legs. I clearly remember their laughter at this "sport". Then boredom set in, they called off the dog and I ran away as fast as I could. I was learning to be "street-wise" and after that I never went round a corner without looking first. I played with my peers and we made up an alphabet about life in Westerbork. My mother made me write it down after the war, and it ended with "Z is the sun which will shine once again." We never gave up hope as we longed for freedom.

Life in Westerbork revolved around Tuesdays. That was the day the trains would leave for the east with anything from 900 to 1,500 people on board. With true German efficiency, these trains were clearly labelled with their destination. Most were heading for Auschwitz and Sobibor. The more fortunate people went to Bergen Belsen and very occasionally to Theresienstadt. Tension would start to build up at the weekend. The transport list of those selected to travel would be posted on the notice board. For those on the list, there was pandemonium as they desperately tried to avoid going, but to no avail. The others breathed a sigh of relief – they now had another week before the next list was published. Many inmates tried to get jobs within the camp, hoping that they were so important that the inflow of Jews from Holland and the outflow of Jews to the east would go smoothly, and they would therefore be spared transportation.

One day in May 1944, as I was entering the barrack around midday, I recall hearing a howling sound from the sky above, followed by a ratatat. As I looked up to the pitched roof of the barrack, I saw lots of holes appearing in the roof, followed by the howl of cascading bullets as they ricocheted off the metal bunks in all directions. Fuelled by fear and panic, I ran across the barrack room to my table under the window. I arrived there unscathed, only to find my surrogate grandfather lying dead in a pool of blood. It was the first time I had come face to face with death, and the loss of a dear, dear old man whom we had come to love so much. But what touched me so deeply was that this man, this Anglophile who loved England so much, was killed by bullets fired from British aircraft and British pilots. It was one of those ghastly accidents of war where a reconnaissance photo provided an inaccurate picture of what this camp contained. It made a deep and lasting impression on me.

And then it happened. On 4 September 1944, when the Allies were already in Belgium and moving into southern Holland, a list was published and we were to go to Theresienstadt.

I remember this journey very clearly. My mother prepared us: three pairs of pants, three vests, three shirts, two pairs of trousers, two jumpers, a jacket, coat, hat, gloves and a very small rucksack. We were herded onto the ramp and into cattle trucks. I remember a black rectangular hole facing me. We were pushed and shoved into the cattle truck, about 60 people in all, and then there was a rumble as the guards rolled the door shut and bolted it. It was very dark in there, but slowly you became accustomed to the dim light that came through four tiny little windows at each corner of the truck. There was pandemonium inside with people shouting and crying. Finally, someone took charge and all the "luggage" was piled up in two corners. This gave some room for people to sit on the floor, but not for everyone. I became aware of a wooden tub which was to serve as our lavatory. We spent 36 hours in that cattle truck with no food or water. The stench that built up – of sweat, urine, faeces and vomit – made breathing air terribly difficult. If we children climbed up the luggage to get to the window, we were pulled back by the others, each gasping for air.

Finally the train pulled into Theresienstadt and they opened the door. It was dark outside, but the blast of cold fresh air into the truck suddenly allowed us to breathe deeply again. This camp was totally different from Westerbork; it had been a garrison town since about 1750, but the soldiers' families had been removed in 1941 by Heidrich, the Nazi head of the region, and it was first turned into a ghetto which housed the elderly and successful Jews of Germany. A great number of academics and musicians were sent there. By the time we got there, most of them had been sent to the killing fields of the east.

We were housed in a very large stone barrack about 200 yards square and four storeys high, with a parade ground in the middle. We slept on the floor with our belongings around us. Realising that life was going to be hard, my mother volunteered to work in the camp hospital laundry, a highly infectious place. But it gave her access to hot water, and when nobody was looking, she would wash our clothes in the hope that this would keep the dreaded insect typhus at bay, as there was an epidemic in the camp and thousands were dying daily. She also washed other people's clothes and bartered this for extra food to feed me and my brothers. We only got one meal a day. We became consumed with hunger. Your stomach becomes concave like a new moon and hunger pain takes over. It was always on your mind, this hunger.

Later, we children lived apart from my mother in a children's home. She would come to the home from time to time, carrying an aluminium saucepan in which she had made a concoction of bread and hot water mixed together to a consistency like wallpaper paste, which she called *broodpap*, bread porridge. With one spoon, she would feed each one of us in turn. I never saw her take a spoonful for herself. I still have very guilty feelings and occasionally dreams about being fed like this, with all the other children looking on as the spoon went into my mouth. All those hungry faces looking on and fading into the dark background. But I didn't care. I was so hungry that I could only think of myself. The pan survives to this day, and every year around the anniversary of my mother's birth, my children and their cousins have a remembrance dinner. One of the courses is served from that old aluminium pan, in remembrance of an extremely brave and resourceful granny.

We had no schooling. We played cards and chess with odd pieces. In those days, children collected stamps, but in the absence of stamps, we collected razor blades, mainly Gillette, and we became very good at spotting a change of print-run on the wrappers depicting Mr. Gillette, so we had swops. A blade in its tissue and wrapper was a first-class exhibit. We made torches from worn-out discarded batteries, wires and bulbs. We used to sleep with the batteries between our legs, and the warmth of our bodies would regenerate them, so we had light for a short time.

On one occasion we were playing in the barrack where my mother lived, and we managed to find a way into the attic. It was great to play in as it was about 200 yards long. We ran about on those nearly 200-year-old ceilings without ever falling through. It gives you an idea of how light and small we were. We came across a trap door which we managed to lever open, and to our surprise we looked down into a large room. Black cobwebs were draped from the wires dangling from the ceiling. from which a lamp-shade and bulb were hanging. But on the floor of the room, there were piles of coats, shoes, dresses, trousers, brushes, combs, teeth, toys and other things. With great excitement we ran back and told my mother, who was luckily not working just then. Clothes were scarce and winter was approaching. She collected together a group of women and followed us to the "Aladdin's Cave", and they lowered themselves down and helped them-selves to as much clothing as they could carry. My reward for having found this treasure was to choose something from the toy heap. I chose a chess set. I still have those chess pieces today and often wonder when I play with them who owned them before me. In retrospect it was obvious that previous inmates of this barrack had been stripped of all their possessions and sent virtually naked in cattle trucks to their deaths in the east.

One incident which moved me deeply was when the Germans came to the children's home to take away some children for transportation. I witnessed a brutal separation of brothers and sisters. They would take away one brother or sister and leave the other one behind. Their crying and pleading still rings in my ears as one child would plead to be allowed to go with her brother on the transport or to stay behind with him. It was terrible to see. For some reason, the Germans were not interested in me.

I witnessed the bombing of Dresden in Germany from our camp in Czechoslovakia. I remember the noise and the crimson-coloured sky. As the war was drawing to a close, many inmates from other camps were brought to Theresienstadt, many in open cattle trucks, most of them frozen to death. Typhus was now rampant and we were so very, very hungry. Early one morning, we were all woken up in the children's home, made to get dressed and taken to the crematorium. Here we were made to stand in a line in an underground tunnel. I remember this black cable running along the length of the tunnel with lights dangling from it at intervals. From my right I was handed a box which I in turn had to pass on to the child on my left. I then took another box from the person on my right and passed it on. We were there for hours. Each box contained the ashes of the dead of Theresienstadt. The box was labelled with the name of the deceased, and the dates of their birth and death. From time to time, I would hear a quiet, restrained sobbing along the line as someone held a box of ashes belonging to their mother, father, brother, sister, aunt or uncle.

Rumours started to abound that the war was nearly at an end, but also that the gas chambers in the camp were almost ready. They were the most up to date system, designed for maximum throughput. So there was great elation overshadowed by a ghastly fear. My mother, who was known as one of only a handful of native English speakers, was returning from work at the laundry one day when she was approached by some Russian prisoners. They begged her to come to their house before 6 p.m. as they wanted to show her something. She duly arrived there and was taken into the attic of their house, where they had hidden a secret radio. She wrote down what she heard. "Yesterday at 2.41 a.m. at Eisenhower's Headquarters......." It was Winston Churchill broadcasting to the world that Germany had capitulated and that at midnight the war would be at an end. She was probably the first person in the camp to know that the war was over. But we were still under German occupation. Were they going to gas us all before they surrendered?

On 9 May, the Russian army entered Theresienstadt. The first troops were a very poorly equipped Mongolian regiment, but they were soon followed by mechanised Russian troops. Not long after, the International Red Cross took over the running of the camp, and it was isolated because of the appalling death rate from typhus and starvation. We remained there for a further month during which a large-scale delousing programme was instituted. Buildings were sealed and the lice gassed. What did they use for this delousing programme? Why Zyklon B of course, the gas which was used to kill my father and so many others in Auschwitz.

My mother was determined to go straight to England as she feared, quite rightly, that there would be no family left alive in Holland. Although the authorities insisted that we had to return with the Dutch to Holland, the country from which we came, my mother persuaded the Red Cross to allow us to go to Pilsen in southern Czechoslovakia which was under American control. There she charmed two British pilots to fly us to Paris and then on to London-Croydon, where we were unceremoniously dumped on the runway. We were home.

My Friend Charles

An eyewitness account by Connie Rosenheimer of life in Theresienstadt,
written, most unusually at the time, in English. Of the 15,000 children who
went there, only 93 returned.

When walking sadly through the street,
I view the people who I meet,
They are so grey, so feeble, so old,
And many trembling from the cold,
No happy faces to be seen
In Terezin, in Terezin.

In the bare park I take a seat,
And speak to several whom I greet,
Sad are the tales of blank despair,
For dear ones gone – they know not where,
No tales of joy of lives serene,
In Terezin, in Terezin.

And stumbling, halting, there they go,
The heroes of the past – so slow,
It fills my heart with pain severe,
For many blind and maimed are here,
There is alas no happy scene,
In Terezin, in Terezin.

With beating heart and troubled eye,
Again I view the passers-by,
Through mud and snow, through storm and rain,
They pass, a melancholy train,
With pan in hand, with hunger keen,
In Terezin, in Terezin.

Oh God, in mercy grant the peace,
That this sad life may shortly cease,
Grant that we once again return,
To those for whom we fondly yearn
To our own house, how humble, mean,
Not Terezin, not Terezin.

Perchance when back in London Town,
A tear will slowly trickle down,
And I will ponder with a sigh,
On the dear friend who said goodbye
Who was my friend – had always been,
In Terezin, in Terezin.

Connie Rosenheimer was born in Sydney, Australia, and married a Dutchman. She was in Holland at the outbreak of war, and was sent to Theresienstadt. She survived and returned to Holland.

The Westerbork Alphabet

(As written down, with spelling mistakes, by Steven Frank in 1945)

A are the *Ardapelen* – Potatoes – on which the Jews have to live.
B are the *Baantjes* – Jobs – which we all desire to have,
C is the *Comandant* – Commandant – whose orders are out,
D is the *Dienst* – Military – that we don't care about
E is the *Eten* – Food – that the Jews love to care,
F is the *Fijant* – Enemy – from here and over there,
G is the *Goelars* – Goulash – which reminds us of meat,
H is the *Heide* – Heath – it's forbidden for our feet,
I are the *Ipa* – Rumours – don't need papers for seeing,
J is the *Jood* – Jew – the dangerous being,
K is the *Kamp, Kofi, Keuken* – Camp, the Coffee and Kitchen,
L are the *Luizen* – Lice – which give us much itching,
M is the *Macht* – Might – of the military police,
N is the *Nethijt* – Neatness – of our WC's
O is the *Orderdienst* – Camp Police – he's so dangerous and cross,
P is the *Prikeldraad* – Barbed Wire – which I hate so much,
Q is the *Qarantene* – the barrack for Quarantine,
R is the *Roodvonk* – Scarlet Fever – which brings us such misery,
S is the *Slapen* – Sleeping – on the ground and bunkbeds,
T is the *Transport* – Transport – oh what a misery,
U is the *Uitgang* – Exit – which we're forbidden to pass,
V is the *Vrijheid* – Freedom – we desire so alas,
W is the *Wacht* – Guard – of the military police,
X is the *Ondergedoken* – man who is living in hiding,
Y is the *Ijzer* – Iron – of beds, rails and train,
Z is the *Zon* – Sun – which will shine once again.

*I dedicate my testimony to five people: to Mr E. Heldring, Mr J.V. Rijpperda
Wierdsma and Mr Arn. J. d'Ailly who with Mr Bob Alvarez-Corea, at great
danger to themselves and their families, petitioned the German authorities for
clemency for my wonderful father and helped my mother so much during and
after the occupation. Through their endeavours I survived. The example of such
loyalty and friendship has been the bedrock of my life ever since. And finally to
my late mother, Beatrix Frank, latterly Sachs, who, with unbelievable bravery
and sheer determination, guided me and my brothers, Nick and Carel, through
the "tunnel of hell" from which we emerged relatively unscarred. She was small
in stature and huge in heroism.
I have a lot to live up to.*

*The old aluminium pan survives to this day, and
every year around the anniversary of my mother's
birthday, my children and their cousins have a
remembrance dinner. One of the courses is served
from the pan, in remembrance of an extremely
brave and resourceful granny.*

Happy carefree days. Steven and his family on a typical holiday before the outbreak of war.

Gina's passport photo taken in 1938, aged 13

My sister Claire, 1939

My mother Berta, 1939

My father Arthur, 1939

GINA GERSON

One of the Lucky Ones?

My name was Gina Bauer and I was born in Vienna into a typically middle-class Jewish family. We were not particularly wealthy, but I do not remember ever wanting for anything. The economic situation was very bad in Austria after the First World War, and my parents tried to live in a way they probably could no longer quite afford. Certainly I was not brought up in the sort of luxury my half-sister, Claire, enjoyed, but I was a much cherished, over-protected and somewhat spoilt child of my mother's second marriage.

My parents were second generation Austrians and like the majority of Jews in Vienna, very assimilated. My mother especially considered herself Viennese first, Austrian second and Jewish way back third. They were steeped in German culture – literature, music, art. We certainly observed the Jewish High Holidays; I was very much aware that I was Jewish, but it did not play a major part in our lives. I remember being the only Jewish girl in my class. I was always somewhat embarrassed to have to ask for time off at school for these special religious occasions, though I cannot really remember any antisemitism personally.

What for me was a very loving and secure future came to a sudden end in March 1938 when the Germans marched into Austria. That things would never be the same again was brought home to me very soon after the *Anschluss* (annexation of Austria by Germany). I had asked a few of my friends to a small party, I no longer remember for what occasion. To my utter astonishment and horror, nobody turned up. I could not understand this at all. I was still the same girl and I thought my friends were still the same people. I suddenly realized I was now a pariah, an outcast. I had not changed, but everything had changed. I was 13 years old.

My parents were of course only too aware of what had been happening in Germany since Hitler came to power in 1933, but these things were kept from me, nor was I at all interested in politics at that age. Yet I do remember my parents giving shelter to a German Jewish refugee family; that was probably sometime in 1935-6. I recall very vividly this small family of father, mother and small boy sleeping in our dining room. Of course I wanted to know why they had come to live with us and I expect my parents tried to explain this to me without alarming me too much. The *Anschluss* certainly did not come as a complete surprise to them. Shortly before the Germans marched in, the Chancellor of Austria, Kurt von Schuschnigg, had ordered a plebiscite or referendum in Austria on uniting with Germany. I remember a Jewish neighbour saying to my mother, "We must all vote – this is terribly, vitally important." Of course the Germans never allowed this plebiscite to take place; they crossed the border the night before.

I remember only too well watching from our window as the German troops marched along our street to the hysterical cheers of the Viennese crowds. There were plenty of Austrian Nazis and they welcomed the Germans like liberators. It all seemed quite exciting – banners flying, martial music from loudspeakers, cheering crowds, but for the Jews life had changed overnight.

In Germany things had of course changed since the Nazis came to power. Restrictions for the Jews were introduced gradually, bit by bit. The Nazis saw what they could get away with and so they added yet more and more anti-Jewish laws. In Austria such restraint was not necessary. They knew only too well that they could get away with almost anything; certainly the Viennese Nazis cheered them all the way. The Germans had nothing to teach the Austrian antisemites.

It became quite a common occurrence in Vienna to try and humiliate the Jews as much as possible, and frequently elderly Jews were forced to scrub the pavements, sometimes with a toothbrush. They were usually surrounded by jeering crowds who would spit at and kick these defenceless people. And I saw with my own eyes German soldiers holding back the enthusiastic Viennese Nazis.

As I said, life for Jews now changed overnight. My father's business had to close before long; I had to leave my school and attend a Jewish school. Jews were not allowed in parks or other public places like theatres, cinemas, swimming pools etc. Many restaurants would have notices on their doors, "Pigs and Jews not welcome here." People we knew before suddenly did not know us any more. All sorts of incredible things happened, like tradesmen turning up at your door insisting that you owed them money. And such was the fear that people just paid up.

Suicide among Jews became a daily occurrence and it also happened in my own family. This event stands out in my memory because of the impact it had on my parents. My uncle, my father's brother, threw himself from the top floor of his apartment block when the Gestapo came for him. It upset me terribly that my 82-year-old grandfather – a lovely, very dignified gentleman – had lived to bury his own son.

Now of course Jews thought only of trying to get out, to anywhere they would allow us in. But countries were not exactly queuing up to give us shelter. The craziest ideas were seriously considered: Shanghai, for instance, where it was possible to 'purchase' a visa for a lot of money and South American countries we had barely heard of. I remember my father writing desperately to a distant relative in Cincinnati – I was not even sure where this was. Anything and anywhere was considered.

My half-sister, who was ten years older than myself, managed to get a Domestic Permit, allowing her to work in England. This was the only type of work available in England where there was quite a lot of unemployment at that time. She left Vienna for a job near London sometime in the summer of 1938 and a few months later she was somehow able to obtain a Trainee Permit for me to come to England for just 12 months. I am not sure what the authorities would have done with me at the end of that 12 months – send me back to Germany? Of course this never arose because the war broke out before that date.

Now there were endless difficulties to get the various documents I needed from the authorities to allow me to leave the country. That was the incredible irony – the Germans wanted to get rid of the Jews, but made it as difficult as possible for us to get permission. I remember vividly queuing with my father from early morning outside the Gestapo headquarters in the bitter cold. It was sometime in December and winters are very cold in Austria. I learned later that the magnificent building where we queued for hours was the confiscated Rothschild palace. I had to have a certificate to prove that I – a 13-year-old child – did not owe any taxes, was not an imbecile etc, had been immunised against various things; the list was endless and I still have most of these documents.

In the meantime, on 10 November 1938, there was the notorious *Kristallnacht* (the Night of Broken Glass). I remember being very alarmed when quite unexpectedly my mother fetched me from school that day, as did a lot of other parents. They must have got knowledge that something was afoot. We were given two hours to pack and leave our home "for our own protection". I remember my mother begging a neighbour, a high-ranking Nazi official, to help us. He would not even listen to her. So we had to leave and I recall that my parents must have realized that in their agitation, they had forgotten to take something important, a document perhaps. They tried to return to our flat, but by then there was already a small paper seal with a swastika over the lock on our door. To get into our own home, they would have had to pierce that paper seal. No way would they have dared to do that. We stayed with friends and I never saw my home again.

At last the day of my departure arrived, 9 January 1939. It is only now that I have children and grandchildren of my own that I can appreciate what it must have meant for my parents to let such a young child travel across Europe by herself. I can only imagine how they must have felt. Children in those days were not as sophisticated as they are now; certainly I had never been anywhere by myself. Flying was not as common as it is today and it was terribly expensive. By now there was not enough money to send me to London by plane, so I was to travel by train. When my own children were about the age I was then, I remember saying to my husband that I could not understand how my parents could let me go, and go alone, not accompanied by adults as the *Kindertransport* trains were. It was a stupid question as my husband quickly pointed out; they had made this sacrifice to save my life. Besides of course, they hoped somehow to be able to join us in England.

Now began my journey to England. I was certainly apprehensive, but also a little excited. At the border town of Aachen, all the Jews had to get off the train. After thorough searches of their luggage, they were all allowed to continue their journey – all except for me.

To this day, I cannot imagine why they picked on me. Possibly they thought I was a very blonde "Aryan-looking" child, whose family was perhaps trying to smuggle things out of Germany – one cannot really hope to follow their reasoning. I only know that I was taken to a small wooden hut where a woman official stripped and searched me – a very frightening experience for a child. But I was really scared when I returned to the office and found the German officials reading my diary. I must have secreted this in my small suitcase. My parents would never have allowed me to take it with me had they known the contents. In the rather graphic style of an impressionable teenager, I had written about the events in Vienna, especially about the suicide of my uncle that had so affected us all. Just a few weeks before my departure, I had had my birthday and been given a very precious "grown-up" present, a manicure set. I was very proud of it. I can see it now – it was in the shape of a heart with a zip all round it. The Gestapo or SS (or whoever they were) cut right round the lining to look for something – I don't know what. Money, jewels? They also cut open the lining of the warm winter gloves my mother had bought me only a few days before, because most of my clothes were still in our flat. They even squashed some chocolates a friend had given me for the journey. All I know is that I was thoroughly bewildered, but in the end they let me go.

By then of course I had missed my train. I had a ticket from Vienna via Ostend to Dover and London, where Claire was to meet me. What to do now? Someone must have told me to take the next train to Brussels and try to get to Ostend from there. So after some hours I found myself in Brussels, where I met the first caring human being, a porter who must have realized my plight. He must have been Jewish because he tried to speak to me in Yiddish, which I did not understand. My schoolgirl French was not much help, but he somehow guessed where I was trying to get to, and he put me on the right train for Ostend.

I only vaguely remember the rest of the journey to England. I recall being very seasick – I had never been on a boat before. I did not speak a word of English, but the immigration officials were kind and my papers were obviously in order. I do remember being rather worried when I got on the train in Dover. Seats on English trains are upholstered even in second class; in Germany, they were wooden benches. I was quite sure I was on the wrong class of train and would have to pay the difference, and of course I had only the very little money that I was allowed to bring. By then I had been travelling nearly 36 hours and I was desperately tired. When I finally arrived at Victoria Station in London, I just sat on my suitcase on the platform and fell asleep. My sister told me later that in her agitation – I was 12 hours late – she ran past me several times before realising that the little figure on the suitcase was me.

The first thing Claire did was to telephone my parents to tell them that I had arrived safely. I can only imagine what must have gone through their minds until they heard that I had arrived, all those hours late. Claire was now working in Woburn House in London and so she took me to her little bed-sit in Kings Cross. I do remember being rather alarmed by the black uniforms of the London Underground guards. Black uniforms meant Gestapo.

My sister of course could not afford to keep me on the very little she was earning. The problem was that nobody was really responsible for me, but I imagine in the end the Jewish Refugee Committee took over. Anyway, I was sent to stay with a Jewish family in the East End of London. Thinking about it now, I am sure the Committee must have paid this family because they were quite poor themselves. In fact I had never seen such conditions in my life. I shared the bed of the daughter of the house, we washed in the sink in the kitchen, the toilet was outside in the yard and we went to the public bath once a week. They were very kind to me, but after a few weeks the Committee must have decided that this was not the right place for me and I was sent to a hostel in Maida Vale.

There the conditions were very different, quite luxurious in fact. Three girls shared a bedroom, we had dancing lessons and at the weekend we were often invited to the homes of some of the Committee ladies for tea, with servants and cucumber sandwiches. I recall thinking even then that fewer luxuries might have enabled a few more children to be saved. I still shudder to remember how the Matron of the hostel gave me a bath and washed my hair when I arrived from the East End home – a very humiliating experience for a child. I knew from the start that my stay at this hostel was only temporary; I was filling in for another girl who had not yet arrived from Germany. So after a few weeks I had to leave and stayed with several families until sometime in May 1938 the Committee found a hostel for me in Southport. There were about 14 girls in this hostel, where we were looked after by a Matron and her elderly mother who did the cooking – themselves refugees.

By now it was pretty clear to all of us that war was inevitable and getting our parents out of Germany was the only thing occupying our minds. There was so little I could do – a child in a hostel. The whole burden was on my sister's shoulders and I know she desperately tried everything humanly possible. To get a Domestic Permit for my mother, though difficult, was just about possible. The problem was my father. He was 60 and not in the best of health. The only way he could get a visa for England was for someone to guarantee that once he was in England, he would not be a burden on the state. In other words, a guarantor had to be found who was willing to deposit £1,000 in the bank. In 1939 that sort of money was an incredible amount, but somehow my sister managed the seemingly impossible. She found a guarantor and I still have all the telegrams she sent to me in Southport. First on 27 June 1939, "Guarantor found", then on 13 July, "Have just posted permit for Papa" and on 31 August, "Parents arriving Wednesday". That Wednesday would have been 6 September, but on Sunday 3 September 1939, the war broke out.

My sister told me afterwards that she phoned my parents in Vienna just before and told them, "War is imminent, for Heaven's sake, just get out." What were my parents supposed to do – go illegally over the mountains into Switzerland? They were no longer young and besides they were law-abiding citizens; it was not in their nature to do anything illegal. They probably told my sister, "We have our permits, we have our tickets, our luggage is packed, it's only another three days – surely – we'll just hang on." But they never made it and so we lost the race by three days.

After that we received the usual ten-word Red Cross messages once every few months until they stopped. It was only in 1956 that we got the following official notification: "According to our records Herr Arthur Bauer and Frau Berta Bauer were deported to Izbica on 5 June 1942 and their names do not appear on our list of returnees."

My sister and I never talked about this; it was too painful a subject. My sister died in 1978 and I regret never having asked her who this person was who was willing to do so much for a stranger. I would have liked to have shaken his or her hand and said thank you. But I never found out and now it is too late.

I am often asked why I am prepared to talk about these very painful memories. I do find it difficult, especially when I recount how near we came to rescuing my parents. There are so few survivors left now and as long as there are people ready to dismiss the Holocaust as something that never really happened, we must speak out; I almost feel it a duty. I am after all one of the lucky ones; I am here to tell the tale. Apart from a very difficult start, I have had a good life. My experiences cost me my childhood and, most important to me, also.my education. I was never able to go to university, something I have never stopped regretting.

Six million Jews killed is a figure that is hard to comprehend, but you begin to understand the immensity of the tragedy when you think of one human being and then another – a writer, a scientist, an ordinary human being who had to perish, not for anything they did, but for who they were. I shall go to my grave not understanding antisemitism. The only time in my life that I felt safe as a Jew was immediately after the war when the camps were liberated and all the horrors came out. I felt – we all felt – that such barbarities could never happen again. How wrong we were. Now, after all these years, once again one fears racial prejudice. It is incomprehensible to me how anyone can look down – or up – to people because their skin is black or yellow, because they are of one race or another. I can only acknowledge one race, the human race, to which we all belong.

To my parents Arthur and Berta Bauer, whom we so nearly saved.

My mother as a young, typically Viennese, woman

Ibi and Waldemar Ginsburg in Munich, 1948

IBI GINSBURG

I Shall Never Forget

I was born Ibi Davidovicz in Hungary. I was nineteen and a half years old when the events I am about to describe happened. I was the eldest of four girls in our family of practising Orthodox Jews.

Until the spring of 1944, I lived with my family in Tokai, a middle-sized town in the centre of the wine-growing region of Hungary. Life was relatively peaceful. Hungary was an ally of Germany, and until 1944 was allowed to run its own affairs. The news of the fate of the European Jews, which filtered through to us in Hungary, seemed unbelievable. So when Germany occupied Hungary on 14 March 1944 and we were locked into a ghetto near our town, our trauma was more connected with our loss of freedom, home and belongings than with fear for our lives.

After a month in the ghetto, we were rounded up like animals and put into cattle wagons. There were 72 of us in our wagon, including babies, children, the old and the ill. The wagon doors were closed and we were left in darkness. The only light and fresh air came through two narrow slits in the side of the wagon. As the long train began to move and gathered speed, taking us further and further away from home, we fell silent. We were filled with foreboding, wondering what the future had in store for us. Our nightmare journey lasted three days and nights before we arrived in the concentration camp, Auschwitz.

As the wagon doors opened, a feeling of panic was added to our shock and disorientation. There were SS men and barking dogs everywhere, and a pandemonium of blazing loudspeakers issuing incomprehensible orders assailed our senses. Emaciated, weird-looking men in striped uniforms herded us out of the wagons. Taking advantage of the commotion, they asked us in Yiddish (the language used by Jews from central and eastern Europe) where we came from and advised the young mothers to hand over their babies to the grandmothers or elderly women. These people who looked so weird to us were actually veteran prisoners. They knew that mothers with babies, children, the old and the ill were taken straight to the gas chambers, and they wanted to save these young women. Their advice was ignored. To us, the whole set-up had the appearance of a lunatic asylum and the advice of these men seemed like the crazy talk of inmates.

Orders came for the able-bodied men to go and stand on the right, and we were separated from our father. The rest of the arrivals were lined up and a group of SS men started the 'selection', directing the fit and healthy-looking women without babies to one side, and the women with children, the elderly and the frail to the other. I became separated from my mother and two younger sisters, aged ten and seven. My third sister was only 13, but looked older and she stayed on my side. My mother's last words to me were to take good care of her. As they were herded to the left, the eyes of my ten-year-old sister followed me until she disappeared from sight. I shall never forget that look as long as I live.

The selection finished and we began to move, with the men following behind us. We saw father and waved. On the way, we marched past an all-woman band, also prisoners, who were playing cheerful tunes. We were told that we were going to the showers.

When we arrived, the place consisted of three large rooms. SS guards with rifles stood all around the room, and in the middle there were hundreds of women in various stages of undress. We all stood horrified, not believing what we were seeing. The veteran prisoners in charge told us to undress, leave all our clothing behind, and just keep our shoes. They warned us to get on with it fast or the guards would start shooting. In a daze, we did as we were told and moved into the next room where our head and body hair was shaved off. Then we had a shower. In the noise and confusion I panicked. I could not see my sister. I was calling out her name and all the time we were under the same shower. I did not recognise her without her hair.

We went into the showers bewildered, frightened and separated from our loved ones. After a short while, we came out into the cold April wind with our heads shaven and only wearing a single shapeless, rough garment, which irritated our bodies. We had been through a process designed to dehumanise us and turn us into 'non-people'.

As we marched through the endless rows of barracks, we realized that we looked just like the strange, shaven-headed creatures who stared at us from across the barbed wire. The only difference was that we still *looked* fit and well fed, although our physical appearance did not show our mental state. We entered our huge barracks which had three tiers of wooden planks, arranged just like a chicken coop. We laid down on the wooden boards and were soon overcome by mental and physical exhaustion.

Our next ordeal was the roll-call, which was to become a twice-daily torment. It started in the small hours. We would stand in the dark for two to three hours while we were counted again and again. We were frozen. Sometimes we would get soaked to the skin and dry out again in the cold wind before they finished and let us go back into the barracks.

At mid-morning on the first day, a group of SS men turned up to see us and politely enquired about our state of health and our requirements. In reply to our request about our families and relatives, an SS officer assured us that all would be well. Sunday was the day for reunions. Just as we cheered up at the good news, our Block Elder (prisoner in charge of the Block), a veteran prisoner from Slovakia, lost her cool completely. She started ranting and raving, shouting that we wouldn't be seeing anybody, since they had all gone up the chimney.

This violent outburst confused and bewildered us; we could not understand why she wanted to mislead us. It took a while for us to emerge from our trance-like state and look around. We noticed that there was not a single blade of grass, neither a tree nor a bird to be seen. The air was saturated with the smell of burning flesh. The sight of two large chimneys, belching out yellow smoke, and flakes of ash floating around us were constant reminders that the Block Elder was right. We understood the purpose of Auschwitz.

After three months, my sister Yudith and I were lucky to be assigned for transportation to the concentration camp Lager 1 near Dachau, where we were used as slave labour. Hunger, deprivation and humiliation were our constant companions, and only hope and our survival instinct kept us going. Liberation came on 1 May 1945.

After the first few days of euphoria, we looked around us and realized the enormity of our losses. Families and communities had been completely wiped out. We became depressed and desolate; we felt guilty at having survived while all around us, our loved ones had died. My sister and I found out that our father had survived and he joined us later in Germany. We were the lucky ones.

At the same time, I met a young man who was a survivor of Lager 1. We became friends, fell in love and married in 1946. For both of us, this was the turning point. We helped each other to exorcise the traumas of the past and began to look forward to a new life. We came to England in October 1948 on a permit to work in textiles, and we found a welcome here. We were pleasantly surprised by the kindness of our fellow workers and the other people with whom we came into contact. The two 'Displaced People' had found a place they could call home and start a family.

Waldemar, aged 17 in Kovno, Lithuania

Waldemar Ginsburg

Journey to Disaster

I come from Lithuania and lived in Kovno or Kaunas, the former capital city of the country. I was born on 9 October 1922. My parents were not religious; they were 'cultural Jews', part of a large secular section of the Jewish community which considered that belonging is more important than believing, and that was also my view. I was an only child, leading a pampered and carefree life. To understand what happened in my town, you need to be aware of the background to my story.

Inter-war Years

At the end of World War I, after 120 years under the Tsarist yoke, Lithuania regained her independence. All minorities were granted full religious and civil rights. The Lithuanian Jews with their high educational level and efficient communal organisation took advantage of the opportunity to reinforce their position as one of the most spiritual and cultural centres of world Jewry. In my town, Kovno, to serve a population of about 35,000 people, there were four full-time Yiddish (the language used by Jews from central and eastern Europe) and Hebrew schools, five Yiddish newspapers, a Yiddish theatre, more than forty synagogues and some of the most prestigious *yeshivas*, Jewish rabbinic academies of higher learning, in the world.

Despite the political, social and economic upheavals in Europe, we lived in peace until June 1940. Then disaster struck: the Red Army marched in and occupied Lithuania.

Facing the Communist Terror

The KGB (state secret police) arrived, sealed the borders and began arresting the 'enemies of the people'. They targeted leading intellectuals, religious leaders, nationalists, Zionists, and so-called 'bourgeois capitalists'. Our family was classed as a 'capitalist enemy of the people', our property was confiscated and we became candidates for deportation to a Siberian slave labour camp. We were not deported; what saved us was Germany's attack on the Soviet Union in June 1941. The Red Army fled in disarray and we had to decide whether to follow or to stay put. We decided to stay. Of the 14 members of our family gathered that morning, I was the only one to survive.

The first pogroms started before the German army arrived. Lithuanian Nazi supporters turned against the Jews, blaming them for the terror of the Communist rule. Thousands of Jews were killed, their property looted and homes occupied.

Facing Nazi Terror

Our new masters, the SS and Gestapo, arrived on the heels of the German army and began terrorising us. By the time the Kovno Jews were locked in a ghetto, 5,000 had already been killed. On 15 August 1941, the ghetto gates were shut and 30,000 hungry and frightened Jews were locked into a prison at the mercy of the Nazis and their allies, the Lithuanian militia. Three days later, 534 Jews were taken to an execution place near Kovno and shot.

After this atrocity, the Jewish ghetto council was instructed to provide slave labour for various jobs in town. Unwittingly, the Nazis threw us a lifeline. We could leave our prison, contact friends, scrounge for food and bring in firewood for cooking. But the killings continued; on 26 September 1,000 Jews were shot; on 4 October, 1,500. On that same day, the SS set the ghetto hospital on fire. The doctors, the nurses and the patients were trapped inside and burned alive. But worse was to come. On 28 October, 10,000 Jews were selected, taken out of the ghetto and executed. Another outrage took place on 28 March 1944 – the *Kinderaktion* (action against children). The victims were the children, the sick and the old.

In July 1944, as the Red Army was approaching the borders of Lithuania, we were taken to Bavaria, to a satellite camp of Dachau, to build huge underground bunkers for the production of Messerschmitt fighter planes. Conditions there were worse than anything we had experienced in Lithuania. When we were liberated by the American forces on 1 May 1945, only about 2,000 of us were still alive.

Life as a Free Man

I was free at last, but it took me nearly half a year to recover from my ordeal. The turning point came in 1946 when I married a Hungarian survivor of Auschwitz and Dachau. We moved to Munich where I joined a radio engineering course at the ORT technical college. On graduating, I stayed on as an instructor. In October 1948 we left for England to start a new life.

Our entry permit was only valid for work in textiles. We had virtually no knowledge of English and we knew even less about textiles, but thanks to the friendly and helpful attitude of our fellow workers and the people in authority, like the police and civil servants, it didn't take too long to settle in. Despite moving to the small town of Elland in West Yorkshire, we didn't feel isolated. We joined the Bradford Reform Synagogue and managed to establish lasting friendships with Jews and Gentiles. The two 'Displaced Persons' had found a place they could call home.

We have been retired for some years now and still live in Elland. When we think back to our dark period when the future looked hopeless, we realize what a gift it is to be living not far from our children and grandchildren, and see them leading a normal, fulfilled life.

In 1992 we received an invitation from the Historical Society of Durham university to talk about our experiences. More speaking engagements followed and they have become quite a time- and energy-consuming task. Our main venue is the Beth Shalom Holocaust Centre in Nottinghamshire. We talk to pupils, to students and to adult audiences (mainly teachers and clergy). We have every intention to continue as long as there is a demand and as long as our state of health allows it.

Waldemar and Ibi at Beth Shalom, 1998

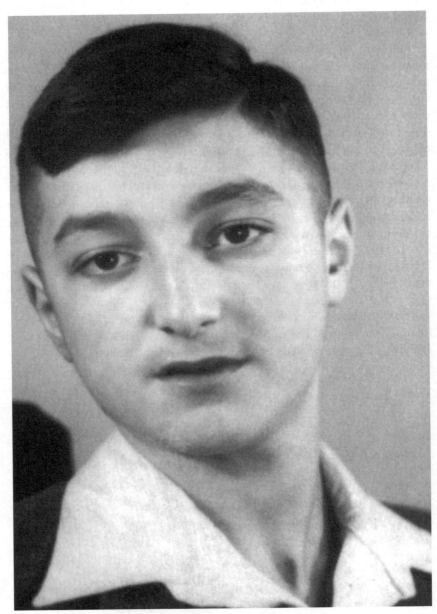

Bernard Grunberg, December 1937

BERNARD GRUNBERG

Lone Journey to Freedom

I was born in 1923 in Lingen-on-the-Ems in north-west Germany, about 11 miles from the Dutch border. As far as I can remember, there were 12 Jewish families living in the city. My father was a very successful cattle-dealer and we had a very comfortable life. I had one sister, who was two and a half years older than me. My upbringing was strict, but I have no regrets about that because I am sure it helped me when I had to stand on my own two feet at the age of sixteen and a half.

The ten Jewish children in Lingen attended Christian schools, but were given religious teaching twice a week by a Jewish teacher from a neighbouring town. I went to the local primary school for four years and then from 1933-37, to a school for higher education. Life was pleasant and, like any other child, I was extremely happy with my schoolfriends and playmates.

Shortly after Hitler came to power in 1933, life for the Jews changed considerably. I lost most of my friends and as time went on, I became more and more isolated because of Nazi anti-Jewish propaganda. I was well treated by all the teachers at my school, and was always told that I need not stay during lessons if they included any Nazi propaganda. But in the playground and on my way home, I was often verbally and physically assaulted, so gradually my education suffered.

Losing my friends did not affect me too much because I had other things to keep me occupied. We kept two cows at home and I learned how to milk them. It now became my job to look after the cows, milk them twice a day and take the surplus milk to the creamery. During the school summer holidays of 1934, 1935 and 1936, my parents took me by car to stay with my uncle, aunt and their two sons, who lived in Groningen in north Holland. My uncle had an upholstery factory and I was allowed to go there. I learnt quite a lot about the business and thoroughly enjoyed my time there. In February 1996, I heard from a friend of mine in Germany who had visited the Transit Camp for Jews at Westerbork in Holland. She found out that the family from Groningen, an aunt, daughter and son-in-law from

Amsterdam were taken to Westerbork in 1943 and from there to the concentration camps of Sobibor and Auschwitz, where they were murdered. It took time and tears for me to get over the shock.

As life was becoming worse for the Jews year by year, my father decided it was a waste of time for me to continue at school. After spending one year at home, I went in April 1938 to a technical re-training school in Berlin with a view later to emigrating to Israel. After giving me some training in joinery and metalwork, the Instructor decided that I was best suited to general woodwork. But in July 1938, a group of Nazi SS entered the grounds of the school and held everyone at the entrance while they set fire to the joinery workshop. Everything – including the valuable woodworking machinery – was destroyed. I remember helping to clear up the workshop, which could never be used again.

Then came the night of 9 November 1938, *Kristallnacht*, the Night of Broken Glass. After the murder of a German Embassy official in France by a Jewish student, many synagogues were set on fire, shops were smashed and looted. Most male Jews were arrested and taken to concentration camps. Many Jewish parents were trying to send their children away to safety.

Through the efforts of the Jewish communities in Germany and Great Britain, the British government allowed children between the ages of two and seventeen to enter the country – on condition that they would not undertake any work, paid or unpaid, nor ask for financial help from the state, and they would emigrate to other countries as soon as possible. So the *Kindertransports* were born. Between 1 December 1938 and the outbreak of the Second World War in September 1939, 10,000 Jewish children and others were allowed to enter this country and were saved from almost certain death.

I came to England with the second *Kindertransport* from Berlin on 12 December 1938, at the age of 15. My father was in Buchenwald concentration camp at the time, and this meant that only my mother had to give consent for me to leave. I went home from Berlin on 10 December to say goodbye to my family, and late that night my father came back from Buchenwald. I had to return to Berlin next morning in order to catch the train that would take me to England. I remember that we were only allowed to take one suitcase, hand luggage, and 10 German Marks. Before our train reached the Dutch border, Nazi guards came on board, opened some of our suitcases and took anything they wanted. Luckily, they did not remove the album of family photos which my mother had lovingly placed in my case.

Our train had to pass very near to my hometown and my father managed to get on board and travel with me for about 20 miles until we reached the Dutch border. This was the last time I saw any of my family. I never thought of this journey as emigrating; to me it seemed no more than a temporary absence from home. It was only much later that I knew different, but I never gave up hope of a reunion with my family.

After crossing the Dutch border, our train stopped at Oldensaal, where we were showered with cakes and hot drinks by the Dutch people on the platform. I have no recollection of crossing the English Channel.

On arrival at Harwich, a group of the older children – including myself – were taken to a summer holiday camp at Lowestoft in Suffolk, very close to the seashore, and we slept in unheated, wooden huts in mid-December. We were given a hot water bottle each night, but they turned to ice during the night. After the experience of the first night, I only took my overcoat and shoes off when I went to bed! One week later, we were taken to Dovercourt, a holiday camp near Harwich, where we found brick chalets and much better conditions. I also spent a short time in a Salvation Army home in Harwich and the treatment was exceptionally good there. Then I was at Waddesdon for a while, on Lord Rothschild's estate, and I also had a short stay in London. I cannot really recall how long I stayed at any of these last four places.

I was in contact with my parents by letter, but this stopped after the outbreak of war, and then you could only send 25 words through the Red Cross. I was also getting letters from home via a cousin in Amsterdam, plus 10 shillings pocket money a month from him. After the occupation of Holland, all contact with home ceased. This played on my mind because I had no idea what was happening there. Every so often I felt I had to be totally alone and cry my heart out; afterwards I could cope again.

In mid-1939 when war became a definite possibility, the government gave us permission to work in agriculture or coal-mining. I was one of about 50 boys sent to a farm-training school at Wallingford, Berkshire, which turned out to be a Borstal Institution (prison for young offenders). I had received a complete set of joinery tools from home and was doing some joinery work at a private house, making and fixing shelves and building a greenhouse. Despite this, being at the Borstal had a very bad effect on me, and I decided that I had to do something about it.

Because of my experience at home with cows, I asked to go to the cow-sheds to prove that I was good enough to be employed on a Dairy Farm. I was in luck. After two weeks, I was given employment on a large, mixed farm in Oxfordshire, which was owned by a real gentleman farmer. I firmly believe that his influence helped me to avoid a rigorous Alien Tribunal and internment as an enemy alien. I was now among strangers and totally on my own, but I was doing work I was used to and liked. I worked seven days a week and was paid 25 shillings weekly. I paid £1 a week for my board and lodgings and was proud to be earning my own living. I felt free.

However, not hearing from home affected me badly and whenever I was alone, the tears would flow. I worked on various farms from Oxfordshire in the south to north of the Scottish border, and always lived in lodgings. It never bothered me whether they were good, bad or indifferent, and the same applied to my employment. If I was not satisfied, I would pack my belongings and move on.

Early in 1945, I met my wife, Daisy Dunnington, born in London, who was in the Land Army during the war. After our marriage in 1947, we set up home and lived in a cottage which was tied to my employment. For nearly 22 years, I worked on a farm at Weston-on-Trent in Derbyshire as lorry driver and maintaining the farm implements and machinery. The last three years before my retirement, I was employed as a lorry driver by a road haulage firm and I also helped with repairs and servicing the lorries. Wherever I went, the other men always treated me as one of their workmates, and some of them became good friends. While working in north Northumberland in 1949, my late wife and I met a young married couple, and so began a friendship that has stood the test of time and is still as strong as ever, although we now live nearly 200 miles apart.

In 1946 or 1947 I received the following information from the Red Cross, "Your parents and sister were deported to Riga in Latvia in December 1941 and nothing further has been heard of them since." At that time I did not know where Riga was, I hadn't even heard of it. I still thought and hoped they would return sometime and we would all be reunited.

In 1986 Mrs Ruth Foster and the City Council of Lingen succeeded in tracing me and I was invited to attend the unveiling of a memorial to commemorate the Jewish families who had lived in the city until their deportation and murder. All my expenses would be paid by the Council. There I met Ruth again: we had both lived in Lingen as children. She told me how she and her parents, my parents and my sister, along with almost 1,000 other Jewish men, women and children were deported in December 1941 to a Labour camp at Riga in Latvia. Now for the first time, I heard from a survivor of the terrible fate that befell my family. It had a very traumatic effect on me, and many tears were shed. I shall never forgive nor forget.

Prior to deportation, all the Jews in Lingen were forced to live in just two houses. All their property, furniture, household goods and valuables were confiscated and sold by public auction, the proceeds going to the state. Special laws had had a devastating effect on their lives. They were not allowed to own any means of transport, to use public transport, go to cinemas, theatres, public parks, nor have any pets. There was a curfew from 6 p.m. to 7 a.m. They had to report weekly to the police, have police permission to travel; they had ration cards marked with the letter J (for Jew) and could only buy their rations in certain shops. They all had to wear the Star of David and the letter J on their outer clothing. Their bank accounts were frozen and they could only draw a fixed weekly allowance for food. Anyone who was lucky enough to be able to emigrate had to pay a special Emigration Tax.

After my first return to Lingen, I was given a lifelong invitation to go to the city once a year, all expenses paid. Each year I have taken up this opportunity and made many friends. After all, I would not – nor could not – blame the children for what their parents might have done. Some of my new-found friends have been to stay with me in Derby; they have visited Beth Shalom Holocaust Centre with me and were highly impressed by what they saw.

Most years in Lingen, I have given talks at schools about my experiences. In 1993, I became an Honorary Citizen of Lingen. Every year Memorial Services are held there on 9 November (Night of the Broken Glass) and on 14 December when all the remaining Jews were deported. A small one-room building, used for religious teaching of Jewish children, and later to stable horses, was purchased and renovated by the city and today houses a museum displaying the life of the Jews of Lingen. I also had a memorial stone placed in the Jewish cemetery to commemorate the murder of my parents and sister, and the cost was paid by the city.

After my retirement, I took up wrought-iron work as a hobby, but I had to give it up owing to my wife's ill health, to be able to look after her and the day-to-day running of the household, until she passed away in 2001 after 54 years of happy marriage. I now live on my own.

I obtained British nationality in 1948 and have lived in Derby since 1971. I will always be grateful to this country and its people for having almost certainly saved my life. I do not look upon Germany as my home country, only as the country of my birth. To me, Germany is just another foreign country. I feel British through and through and am proud of it. At the end of the war in Lingen, there were only five survivors from the twelve Jewish families that had lived there before the war.

I dedicate this chapter to my parents and my sister who perished in the Holocaust: to my father who died in Riga, Latvia, and my mother and sister who were murdered in Stutthof extermination camp.

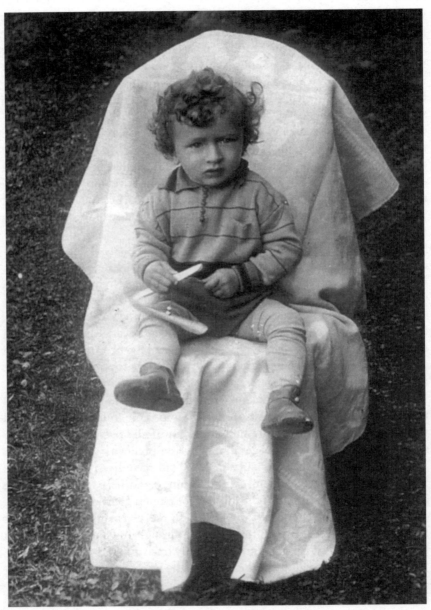

Roman, aged 1 year plus, in 1928 in Chodecz. Photo obtained from his aunt who lived in Switzerland.

ROMAN HALTER

The Kindness of Strangers

I was 12 years old in September 1939 when Hitler's troops entered Poland. I was the seventh child in our family and the youngest. My family and relations lived in the north-western part of Poland, in a town called Chodecz (Godetz in German). The area where I lived was made an integral part of greater Germany in 1939 and the "clearing-out" – the murder – of the Jewish people began almost immediately. Before September 1939, Poles, Germans and 800 Jews lived in my town. Murder began as soon as the SS police took charge of the town, towards the end of September 1939.

First of all, the SS rounded up all the potential Jewish and Polish leaders in our town and shot them. And they did the same thing in the adjoining towns. Then they took all the able-bodied Jewish men and women to work, either building the Berlin-Pozen road and railway line, or on the construction of the first extermination camp in Chelmno (German Klumthof), built to murder the Jewish communities of north-western Poland.

For those of us who remained in Chodecz, our properties were taken away and we were relocated in hovels on the outskirts of the town. We were made to wear armbands with the Star of David on them and to walk in the gutter. By the following year, autumn 1940, of the 800 Jews who originally lived in our town, 360 were left; and we were all sent to the ghetto in Lodz.

When we arrived there, the Lodz ghetto was overcrowded and could only accept 120 of us. My grandfather, father, mother, half-sister and two of her children, and I were amongst the 120 taken in, but the remainder were taken away and shot. The Lodz ghetto was an unjust and unequal society. Those who ran it under Mordechai Chaim Rumkowski, along with their friends, relations and acquaintances, managed to eat adequately; the rest starved. Those of us who were outsiders starved from the first day.

My grandfather, to whom I was very close, died two months later, in October 1940. He told me that *when* I survived – not *if* I survived but *when* – I must tell the world that the German Nazis were murdering all the Jewish people. As early as October 1940, he had understood this, and his words helped me to live because I believed what he said to me.

The Lodz ghetto set up factories to produce things needed by the German forces. I succeeded in getting a job in the metal factory. In addition to the starvation rations, those who worked received soup, a watery soup, but soup nevertheless. Even with the extra soup I looked like a skeleton, and so did my father, mother, half-sister and her two children. My father died of starvation in spring 1941. My mother's legs were swollen from hunger and she moved with great difficulty.

In Spring 1942, my mother, my half-sister, her two children and I were all selected to be taken to Chelmno to be murdered there. My half-sister could have saved herself, but when they took her two children, she chose to go with them. My mother told me to escape and hide till the selection of our area of the ghetto was over. "Run in a zigzag," she told me, "and don't stop when they shoot or shout 'Halt!'" I did as she asked and escaped that selection, but my mother, half-sister and her children all perished there.

I continued working in the metal factory till the Lodz ghetto was emptied in Autumn 1944. When this happened, 500 men, women and young people, the most skilled from the metal factory, were selected to be transported as slave labour. I was amongst them, and we were going to make munitions somewhere in Germany.

First of all we were sent by cattle truck to Auschwitz-Birkenau. On the train there were 500 metal workers like me and 2,300 people from the Lodz ghetto, most of whom had been in hiding inside the ghetto. We were packed into the cattle trucks, 80 people per truck, 35 trucks. In the camp at Auschwitz-Birkenau, the 500 metal workers were put to one side as the others, the 2,300, were led to the gas chambers.

From Auschwitz we metal workers were then transported to Stutthof – a brutal and murderous concentration camp. There we found out that the munitions factory was supposed to be north of Pozen, but there was to be a change of plan because the Russians were advancing rapidly westwards. The machines were now to be packed and sent to a factory in Dresden. Thirty-two of us were dispatched to north of Pozen to clean, dismantle and pack the machines. It took us six weeks to do this. During that time, we lost about 120 people in Stutthof from our original group of 500. Auschwitz was then asked to select 120 'tough' new people to make up the figure of 500 workers in accordance with the orders of Albert Speer's Ministry of Armaments.

We arrived in Dresden on 24 November 1944. As we were marched by the SS from the railway station to the factory on 68 Schandauerstrasse, starved, thin and weak as I was, I was nevertheless overwhelmed by the beauty of the town. Chodecz was a *shtetl* or little town in Yiddish. The

Lodz ghetto was squalid and ugly, but Dresden was a beautiful city. I looked to right and left as we were marched along and I promised myself that when I survived, I would become an architect.

On 13 February 1945 Dresden was bombed: it was not touched till then. The factory in which we worked as slave labourers under SS supervision was damaged and put out of action. The SS made us clean the machines and repair the damaged building, and we had to spend many days and nights doing it.

Eventually the SS realized that it was a hopeless task and one day towards the middle of March 1945, they marched us in a southerly direction. It turned out to be a death march. Those who were weak and could not keep up with the pace of the march, were taken away and shot. We all realized that our usefulness as munitions workers had come to an end and now the SS would take us to some ravine where we would all be shot. It was this certainty that made a few people try to escape on the third night of our march. I was amongst them.

Our plan was to get to Dresden and hide in the ruins, but daylight overcame us when we were only eight kilometres from the city, and we had to take shelter. In a place called Oberpoyritz not far from Pilnitz Castle, three of us were taken in by a childless, German couple called Kurt and Hertha Fuchs. My two colleagues were called Abram Sztajer, who was 30, and Adam Szwajcer, who was 31; by then I was 17. Adam had been in Auschwitz-Birkenau from the beginning of the camp and his arm was tattooed with No 57.

Mr and Mrs Fuchs looked after us for weeks. I slept in the greenhouse/shed and worked all day in their vegetable garden at the back of their house. With the help of Mr Fuchs, my two friends found work with a nearby farmer, and came back each evening to the Fuchs' house.

Russian troops passed through the village of Oberpoyritz on 4 May 1945. That night my grandfather came into my dreams, telling me to go back to Chodecz. The dream was so vivid that I got up in the middle of the night and began dressing, and only then realized that I had been dreaming. The next morning, I told Mr and Mrs Fuchs and my two colleagues that I was leaving that day for Chodecz, my town in Poland, to meet up with members of my family. I explained that as I was the youngest of seven children, I had hopes that some of them might have survived... Or some of my cousins or uncles... The prospect of going home made me feel dizzy with longing.

When I told Mr and Mrs Fuchs and the others that I was preparing to go, that very day, they thought that I had gone mad, that I had lost my senses. They advised me to wait a week or two, or a bit longer, and then leave. I stayed just one more day – persuaded by the meal which Mrs Fuchs was preparing for that evening to celebrate the end of the war.

The following morning I left. I eventually reached my home town of Chodecz, some 460 kilometres as the crow flies from Dresden. I discovered that of the 800 Jewish people who lived there before 1939, only four had survived – myself and the three Pinczewski sisters who now live in Melbourne, Australia. All the Jewish people from the adjoining towns had also been murdered. Jews had been living in Poland for a thousand years, and now all the thriving communities had been wiped out. Finding nobody at home made me wonder about my own survival. What had kept me going during those black years? I knew that my grandfather's words helped me greatly because I believed him totally. Then there was my own will to live and my love of life, my innate optimism, the courage to take risks, and perhaps – not least – the fact that I had been so loved by my family when I was a child.

The Polish people of my town did not give me a friendly reception: in fact, I was in fear of my life. The whole area felt to me like one big grave-yard. I left Poland and went to Czechoslovakia (now the Czech Republic), and with the help of a kind Red Cross lady in Prague, I managed to get some foodstuffs which I decided to take back to Mr and Mrs Fuchs. With this modest parcel of edibles, I wanted to say thank you to them. The trains were running but they were infrequent, and those that came were over-crowded. I noticed people sitting on the roof of the train, so I too climbed up and travelled like that all the way to Dresden.

When I got to the village, Mrs Fuchs was dressed in black. Five days after I had left for my home in Poland, local men who had been in Hitler's SS during the war had learned that Mr and Mrs Fuchs had sheltered Jews. Although the war was now over, they had come and taken Mr Fuchs, Adam and Abram to a nearby field, where they shot and killed Mr Fuchs and Adam, and took Abram away with them. He survived and lived in Israel until he died in 2003. It took me many years to find him because he changed his name slightly. Mrs Hertha Fuchs was honoured for her brave actions and elected Righteous Among The Nations by Yad Vashem, Jerusalem.

In October 2002 I visited Dresden and went with a television crew to see Mrs Fuchs, who died aged 95 in December 2003. I asked her why she had taken in and sheltered the three of us. She paid for it so very dearly with the death of her husband, Kurt, and we had nothing to give her but our thanks. She answered that both she and her husband felt they had to do it. "You see," she said, "although we are Germans, we were not Nazis; our minds were not poisoned by the 12 years of propaganda, and all the

Nazi screeching against the Jews. It was our impulse to do this, to take you in and save you. You would do the same, I think, Roman."

I replied that after the wonderful example she and Kurt had shown, I would like to think that I would do the same. But I know that it is easier to say yes than to do it. I often ask myself if I would have the courage, the sense of what is right and what is wrong, the humanity, to take in strangers and save them, when such an act was punishable by death for all. I would like to believe that I would.

I dedicate this story to my lost family, to my children and grandchildren.

Roman speaking at Beth Shalom in 2001

Kitty on a visit to the former concentration camp Gross Rosen whilst filming 'The Death March' in 2001

KITTY HART-MOXON

Obey and Die

I was born Kitty Felix in a town called Bielsko in Poland, which in 1939 was very close to the German and Czechoslovakian frontiers. My brother Robert was five years older. We had a wonderful and most interesting childhood. Because our town lay at the foot of a mountain range, we had numerous sports facilities and most of the inhabitants spent their leisure time in the mountains. In winter there was skiing, tobogganing, and ice skating. In summer everyone went hiking and climbing. And we also had swimming, athletic and gymnastic clubs.

I was 12 years old at the outbreak of the war in 1939. The German armies invaded Poland very close to our town. Because we were so close to the frontier, most of the population started to flee days before the invasion.

My father decided to head for the centre of the country to a town called Lublin. I was quite unable to grasp what was happening. But as the Germans brought the war ever closer and the town was bombed daily, I began to suspect that there was something terribly serious happening.

Within weeks German troops entered the city. Soon after the occupation, posters were put up, decreeing that the Jewish population had to register. Without registration it was impossible to get ration cards and thus obtain food. Many young people began to flee to the East, including my brother Robert. Every day brought new laws and restrictions. We had to wear armbands with the Star of David clearly displayed. Soon a small section of the town was allocated to the Jews and we all had to move into this section – which became the Lublin Ghetto. Leaving the ghetto area was punishable by death.

Children were not allowed any schooling and my father was no longer able to carry out any work and earn a living. Any man outside in the open was liable to be grabbed and carted off to shovel snow, and often never returned.

Soon the ghetto became overcrowded as the Germans began to bring in people from many parts of Europe and simply dumped them in the ghetto streets. Living conditions worsened day by day; there was total chaos. The newcomers could not communicate with the local population and their currency was not valid in the ghetto. Soon there was an epidemic of typhus and cholera.

But worse was to come. There were almost daily raids into our homes by special action Storm Troopers called *Einsatzgruppen*. They would smash their way in without notice, beat up everyone, confiscate the food they found and often throw people down the stairs and out of windows. Mostly the people in a cordoned-off street were forced to line up, pushed onto lorries and deported to unknown destinations. They were never seen again.

It was often the children who kept life going. My father, for instance, would send me with whatever he still possessed to smuggle my way into the Aryan sector of the city to barter some goods for flour, bread or potatoes. I would go down a manhole through the city sewers and bring back a little food.

My mother, who was a qualified English teacher, made contact with a Catholic priest whose vicarage was opposite the Gestapo headquarters. She gave him English lessons in return for food. Crawling through the city sewers, she too risked her life, but without our endeavours we would have died of starvation.

The ghetto's main street was always patrolled by the SS Action Troops and one had to bow to them and step into the gutter. On one occasion, when nearing a patrol, my 15-year-old friend failed to step off the pavement and was shot dead in front of me.

People began to build barricades and hiding places in their homes, but my father thought that the only way to survive was to escape from the ghetto, even though this was punishable by death. Yet we took the chance and attempted several escapes.

The first was in the winter of 1940-41 when we tried to reach the then Russian frontier at the river Bug, east of Lublin. We travelled by horse and cart over several days, mostly cross-country since it was forbidden for us to be outside the ghetto and on main roads – there was a curfew and anyone found after dark was shot dead on the spot. Unfortunately by the time we reached the frontier town of Dorohusk on the river Bug, it had been closed 24 hours before. Unknown to us, the Germans were already preparing for the invasion of the Soviet Union in June of 1941.

We waited for the river to freeze and then attempted to cross it illegally to reach the Soviet Union by horse and sleigh. We had almost reached the far bank when shots rang out from both sides. We crouched in the sleigh, but the guide swung round and took us back to the German side. There was no alternative but to return to the Lublin ghetto.

Conditions were now intolerable there and we could not find anywhere to live even though there were constant deportations. Once again my father decided to take us out of the ghetto. Disguised as peasants with bundles on our backs, we walked out before the ghetto was completely sealed off from the outside world.

We reached a small village south of Lublin called Zabia Wola where we found a small Jewish farming community. It was the summer of 1941. My father found work at a nearby Estate library and my mother once more gave English lessons for food. Soon the Germans began to blackmail the Jewish population to give up articles or food every day – wedding rings, shoes, eggs etc. We were constantly threatened with deportation to unknown destinations unless we satisfied the demands. We did not realize at the time that we were not many miles from the killing centre of Belzec. Most of the Jews from the neighbourhood had been deported there and killed instantly on arrival.

In August 1942, we realized that a deportation was imminent. My father decided to leave, but we still had my grandmother with us, and she now refused to go anywhere. There was no option: she had to be left behind. As dawn broke my father, mother and I escaped into the forest nearby.

We watched in horror from a clearing in the woods as the whole village was surrounded by troops in helmets, carrying pointed guns. There were screams as people were thrown onto carts and lorries and driven away. We now know they were all murdered in Belzec that day, 12 August 1942.

We hid in the forest some three weeks, living mostly on berries. Eventually we made our way back into Lublin – not to the ghetto but to the vicarage of the Catholic priest, who had obtained non-Jewish documents for us that were to help save our lives. I now had a new identity. My name was Leokadia Dobrzynska, born in Lublin.

The priest had worked out a survival plan, but we would have to part, as together we were unlikely to survive. My father was to go to Tarnow to be employed in a sawmill. My mother (now my aunt with a different name) and I would to go into a Lublin collection centre where the SS were holding non-Jewish Poles they had grabbed off the streets to dispatch them to work in German factories. We got to the centre and soon found ourselves in a train, on our way with a group of Poles into the German Reich.

Our destination was Bitterfeld, the ammunition plant of IG Farben. As I spoke German well, I was to work in the offices and was given the task of issuing meal vouchers, enabling me to eat in the canteen reserved for the German staff. The women had the dreadful work of shaking aluminium dust from sacks, which was very harmful to the lungs. My mother, being the eldest, did not have to work at all.

We would have survived the war there quite well, but it was not to be.

A spy had been planted among us and soon it became clear that we were not the only Jews among our group of 50 women.

On 13 March 1943, I was called to the chief's office. On the table lay a cap with skull and crossbones. I knew at once that we had been betrayed. Thirteen of us were driven to Gestapo headquarters and interrogations began to find out where we had obtained our documents. Our greatest fear was that they would pick up the priest and also my father. Mother and I decided that we would never confess, come what may! We were separated and put into solitary confinement.

Some days later we were charged at a trial. We had committed three offences:

    1. We entered the German Reich illegally.

    2. We were in possession of false documents.

    3. We were Jewish.

These crimes all carried the death penalty.

Our execution was to take place next morning. I was 15 years old and not ready to die.

We were led to a courtyard at dawn and made to face a brick wall. We stood on sawdust to mop up the blood. The guns were in position. The order was given to fire. As the shots rang out, some girls crumpled on the floor beside me and my first thought was that I had been missed. But no! They actually fired into the air. It was a mock execution to show us what was to come if we didn't cooperate. In fact our death sentence had been commuted to hard labour for life in a concentration camp and the camp Gestapo were also to interrogate us by "special means" about our false documents.

We were moved to prisons in Halle, Leipzig and Dresden, and then travelled in a specially constructed prisoner train fitted with interior cages. We were delivered to the gates of hell – Auschwitz.

Auschwitz is not something that I can possibly describe in a few pages and there is no language that can adequately explain it – other than to say that we were now on a different planet! No one could possibly have imagined what was to come.

Most people who entered through the gates of Auschwitz-Birkenau were confronted with an immediate 'selection': either to be admitted to the camp or to be killed by gas on arrival. However, having come from prison, we were not subjected to immediate selection. We were still to be questioned by the camp's Gestapo. This is how my mother entered the camp with me: had there been a selection, she would have been killed on arrival as only young people were admitted into Auschwitz.

Screaming women prisoners with whips, and SS guards with howling

Alsatians greeted us on arrival. We were marched to be stripped, shaved of all hair and tattooed on our left forearms. From then on we had no names. I was now number 39934 and my mother 39933. We were thrown khaki breeches, uniform tops from former Soviet prisoners of war who had been murdered the previous week, and wooden clogs for our feet.

Our sleeping quarters, the stone hut called the Block, already held 1,000 women – it had three-tier platforms, each to sleep eight people, but they were all occupied and we sat all night on the stone channel that ran right through the Block.

It was still dark when whistles blew and there were screams of "*Raus*" – Out! It was *Zahlappell* – roll-call. This ritual took place twice a day, morning and evening, when the whole camp stood to attention, anything from 2-4 hours, waiting to be counted by SS personnel. There was no water to wash or drink and no lavatories. Latrines were built some time later, but access was restricted and only possible with payment, usually by bartering our bread ration.

The small bread ration was handed out after evening roll-call and the camp soup at midday. This was the only food distributed and it soon became apparent it would not sustain life for very long.

I was soon put onto hard labour – marching many hours in wooden clogs and then digging trenches or carrying heavy stones. I realized that it would be impossible to stay alive very long working outside; somehow I had to find a way out. Fortunately, I managed almost immediately to get my mother to work in the hospital compound. At least she was not exposed to the elements and hard labour and did not have to stand for roll-call for hours on end. The counting took place within the hospital block.

Newcomers to the camp were considered the lowest form of life and much despised by the ruling prisoners. It was imperative to get proper clothes and give an impression of being "streetwise" and thus not be at the mercy of the ruling prisoners who had the power over life and death.

For many months I worked in dozens of work groups: carrying shit in buckets to the cesspool, loading dead bodies, working on the construction of the railway, digging trenches, or working in potato fields which enabled me to smuggle some potatoes back into the camp. Whenever possible I hid and did no work at all, just trying to conserve as much energy as possible.

There was an epidemic of typhus and many other infectious diseases and in the later part of 1943 I went down with typhus. Most people did not survive when they fell ill as treatment was non-existent. But I was taken to my mother who looked after me and hid me during the daily selections for the gas chambers.

I had many complications and partially recovered after some three months. I was lucky, and managed to stay and work as an orderly in the dysentery hospital block. The daily death toll was horrendous and my main duty was dragging the dead out of the hut. Every day the SS Dr Mengele – named "The Angel of Death" – would carry out selections, walking from bunk to bunk pointing to those he sentenced to die.

It was early spring 1944 when he announced that the whole block was to be emptied, which meant that all patients were to die. We, the "staff", were to be transferred. A new work group, the *Kanada Kommando*, was formed consisting of 400 girls. On a fine spring morning, we were marched out, totally unprepared for what we were about to experience. We had heard about the *Kanada*. It was a nickname given to the group of men and women who sorted the possessions of the people brought to Auschwitz from all parts of Europe. These workers had access (though strictly forbidden) to clothes and food and because of that had a better chance of survival. But they were extremely secretive about the nature of their work.

We were marched to a relatively small wooded area where we saw four brick structures with very tall chimneys. These were the four crematoria housing the gas chambers. Many sections were cordoned off with electrified fencing. There were some 30 wooden sheds and at the top end a large L-shaped building, the *Sauna* or "bath house". We were now in the Kanada Section of Birkenau: the extermination centre.

All the wooden sheds were jam-packed with belongings of all descriptions. At the far end was a gigantic pile of jumble some three-storeys high of everything imaginable that the deportees had brought with them. Food of every description was rotting on the pile, yet it was inaccessible to the starving prisoners.

We were housed in the first two sheds, where I had a direct view of Crematorium IV. I was on nightshift. My task was to find men's jackets in the jumble, form bundles of twelve in a given time, sign with my number and hand them in for disinfection. Every jacket had to be searched for valuables. Often by the end of a shift, four of us would carry jewellery and currency that was found in the clothes in blankets and buckets.

Over the other side of the high tension electrified fence was the wooded area. Thousands of people, including children, were gathered there. They imagined they were going to be showered and admitted to the camp and had no conception of what was to come. In fact they were waiting their turn to go into the gas chamber and die of suffocation.

Small groups one at a time were led into the gas chamber. Day in, day out, we observed in horror as men in green uniforms donned gas masks, climbed ladders and emptied tins of white crystals into an opening in the roof of the building. Soon screams could be heard – it varied how long this lasted. Smoke and fire began to belch out of the chimney and soon ash was dumped in the pond behind crematorium IV. Often there was insufficient capacity to dispose of the dead and piles of corpses lay outside the building waiting to be burned.

My time in the *Kanada Kommando* lasted eight months. During that time we witnessed the killing of more than half a million people. We knew how many trains arrived daily and roughly how many people were packed in the numerous cattle trucks. There were days when an unbelievable number of some 10-15,000 people were gassed. All the Jews of Hungary. Everyone in Gypsy Camp. All the inhabitants of the Lodz Ghetto, the inmates of Majdanek, Theresienstadt and people from many other locations.

We girls could not take in what was happening – even though we *heard the screams as people were dying*, it was just too unreal and our brains could not accept what we were witnessing. But it sank in eventually when we saw the people disappear before our eyes, never to be seen again except for the piles of belongings left behind.

On 7 October 1944, loud explosions were heard from Crematorium IV and the huge chimney toppled to the ground. It was an uprising, but we did not know it. We believed the SS were bombarding the whole area as we had been told they intended to raze the whole camp to the ground and kill all the inmates.

In the ensuing battle many SS personnel and all the male prisoners lay dying. The uprising was started in crematorium IV by the men who worked inside, but it was only made possible because of four girls who worked in the ammunition plant. They supplied the material for the explosives. One girl was from my group and in a way we were all implicated. We supplied many valuables for the purchase of explosives.

Afterwards, there were reprisals and interrogations. The four girls were found, tortured and hanged in full view of the entire camp. I was transferred back into the main camp.

The Russian forces were fast advancing from the East. The SS were determined that none of the inmates would be liberated by the Allies, and so they ordered the evacuation of the whole Auschwitz complex. Prisoners were transferred by cattle truck or on foot westwards to other camps, or to the numerous ammunition plants inside Germany where they were used as slave labour.

On 11 November 1944, I was marched to the cattle trucks with my mother and 100 women to be transported to the base camp Gross Rosen in south-eastern Germany. Over 100 sub-camps had been built in this mountainous area, many situated in caves. We were sent to the nearby town of Reichenbach to the Telefunken-Phillips electronics factory.

Obtaining any extra food was impossible there and soon many of us were on the verge of collapse due to starvation. But I had a saviour: a German civilian woman working next to me placed herself in grave danger for me. She would bring a sandwich daily and hide it at the back of a shelf. In the three months at the factory, she saved both my mother and me from total starvation.

The Russian Army was advancing and closing in. Gunfire could be heard in the distance and liberation seemed close. Without warning, we were lined up outside our hut on 18 February 1945, on my mother's 55th birthday. We were to be evacuated on foot. Soon we were on the death march, heading into the wilderness of the Sudeten mountain range, the Eulengebirge. Our column was joined by hundreds of women from the neighbouring camps and stretched as far as the eye could see. The snow was some two feet deep and it was still snowing heavily. Most of us were barefoot and with hardly any outerwear. Soon we were drenched. No food was issued. By the first evening, most of us were completely exhausted and near collapse, but it was imperative to keep going and be at the front of the column. Everyone who lagged behind was shot dead by the guards at the rear. The nights were spent in the open sleeping on frozen ground, but whenever possible some of us would stray from the column to find shelter in barns or sheds, and forage for food while the guards were asleep.

There were occasions when we attacked passing peasant carts carrying potatoes or other farm produce. Then the guards would lash out and once I was struck with a rifle butt on my head and knocked unconscious. My friends carried me and dragged me along for many hours.

We began to climb the "High Owl" mountain, the highest peak bordering Czechoslovakia. It was dawn when we reached a plateau and quite unexpectedly met convoys of German refugees asleep in horse-drawn carts. We saw meat and sausages hanging from the sides of the carts. Nearby were cows to be milked! In a flash we attacked and overran them; it was our first sight of food in days.

By this time our column had shrunk drastically. Many women had collapsed from exhaustion and lack of food and did not get up again. Others froze to death during the many nights in the open in temperatures of minus 10–15 degrees. We had covered some 100 kilometres of mountainous terrain by the time we reached Trautenau, a camp in Czechoslovakia.

The very next day those still on their feet were forced into open coal trucks. The few hours in Trautenau enabled me to obtain a loaf of bread bought with the single gold sovereign I had brought from *Kanada* – a huge risk punishable by death. This single loaf saved my mother and me from complete collapse in the next six days.

Our nightmare journey had begun. We were packed like sardines and had to take turns to sit on the floor of the truck that was now also our lavatory. We passed no stations or towns; travelling through open country it was impossible to tell where we were heading for. The Allies mistook us for military convoys and bombed the train, the track was blown up and the train headed backwards. Gradually our truck started to empty as many of our friends began to die of cold and lack of nourishment.

After six days and seven nights in the open, we at last reached a destination. The sign read Porta Westfalica. We had travelled 1,000 miles to the north-west of Germany. By this time only about 200 of us were still alive.

We were marched to a small camp at the edge of a forest and soon the guards took us to our place of work inside a mountain cave. It was another Philips electronics factory. We were lowered down on platforms, 11 levels deep underground. At that depth, breathing became very uncomfortable due to poor ventilation, but we were made to work 12-hour shifts.

At the beginning of spring 1945, the Allies were closing in from the west, and we were again evacuated, this time eastwards to Belsen. But because of overcrowding there, we were forced to run into a siding. From the stationary cattle trucks we heard sounds of people's cries for help. Before we knew it, we too were pushed into cattle trucks and the doors were bolted. It soon became apparent that we were sealed inside an airtight truck – to be abandoned and left to die of suffocation.

It was pitch dark inside the truck and panic broke loose; the walls were wet with condensation and soon we were gasping for air. It was not long before many of us became unconscious. I was fortunate to possess a small knife. Pressing to the floor of the truck, I enlarged a small gap which allowed my mother and me to take turns to breathe. The train began to move. It was impossible to know where we were going, but suddenly it stopped. We had been sealed for many hours when we heard footsteps outside. We screamed for help. Someone unbolted the doors and we simply fell out of the truck, onto three men in German uniform. They seemed completely taken aback at what they found and soon we demanded to be taken to the nearest camp.

Much later it came to light that our truck was the only one opened. After hostilities had ceased, 240 bodies had been found in the train and later a memorial was erected to commemorate the horrific event at the siding on the outskirts of Salzwedel.

The soldiers who opened our truck escorted us to a nearby camp in Salzwedel. The women in this camp were brought here from the Lodz Ghetto and had worked for one and a half years in chemical factories.

It was now April 1945. We were told that no more food would be allocated from now on. By this time our group had become too weak to move about as we had been without nourishment for many days. We heard that the camp was mined and the authorities intended to blow us all up.

One day leaflets fluttered down from the sky. They came from French prisoners of war who had already been freed and promised to cut the high tension electricity in the fence and rescue us. Liberation was close. Once more we could hear the gunfire and shells, and bullets passed over our heads. This time the SS abandoned the camp and disappeared.

On Saturday 14 April 1945 strange tanks rolled past and did not notice us! But suddenly a tank swung round and burst through the gates of the camp. The American 84th Division had arrived and saved us just in time from certain death. They immediately announced that they had no food and we would need to find some from the local population. Those still able to walk rushed into the town. There followed a three-day rampage in Salzwedel. We entered homes in search of food and clothing, but also destroyed everything that we could see.

Soon the Americans were due to leave the area and hand over the town to the Russian Army. We panicked, since no one wished to remain under Communist occupation. The Americans took us on their tanks and dumped us in the territory occupied by the British Army.

My mother and I soon began to work as interpreters to the British Military Government, then we moved to the large Displaced Persons Refugee camp to help the Quaker Relief Team to set up and run the camp on the outskirts of Brunswick. Families that were scattered all over Europe had to be reunited. For Mother and me that was not to be. We soon found out that my father had been murdered and my brother Robert killed in action. About 30 members of our family had perished in Auschwitz. It was a year and a half before we finally obtained special permits to join our only relatives who were still alive in the UK.

My uncle was at the quayside in Dover to meet us. His greeting was chilly, "*Welcome to England. Understand that in my house I don't want you to speak about anything that happened to you. I don't want to know and I don't want my girls upset.*" Mother and I were stunned!

We realized that a difficult future lay ahead, but we were appalled and unprepared to discover that this attitude of indifference and often antagonism towards survivors was almost universal. Naturally, there were some individual acts of kindness, but little practical help or financial support was available from charitable organisations to the few survivors here in the Midlands. It was a devastating start to our new life.

In September 1946 Britain was an uncaring society, unwilling to listen to survivors. The government too was unhelpful and even imposed restrictions on the type of employment survivors were allowed to take up. There were no government grants, no welfare payments and no counselling was offered to help survivors come to terms with their traumatic past. We were simply left to cope on our own. I had lost all my teenage years; instead of studying, I had spent six years fighting for my life. For me, *Auschwitz was my university*. It certainly equipped me to cope with whatever life would throw back at me.

Some four decades passed before people recognized the urgent need for lessons to be learned from the Holocaust, if history is not to be repeated. Being the worst example, the Holocaust is central to understanding the causes of the genocides that have occurred in many parts of the world since the end of the Second World War.

I dedicate this chapter to the memory of the grandparents of my sons, David and Peter, as well as to the youth of today. In particular to my grandchildren: Lucy, Jonathan, Sophie, Simon, Daniel, Juliet and Michael.

My father, brother Robert, my mother, grandmother and me on holiday in Karlsbad in the 1930s

Arek at Beth Shalom, 2003

AREK HERSH

Growing Old Fast

I was born in a town called Sieradz in central Poland, which had a population of 11,000 – 6,000 Christians and 5,000 Jews. I was the fourth of five children, with one brother and three sisters. When I was two, we moved to Konin, where my grandmother lived. I started school there, but in 1937, when I was just eight, we moved back to Sieradz. My childhood there was very happy. All round the town there were forests in which we played, and in winter we skated on frozen rivers, rode on sleighs and made snowmen. We were Orthodox Jews and our religion was very important to us.

By 1938, German Jews of Polish descent started coming to Sieradz from Germany. They told us about the Nazis' inhumanity and how badly they treated the Jews. Another sign of growing Nazism was the greater degree of antisemitism amongst the *Volkdeutsche*, the ethnic Germans, living in and around the town. I remember one market day going into a shop and hearing two Christian Poles say, "Don't go into that shop, it's owned by Jews." Even amongst children, antisemitism began to increase. But we still had many wonderful non-Jewish friends.

Storm clouds were gathering over Poland and men were being called up to the army. Hitler was ranting on the radio about what he was going to do to Poland and the Jews. At the end of August 1939, I remember sitting outside our house with my older brother. Suddenly, we heard the sound of a plane, followed immediately by a barrage of rifle-fire. It was the beginning. The Polish army put up a very brave fight, but they were quickly defeated by the German army.

On 31 August 1939, the whole population of our town was ordered to leave. The following day the Germans attacked from all sides. They strafed the roads, bombed at will and their planes created so much havoc and panic that we did not know which way to run. We made our way to the large city of Lodz where we had cousins, and got there after walking for several days. But the Germans arrived a few days later. It wasn't long before they caught a few religious Jews and cut off their beards with large shears, watched by other soldiers who laughed and photographed the spectacle. My father decided we would return to Sieradz.

The Germans were planning how to liquidate the Jews of Poland and the rest of Europe. They plundered houses, shot or hanged hostages and rounded up people in the streets. You had to hide to avoid being caught. One day, I watched as German soldiers dragged Jewish men from their houses, kicking and beating them in the street. With horror I noticed that my father was amongst them. The men were forced to run to the market place, where two rows of soldiers kicked and clubbed them with rifle butts. My 21-year-old cousin was kicked to death.

The men were taken to the army barracks and held there overnight. It turned out that some Jewish men were accused of firing at a German soldier. Not knowing who was responsible, the Germans were holding all Jewish men as hostages. Fortunately some Polish Christian women saw the incident and told the German police the truth. A Polish Christian man – not a Jew at all – was guilty. After this, the men were released, some with broken arms and legs. My father got off lightly with a few bruises, and thus ended a tragic episode in our town.

The war began in earnest and at the age of 11, I was growing old fast. The Germans set up a committee, a sort of Jewish police force, to supervise the Jewish part of the town. It had to supply a Jewish labour force to the Germans for local work. Then one day, they were ordered to supply strong men to be sent away to work.

One night they came for my father, but he managed to escape in the dark. Instead, they took my brother, Tovia, who was only four years older than me. He escaped as well, so the German police came for me. I was only 11 and I was sure they would not take me. But I was wrong. They marched us all to the railway station and there I noticed Tovia hiding near a building, beckoning to me. He wanted to take my place, but I thought I would have a better chance to survive, being so small. So I persuaded him to go home.

We boarded the train and eventually arrived at a station called Otoschno. They marched us towards four wooden barracks, guarded by black-uniformed SS men carrying whips. As we approached the gate, they started to beat us mercilessly – that was our welcome to the camp. There were 2,500 men there, working on a new railway line to Russia. We worked 10-12 hours every day with terrible beatings and hangings, and little food. After 18 months, of the 2,500 men who started work there, only 11 were left, including me.

When our part of the railway line was finished, the camp commander sent me back home. I got there to find that my father had been taken six months after I was sent to Otoschno. Nobody knew where he was. By then the ghetto in Sieradz consisted of only 1,400 Jews of the 5,000 before the war.

After I had been home only two weeks, in August 1942, the Germans ordered us to go to the square at 8 a.m. They then marched 1,400 of us to the church and we had to file out of the building one by one. As I went out, I noticed two high-ranking SS officers. One of them shouted at me, "What's your profession?" and I shouted back *"Schneider"* (tailor). He sent me back inside with my mother, brother, sister and most of my family. Outside, they selected 150 people fit for work. I was very nervous and thirsty, and went outside again to get some water. The SS officer asked me my profession again. I repeated that I was a tailor, but this time he told me to join the group outside. Little did I realize that I had just saved my life. The Germans eventually took about 4,000 Jews to the church and kept them there for 48 hours without water or food. Then SS men arrived with lorries and took them to Chelmno extermination camp, where they were all killed.

The 150 people selected were taken to Lodz ghetto, which was completely fenced off from the rest of the city. There were Jewish policemen inside the ghetto gates and the German police and soldiers outside. The people I saw in the ghetto were thin and undernourished, some just like skeletons. We were taken to a large block of flats where we slept on the floor on straw mattresses. I could not sleep that first night and thought only about where they had taken my family. As the days went by, I watched every transport that arrived at the ghetto, searching for someone from my family. I hoped against hope that another group of people would be brought from Sieradz. But they were all murdered in Chelmno.

After some time, in September 1942, the Germans put up notices, saying they wanted people – the sick, the elderly and children – for "resettlement". We were not fooled. We knew by now that this was simply another word for death. I hadn't been in the ghetto long enough to be allocated any work. Hearing whispers about "resettlement", I decided to play it safe and find a hiding place. That night, I heard shooting from several blocks away and screams as the soldiers came nearer. I decided to make my move and climbed over a wall to hide in the cemetery. I stayed there, paralysed with fear. I waited until the shooting had died away and only then went out.

The situation in Lodz ghetto was appalling. There was overcrowding, insanitary conditions, endemic diseases and starvation rations. We had to work long hours, and every day was a struggle to survive. I witnessed public hangings, and the bodies were left there for days, making us feel there was no hope in resistance. Physical exhaustion, fear, trauma and the inhuman conditions made life harder and harder. There was less food each day and I became more and more hungry. I began to lose all hope.

Sometimes I would look through the fence and see people on the outside walking around and travelling on trams. How could it be right that they were free and we were fenced in?

One day as I was standing at the fence, I felt great despair and began to cry. Suddenly, I felt a hand on my shoulder and saw a woman standing over me. She was about 40, tall with grey hair and dressed in a black coat with a fur collar. She asked me why I was crying and I explained all that had happened to me, that I had no parents or family to turn to for help. Suddenly, she took my hand and said, "Come with me." She and her daughter lived several blocks away. As we walked upstairs together, I had a sudden feeling of "belonging" and that someone cared for me. I stayed with them for several months.

Eventually I applied to enter an orphanage and was accepted. I was happy to start this new chapter in my life. I was with children of my own age and was given a job in the textile mill. The work was hard but I had food at the orphanage and made friends. Yet the events of the past few years still haunted my mind. My nights were often filled with terrifying nightmares.

My friend Szymek in the orphanage introduced me to his sister, Genia. Immediately on meeting her, I knew I was in love! Genia made life in the ghetto so much easier to bear. She was a beautiful girl, with big brown eyes, black, curly hair and a delightful smile. I often used to walk through the ghetto with her. Everything around us was so drab, dirty and overcrowded, but when I was with Genia, it did not seem to matter. We talked about what we would do after our liberation and about our future.

In the ghetto we were forbidden to practise our religion. The worst part for me was being unable to have my barmitzvah, when at 13 a Jewish boy is accepted as a man. It is a great religious step in a boy's life. I had no parents, nobody to guide me and could not have this honour.

By June 1944 there were rumours of Russian armies advancing on Warsaw and we felt sure that we would soon be liberated. But the Germans started to liquidate Lodz ghetto, where there were still 70,000 Jews. Each day more and more people were taken out and transported to unknown destinations. In August, when I had been in the ghetto for 23 months, orders came through for the orphanage to be closed. All the children were to be "resettled" and we were told to collect our belongings together. On 25 August, we assembled outside the orphanage. There were about 185 of us and we made a pitiful sight – thin, undernourished and nervous. Everyone was wondering where the Germans were taking us. Some of the younger children were frightened and we did our best to comfort them. I think I was more scared than most, because I knew what "resettlement" meant.

We set off, carrying the few belongings we possessed. Over my shoulder I had a little blue bag containing all my worldly possessions – one shirt, one pair of underpants, two handkerchiefs, one pair of socks and a half-finished wooden horse I had been carving. Also in the bag were my most cherished possessions – a number of family photographs. I looked at the photos of my parents and thought how much I needed their guidance just then. I was 15 years old, a boy trying to be a man.

We were marched towards a small railway station. I remember people opening their windows to look at us as we went past, their faces solemn, their heads bowed. This confirmed my worst fears and I looked round at my friends, wondering if they realized what "resettlement" really meant. It was very hot on the march and we were all tired and sweating. All at once the hopelessness of the situation overwhelmed me. I thought "I am only 15. I don't want to die yet."

We were put onto a lorry and continued our journey for about half an hour till we came to a small railway station. There were people milling about everywhere, being herded into cattle wagons by SS men with guns. The shouts of the guards, *"Schnell, schnell!"* (Quickly!), the grinding of the shutters as the wagons were closed, the frightened cries of children and moans of other people were very disturbing. We were forced to get in line and shuffle forward as the wagons were filled. Our turn came and we were herded into a wagon, about 100 of us, orphans and strangers alike. The shutters were closed, trapping us in humid semi-darkness. "How will we breathe?" I thought. There was no room to sit down. "How will we sleep? What will we eat?" There was only a tiny window with no other light or ventilation.

Through the crowd I noticed Genia and her brothers. My heart leapt. At least we would be together, there would be someone to talk to and care for. I made my way over to them as the train began to move. As the journey progressed, it got hotter and hotter in the wagon. Little children began to cry, elderly people began to faint and many people were desperate to go to the toilet. All we had was a bucket with a blanket round it to help us retain the little dignity we had left. After a while the stench from the bucket was unbearable. We could not sit down because the wagon was too cramped and we were all very hungry and thirsty. An old lady collapsed and died. I began to pray as never before, "Please God, let us reach our destination soon," but the long day dragged on and on.

Eventually you reach a stage where you resign yourself to a certain situation. During that long, terrible day, I reached that stage for perhaps the first time since the war began. I began to care little for my own fate; I just wanted the horrendous ordeal to end. Perhaps the only thing that

stopped me giving up completely was the responsibility I felt towards Genia
and her brother. Genia was nervous and trembling with fear. She had never
been in a camp before and did not know what to expect. I held her hand
and assured her that we would be all right. Gradually I was able to calm her
down a little. The heat in the wagon was horrendous, but at last night fell
and it got a little cooler. We slept, half-standing, leaning against one
another, but our sleep was punctuated by moaning and the smell of sweat,
death and human waste. The night that lasted a year.

Abruptly, the train began to slow down and we came to a stop. I saw a
camp, barracks, high fences, guards, watchtowers, and people walking
about in striped suits. We had arrived at our destination. Then we heard
German voices and the noise of doors being pulled open. We screwed up
our eyes at the brightness that hit us and gulped in lungfuls of the wonderful air. The Germans began to shout at us, herding us into queues. There
was commotion all around.

There were several thousand people on the transport and endless lines
of people streamed along the long, concrete ramp. We had to wait in a
queue for our turn to ascend the ramp. I saw one young mother screaming
and clinging to her children as the SS tried to take them away. They began
to thump and kick her, knocked her to the ground and carried on beating
her. I turned away, sickened and guilty for not going to her aid, but
knowing there was nothing I could do.

Eventually our queue began to move and we were herded along the
ramp. I realized that the Germans were separating people into two rows, to
the left and right. The left was full of children and old people and I knew
I had to avoid that one at all costs. As I came near the two officers who were
directing people, I drew myself up to my full height, trying to give an
impression of my strength and fitness. To my horror, the SS man barely
glanced at me before indicating that I should go to the left. There was
nothing I could do or say. My mind was numb. I saw other children from
the orphanage in this row and joined them with an awful sense of terror.
Suddenly a commotion began behind us and when the guards' attention
was distracted, I crossed to the right-hand row. I merged with the people
there, my eyes downcast. I shuffled in through the camp gates, still not
fully aware that I had just saved myself from certain death in the gas
chambers. A man in a striped suit told us we were lucky to be in this group.
We were in Birkenau, Auschwitz.

Our group was all men and we carried on walking until we arrived at a
small square surrounded by electrified fencing and barracks. Then we
stood there for about an hour. Suddenly a door opened and a group of
women, their heads shaved, ran out. Behind them were some SS men,

herding them along with whips. From the reactions of many men in our group, it was obvious that they were seeing their wives and daughters.

We were then taken into a large hall, where we had to undress and leave all our clothes and belongings in front of us. They took away the only photographs I had left of my family, my only link with home. Of all the black days in the war, this was one of the blackest. Every one of my friends – Heniek, Szymek and Genia – and all but three of the orphanage children, went to their deaths.

We were led from the hall into the showers and then to another small room where numbers were tattooed on our left arms; mine was B7608. From there, we went to the *Cygainer Lager*, the Gypsy Camp. Before our arrival, it had housed 4,500 gypsies and their families. One day, the Germans had assembled them all and taken them to meet their fate in the gas chambers.

The Gypsy camp was a disease-ridden place. The Germans took away every last vestige of human dignity and the food we received was just enough to keep us alive. Prisoners were just human skeletons walking around in the compound. During the daily roll-call, which usually lasted several hours, many collapsed from exhaustion. There wasn't a blade of grass to be seen anywhere – the starving prisoners had eaten it all. And we could see the crematoria and open ditches burning the new arrivals every day. The foreman had told me what happened to the people who went to the left. Daily we watched clouds of smoke belching from the chimneys and smelt the awful stench of burning flesh.

On the evening we arrived, about 1,000 men were put into our barrack. We were horribly overcrowded, but at least we were alive. We slept on three-tier bunks, ten men to a bunk, and if one moved, we all had to move. My mind was in such a turmoil I just couldn't sleep. I was thinking about what the foreman had told me about the crematoria.

The next day we were woken very early. We were given black "coffee" made from burned wheat and a piece of bread. We then had to gather for roll-call and stand in straight rows to be counted. Afterwards, we wandered around aimlessly until we were given some watery soup in the afternoon. I had two pieces of turnip at the bottom of mine and had to use my fingers to eat them.

As we were queuing for this food, I met another boy from Lodz called Natek, and we became good friends. We decided to stick together, along with Krol, another of my orphanage friends. Of all the children from the orphanage, we were the only ones who had survived. After we were tattooed, they cut off our hair and issued us with our concentration camp suits and shoes.

After two weeks in the gypsy camp, all the young people in my block had to report for a roll-call to be selected for work. The SS officer looked up and down the columns of boys. He picked out several and told them to wait on the other side. He passed us several times, but didn't choose me, so I decided to stand on my toes to try to be noticed. He passed me again, then stopped, looked at me and told me to join the others. It had worked. I had survived again. Natek and Krol also got through.

After half an hour, we were marched off. We didn't know what camp we were going to, but after a while we noticed brick buildings in the distance. We approached a large gate and above it the sign *"Arbeit macht frei"* (work brings freedom). We had arrived at Auschwitz I, the main camp, and were taken to Block four. We were all young boys and we were housed several to a room. Luckily Natek and Krol were in the same room as me.

When we went outside to have a look around, I saw prisoners who were so thin they could hardly walk. Everyone was dressed in the familiar striped uniform. Behind the block, there was electric fencing, a high wall and tall watchtowers manned by SS with machine guns. The sanitary conditions were dreadful. Outbreaks of typhus, transmitted by lice, killed thousands of prisoners. Everyone was weak and undernourished so their resistance was very low.

I stayed in this central camp for three weeks and was then transferred to a sub-camp called Budy, which was about five kilometres away. It was mainly an agricultural camp where cows, horses and pigs were bred. I looked after the horses, feeding and grooming them, and cleaning out their stables. After a while I was ordered to plough the fields. We were given sacks of fertilizer to use on the soil. I noticed that there were small bones mixed with the powder and was told it came from the ashes of thousands of people burned in the crematoria at Birkenau.

From there I was sent to a fishing commando with four other boys. Our life in Auschwitz was a rapid disintegration of mind and body. They dehumanised us completely. Starved and deprived of all human dignity, we quickly became used to the horrors we saw every day. We were reminded daily about going up the chimney, but it soon lost all meaning as we just didn't care any more.

December 1944 and Christmas were approaching. We had news through the partisans that the German army was getting a good hammering on all fronts. We knew it wouldn't be long before the war came to an end; we just had to be patient. We heard that the Red Army was not far away, which meant that we might soon be liberated. In the meantime life continued as normal – out at 6 a.m. with a cup of black "coffee" and a piece of bread to sustain us for many hours in sub-zero temperatures.

On 6 January 1945 our group from the fishing commando was transferred to another sub-camp called Plawy. We were there just 12 days. Then we began what was to become a death march towards Germany. At the time there were about 42,000 men and 18,000 women in Auschwitz. There was no rail transport available and thousands of prisoners had to start marching, guarded by the SS. Auschwitz was liberated on 27 January 1945, just nine days after our death march began.

With a few SS guards, we started our march out of Auschwitz. It was a severe winter. We had no way of keeping warm except to continue moving. Some prisoners began to falter and asked the guards if they could rest for a while, but they just pushed them on. Those who could not walk any more were shot in the back of the head. I plodded on, almost dropping from exhaustion. On both sides of the road, people lay dead, shot for not being able to walk any further. We kept on walking. The guards began to push us more and more, but through half-closed eyes I was able to watch the retreat of the German army and this sight spurred me on.

As we marched, we heard an aeroplane approaching. It fired a rocket which lit up the whole terrain. In spite of the danger, we were exhilarated. I became more and more tired, but I tramped on, not daring to stop. I had seen what happened to people who stopped. We had been on the march for about 12 hours when we were taken to an empty school to rest. Natek and I ate some semolina that he had stolen from the SS warehouse in Auschwitz. That kept us going.

As we marched on, more and more prisoners were being shot and their bodies kicked to the roadside. Deep snow covered the ground and the frost and wind lashed our frail bodies. We had no energy to talk to each other; we were just walking skeletons. Many gave up; we heard more shots, each one spelling the end of another prisoner. The SS wanted to leave no one behind to tell about Auschwitz and the horrors perpetrated there. Once again, at nightfall we were told to stop, this time in the open. We just sat there in the snow to catch a few moments' sleep. I found that my mind was no longer working. I fell asleep.

We were awakened by shouts from the guards, *"Schnell, schnell!"* (Quickly). We stumbled to our feet and moved on, passing several villages. I thought of making a run for it, but with the number on my arm and my shaven head, I knew I would not get far. Eventually we reached a large town called Katowice. There we were marched to the railway sidings and put into goods wagons. The journey in those wagons, destination unknown, lasted for several days. Still we were given no food, and Natek and I staved off hunger – and were probably kept alive – by eating the rest of the semolina.

We eventually arrived at our destination, Buchenwald concentration camp in Germany. We were unloaded like cattle, frozen, half-dead and desperate for food. We were immediately taken to a building to be deloused and go through a shower. The feeling of hot water on our bodies was unimaginably comforting. Then we were marched off, and my column was taken to a block half-filled with Russian prisoners of war. Natek and I stuck together like Siamese twins.

So life began in Buchenwald. Terrible as it was, at least we had shelter, a small amount of food and the opportunity to sleep. Much of what I saw in Buchenwald was similar to Auschwitz. Every day we saw little pushcarts taking dead bodies from the blocks to the crematoria. The bodies were piled ten to a cart and were generally no more than skeletons. There were roll-calls, and we were given a little food, usually watery soup.

April 1945 arrived. One day, I saw people talking in excited groups, saying that the Germans had decided to evacuate Buchenwald. I thought it was terrible news. People were talking about American tanks that could only be 20 kilometres away and would liberate us before the SS could evacuate us all. I went into our block and saw my friends gathering their few belongings together. I could not believe this was happening. At last 200 armed SS men came into the camp to clear us out. There were 4,500 of us and we were on the march again.

It was now 7 April and I began to wonder how much longer I could survive. They marched us towards the city of Weimar, then to the railway sidings and loaded us onto open wagons. We were crammed about 120 to a wagon. All my block was loaded together, so all the boys were on the same wagon. Several had brought blankets from the camp, but we were still cold, wet and cramped. Evening approached and it grew much colder, but we were given neither food nor drink. The SS guards shut all the doors and we started to move. The night was long and we spent it standing up, half-asleep. The train sped on, further and further from Buchenwald. We all wondered what our fate would be. I was tired, hungry, cold and miserable; I felt half-dead. I was only 15 years old and I had seen some of the worst horrors that man has ever perpetrated against man.

Dawn came and the train started to slow down. As it came to a halt, the SS began shouting. Our door was opened and I saw there were no houses in sight, just fields and a stream nearby. We were told to have a drink of water and a wash. Then the train set off again and looking up, we saw some American fighter planes which swooped low a number of times, then disappeared. Our spirits rose; they must have known we were prisoners by our camp clothing. On the train went, hour after hour; still we were given no food and the night air was freezing. Many men died that night.

On the third afternoon we were given a piece of bread and a cup of black "coffee". We passed towns and villages where everything was green and healthy; we saw people walking freely and well-fed animals in the fields. The train stopped in the countryside at a small station. We ran to the field nearby and I decided to pick some grass and try to cook it. I had to keep an eye out in case anyone tried to grab it from me. This is what hunger had reduced us to. Soon the guards ordered us back onto the train. Each night more people died.

One morning we stopped at a small station. The Germans brought us some bread to eat and we stayed there for a few hours. As night fell, we had to climb back onto the wagons, but about midnight we heard the guards walking about outside. Then our door was pulled open and to our delight, we saw large containers of soup, which we devoured quickly. But the soup was horribly salty. It was so bad that it burned our stomachs and we had no water to quench our terrible thirst.

The train started moving again and next morning we stopped at a river. As soon as we were let off, we raced down to the river to drink. The water was not very clean, but who cared? It tasted wonderful. As we were drinking, the guards opened fire on us and killed ten people. They were probably bored and shot at us for fun.

We climbed back on the train and the nightmare journey continued. One day, one of our men got news that the Americans had liberated Buchenwald on 11 April. We were the last transport to leave. All those who had stayed behind had been liberated. We were dejected at this cruel piece of luck. I looked at the boys in our wagon and wondered if any of us would last out.

After a while it started to rain. I looked up at the sky. There had been little opportunity for prayer since the time I had left Lodz ghetto. Now I found myself talking to God. "If you are up there in heaven, why don't you help us?" I asked what crime I had committed to be punished like this. I was still not 16. "I've suffered more than most people of 90," I protested. "And my only sin is being born of Jewish parents." I was so desperate that I sat in the corner of the wagon and wept.

After three and a half weeks on the train, we arrived in the Sudetenland in Czechoslovakia. On 4 May 1945, 600 of the original 4,500 men from Buchenwald arrived at Roundnice. The Czech people wept when they saw what we looked like. Our train was finally taken to the Theresienstadt ghetto, where, four days later, on 8 May, we were liberated by the Russian army. I had survived, but virtually all my family had been murdered. The only relative who survived was Mania, my eldest sister, whom I found in Ulm, Germany, in 1947. My friends Natek and Krol also survived.

I now live in England with my wife, Jean, near Leeds. My years since the events described have been quiet and happy. I have lived, worked and appreciated every moment of the life I now enjoy. For this reason, now that I have retired, I spend much of my time working with young people, sharing my story and reflecting with them on its meaning, past, present and future. I do remember the past. I also think about the future.

In memory of my mother Bluma and father Szmuel,
sisters Mania, Itka and brother Tovia, and my little Dvora.
Deprived of life.

Dedicated to my wife Jean,
my daughters Susie, Karen and Michelle, the new generation,
and to my grandchildren
Alex, James, Nicolo, Liora, Avital, Natasha and Galit.

The only surviving photograph of family members. These are my cousins posing by a family gravestone in 1935. All my other photographs – the last link I had with my home – were taken from me the day I entered Auschwitz.

Outside the church in Sieradz where I was selected to join a work group. When I left, I did not realise I would be separated from my family forever.

Edith in 1950

EDITH HOFMANN

Unshed Tears

When Edith Hofmann wrote her story in 1950, she was a 19-year-old coming to terms with her own survival. The cruel reality was that no one wanted to hear. Her story is written in novel form, but it is certainly not fiction. Scared for her own safety, Edith chose to write in the third person rather than pen a memoir. The following adaptation from her book, Unshed Tears (Quill Press, Newark, Notts, 2002) describes her deportation from the Lodz ghetto to Auschwitz in the summer of 1944 and her arrival there.

... There were sixty people to one waggon. As soon as the people got used to the darkness, the scramble for places around the walls began. Then at last they threw their luggage on the floor and sat down on their property, exhausted after the nightmarish drive to the station. In the middle of the wooden floor stood an urn filled with black coffee and a Jewish ghetto-policeman came and began to fill the little pots or mugs of the prisoners with the dark bitter liquid. Then the urn was taken out and the same policeman reappeared with a bowl of thick wedges of bread. He gave one to each. After this he jumped out and a minute later the sliding door was closed with a thump, and sealed, and the 60 victims found themselves helpless, overcrowded, enclosed by darkness and unbearable heat.

Judith wondered whether it was all a nightmare. She was frightfully thirsty, but did not want to touch the little amount of coffee they possessed and she could not even eat the bread, her throat was so dry.

At last darkness began to creep in and the prisoners settled down for the night. They found places on the floor, supporting their heads on folded-up pieces of clothes, satchels, or someone's arm, leg or other part of the body. Most of them clutched their belongings with eager hands, protecting them against possible loss. With the passing hours, a cool breeze found its way into the stuffy box, bringing relief to those inside it. One by one they drifted into slumber and heavy breathing mingled with snores began to fill the place. By midnight, hardly anything stirred within the rocking train. They were heading south-west.

Towards midday next day the heat became unbearable. There wasn't a drop of water to be found anywhere inside the stuffy waggon. People sat still and silent, for every movement was too much of an effort. Those who had some bread left did not eat it for their tongues were too dry to munch it. They did not know how much longer they were going to be enclosed in the dark oppressive box that was throwing them from side to side, but many of those whose eyes yesterday had been shining with a resolution not to give in, were by now resigned to their fate. There was not much strength left in them to struggle.

It was about two o'clock when the train began to lose speed. Automatically people lifted themselves up from the dusty floor and gathered at the little barred windows. The shabbily clad figures pressed at each other, those at the back attempting to push their way forward with their elbows, their eager eyes looking in one direction. Was there a town which was to be their home in the future? Were they at last going to step out of the smelly waggons and find themselves in the light and air?

A complete silence fell on the prisoners as sight and mind made an attempt to take in the strange picture that unfolded itself in front of them. Their eagerness was gone, a look of meekness and surprise took its place. Judith stood on tiptoes to get a glimpse of the spectacle that had brought this sudden hush about.

Outside the barred holes a strange world was spread in front of them. The hot sun was scorching the yellow sand that stretched for miles like a desert on which stood this incredible town that was no town at all. It was enclosed in barbed wires, strewn with hundreds of wooden huts placed in rows and swarming with people who resembled human beings very little. They were all dressed in a sort of striped pyjamas. Their cheeks and temples were hollow; their heads were shaved! They dragged their feet behind them as they walked, apparently aimlessly, from place to place. There wasn't a tree or plant in sight. The air was still and a deadly threat hung over the endless place.

The train stopped, and a mixture of noises composed of sharp German commands, the howling of dogs and cracking of whips, filled the immediate surroundings. Within seconds the doors flew ajar, unbolted by skilful hands that had undoubtedly done such jobs many times before.

An unearthly chaos followed. There was no time for the prisoners to think, no time to make decisions. The light that flowed into the dark interior of the waggons almost blinded them. "Get out! Get out! Hurry up! Quicker! Quicker!" Whips cracked, dogs barked.

"Leave your luggage behind! Hurry! Hurry!"

Those who stood at the back of the waggon managed to snatch their bread, or an object that was very precious to them and hide it in their clothes. Young and old, helpless people, without defence, all poured out of the wide opening, hardly knowing what was happening to them. And then, suddenly, unaware of the true meaning of it, they found themselves at the crossroads. The look in the eyes of the Germans filled them with terror and foreboding. Having no other option, they followed the direction of a whip, gun, or outstretched arm. "Left! Right! Over here! Over there!"

Brutal pushes, or kicks with leather riding boots, helped the stragglers to get to their appropriate place in good time. The Germans took great pride in being good organizers, and although the procedure looked chaotic to the frightened prisoners, everything went according to plan. Within a few minutes several groups stood ready, waiting for the next move. On one side were the young and healthy-looking men, separated from the women. On the other side old men, women, and mothers with children formed three groups of their own. The sun shone mercilessly upon their heads, the still air filled with a gruesome strangeness; in the distance thousands of broken, shabby figures were moving aimlessly from place to place. This was Auschwitz, the concentration camp.

The harsh order was given, and the groups in lines of five marched off in different directions. Anxiously, heads turned all ways trying to snatch a last look from a beloved one, and then there was nothing but the road ahead, lined with huge SS men on motorcycles or marching with police dogs at their sides, nudging them on, making them walk faster and smarter.

Judith was in a procession of young women, of whom about 50 were Czech. Many of them knew each other and now at the critical moment automatically huddled together. As they marched along towards a huge iron gate, they found it hard to believe in the reality of the moment.

Two guards who were on duty by the gate held it open for them, and the procession made its way through. From high above, the inscription *"ARBEIT MACHT FREI,"* (Freedom through Work) grinned down upon them. New to the place, however, they failed to see the irony of those three words.

As they walked along the dusty camp road, crowds of people gathered along the barbed wire which stretched on both sides of it. Some glared at them with an empty look; others who had any energy left, waved and shouted at them, urgently beckoning them to throw over some of their bread or other precious belongings. With hostile eyes they surveyed the pleading prisoners and clutched their treasures closer to their bodies.

At the end of the long road stood a group of buildings. Relieved to get out of the scorching heat, the women entered one of them and found themselves in a large stone hall surrounded by bellowing men and women in the

SS uniform. "Take your clothes off! Faster! Don't dawdle. Put it all on that heap there, together with all your belongings. Bring jewellery to the desk! Hurry up you dirty Jewesses!"

That was the beginning of the 'bath'. With satisfied grins the huge men with their arms folded on their chests watched the women discard one piece of their garments after another, until, naked, they stood waiting.

Next came the hair treatment. It did not take long. Skilled hands, a pair of clippers and the women were deprived of the last thing left to them to give them a feeling of self-respect. And then the hairs of the body were removed in the same way.

The general inspection was next on the list. Every inch of the body, including the ears, mouth and the most incredible parts were searched for jewellery or other hidden treasures. With a blank look on her face Judith followed the rest into the shower-bath hall. Hundreds of showers were turned on at the same time and the officers made sure that everyone obeyed the order "Wash yourself!"

As they filed past a desk after leaving the bath, each was thrown a frock and a pair of clogs, regardless of size. A fashion parade followed.

The women crept into their new attire examining each other not without a sense of humour. Some even passed a few jokingly rude remarks while others commented on the absurdity of the situation. It was quite a pitiful sight – the bare heads, the ridiculous frocks, the large clogs and even the perverted smiles on their faces.

Judith, in her new pale blue dress which reached high above her knees and had short sleeves, kept close to the group of Czech women.

The whips cracked and the procession moved back towards the camp. Now they knew why the prisoners had the audacity to ask for their bread. A gate opened for them again and they found themselves inside a women's camp. It looked like all the others. Long huts were on either side of a narrow dusty road. There were about two dozen of them. All around were similar camps, separated from others by the same dangerous wires. At one end of the camp was an open space and on that the large group was told to stand at attention in rows of five.

It was early afternoon and the scorching sun shone upon their bare heads. The sand beneath their feet was hot and there was no plant in sight. The hours followed each other and nothing happened. The other prisoners were moving about the camp regardlessly or sitting leaning against the wall of the hut. Some even lay in the sand sleeping.

Not far away was a men's camp. All the men wore striped prisoner's garments. Some activity was going on there; huge boulders were being carried to one place and after the last piece had been placed on the heap, the work began in reverse. Another two hours, and the boulders were gone. The hours dragged endlessly. Thirst and a feeling of weakness caused by the heat tormented them.

After six o'clock the most incredible and horrifying thing happened. Down the main camp road came marching a group of prisoners, preceded by a band playing a well-known march. And then another group and another as they returned from work. The gay music made Judith's blood curdle. The endless, bare, cheerless plain, the animal-like prisoners, the cropped heads, the stillness in the air above, the whips and terror of the unknown and music made a most gruesome combination. In a girls' camp nearby another band struck the first note and proceeded to play Mozart. Judith shrank into herself and a dreadful loneliness overcame her.

That circus lasted for about an hour after which there followed a commotion in camp, accompanied by shrieks and commands. Within a few minutes groups of a thousand each stood in ranks in front of their barracks in a deadly hush. That was *Appell* – roll-call. In front of each group three or four women were running up and down securing order with a whip.

For the eye which met the spectacle for the first time, it was an unforgettable experience. All the camps, stretching under the endless skies, forming one unit, followed the same pattern. The silence was a ghostly one. All eyes were turned in one direction from which the self-satisfied figures were expected to appear and count them, and thus relieve them of the tedious task of standing in one place absolutely still.

The sun was beginning to go down when four tall men in uniform strode into the particular camp. With chins up, they counted the rows of five and marched on. They moved from group to group, taking their job very seriously. When at last every one in the camp was counted and re-counted the *Appell* was over and the most sought-for moment was within reach. Everyone retired to his particular barrack or block – as it was called. A few moments later, monitors from each block reappeared on the camp road and made their way down towards the canteen where huge cans filled with soup were waiting for them to be taken back to the hungry mob.

Judith and the rest of the group were led into an empty barrack. It was one large hall with a stone floor and very small windows by the roof. Except for two cubicles by the door and a stove whose brick pipe ran along the centre of the floor, thus dividing the hall into two parts, it was absolutely bare.

Five wild women with violent gestures and rough speech were giving orders. One was the block leader, a beautiful dark-haired girl from Slovakia, the others were her helpers. All were prisoners but had managed in one way or other to gain the privilege of their status. It seemed they had forgotten that the helpless prisoners they were now bullying, and beating, and pushing around were there for the same reason – Jewish blood was flowing through their veins. But then of course, they would have never risen to their rank had their conscience allowed them to soften toward their fellow prisoners.

In files of five they were seated on the cold, hard floor. There was hardly an inch to spare between them on either side, as all thousand women had to be accommodated in the one hall. How they were to lie down and find room for sleeping, nobody knew. Several new monitors were picked, some to go and collect the soup, others to give out the basins, one for each line of five.

After about half an hour the performance started. Several baskets with slices of coarse brown bread arrived, followed by the cans of soup. Everyone's interest was aroused at that moment, and a hush dominated the place. The baskets were taken round along the narrow passages and the barrack supervisors threw the slices to individual prisoners who fell upon their share with a ferocious gusto. The first in each file lined up for the soup which was being shared out by the block leader. With the ladle she reached down to the bottom of the can and brought out the solid potatoes and vegetables with which she filled a saucepan of hers and those of her fellow-helpers. Hostile eyes followed her action and rebellion rose in the minds of the prisoners.

One after another the women with their little basins filled returned to their places. There were no spoons and to make the distribution just, the sips which they had to take from the edge were counted. Judith's turn came and all eyes this time were fixed on her. One, two, three, four, five – and no more, for the time being anyway. Under the strictest supervision of others' stares, it was impossible to get away with an extra drop. Small and large quarrels arose in various parts of the block, for some people managed to get a larger mouthful than the others. The basins licked clean, the pilgrimage to the latrines followed. It was part of the daily routine and everybody had to participate. The latrines were housed in a barrack and there were rows and rows of them. It seemed as though the whole camp and all the others were engaged in the same sort of activity.

With that behind them, it was back to their block and time to settle down for the night. There was a certain art in this, for there wasn't half the room on the floor for everyone to lie down. The newcomers found it especially hard to puzzle out the problem. Quarrels livened up the place, which brought the block leader and the others along with whips and buckets of cold water, which they readily emptied on the helpless crowd. "Shut up, everybody! Quiet! Or I'll send you into the chimney."

Half an hour later the floor was a mass of intermingled legs, arms and bodies. Judith, with her head resting on someone's body and her own covered up with other people's limbs, her skirt soaked with cold water, lay awake for a long, long time. "What was it all about?" she asked herself. Why did they lie here like this on the cold, stone floor soaked with water? How could those Czech girls betray them and treat them in such beastly fashion? Where would it all end, and what did she mean by "I'll send you into the chimney? The chimney ... what was the chimney?..."

Exhausted and soothed by the bromide [sedative] that had been one of the soup's ingredients, she fell asleep.

Dedicated to all the children from Prague who did not come back.

The Final Journey 1944: painting by Edith Hofmann

Amélie, 1999. Photo by Sidney Harris

AMÉLIE JAKOBOVITS

Escape to Switzerland

Paris 1936. The city was enjoying its last few years of freedom before falling to the Nazi invaders. Amélie Munk, an eight-year-old Jewish girl had just arrived with her family from Ansbach, near Nuremberg in Germany – where Nazi antisemitism had turned increasingly vicious.

Rabbi Elie Munk and his wife Fanny (née Goldberger) had first settled with their baby daughter Amélie in Ansbach, Bavaria. By 1933, the Jews there had long sensed slow but growing antisemitism. Posters declaring them a national enemy had appeared as early as 1923. Four years later, Jewish cemeteries were being desecrated and even before the National Socialists came to power, local Jews had to endure antisemitic jibes. Bavaria was the central point of Nazi antisemitism.

Against this background, Amélie's first years at school were, in her own words, "absolutely horrendous". The kindergarten which she attended at the age of four was already under the influence of the Nazis. The teacher would go over to the Jewish pupils, order them to stand up, and then she would rap them on the head and over the knuckles with a ruler. Amélie and other Jewish children would be punished just for not being able to answer a question. It was a humiliating experience which remained permanently with her.

To try to forget the horrors of school life, Amélie would go ice-skating on the lake. But little by little such pleasures were prohibited to the Jews. The Nazis began forbidding "Jewish children and dogs" to enter certain parts of the villages, so that Amélie could no longer play in the village gardens. Notices banning Jewish children from playing in the parks of Ansbach also appeared overnight. Gradually this antisemitism became more open. By 1934, laws were passed forbidding Jews to congregate in groups of more than three. A banner floated across the entry to the town proclaimed, "The Jews are our Misfortune."

As life deteriorated for the Jews of Ansbach, Rabbi Munk was asked to lead a community in Paris and the family moved there in 1936. Amélie was fortunately brought up to speak French, and her school experiences in Paris were a dream compared to the antisemitism she had suffered in Germany. Yet despite this new sense of freedom the first years in Paris were turbulent. The war moved in Germany's favour and the Germans invaded France on 15 May 1940.

Amélie walked down the street one day to find huge posters calling on Jews to register with the local mayor and produce identification papers. The shadow of Ansbach suddenly returned to haunt her in Paris and it became still more ominous the next day. The local streets were plastered with notices forbidding Jews to visit certain parks in Paris, forcing them to register once a week and to wear the yellow star.

Rabbi Munk had already volunteered to join the French Foreign Legion and was sent to a training camp in the south. Amélie's mother decided to leave the capital. She took the family to the Gare de l'Est, along with thousands of other refugees, Jews and non-Jews, who were attempting to flee the Nazis. The Munk family just managed to catch the very last carriage of the last train as it pulled out of Paris – two hours before the German bombs rained down on the French capital.

The train was supposed to take all the refugees down to Spain, travelling through France over the Pyrenees mountains. The journey itself was a terrible experience with thousands of people in each carriage. In the event, the family got off the train at Albi, a small town north-east of Toulouse. They were still far from the Pyrenees border, but Mme Munk had suddenly remembered that her last letter from her husband was postmarked Albi, so she decided the family must get off there. Like all the refugees, they were accommodated in a refugee centre. Mme Munk settled her family down and next morning told Amélie to find a bicycle and go in search of her father.

Amélie found the military compound – and her father. Rabbi Munk had not known whether the family had remained in Paris or been forced to flee. Nor had he realized the extent of the German threat against the Jews.

Life in the refugee centre was not too terrible, but after a few days it was emptied and the refugees were taken on 50 huge trucks to different villages around Albi. This had to be done every few days to prepare for the arrival of more refugees from the north of France. The Munk family were taken to a village called Milhras, which had 50-60 inhabitants who were mainly farmers. Each villager was expected to take on a refugee family and the Munk family were looked after by the Mayor.

After a few idyllic weeks there, the refugees were on the move again – to make way for the next contingent of refugees. The cycle of movement from flight to refuge, refuge to flight, overtook them once again. But the Mayor had grown attached to the Munk family and simply moved them to an attractive cottage surrounded by fields in the same village. Amélie has very fond memories of the months in Milhras, in which she and her family became very close friends with the village people. One afternoon when she and her sister were hanging out the washing, she suddenly saw her father appear. Since France had lost the war against Germany, his military services were no longer required and he was able to rejoin the family.

The family remained in Milhras until the approach of the Jewish High Holidays in early October 1940, when Rabbi Munk decided that they should move on in search of a Jewish community. Their destination was Toulouse, where the community officers eventually found them an apartment. They stayed there until just before the Jewish New Year of 1941. Elie Munk had heard rumours that Jews were about to be arrested all over France and taken to Germany. News filtered through that those arrested would be transported in cattle trucks. The rabbi had the foresight to urge his fellow Jews to leave and hide in small villages around the city. It was time for the family to be on the move again.

Amélie and her family headed west on foot towards Marseilles. They stopped at a small town where they were accommodated in an old factory with other refugees. They remained there for a few days and then made for Marseilles itself, which had a Jewish community. However, on arrival there, the family did not feel particularly welcome and Rabbi Munk found the money to travel from Marseilles to Nice in the spring of 1941.

Times were difficult: France had surrendered to the Nazis, and the south of the country found itself divided up between Germany and Italy. But under Italian jurisdiction, the Jews were comparatively free. It was only later, when the Italian leader Mussolini capitulated in 1943, that the Germans occupied the whole of France and life for the Jews changed drastically. The gradual decline towards the deportations and death camps had begun. Sudden arrests, shootings, the constant fear of transports to the unknown – this was the climate.

After the Germans took over, the small Jewish community in Nice bribed the French police to give them prior warning of any forthcoming harassment. On 15 July 1942, Elie Munk was told that the first mass arrest of Jews – 800 people – would take place the following night. However, he was assured that any French-born French citizen would be protected. So while others scurried to cellars and forests, Rabbi Munk, French-born with three French-born children, stayed in his home. Unfortunately, his confidence was ill-founded.

At 2 a.m. the following morning, there was a knock at the door. Five menacing Nazis and one obvious collaborator in a French uniform came in to arrest the entire family. However, the French soldier saw Mme Munk with her twin babies, then aged 2-3 months, and took pity on her, and these three were eventually given permission to remain at home. But Rabbi Munk, Amélie and her sister Ruth were all arrested.

They were taken to the place where the 800 other Jews were held, then herded into lorries and driven to a huge shoe factory outside Nice which the Nazis had requisitioned. It was a scorching hot day and all 800 people were assembled in the courtyard and called into the office alphabetically. It was 3 p.m. by the time the name Munk was called, during which time they had had absolutely nothing to eat or drink. At the end of the interrogation, Rabbi Munk was told to say goodbye to his children, who were free to go. Amélie made a terrible scene, crying, shouting and stamping her feet in protest. She refused to leave the building without her father, but Rabbi Munk convinced her finally that she had to go home.

After the ordeal of the interrogation, the Jews were herded into cages filled with straw for the night. Then a rumour was passed around that if anyone had a French connection, they should write a little note to that effect with their own name on it. Rabbi Munk wrote, "Elie Munk, born Paris 1900, cité de Trevise, Paris, father of three French-born children." This small note obtained his release and he walked back home to his family. Apart from the Munks and two family friends, none of the other 800 Jews arrested that night was ever seen again.

A few months after this, the rabbi went to the synagogue one day and met a young Jewish student who described how he had been arrested and taken to SS headquarters. During his interrogation, the student had noticed a file on the officer's desk with the name Munk on it. When the officer left the room for a moment, the student found the courage to open the file. It said that Rabbi and Mme Munk were to be deported two days later to a camp in Germany.

Rabbi Munk immediately went to the underground movement, the Maquis, who gave him a total change of appearance to make him virtually unrecognisable, and helped him plan the family's escape to Switzerland. He explained to the family that their ration cards had been taken away by the underground and replaced with new ones in the name Martin instead of Munk. They had also given him false identification papers, plus a certain amount of money to pay for the trip from Nice to Geneva over the Swiss border. He handed his family their passports with the name Martin and gave them instructions about their escape.

They pored over the map given to Elie by the underground and were shown the little farm near the Swiss border where they were to meet on Thursday night, 14 September 1943, after travelling separately by train from Nice to Geneva. Amélie was to take her sister Ruth and brother Jacki.

Rabbi Munk was to bring three-year-old Françoise, his wife and the baby twins.

They left separately next morning with almost no luggage. The family reached the station and caught the train, but were immediately separated by the sheer numbers of people on it. The journey itself was a nightmare for Amélie. All the time the family remained apart. Their plan was to pretend not to know each other if they met accidentally because there was nothing as dangerous as a complete Jewish family together on a train.

Amélie reached the farmhouse, where she met the others at about 11.15 p.m. There was nobody else there. Rabbi Munk could not believe that the underground had let them down. They waited until past midnight, but he did not feel confident enough to find the border with Switzerland without their help. This meant perilous hours spent in the forest trying to find where it was. There seemed nothing else to do but spend the night in the empty farmhouse, praying that they would not be discovered.

The next morning, Friday, they hitch-hiked separately to nearby Aix-les-Bains, where they hoped to spend the Sabbath. Even at times of such danger, the Sabbath was of paramount importance to Amélie's father. They stayed at the Hôtel de la Paix: the Nazi headquarters! Under the assumed name of Martin, nobody asked any questions at the hotel, but the Nazi presence was very high-profile. Meanwhile the tiny community in Aix found them another underground contact, and the family arranged to meet them on the Sunday at the same farmhouse.

The meeting was fixed for 11.30 p.m. The family once more made their way separately. Every move during that day as they tried to reach Switzerland felt like an eternity. The Maquis turned up – two huge men with a revolver each and they told the family to follow them through the forest without making a sound.

The Resistance men took the twins on their shoulders while the rabbi carried Françoise. Ruth walked with her mother just ahead of Amélie, who remembers every emotion she felt at the time. It was 11.45 p.m. Amélie walked on the right of her father with Jacki on his left. Elie Munk held a little book of Psalms in his hand and they very quietly read them together.

The Resistance men left them for a moment and when they returned, they told them where to find the hole they had cut in the barbed wire. They then said, "You will have to negotiate the hole one by one, and then you must roll or walk down a hill. When you come to the bottom of the hill, you will be free and out of danger. Switzerland and the Swiss citizens will take care of you."

The family found the hole in the barbed wire. One after the other, the children squeezed their way through, tearing their clothes and getting scratched, but not caring about anything except getting into Switzerland. Some of them rolled down the hill, some walked, but when they reached the bottom, they found something which the men from the Maquis had failed to mention – a river.

It was too dark for them to gauge its width and depth. How could they negotiate it? Neither Mme Munk nor the twins could swim. Baby Max started to cry inconsolably. They took it in turns to walk him up and down, but the child continued screaming. Amélie recalls that she looked at her father and understood that this was the most dangerous moment of their lives.

She suddenly saw a light some distance away and began to point it out to her father when he put his hand over her mouth so that she wouldn't make any noise. The light went off and a moment later went on again; it went on and off again, getting closer and closer. They had no idea what was happening. Amélie and her father were petrified.

Then a voice said, "I am a Swiss soldier. I heard that baby crying. I want you all to follow me." He picked up little Max and they all followed him. They followed him across the river, which turned out not to be so deep and wide as they thought. Then they found themselves on the main road.

The Swiss soldier turned to Amélie's father and said, "I am the father of seven children. I couldn't bear to hear the baby cry on the other side of the river, which is no-man's-land, where the Nazis come with their dogs on the dot of midnight. Had that baby not cried, I would not have asked permission from my Commander-in-Chief to cross the river and pick up the baby who was crying so desperately. I had no idea that there was a whole family with that child. Never forget that you owe your lives to that little baby boy's crying."

Adapted from *Amélie, The Story of Lady Jakobovits*, by Gloria Tessler (Vallentine Mitchell, London, 1999)

To my husband

Rabbi Dr Elie Munk (Amélie's father), re-dedicating the Ansbach Synagogue, 1964
Photograph from Diana Fitz

Idel Kagan (Jack) on the left, with his friend Tevele Niankovski, a photograph taken in Moscow in 1944

Jack Kagan

Surviving the Holocaust with the Russian Jewish Partisans

I was born in 1929 in Novogrodek, Belorussia, into a unique family. Two brothers married two sisters and harmony reigned in the house! Even though we had two houses, we lived in one! Everything was togetherness. The most important thing in life was family. My father Yankel was a businessman. My mother Dvore was a businesswoman who looked after our two shops, where we sold the saddles and sandals produced in our workshops. I had a sister, Nachama, two years older than myself.

We were a middle-class family; not short of anything. Novogrodek had a Jewish population of between 6,000 and 6,500, which made up half of the town's inhabitants. There were really no problems between the Jews and the local population. But from 1935 the situation began to change. Poles from western Poland started to settle in our town, bringing strong feelings of antisemitism with them. The Jews lived in the centre of the town and most of the shops belonged to them. They formed the majority of the professional people. Jewish community life was organised through the synagogues and unions. There were all sorts of Jewish institutions – hospitals, Hebrew schools, orphanages – and there was a Jewish theatre, a library, a bank and Jewish newspapers.

All this changed on 17 September 1939. War had broken out on the first day of September. We were very worried about a probable German occupation, but on the afternoon of the 17th we heard the roar of Soviet tanks coming down the street. Some Jews cried with joy because the alternative to the Red Army was occupation by the Germans. But our life changed. We had to run down our shop as private enterprise was not allowed. We then had to close our shops and workshops and stop going to the synagogue because Hebrew was not allowed. Everything Jewish connected with religion or Palestine had to stop. Every institution that was Jewish had to change. It became a different life. The rich business people were arrested during the night and sent to Siberia, together with the leaders of the community. Thinking back on it now, the Russians wanted to destroy our rich Jewish culture.

Then the war between Germany and Russia broke out on 22 June 1941. Already the following day, the whole Russian army was in retreat. We knew that we would suffer under the Germans. We expected labour camps and imprisonment, but could not imagine that they would try to liquidate us all. I remember the discussion between my father and my uncle. "There is no point in running. We are used to work, they won't kill us!"

And so we stayed. On 24 June 1941 the town was bombed. Four days later, planes flew overhead and dropped fire bombs. Most of the town was burnt down. Large numbers of people lost their lives. We, the Kagan family, lost everything. I was left with a pair of short trousers and a shirt. We found an empty house and moved in with about eight families.

The Germans entered Novogrodek on 4 July 1941 and immediately started enforcing anti-Jewish laws. Yellow stars had to be worn on the front and back of clothes, Jews were not allowed to walk on the pavement, everyone from the age of 12 to 60 had to report for work. Jews lost their rights of citizenship, which meant that if someone wanted to rob you (and many did), you could not complain to the authorities, for you had no protection.

My father and uncle were working as saddle-makers. My mother, aunt and others, including myself, were working on clearing up the bombed streets. For that we were issued food cards for 300 grams of bread and potatoes.

On Saturday 26 July 1941, some Jewish men were rounded up by the local police and taken to the market place, where a group of SS men were waiting. I was in the market place at that time. I hid behind the ruins of a burned-out house. I heard shots being fired and an orchestra playing music. I waited there quite a while and when I reached home, I heard the awful news that the SS had selected 52 men and shot them. Jewish women were ordered to wash the blood off the cobble stones. From time to time after that, groups of Jews were caught in the street and told that they were being sent to work. But later we would find out that they had been shot a short distance from town.

On Friday 5 December 1941, posters appeared stating that as from 6 o'clock that evening no Jews could leave town, and the next morning all Jews must assemble at the court-house. They could only take with them whatever they could carry. Saturday was a bitterly cold day, minus 20 degrees Centigrade. The 6,500 Jews assembled in the yard of the courthouse. We waited all day in the cold. Late in the afternoon, they opened the doors and there was just about room for us all to stand inside. There was no sleep that night. We were locked up there Saturday and Sunday.

On Sunday, the *Wehrmacht* (German army) arrived and took a party of about 100 men to build a fence around 28 houses in the suburb of Peresika. They were creating a ghetto. Early on Monday morning, 8 December 1941, lorries arrived with the SS and local police. We had to form a line, families together. The head of the family had to approach the SS man, and two questions were asked: "Profession?" and "How many children?" From the SS man, there was just a sign with the glove, right or left: life or death. My uncle went first with his family. "Profession?" "Saddle-maker." "How many children?" "Two children." Sign from the SS man to the left. My father followed: Saddle-maker; two children, sign to the right. As my uncle with his family were walking to the yard, a German officer shouted that he needed an auto-mechanic. My cousin Berl answered and this saved his life. Five thousand, one hundred people were selected to the left and taken to the village of Skridlevo. They were beaten up on entering the forest and ordered in parties of 50 to lie face down on the ground. From there, again in parties of 50, they had to give up all their valuables, undress in the bitterly cold weather and were driven to the pits where they were shot. That day we lost my uncle, aunt and their family. It was an appalling blow to us all.

The remaining 1,500 of us were taken to Peresika, where the ghetto was formed. It was small. Bunks were built: 60 cm (approx. 2 feet) of space per person. If you had to turn over in the night, you would wake up the nine people who slept in your row. It was an open ghetto, which meant we had to go out to work. My father worked as a saddler, and my mother stitched fur gloves for the German army. I worked in the Russian barracks, along with about 250 men. The work was difficult and I had a four-kilometre walk to work. I was barely 13 years old – I believe I was the youngest worker in the barracks. After a while I was transferred to a better job – wheel-barrowing stones. This work was also hard and I received plenty of beatings.

Various regulations were coming out daily against the Jewish population. Jews from the little surrounding towns and villages were brought to Novogrodek, starting at the beginning of May 1942. Altogether the ghetto now held about 6,500 people. Every centimetre of space was utilised. It is difficult to describe the misery of that time. People were walking around aimlessly knowing that they were sentenced to death, but not knowing when the execution would take place. Yet there was nowhere to run to.

One day at the beginning of July, we arrived at work as usual. At lunch time, I drifted away from the workplace as I had done every day, to search for cigarette ends or pieces of bread which the German soldiers would throw out. Suddenly, out of nowhere, a German soldier jumped at me, shouting *"Raus, raus du verfluchter Jude!"* (Out, out, you cursed Jew). I felt a crack from his rifle butt and he pushed me into the middle of the barracks square, together with about 50 other people. The SS troops surrounding our group shouted insults at us and made us line up in a single row. Within a few minutes a machine gun was assembled and I thought they were going to shoot us. My legs became like jelly. They kept us there for a long time. Eventually, a high-ranking SS officer arrived. He did not say anything but just released us and we went back to work. After that, I went to work with my father to learn saddle-making. Father was friendly with the foreman and he had given permission for this.

On 7 August 1942, we arrived at work as usual. Immediately we were surrounded by the police and the SS. There were about 500 of us, men and women. At the same time they surrounded the ghetto and barracks. The Germans took everybody from the ghetto to Litovka, two kilometres away, to prepared mass graves. They killed everybody from the ghetto: all my relatives from Karelitz, including my old grandmother. On that day, 5,500 men, women and children were killed in Litovka.

That same evening everybody in the workshops had to line up and be inspected. I stood next to my father, dressed in his jacket and long trousers to look older. The Nazi chief passed and did not say anything, but all the children hidden in the loft and basement were found and thrown out of the windows. Then they were taken by lorry to Litovka where they were killed. From that day the ghetto in Peresika contained 500 Jews and the court-house 500 skilled tradesmen. I was one of the youngest among them. From our family, my mother, father, sister, cousin Berl and myself had survived so far.

We were kept locked up for a number of days without food and water. Then a van was driven into where we were assembled and loaves of bread were thrown at us. The Germans took pleasure in seeing us struggle to get hold of a piece. Then the camp commandant told us we were the lucky ones; we would remain alive because the Reich needed us, but we would have to work hard. Numbers were issued. We had to stitch one on the back of our clothes. Mine was 334.

Now it was no longer a ghetto, but a work camp. We were enclosed by two circles of barbed wire with a wooden fence on the outside. Towers with searchlights and machine guns were installed. The camp had no water facilities. Every day a number of workers had to fetch drinking water. This was our contact with the outside world.

After the second massacre, young people began to escape. There would be a lot of whispering, then they would disappear at night. Contact with the Bielski partisans in the woods had been established, and the young prepared their escape. The Bielski brothers gave me a hope, a place to run to.

I knew the youngest brother, Archik Bielski, very well. We went to the same school and were in the same class. The four Bielski brothers had refused to submit to the German terror and had gone into hiding in the forest. They were joined by other families and people from the ghetto in Novogrodek, and the Bielski brigade was formed. Once it became known in the ghetto that there was a place to run to, people began to take the chance.

By the end of October 1942 the Bielski group consisted of more than 300 people. I started to prepare myself for escape, too. Getting out of the camp was still quite easy. The danger was that in winter you could freeze to death. Then there was the problem of food, and the fact that the outside world was unfriendly. People were ready to sell you to the Germans or just give you away for the sake of it.

I got friendly with the warehouseman in charge of the store of felt boots. He had lost a son of my age and therefore wanted me to succeed in my escape. He risked his life and gave me a pair of the most beautiful, hard felt boots. I told my parents that I planned to escape and they gave me their blessing.

On 22 December 1942, the gates were opened to let in lorries to unload raw material. It was very cold. I put on my special felt boots, loosened the yellow star and number, and tore them off when I got nearer to the gates. There were no guards to be seen. I walked through the gates without looking back. I crossed the highway and went on to the small forest where a few people were already waiting. By the afternoon there were 14 of us. We waited until dark, then started to skirt around the town because a rendez-vous had been arranged with the partisans at midnight.

The going was very difficult, with waist-deep soft snow. We had to cover approximately eight kilometres. We reached the little river Britanka. We felt the ice under the snow, but suddenly the ice gave way and most of us fell in. I was the worst off. I had felt boots and the fabric immediately absorbed the water, and snow started sticking to my boots. Each step became more difficult.

We all reached the rendez-vous place but too late! The partisans had not waited, but were due to come back three nights later. We were advised to wait in the small forest for the next three days. After a while, I just wanted to sleep. I started to dream and realized immediately that if I fell asleep now, it would be forever. I fought hard with myself and made a decision: I must return to the camp. Otherwise I would freeze to death.

I crawled to the road and put my life in the hands of fate. I was fortunate. A peasant passed by in his sleigh. He didn't notice me when I climbed onto the back. When we got near the camp, I just fell off and started walking towards the well. I knew that in a few hours' time the first party would come to fetch water. I waited in the bitter cold.

Eventually they came. The guards were so wrapped up that they could not see anything. I moved forwards and was noticed by one of the carriers. He must have immediately told the others, as I found myself in the middle of the group. Before I knew what was happening I found myself back in my room.

My father tried to take off my boots but it was impossible. A file and sharp knife had to be used. My toes were black with frostbite on both feet. There was no doctor to help and no medicine, no bandages, nothing. After a few days the flesh started to rot, and my toes had to be amputated. I felt sure that I had signed my own death certificate – by being in a camp, unable to walk. The strain on my parents and sister was unbearable. If I couldn't work, I couldn't bring in any food, which meant a decrease in rations for them.

I gradually started to feel better, but a new enemy began to show up – bugs, millions of them. They made my life a misery. Because of the dirty conditions, lice and bugs reigned. They got under the so-called bandages and disturbed my wounds. I had to scratch and with the slightest scratch the wounds would bleed again.

In April 1943, there was a new announcement that specialist workers – including my father – would receive extra food rations. On 7 May 1943, my window was open and I watched the workers going to get their extra rations of food as usual. Suddenly I saw local and foreign police running about, hitting out with their rifles. My mother came to the window to reassure me. I was sure she had come to say goodbye (you had a feeling about things then, and when my mother came to me like that, it was as if she were saying goodbye). I could no longer stand hearing the shouting and seeing the beatings. I turned towards the wall, covered myself, put my fingers in my ears and lay quietly, crying my heart out.

Suddenly I heard guards coming into the room. They had killed everybody and were now coming to rob, but we didn't have anything. They took some belongings and threw them on the top bunk and so covered me even more. How long I lay there I don't know, but soon I heard crying and realized the workers had been sent back, my father among them. All the others, including my mother, sister and aunt, had been taken just outside the camp and killed.

After this food was cut down to 125 grams of bread mixed with straw and a bowl of soup a day – a slow starvation diet. It was impossible for me to get used to the hunger. I was not occupied and the days passed very slowly, waiting 24 hours for the next slice of bread.

An escape committee was formed because it was now certain that nobody would be left alive at the end. The first plan was to wait for a dark night, throw hand grenades into the guardroom and escape. Some would definitely reach the forest. But what about me? I could not run and could not let myself be taken alive. So my father prepared two nooses. As soon as we heard the first explosion, we would hang ourselves. After a while, this plan was dropped and a new one devised: to dig a tunnel 100 metres long to the other side of the barbed wire into a field of growing wheat. Work started sometime in June and went on around the clock.

At the beginning of July 1943, my father came to me during the working day, took some belongings and said goodbye. He told me that they were sending him for a short while to a different camp. It was a very sad day for me, the parting was so quick and to this day I can see him with his small packet in his hands, putting on a brave face, saying he would see me soon, knowing very well that this was goodbye forever. He was killed sometime in February 1944.

When I felt better, I started to test my strength. After six months of lying still, I felt pins and needles and pain when I lowered my leg. I was very weak but tremendously determined. I was still only 14 years old. For me, life was hard then. I could more or less get around on crutches, but I was just like a skeleton. I had to live completely on charity for a slice of bread and some soup water.

The digging of the tunnel progressed very well. We were nearly 100 metres forward and well past the barbed wire. Nobody can imagine how much earth accumulates from such a project. First the loft was filled, then double walls were built and filled. At the end of August there were further problems: rain was seeping through and earth was falling from the roof of the tunnel. Wood had to be stolen and some bunks destroyed to make supports. In the middle of September, a meeting was called and a vote taken. There were still some people who said it was better to die in the camp than to run, but the majority preferred escape. A list was drawn up. The first to go through would be the tunnel diggers, followed by five armed men, then the strong ones. I would be among the last, along with my friend Pesach who had also lost some toes. I had to make a trial run and it went perfectly well. I was already walking without sticks.

On 19 September 1943 a meeting was called and we were notified that the tunnel would be completed the following week. So started the longest week in my life, but I was not scared. People were saying goodbye to each other, exchanging tips about the route and the best way to go. It was thought that if we all went our separate ways, we would stand a better chance of survival.

26 September 1943 – our chosen day of escape. We assembled in the loft at about 8 p.m. It was a dark and stormy night, the searchlights had been cut off and some of the nails removed from the zinc roof, so it would rattle a lot in the wind. We assembled in a long line and waited about an hour. At about 9 p.m. a small hole was made for ventilation and the line started to move forwards.

About 120 people went down into the tunnel. They sat in there for about 10-15 minutes until the final hole was punched through and the line started to move forward. But we had not reckoned on the effect of the lighting in the tunnel. When people came out at the other end, the sudden darkness after the brightness in the tunnel disorientated them and they ran towards the camp, whereupon the guards opened fire. Although the searchlights were cut off, the guards still saw movement in the dark and probably thought partisans had come to liberate the camp.

When I came out of the tunnel, I could see the whole field ablaze with flying bullets. I saw figures in the dark running towards the forest and was certain that in the morning the Germans would search that area. So Pesach and I planned to skirt around the town and wait on the other side. We stuck together. The fields were recently ploughed so walking was difficult. We took the same route as I had taken on my first escape and crossed the same river.

Morning started to break. We lay behind a bush and stayed there all day, about two kilometres from town. As soon as darkness fell, we got up and went to the nearest house and asked for food. A man gave us a loaf of the most beautiful bread and milk. We walked for five nights in the same direction. It rained a few nights and I was afraid to take off my torn shoes. Around the hole I could see hardened blood. On the morning of 1 October 1943, we started to rest after a night's walk when we saw a group of people with a cart and horses. We hid ourselves but then we heard them speaking Yiddish and I recognised one of the partisans. These fighters were back from a mission and we were very lucky to have met them. It is impossible to calculate the odds of going into that forest, without really knowing the way, and reaching the group we were searching for.

The partisans took us to the base and there I was reunited with my cousin Berl. We laughed and cried at the same time. I had reached the Ordzhonikidze detachment of the Kirov brigade. This was the name of the ex-Bielski fighting group of 180 men and women. Soon after, Berl decided that we should join the family group of the Kalinin detachment, better known as Bielski, so that we could stay together. He got permission for us to transfer and we left the fighting group. We only had a short, two-kilometre walk to reach the Kalinin group whose commander was Tuvia Bielski. It was strange to see so many Jews in this place, quite unafraid, although it was so close to German police stations.

The reconnaissance arrived and told Bielski that the Germans and local police were on the move. That meant immediate evacuation of the camp. It could not have happened at a worse time for me. My wounds were just beginning to heal. We moved out slowly in the middle of the day, a large convoy. The danger was great because we had to cross major roads. Berl decided that he and I should leave the convoy because if shooting took place, I would not be able to run. He found out the route the convoy was taking and we left on our own.

Berl knew the way and we walked slowly. We met the group on the following day and heard that shots had been exchanged with the local police. We had something to eat and moved on again to the next meeting place. I got used to sleeping in the forest without fear. So we carried on moving for the next few days until we reached the base in the huge Naliboki forest. We arrived late and I was very tired. With difficulty I took the outer rags off my feet. I took off my sweater and wrapped it around my feet, then covered myself with an overcoat and fell asleep. I woke up early in the morning. The pain from my feet was unbearable.

The Bielski base in the forest developed into a little town with a bakery, a salami-maker, shoe workshops, tailoring and engineering workshops and, later, a tannery. Partisans from all over the region used to come to repair their guns, shoes and uniforms, and exchange flour for bread, cows for salami. I did all sorts of work in the camp.

In the forest the Jewish partisans had another enemy – the White Poles. Their slogan was "Poland without Jews and Communists" and many Jews who managed to escape from the ghettos were killed by them. The Bielski group took an active part in fighting the enemy and in committing various acts of sabotage, which included blowing up bridges and cutting down telegraph posts. Over a period of six months in 1944, the Bielski fighters stopped the German trains for 51 hours, which was a great achievement.

At 4 o'clock on the morning of 22 June 1944, exactly three years after the Nazis started the terrible war against Russia, the Red Army began its great offensive on the Belorussian front. On 3 July Minsk was liberated. When lying on the ground, we could already hear the sound of artillery. We prepared for a fight with the German army as we knew their retreat would be through the forest. Sure enough, one morning a large retreating group of Germans broke through our reinforcements. Unfortunately, ten of our members were killed.

On the following day, we heard that the Russian army was in Novogrodek. We were pleased that the nightmare was over, but each one of us felt terribly sad. We all knew what we would find in Novogrodek – a destroyed town without Jews and the people we had known before the war.

It was decided that we would return to Novogrodek. Bielski requested that everybody should march out from the forest in an organised body. And so it was. I walked without difficulty the 100-120 kilometres to the town. Thanks to the Bielski brothers, 1,230 Jews arrived in the suburbs on 16 July 1944. Although we were free, nobody talked or laughed or sang. We were all sad.

Long columns of German prisoners of war were led through the streets of Novogrodek. They were a scruffy lot, no longer the victorious army. I saw a high-ranking officer marching with the men, in a nice pair of boots. I called the Russian guard and asked his permission to remove the boots. The soldier smiled with full approval, "Please help yourself!" I caught up with the officer and spoke to him in Yiddish, which is similar to German. I wanted him to know that I was a Jew. I told him to stop and remove his boots, saying they were too good for him, then the Russian soldier approached and gave him a push with his rifle, whereupon he sat down and pulled off his boots. I wore them for a long time after that.

In fact, I was still wearing them when I eventually arrived in England in 1947! When I first came here, I found a job as a cutter in a handbag factory, then after 15 months, I started my own company, Princelet Handbags, followed by another one, Hi-speed Plastics. I started up a number of successful companies after that.

I met Barbara Steinfeld, fell in love with her and we were married in 1955. We have two sons, Michael Leon and Jeffrey David, and one daughter, Deborah Judith, and between them all, we have ten grandchildren.

I eventually settled down to a normal life, but I can never forget the past. I regret missing out on my youth and educational opportunities. But I continue my study of Resistance in the Holocaust and enjoy speaking to groups about the role of the remarkable Bielski brothers. To me they are among the greatest of Jewish heroes.

Adapted from *Surviving the Holocaust with the Russian Jewish Partisans*, by Jack Kagan and Dov Cohen (Valentine Mitchell, London, 1998).

To the lost Kagan family

Jack Kagan's cousins, a pre-war photograph.
Front row: Shiendl Sucharski, Leizer Kagan,
Nachama Kagan, Berl Kagan. Second row:
Srolik Sucharski, Leizer Senderovski, Idel Kagan.
Only three in this photograph survived the war:
Leizer Senderovski (Sadan), Idel and Berl Kagan.

Jack and Barbara on their wedding day, 1955

Reunion – Hille and Anne (on the right) in England after the war, c. 1950

ANNE KIND

A Long Journey to Reconciliation

I was born Anneliese Rosenberg in Berlin in 1922 at a time of great turmoil, four years after the First World War and the Versailles Treaty. I remember my mother telling me how people were starving and unemployment was high. All the terrible things which happened in Germany after that time were probably due to the economic conditions in the 1920s.

My parents were Jewish but we did not eat kosher food and only went to synagogue on high days and holy days. I learnt Hebrew in order to follow the service at festivals. I was German first and then Jewish.

Writing and reading my poems to small audiences has helped me to come to terms with Germany, the country of my birth. I've been back three times in order to come to terms with all that has happened. I wanted some sort of reconciliation. I looked up the word in the dictionary. It means 'to become friends after estrangement'.

It's been a long journey.

NO CHOICE

When people say: "Jew"
and I say nothing
so laying the foundation
of another pogrom;

when I see surprise in their eyes
on hearing I'm a Semite
born in Berlin
fled, you know who
it's because they see
that which I've hidden.

Before the Nazis existed
I didn't know
that I was different.
Lay the blame on my mama, papa
they didn't teach me
how to be an outcast.

We lived in a suburb of Berlin. Hermsdorf had been a village and still has that feeling about it. I loved the house and the place and I loved my childhood in Germany.

Next door was a baker's shop. They sold wonderful cakes and I went there on a daily visit.

PREMONITION

Each morning I fetched milk
from Bese's shop
they sold lovely things
crisp rolls, chocolate-iced buns.

Herr Bese, dark baritone
Dipped the litre measure
into the churn
his voice carried us
from Figaro to Butterfly.

"Gnädige Frau" he'd say to my mama
"taste the butter or the cheese"
to please him she'd oblige
her jaw moved up and down

tasting as if it were wine
recalling millions, starved, in the twenties.

Herr and Frau Bese smiled at me
in their snow-white coats, so polite.

I could never understand
why my young sister disliked them so.
One day I saw a swastika
flying from their sun-blind canopy.

New Year in Germany was special. We children were very excited to be allowed to stay up to see the New Year in. A special ceremony always took place on Sylvester night. A small amount of lead would be heated up in a saucepan until it had become liquid. Everyone in the family would take a spoon to ladle lead and then drop it into a bucket of cold water. Whatever the shape turned into was going to be your good fortune or otherwise for the next year. Rather like reading tea leaves in a teacup.

TEUTONIC NEW YEAR

I was a child on New Year's Eve
Berlin in nineteen thirty three
before the Brown Shirts came
who didn't like my name.

Paper streamers everywhere
people shouting in the square
where on that morning Mutti bought
traditional carp
which had just been caught.

Drinking punch or pouring lead
we children joined in
weren't sent to bed.

Lead shapes like tea leaves
could not foresee
the imminent inhumanity.

Bells ringing
voices singing
frohes Neu Jahr
prosit Neu Jahr

good will to all men
so said we all
but when....

We spent summer holidays in Heringsdorf, a small fishing village on the Baltic Sea.

SUFFOLK   DÉJÀ VU

On the Baltic strand at Heringsdorf
Holidays were spent when I was young.
Striped awnings, sun and soft yellow sand.
My mother lounging in a trouser suit
So elegant in nineteen twenty six.
Uncles, aunts, cousins, friends all mix
With children digging holes,
Fill them with sea, get pushed in, jump in
Playing 'it'. Behind us dunes and flat, flat land.
Bright poppies in a field of corn
This was the place where I was born.

Fifty years pass and on a beach in Suffolk
Two young girls lie giggling in the sun
Strong winds, loud waves drown stories of their fun.

This part of England mirrors the coastline of my youth
And in a hide at Minsmere
the past echoes the noise of tramping boots.

Walking barefoot on the beach
Letting waves wash my feet
I think of childhood holidays
Spent by the Baltic Sea
And all the aches of getting old
Leave me.

My best friend Hille lived in the ground floor flat in our house. Her father owned the hairdresser's shop where my mother went to have her hair done. I loved Hille, she had great imagination and we played together whenever we could. What I did not realize was that she was German; I thought I was until Hitler came to power. Hille had to join the Hitler Youth and wear the brown uniform with the swastika on the armband. We both felt uncomfortable and embarrassed about it. It was never talked about.

HILLE

I remember you well
me running, you never catching me
I was healthier and younger.
I never questioned
why your breathing
was not like mine.

Your thin blond hair
blue Aryan eyes
ears pierced for rings.

I looked up to
your imagination in
the games we played,
dressing up.
Thin body, spindly legs.

Our games became real
when in your Nazi uniform
you crept up to our apartment
to say goodbye.

Thank you
for that gesture of defiance.

DRESSING UP

You were Madame le Blanc
In our charades
While I was in the kitchen
in white apron and white cap
waiting for your call.

You pressed the bell
I came to meet your every whim
far travelled, fashionable, trim
you lounged
the baby playing at your feet.

You, I and my young sister
played endless games
evoked by tantalising glitter
of the outside world.

And when your enemies
were at your door
you dressed up
to masquerade as male
avoided rape,
the victor's revelry.

Madame le Blanc
I hear you crying
for all that degradation
all that dying.

Herr Techam, Hille's father, was a good hairdresser. My mother thought well of him. When she had her hair done, I wasn't always allowed to see what was going on behind drawn curtains. I used to watch when he plaited hair and made wigs on models.

HERR FRISEUR 1930

I thought he would always be there
cutting and waving mother's hair.

I remember him
tall, fair, slightly bald.
I watched him making wigs
with deft hands.

He sent us away to play
to do what had to be done
behind closed curtains.
A secret.

Once, when his back was turned
I peeped and saw her wearing
a mysterious black cape.
He was dying her hair.

What happened to you Herr Friseur
did you shave innocent heads and
did you charge the state for your service?

Another friend was Britta; she lived next door but our relationship had its ups and downs.

WHITE LIMOUSINE

She held such power over me
owning that pedal car.
It was all I ever wanted.

Britta, why didn't you
let me have a go
why did you always say No.

We quarrelled fiercely
over that white car
your status symbol, my envy.

We were eight years old.
Where are you now Britta Schmidt?
I wish I could talk to you.

I lied when I took die Zeitung to your Dad
told him the paper woman was too lazy
to climb your stairs.

I had to make my mark somewhere.
That senseless lie made quite a stir
I got a telling-off from 'her'.

Britta what happened to your pedal car?
but most of all, I wonder where you are.

I started school in 1928. My first teacher was Herr Heinrichsohn, a gentle, kindly man who encouraged us in everything. I have remembered him all my life.

JUDEN 'RAUS★
January 30th 1933

I started school in 1928.
My teacher, Herr Heinrichsohn
fair hair, blue laughing eyes
laugh lines, loved him all my life.

In the cold airy hall
I looked towards the floor
not at the Head who spoke
in flowery terms of saviour
rescuer, sieg heil.

He sent us off to see a film
a Hitler youth, murdered
by Communists and Jews
we children wept.

People wore swastikas in their lapels
Flags flew from windows
neighbours didn't speak
although I curtsied (small girls did)
there was a feeling in the air
embarrassment
unwelcome mats put out.

Years later on a visit to Berlin
Tiergarten Park
I sat on a bench
that would have been reserved
for Brown Shirts, not for Jews
"Juden 'raus" it used to say.

I often think of you
Herr Heinrichsohn
did you salute
and wear a swastika
when fear and power took command?
I'm glad I'll never know.

★'raus: from heraus....get out!

On 31 January 1933 everything in my life changed. Suddenly swastikas were being flown from roofs and houses. People were wearing swastika badges in their lapels and some of the children at school didn't speak to me any more.

LAST HOLIDAY 1933

'The little Alps' they called Rupien
where holidays were spent
before I left the land where I was born.

I met a boy, swam in blue water
Swore he loved me
Said it was forever.

We wrote
Distance grew between us.
The war intervened.
When it was over
It was all over.

One day a knock came on our door.
When I saw him again
He was short and plain.

I saw the scars
Weals on his back
Tattooed number on his arm.

I cursed the soil
Where we were born.

BERLIN, 30 JANUARY 1933

At school assembly
I couldn't raise my arm
for that infamous man.
and so it all began.

Took all we had
said our goodbyes to
loving aunt, best friend
(she dared to visit me)
where no one understood
my words.

I made my father choose
Christmas or Chanukah
both Festivals of Light

Orthodox, Progressive?
chose neither
I'm on the outside looking in.

I hid my true identity until
my gentle Englishman
taught me to be.
I wear my house around me
like a snail
it's crowded being me.

My father had business connections in England and had travelled to London on many occasions. He could see from afar how the Nazis were taking over Germany and what Hitler had promised to do to the Jews.

In February 1934, my parents, my sister and I left Berlin forever. I did not want to go to England where I knew no one and where I would not understand the language. On our way from Southampton where we had landed after a horrific sea journey, I asked my father "Why are all the stations called 'Bovril?'"

My father had rented a house in South London and we were sent to a small school to learn English. I remember saying to my sister, "What is that word that keeps cropping up on every page of this book?" The word was "the". I made a decision to learn to speak English as soon as possible and without an accent. That was my goal. I was really excited the first time I dreamt in English.

After about a year, people who did not know about my background stopped asking "Where did you come from?" because I had become fluent without an accent. I felt a great sense of achievement. We spoke German at home but more and more I wanted to speak English.

My favourite great-aunt was Mathilde. We were all upset at leaving her in Berlin. After we had been here a year, she came to visit us. She must have been 72 years old and very frail; however, she had withstood the journey and we all begged her to stay with us. She refused because she had a small pension and she did not want to be a burden. That was the last time we saw her.

GREAT-AUNT MATHILDE

Gentle, dainty
darling of my childhood,
fairytales, Anderson and Grimm
did the horror come true for you?

We begged you to stay
where it was safe
but no, you would go back to Berlin
and your old age pension

didn't want to bother us
left us full of guilt.

You with your white hair
piled high like a castle
black silk dress
white lace jabot
high button boots
smiling eyes
darling of my childhood.

DEAREST GREAT-AUNT

Grosstantchen Mathilde
was killed in a camp
Theresienstadt, Terezin?
Today I heard,
her Viennese lilt
asking for her pension
a day early
to save her weary feet.
I had to speak to the stranger
knew our paths would meet.
"Please help me across the street
I can no longer see so well, nor hear.
Come and visit me," she said,
"don't say you will
just to be polite."

We looked into each other's eyes, smiled.

I took her thin arm,
so well remembered
held up my hand to stop the traffic
like Moses, parting the water.

After many years of trying to find out what had happened to Mathilde, I got a letter from the International Red Cross in 1997. It was a reply to my letter to them in 1992. This is what it said:

Dear Mrs. Kind,

Re: Mathilde Rosenberg born 7.8.1860 in Prague, unmarried, no profession, last address Berlin W 50, Marburger strasse 5, was delivered on June 11 1942 through the Secret Police of Berlin, through Transport 1/5 into the ghetto Theresienstadt. On the 19th September 1942 through the transport BO she was sent to Maly Trostinec.

Category: JEW

Through the information of the Czechoslovakian Red Cross in Prague, 25th May 1951, we heard that the transport BO must be accepted as a death transport as less than 10 per cent of those deported came back after the war. We remain with friendly greetings (signed) for the archives.

CATEGORY.... JEW

Mathilde, I buried you today
In my mind,
forty years late.
The letter told me
what they did to you.

"We regret
less than ten per cent
came back from that camp."

Grosstante,
you were aged eighty two
you nursed me
through childhood days
they dragged you into trains

bundled you
with hundreds, thousands
into one category
Jew.

Meanwhile in Germany things were happening and changing. I wrote to Hille and saved up my pocket money, and with the help of my father, I sent her the ticket to come and visit us in London. That was in May 1936. Looking back, I think how naïve we were.

She stayed with us for two weeks and we had a wonderful time. I tried to teach her English and showed her London, and begged her to come and visit us again. After she went back, I did not hear from her again. I was upset about her silence but I was 16 years old and had other diversions; and then the war came.

Good and bad came out of the war for me. I took up nursing and met a doctor at the hospital and fell in love. We got married in 1943. I did go to the Rabbi at the synagogue in London where I had been to Hebrew classes. When he heard that my husband to be was not Jewish, he did not want to know me any more. My parents accepted Bill, as his parents accepted me. In 1944 my father was killed in the Blitz in London. The irony only hit me many years later. I went to live with my mother while Bill was in the Royal Army Medical Corps. Both our children were born in London and I am so happy that they are English. I suppose what I'm saying is, I'm glad they're not German.

One day after the war, I received a letter from Berlin; it was from my friend Hille. I was overjoyed to know that she had survived the war and within a few weeks she came to visit us. She told me the most horrendous stories and how she had lived dressed as a man for months on end in order to avoid being raped by Russian soldiers.

To my question about why she did not write to me after her visit to us in 1936, she replied: "When I got back, my father told me that the Gestapo had paid them a visit and insisted on searching my room. They found your letters and photographs and destroyed them and warned my father to tell me never to get in touch with you again, otherwise I would be sent to a concentration camp. I was terrified. That's why you did not hear from me after that lovely holiday in London."

For many years I told no one how I felt about being Jewish and German. It was my secret. I never denied it if asked, but if the conversation came around to the subject of religion or origin I kept quiet. My husband found it sad on my behalf.

In 1985 we decided to go to Berlin after much soul searching, to look for the house where I had lived as a small child and to try to find my roots.

LOOKING FOR ROOTS 1985

In what sort of country am I
where baroque figures dance
on roofs and ceilings?

where statesmen and militia
stand motionless among trees
lining a royal route?

where memorials are seen
 in abundance to the dead they killed
and kept a record of their deeds?

All is neat and tidy here
where I was pushed in my well-sprung pram
across roads made for triumphant victory.

Unter den Linden
where the Adlon reigned supreme among hotels
Berliners sit as before

under striped awnings, serious
drinking strong brown coffee
matching the tyrant's uniform.

This is where flags and eagles
parodied ancient Rome
where pride became a theatre of power and fear.

I've come to see
all that it means to me...
dear God, my roots are here.

I have been back three times. I knew I had to do that. I wanted to be reconciled with the country of my birth, but I found it very hard to do. Not only on my own behalf, but on behalf of the millions who were killed for no other reason than the fact that they had Jewish blood in their veins.

In the early 1990s, I was invited, among many others, by the Mayor of Berlin to go back and to see all that was being done to 'make good' the evil that had been committed by the Nazis. At first I didn't want to accept. I had such mixed feelings, but then I did accept and went with my son and daughter. I am glad that I did.

It took another visit in 1999 to become friends.

LOOKING FOR FEELINGS IN BERLIN

The Senatskanzlerei invited us
To look at feelings
Of murdered childhood.

We travel through the old Jewish quarter
Broken down houses, shuttered windows
An occasional cry from one of our group
"that's where I lived."

Those words moved me to tears.
A taut spring, released.
So much hatred had been poured on us
Left me with guilt and shame.

Today we're living in the past,
Victims and perpetrators.
The present and future infest
The debris of our lives.

Fairy tales remind us:
Goodies always win.
This is no fairy tale
Only history repeating itself
Over and over and over again.

BERLIN
FASANENSTRASSE, SYNAGOGUE, 1999

Kristallnacht 1938, they burnt it down
rebuilt, and now, Schutz Polizei
reminds us...

It's Friday night, we enter
and they screen us
to make sure
we're honest Jews.

Drab outside,
brilliant lights inside the shul
the rabbi prays
in his black and white striped shawl.

The cantor chants.
The choir sings in Hebrew
I can still follow

Shma Yisrael, Adanoy
Elouhenu, Adanoy Echod.

My roots are here.

If the horror were to start again
the rabbi with shawl over his head
leads the congregation,
Kaddish, prayer for the dead.

AUGENBLICK

They've forgiven us
It's official
acclaimed by the Senatskanzlerei.

We were never proved guilty
although Jesus of Nazareth
remains a problem between us.

Thoughts unwind
like a bandage across the eyes.
The wound is weeping.

Who was waving flags
daubing stars, throwing stones
on Kristallnacht?

No one claims that notoriety.

In the blink of an eye
sight is restored
the bandage is rewound.
Scar tissue acts as cover-up.

STRING OF PEARLS

You, whose loved ones
have not known Auschwitz
whose forebears can be seen
to go back a long time
neatly tucked up in rows
declaring you present

I expect you
to make up for those
who ill-treated mine
cutting off my past.

If I am out of humour
bear with me
I expect you to set
an oyster before me
with its shell open
showing the pearl.

RELEASING THE ENEMY

During a game of Bridge
my German partner opens the bidding
"two hearts"...

Above her, where I look
rather than into her eyes before replying
hang the stiff Germanic heads
of her ancestors, not a smile among them.
Suddenly a wave of affection
having resented her Prussian background
her complaints about Russians
pillaging her grandfather's farm,
after they dragged him into the wood.
Shots, silence;
she and her sisters refugees...

I had heard that story years ago
only today it penetrates my soul
Two hearts; a strong call.

HERMSDORF BEI BERLIN May 1999

I sit on the well-worn terrace
Of my childhood, sipping coffee

Your street and mine, Hille
At the right angle of life.

We didn't mind cycling
On cobbled stones
The only smooth surface
Red tiles on the terrace.

That's where we played
With whips and tops
Hoops and sticks
Even the Nazis couldn't stop us.
Alone
I'm hop-scotching into old age.

I must add a postscript. I've been so fortunate in having had a wonderful husband who encouraged me in all my interests and supported me when I needed it. Through his profession I worked for 27 years for the Family Planning Association and then for nearly 7 years for the Leicestershire Organisation for the Relief of Suffering (LOROS), a charity whose aim was to build a hospice. I was their fundraiser and administrator and set up 64 support groups right across the city and county raising £1.5 million. In 1986 LOROS was opened officially by the Prince and Princess of Wales. In 1990 I received the OBE.

In memory of two special people:
my Great-Aunt Mathilde and my best friend Hille,
who both contributed in their way to the person I am today.

Anne's first vist back to Berlin in 1985 after 51 years

Some of Anne's poems have previously been published in:
Charnwood Writers, Iota, New Hope International, Momentum, Other Poetry, Omens, Stand, Staple, Wayfarer, Anthology: Beyond Lament... (Northwestern University Press, USA).

Freddie aged 24, after Liberation

FREDDIE KNOLLER

Desperate Journey
Vienna–Paris–Auschwitz

I was stunned looking at a bundle of letters and seeing the unmistakable, elegant handwriting of my father who perished in Auschwitz in 1944. He and my mother wrote over 100 letters to my brother Eric who emigrated from Vienna to the USA in December 1938. Eric died in 1996 and never disclosed that he had kept these letters dated 1938-1941. They were found by his widow when going through his personal effects. Why did he never tell me about the letters while he was still alive? Did he have the same guilt feeling all Holocaust survivors share in varying degrees? Why did it take me over 30 years to tell my family and the world what I went through? Is it the same guilt feeling?

My book, *Desperate Journey*, which was written with the help of my friend John Landaw, tells the story of a young, naive boy, just 17 years old, forced to leave the strict parental home. There I was, like a bird leaving the nest for the first time, wanting to taste all the things which a boy, in normal circumstances, would not have been allowed to experience. My attitude of hope and optimism helped me to overcome fear and perils and was one of the reasons why I am still alive today.

My father was an accountant and quite strict. My mother loved life, she was very easygoing, always happy and very musical. She made sure that her three sons received musical tuition. My oldest brother Otto played the piano, Eric learned to play the violin, so naturally I had to learn the cello at the age of six. By the time I was ten, we performed on the stage and at various charity functions.

From early childhood, my family and I were subjected to antisemitism, for which the Austrians were so well known. I was set upon ever so often by Christian children on my way to school.

After the *Anschluss* (annexation of Austria) these attacks became even more virulent. On the night of 9 November 1938, when the Nazis burnt down all the synagogues, my parents insisted that we, the children, should emigrate.

I was the first one to leave, going illegally to Belgium. Eric was next and left for Florida, USA, having been supplied with an affidavit by a friend of the family. Otto was the last to leave our parents; he went illegally to Holland and from there to England. My parents did not want to leave, saying that they were too old for anything to happen to them. Father was 56 and mother 53.

My destination was Antwerp, where I was given the address of a diamond dealer, who helped me morally and financially. The Jewish Committee provided living quarters which I had to share with two other refugees of about my age. In their company, I learned how to play poker, and how to smoke. They also introduced me to alcohol and bad women. Luckily, this freedom was stopped when the Jewish community gave me the choice of either joining a camp for Jewish refugees or of being without further assistance from them. I decided to join the camp of Merksplas and later Exaarde, where I joined the camp orchestra.

When the Germans invaded Belgium in May 1940, everyone in the camp fled on foot to France. At the border, I was arrested by the French as an enemy alien and taken to St. Cyprien Internment Camp for the enemies of France, regardless of whether they were Jewish or real German Nazis. The food and hygiene at this camp were disastrous and soon typhus broke out. I escaped during the night, walking 10 km to the next town, Perpignan. From there, I proceeded to Gaillac, where my aunt, uncle and cousins lived.

In the meantime, the Germans had occupied Paris and the northern part of France, but Gaillac was still in the unoccupied zone, ruled by the Vichy Government. I became bored, craving for new adventures. I decided that I must see Paris, the town of my dreams.

My relatives fought with me and tried to stop me going into the "Lion's Den". However, I insisted and off I went. In Paris I became fascinated by the night life of Pigalle and earned my living by taking German soldiers to night-clubs, to brothels and cabarets. I earned a percentage, at these places, of whatever the soldiers consumed. I organized myself with false identification papers and became "Robert Metzner" born in Metz, Alsace-Lorraine. I met all kinds of people: decent German soldiers, homosexuals, abusive Nazis and French collaborators. I met a wonderful Frenchman who worked in the Resistance. I met some very nice women and some tough prostitutes.

On one occasion, I was arrested by a Gestapo officer who claimed that he could accurately distinguish between the head of a Jew and that of a true Aryan. While he was telling me that, he went behind me, took my head between his hands and I felt his fingers start to trace, then stop and trace again round the circumference of my skull. He then agreed with my contention that I was born in Alsace-Lorraine, that my ancestors must have been of good German background. He could recognise this from the shape of my head. The officer warned me not to go back to Pigalle, but to work for the German Reich. From then on, I could not continue my work and in May 1943 I joined the Maquis, near Figeac, in south-west France and lived in an abandoned shepherd's hut on top of a hill. Among us were a number of Jews, quite a number of French Communists and some young people who did not want to work in Germany under the new law of *"Service du Travail Obligatoire"* (Compulsory Labour). Apart from political discussion and arguments, we did not do much resisting except for an attempt to blow up a German troop train. We did, however, work for the peasants and farmers in the region who paid us with food.

I had a relationship with a young girl from the next village, with whom I thought I was in love. Like a fool, I admitted to her in a moment of love-making that I had false papers and that I was hiding because I did not want to work for the Germans. One day we had an argument and I told her that I did not want to see her again. A few days later, I was arrested by the French police. When I showed them my papers, they just laughed. They asked me for names in my Resistance unit and wanted to know where I came from. When they started to torture me, I told them that I knew nothing of a Resistance unit, but that I was a Jew from Vienna hiding up in the hills. They took me to the Gestapo and I was then taken to Drancy, the infamous transit camp for the east.

At the beginning of October 1943, my name came up for deportation to the east. We were taken to the railway station and 100 people were squeezed into each cattle wagon. There was not enough room for everyone to sit on the floor. We youngsters made room for the old people, women with their babies and the infirm. In the wagon there was one bucket with drinking water and one empty sanitary bucket. We travelled for three days and three nights to our destination. I will never forget the stench, the arguments, the screaming of the babies and the moans of those who were dying. I was squeezed against a middle-aged Frenchman called Robert, a gentle person who looked very much like my father. I took a liking to him and made him as cosy as I could. We became good friends. He told me that he was a doctor and I did not realize then that it is because of him that I am alive today.

When we arrived we saw a sign "Osviecim" on the railway platform. We guessed that we were somewhere in Poland. The platform was full of SS with dogs and we saw some young people in striped prisoners' clothes.

The SS selected the younger people who were to walk to the camp, but the older men and women with their children were taken away by trucks.

This was the time when we were taught German discipline through blows and killings.

We heard some alarming rumours about the older men, women and children transported by trucks, but very few believed them. Others, however, who gave credence to the rumours, killed themselves by walking straight into the electrical fences.

I realized that there were two choices: you could either give up and within 2-3 days you would be dead, or you could fight to live and try to adjust yourself to the situation "by hook or by crook". I chose the latter.

I did not look at others who suffered and moaned about hunger, or those who neglected their personal hygiene – a sign that they had given up. I had to take care of myself – I was number one. I had one mission only, to survive, in order to tell the world about the barbarism of the cultured people of Germany.

On a visit to the hospital, I saw my doctor friend, Robert, from the train. He told me that he had been put in charge of the camp hospital and as I took care of him in the train, he would help me with some extra food whenever possible. I was told to go to the hospital every evening when I returned from work.

At work, I had to carry cement bags weighing 25 kg on my back, day-in, day-out. To do this work and survive with the minimal ration of food we were getting was not possible. People dropped like flies. The extra food I received from my friend Robert was surely the reason for my survival.

When the Russians approached Auschwitz, the whole camp was evacuated. The date was 18 January 1945. We were lined up in rows of five and were told that we would have to walk, and that anybody trying to escape would be shot. It was very cold and it was snowing.

We went westward, walking in our wooden shoes on icy, snow-covered roads. We were still in our striped, thin clothes. Many collapsed and were immediately shot on the spot. We had to take the corpses and throw them into the ditch next to the road. The SS surrounded each of our columns and were ready with their guns.

After walking for the whole day and part of the night, we reached a brick factory where we were allowed to rest and sleep under cover. Only half of us were still alive when we arrived at the factory. One in our group, a French political prisoner, did not wake up. He was dead, frozen stiff. I took his red triangle from his tunic, showing that he was a political prisoner, put it in my pocket hoping to exchange it later for the Star of David insignia. Finally, we were taken to a railway station and squeezed into an open cattle wagon, standing room only. We thus travelled through Austria and Germany, seven days and seven nights, until we reached our destination. Nine people in our wagon died during the journey.

Our new camp, Dora-Nordhausen, was the place where the V1 and V2 rockets were manufactured beneath the Harz mountains. We worked in the tunnels, pushing wagons on rails and carrying heavy metal objects. We experienced a lot of hangings of prisoners, Russian prisoners of war and even civilians, who were supposed to have committed sabotage. One night, the Allied planes bombed the entrance to the tunnels. Many of our comrades who worked there on the night-shift, died. The next day, we were given tools to repair the damage.

As the American troops were nearing our region, we were evacuated to Bergen-Belsen. There was no more food available, and the beatings stopped. The German SS disappeared, and we were now guarded by Croatian and Hungarian SS units. We dug into the ground to find some edible roots. Many collapsed from hunger and dysentery and died where they collapsed.

On 15 April 1945, British troops entered Bergen-Belsen. We were given hot milk with rice, which we devoured like wild animals. Many inmates died, having stuffed themselves with food which the stomach could not digest. A British officer asked for volunteers to go to nearby farms and bring back any food we could find. I joined this group, with a soldier carrying a gun. We searched for food, loaded it onto a trolley in view of the protesting farmer and his wife. When I found a large photo of Hitler hidden behind a wardrobe, I took a knife and cut the photo to pieces. The old farmer went red in the face and shouted at me: "*Du Sau Jud*" (You filthy Jew). I just could not stop myself. After all that happened to me as Jew, my emotions overtook me and I sank the knife into his belly. We left the farm soon after this.

I returned to France. With the help of the American Embassy in Paris, my brother Eric found me in a little village where I was sent by the French government to recuperate. Our reunion was very emotional. Eric was a soldier in the American Army and was ordered by his Commanding Officer to search in all the concentration camps for our parents and myself. He went to Vienna and found that our parents were deported to Theresienstadt. He also told me that our brother Otto became a doctor, and lived in New York.

In 1947, I emigrated to the USA and became a naturalised US citizen. In 1950 I met my wife, Freda, an English girl, on a blind date. We got married on 31 December 1950. After two years in Baltimore, my wife became homesick and we made our way back to her parents in London. We have two daughters Marcia and Susie who were born in England.

*I dedicate my story to my daughters, Marcia and Susie,
and to my grandson Nadav.*

Freddie aged 82, in Totteridge, May 2003

My first schoolday, 1930

LOTTE KRAMER

Surviving Circles of Hell

Lotte Kramer was born in Mainz, Germany, and came to England as a child refugee on a *Kindertransport* in 1939. She worked as a ladies' companion, in a laundry and a dress shop while studying Art and History of Art at Richmond Institute. Her poetry has appeared in a wide variety of magazines and anthologies in England, Canada and the USA, and she has frequently exhibited her paintings. She has published nine books of poetry including a bilingual edition in German. She is married and now lives in Peterborough where she is a voluntary worker in the City Museum.

Lotte lost her parents and 13 members of her family in the Holocaust.

GERMANY 1933

The air was dank with fifty little girls.
Spell-bound they listened to their teacher's tale
Of one young martyr*, one who gave the name
To that new hymn. They wept for him. He burnt

An early hero into ready minds.
And then the oath – they hardly knew what for –
Of loyalty to him whose massive roar
Bludgeoned their ears. There was no choice, no sign

Of something sinister. They longed to serve,
To sing in great processions, hold a flag,
And feel secure under this pagan tag.
A slag-heap waiting for a willing herd.

'Now choose the one to lead, to march ahead,
To keep your trust, unfurl the swastika.'
The teacher urged a ballot on the class.
'The one you like the most' he archly said.

The children chose and named a jewish child.

* *Horst Wessel*

239

A NEW SUBJECT

'Today we start a subject that is new
To everyone. As your new master now
I've come to tell you something of those true
Great ancestors we have. You must be proud,

You boys, our fatherland, our new decade,
Is nurtured by a giant race: red-blond,
Eyes blue, a strong physique and unafraid.
The finest ethnic heritage is ours.

Let's see the type of man we used to be –
Yes you – just there – behind that darkish head,
You in the seventh row – get up, come here!
What is your name? Ah, Heinz, ah, very good.

Now face the class. You see in this blond boy
The perfect specimen of purest race;
His bones are powerful, his hair is fair,
His eyes are blue set in an eager face.

No shameful mixture in his blood or breed.
This is your future now, our Germany!
You grin – you laugh – you too – I'll have no cheek
From anyone! What is the matter, speak?'

'Please Sir, it makes no sense, it's true, you see
Heinz is a Jew.'

THE NON-EMIGRANT

(my father in Nazi Germany)

He left the application forms
Hidden inside his desk and missed
His quota for the U.S.A.

He thought he'd stay and wait and stare
The madness out. It could not last.
He would not emigrate, not lose

His home, his language and his ground.
Beside his armchair sat a pile
Of books: the smoke from his cigar

Fenced comfort with a yellow screen.
His daily walk was all he'd need,
He thought. Abroad was where he'd been.

THE RED CROSS TELEGRAM

The red-cross telegram
Read when it came
Those five and twenty words;
The terror, fear,
Was there; I did not dare
To grasp the cruelty
That now I know
It did contain:
'We have to move,
Our residence will not
Remain this town,
Farewell, beloved child.'
How can I ever sing
A requiem
In silent, dark despair,
Transfiguring
Your calvary of nails
And gas and graves.

DEPORTATION

What do we know of nights in cattle-trucks,
Of fires dying on a wire fence,
Of their despair,
Or their release in fumes,

Of their suspended sentence, freezing stance,
And hunger in the ruins of their flesh,
Or of their souls,
Could they still hear the chant?

Some days the lash tears at my skin and bones.
What right have I to soak defeat in fears,
Wet with my tears
My well-fed, balanced face?

I want to lie with them in unknown graves
And bury freedom of indulgent years.
There is no judge
To hear and end their cause.

[All the above poems were published in *Selected and New Poems 1980-1997*, Rockingham Press, 1997.]

KINDERTRANSPORT REUNION

A doddery crowd with the same history,
We hug shoulders and clasp hands,
Weeping, laughing at new nearness.

The same faces with stencilled age
We are survivors of circles of hell
Having slid through some six decades

With the usual joys and losses as shadows,
Able to look back at spontaneous goodness
That has confronted our sceptical childhood.

Whereto now as a new century
Is taking hold with much talk
And almost indecent heralding haste?

Begin again in wonder at the brain's
Possibilities, stare at the lilac's candles
Renewing their perfume each spring.

[Originally published in *The Phantom Lane*, Rockingham Press, 2000.]

In memory of my parents

Lotte Kramer, photograph by Beata Hörr

Myself in 1996 (Photograph by David Jacobs)

ANITA LASKER-WALLFISCH

Inherit the Truth

I was born in the town of Breslau, which was German then and is Polish now. My father was a lawyer and my mother was a beautiful lady and a very fine violinist. We had a very happy home. We were three sisters and we all learnt to play an instrument. I played the cello. There was no particular emphasis on being Jewish. We were a typical completely assimilated Jewish liberal family.

"Culture" was a very important part of our lives. We read the classics every Saturday afternoon, a great deal of chamber music was played in our home and we were brought up speaking French. In fact, there was a rule in our house that on Sundays French only had to be spoken. My father maintained that people have as many souls as they have languages. Life seemed normal and it was inconceivable that it should not continue to be so.

My first encounter with antisemitism was at the school I attended. I was eight years old. I was about to wipe the blackboard and one of the children said, "Don't give the Jew the sponge." This is a long time ago, but I have never forgotten it. Then suddenly some children spat at me in the street and called me a dirty Jew. I did not really understand what was going on. One just had to accept that one was *different*. One did not belong to the *master race*.

When I was 12 years old, it became impossible to continue my cello lessons because there were no Jewish cello teachers left in Breslau, and it had become too dangerous for an "Aryan" cellist to teach a Jewish child. With some difficulties, my parents got permission for me to leave school and go to Berlin, where I had private tuition in school subjects and lessons with the only Jewish cello teacher still living there.

This came to an abrupt end on 9 November, *Kristallnacht* (Night of the Broken Glass). Herr vom Rath, a minor official at the German Embassy in Paris was shot by a Jew, a young man by the name of Herschel Grynszpan. This incident "spontaneously enraged the German people," as the press put it at the time, and the first major pogrom of the Nazi era took place. It served as an excuse to unleash the worst instincts in brainwashed hooligans who were acting on behalf of the government at that time. Synagogues were burnt down, Jewish shops smashed up and looted, and private homes invaded and demolished. The majority of the male population was arrested and the expression "concentration camp" became part of the vocabulary.

The *Kristallnacht* was a kind of dress rehearsal for things to come. A test. How far can we go...? The willingness of the mob to attack undefended targets was a green light for the Nazis. There were no limits to what could be done in the pursuit of torturing Jews, and it became patently clear that one could no longer remain in Germany. Frantic efforts at emigration were made, but as night follows day, it became more and more difficult to find a safe haven. Frontiers closed and the difficulties one had to overcome to obtain entry into another country became well-nigh ludicrous. Enormous difficulties were also made by the Germans themselves – who were so keen to get rid of us. If you wanted to get away, you had to pay. Many people did not get away, and I assure you that it was not for lack of trying. My family was among those.

Public places displayed signs that Jews were not welcome. We were not allowed to own radios; bicycles had to be surrendered; we had to add the name Sara or Israel to our names; we had to wear the yellow star on our clothes and so on. The war broke out and we were finally trapped.

Life still had a semblance of normality although one's concept of normality was greatly distorted by then. After my return home from Berlin and realising that emigration was out of the question, I tried to go back to school. This time a Jewish one. Eventually Jewish schools closed and I was conscripted to work in a paper factory. We had to leave our home and move into a flat with my aunt, which was already hopelessly overcrowded. The deportation of Jews started in earnest.

On 20 January 1942 a conference took place in a suburb of Berlin, called Wannsee. At this "Wannsee Conference" they discussed – and it took just one hour and a half – how to exterminate European Jewry: and we are talking here of a matter of 11 million people...

On 9 April 1942 my parents were deported and sent on a transport to the East, to a place called Isbiza near Lublin. Of course we wanted to stay together as a family. My sister Renate's and my name were not on the list, but if we had simply presented ourselves, we would hardly have been sent back. But our father did not want to hear of it. "It is better that you remain. Where we are going, one gets there soon enough." Needless to say that I never saw them again. I was 16 years old.

After the war I went to the Wiener Library [a documentation centre in London dealing with the persecution of Jews], and learnt that the method of murdering where my parents went was that the victims had to dig their own graves, undress and be shot into these graves. A very messy way of eliminating human beings. A more efficient way had to be found – gas chambers.

My aunt, uncle and grandmother had also been deported and now we were completely alone. We continued working in the paper factory. The workforce there were Jews, Poles and French prisoners of war. I could never accept that I should be killed for what I happened to be born as, and decided to give the Germans a better reason for killing me. I involved myself in clandestine activities – forged papers for French prisoners of war to escape with. Eventually, I tried to escape myself with forged papers.

These papers were leave passes for French civilian workers, who – unlike French prisoners of war – were allowed to go on leave from time to time. It was of course strictly forbidden to talk to the prisoners. We chose to ignore this and developed an extremely ingenious way of communicating with them. There were segregated toilets in the factory. In the toilet for Jews, the bracket holding the chain for flushing had become loose and you could pull it straight out of the wall, leaving a hole in the wall. On the other side of this wall was the refectory of the French prisoners. We developed a sort of sign-language, whereby a prisoner and I would go to our respective locations, and communicate through this hole by whispering almost inaudibly into each other's ear or putting messages through it. My main occupation was to produce civilian clothes and forge the writing on the papers which were given to me. I was able to write the German script and I still had a typewriter.

One day, I found that the hole had been blocked up. We had obviously been observed. That was when we decided to make a run for it. The idea was to get somehow into the unoccupied zone of France. It was not exactly the most thought-out escape plan, but one didn't think too far ahead in those days. There was only one overpowering thought in one's mind: to get out of Germany.

We did not get very far – to be exact, no further than the railway station. I had obviously been watched by the Gestapo for some time. I was arrested and sent to prison. I had committed a criminal offence. Forgery, Helping the Enemy and Attempted Escape were my indictments when I eventually appeared in court to be sentenced. The absurdity of my situation was that having committed a criminal offence on top of being a Jew – which was bad enough – actually helped me rather than hindered me. It permitted me to stay in prison for over a year, postponing my arrival at a concentration camp. When I was eventually sent to Auschwitz-Birkenau, I did not have to go through the usual selection on arrival at the notorious ramp, where the SS chose who should live and who should die in the gas chamber. I had a criminal record – I was a *Karteihäftling*, a prisoner with a file, and they did not get gassed automatically. In other words, it was preferable to arrive in Auschwitz as a convicted criminal rather than an innocent citizen...

That I survived nearly one year in Auschwitz is without any doubt due to the fact that I became a member of the camp orchestra. As long as the Germans wanted an orchestra, it would have been counter-productive to kill us. Our task consisted of playing every morning and every evening at the gate of the camp so that the outgoing and incoming work commandos would march neatly in step to the marches we played. We also had to be available at all times to play to individual SS staff who would come into our Block and wanted to hear some music after sending thousands of people to their death. Although we were somewhat privileged, we had no illusions that we would end up in the gas chamber eventually; we were all of us under sentence of death. It did not seem remotely possible that anyone would come out of Auschwitz alive. But a miracle happened. The Russians advanced, and we were shunted westwards to Bergen-Belsen. No one had ever heard of it.

Bergen-Belsen was very different from Auschwitz. In Auschwitz, people were murdered in the most sophisticated manner; in Belsen, they simply perished. There was no orchestra there. We sat about and waited and watched each other deteriorate. Belsen was totally ill-equipped to deal with the thousands upon thousands of miserable skeletons who arrived there because of the ever-advancing Allied troops. The last weeks in Belsen saw the arrival of the death marches from all over Germany. Half-dead people dragged themselves into the compound. They had been marching for days on end and what arrived at the camp were just the remnants. The rest had died on the way.

There are no words to describe this inferno. The dead bodies started piling up, there was no food, no water – nothing. It was clear that we had come to the end of the line. It was very hot that April and the effect of the temperature on the mountains of bodies was horrendous. Feeble attempts were being made to move the corpses. Those of us who could still walk were given some string. We were to tie the arms of the dead together and drag them along the road to a big ditch. But this operation was soon abandoned as futile. We were too weak, and the bodies remained in the camp. The state that square mile was in, in early 1945, beggars the imagination. However, corpses were so much part of the landscape that we – the inmates who had been living like this for weeks and months – no longer noticed them as anything unusual.

We had neither food nor water, and clearly it was only a matter of time.

We heard a lot of shooting and rumbling noises in the distance and it was suggested that this was the noise of tanks. But whose tanks? After so many years, my memory of details is somewhat blurred, but I do remember distinctly that I was furious most of the time when someone suggested that these tanks *might* be British. I did not want to hear it. I felt more "at home" so to speak with the thought of impending death than the thought of being liberated by the British army.

It was about 5 p.m. on 15 April 1945 when the miracle actually happened: the first British tank rolled into the camp. We were liberated! No one who was in Belsen will ever forget that day. We did not greet our liberators with shouts of joy. We were silent. Silent with incredulity and maybe just a little suspicion that we might be dreaming.

In March 1946 – eleven months after the Liberation – I finally managed to come to England. I became a professional musician. I married the pianist Peter Wallfisch in 1952 and have a son and a daughter. My son and two grandsons are also musicians and my daughter is a psychotherapist.

The story of Anita Lasker-Wallfisch is told in her book, *Inherit the Truth*, 1939-1945 (dlm, London, 1996).

The family in 1939, left to right: myself, Renate, Marianne, my mother and my father

Michael in his studio

MICHAEL LEE

A Survivor from Lodz

Michael Lee (Lewkowicz) was born in Lodz, Poland, the eldest of two sons born to Zisman and Dvora Lewkowicz. Michael was born on 22 March 1924 and his younger brother, Joseph, in 1933. Zisman came from a *shtetl* (little town) called Wielun in Poland and Dvora from Vitebsk in Russia. She had gone to Lodz shortly after the First World War in search of work as a dressmaker. Zisman worked for a Jewish welfare organisation called Tomchei Orchim.

Lodz was an industrial town full of textile factories, with a population of 700,000, one third of whom were Jews. The family lived there in one room on the fourth floor of a tenement block, with no running water, and toilets outside in wooden shacks. The tap with a sink underneath it was on the corridor, used by everyone who lived on the fourth floor. Michael remembered his mother waxing the floor of this room with a red floor polish. During one of his visits back to Lodz, he managed to gain access to the room and felt very emotional when he saw that the floor still bore traces of the red floor polish.

One of his earliest memories of his former home was visiting the studio of the artist Arthur Szyk who worked in the adjacent building. His mother took in sewing to pay for his schooling, so that he would be able to attend a better school. Despite the fact that his parents were poor, Michael was sent to a fee-paying school called Yavne. It was Zionist-oriented and Hebrew was the main language there. Michael became a member of a Zionist youth group, Hanoar Hatzion. The family were semi-observant Jews: they kept a kosher home and celebrated the festivals. They did not socialise with their Gentile neighbours.

On 1 September 1939, Wielun was bombed by the Germans and Michael's paternal grandmother was killed. A week later, the Germans arrived in Lodz. By then, Michael had been attending a trade school for one year, where mornings were devoted to academic studies and afternoons to practical work with metals. Once the Germans occupied Lodz, the school was closed and used as a barracks for the German army.

By 1 May 1940, all the Jews in Lodz had to move into the ghetto and the family lived in a small room in a wooden house. They tried to take as many of their possessions as possible with them. Michael was 16 years old then and remembered his parents organising a kind of sleigh to take their belongings into the ghetto.

Because of his experience with metalwork, Michael obtained a job in a metal factory on 68 Kagiewnicka Street in the ghetto. Payment was a little ghetto money and a bowl of soup. One of the jobs was to make iron bars and occasionally they were taken out of the ghetto to work: once, for instance, they were taken to Gestapo headquarters to fix bars on the windows there. Michael's father, Zisman, managed to find a job in a food distribution centre and got a little extra food for the family. They were always hungry.

Conditions in the ghetto became worse as more and more people came in from other countries. They lived in constant fear of deportation, although at this time they had no idea of the existence of extermination camps.

In September 1942, there was a curfew lasting several days and during this time, the ghetto's children, elderly and infirm were taken away. The Lewkowicz family managed to stay together and Michael continued to work in the factory. Some of the young people organised themselves into a kind of resistance. When the foreman pushed them to work harder and harder, their aim was to go slow because this would obstruct German production. Michael said this wasn't officially sabotage, but it also helped them because by working more slowly, they conserved a bit of energy.

Life continued in the ghetto, with ever-worsening conditions, until late August 1944 when the family were rounded up by the Jewish police, herded into cattle trucks and taken to Auschwitz. This was the last time Michael saw his family.

At Auschwitz, Michael was tattooed with the number B8405 and then transferred to a nearby camp called Gleiwitz. From there, he was marched every morning in a line of prisoners to a factory where trains were repaired and serviced. He was allocated as a labourer to a German who specialised in repairing train wheels. At midday the prisoners were given a bowl of soup. At the end of the day, they were marched back to Gleiwitz, where they were fed a bowl of soup and piece of bread.

Gleiwitz was evacuated in January 1945 when the Russians were approaching. For the next two weeks, the prisoners were marched in freezing weather away from the advancing Russians. This was one of the notorious death marches, and anyone who could not keep walking was shot on the spot.

They eventually arrived at another camp called Gross Rosen, which Michael always said was the worst camp he was in, "a hell on earth". After a few days there, they were put onto open rail trucks and taken to Weimar, and from there to Buchenwald. After several weeks in Buchenwald, he was then transported to a satellite camp of Dachau called Allach.

Towards the end of April 1945, Michael was once again put onto a rail truck, and this time the plan was to take the prisoners into the mountains and kill them. The train was shunted back and forth as the American army was advancing. Then one morning, the prisoners awoke to find that all the German guards had disappeared. For the first time in years, there was no one giving Michael orders. He always said how strange that felt and for the first time in years he cried. He joined up with a group of Russians and they walked until they came across a farm. On the way, Michael found a boot lying in the road which he put on. A little further along, he found a dead German soldier lying in the road with the other boot still on. He then had a pair. Once at the farm, they killed a pig and ate it. Not used to this type of food, he was then very ill.

The following day he was picked up by the Americans and taken to hospital, where he remained for some time recovering his health. He was then placed in a Displaced Persons camp south of Munich, which was run by the United Nations Relief Organisation. He stayed there for two years, and during this time the Red Cross traced some of his relatives in England. There were no other survivors from his father's large family in Wielun or his mother's in Vitebsk.

Michael came to England in 1947 to live with an uncle. His father was the youngest of twelve children and some of his brothers had come to England before the war. He settled with his Uncle Max and found employment working in a leather goods factory. After a few years, he and one of his colleagues decided to go into business on their own and started their own factory, manufacturing handbags and purses. He bought his own house in the same road where he had lived with his uncle. He married his wife, Ivy, in 1963 and their daughter, Dvora, was born in 1966.

As he neared retirement, Michael took up painting in oils and attended evening classes learning about the history and architecture of London, a city he loved. He was granted the Freedom of the City in 1989. Once he retired at the age of 70, he pursued his love of the arts, visiting art galleries, enjoying the theatre and concerts, especially opera.

He returned to Poland a few times: the first time with a group of fellow survivors in 1990 and the second with his wife and daughter. He told his story at Beth Shalom Holocaust Centre and accompanied a group of teachers to Poland. Stephen Smith, co-founder of Beth Shalom, once asked Michael how he had dealt with memories of the Holocaust period, personally, emotionally and psychologically. He replied, "I have tried to analyse how I dealt with it. Probably by forgetting. Erasing a lot of things from my mind. When I went to Auschwitz some years ago, another member of the group asked me, 'How come you are so normal?' Now I never considered myself to be either normal or abnormal. So maybe the answer is that I've erased a lot of things from my memory."

Michael told Roman Halter, a fellow survivor, that he had a special feeling at Beth Shalom. "My family who all died in the *Shoah* [Holocaust] have no grave. Whenever I go to Beth Shalom, I somehow feel that their souls are residing there. It is for me an important place of calm – *Shalom* – dignity and spirituality. I hope that it continues to be that in times to come."

Michael died on 17 July 2002. His story was written by his daughter, Dvora.

In memory of my grandparents Zisman and Dvora Lewkowicz, Uncle Joseph and the family from Wielun and Vitebsk who perished in the Shoah. I shall always miss not knowing you.

Michael's father Zisman with his brother Joseph

Michael after Liberation, Felderfingen, 1946

Trude lighting a candle at the Yom Ha Shoah commemoration, Beth Shalom, 2002

TRUDE LEVI

"She Isn't Worth a Bullet"

April 23 is my birthday. Every year it reminds me of my 20th and 21st birthdays.

I was born and brought up in Szombathely, a provincial town on the Austrian border in Hungary. My mother came from Vienna and was a language teacher. My father was Hungarian, a gynaecologist, but he also worked as a general practitioner. We had many books, made music and altogether I grew up in a highly interesting and cultured environment. We had little money because my father was a left-wing socialist and he treated many of his patients without asking them for payment.

From 1938 onwards, when Hitler annexed Austria, and throughout the war when he occupied European countries, refugees came to Hungary. They told us stories about Jews being beaten up and dragged away, never to be heard of again. In those days there was no TV, and without seeing starving children, emaciated and murdered people for ourselves, we simply could not imagine that man's inhumanity to his fellow man could be so great. We didn't believe the stories we were told.

In 1944 I was nearly 20 years old and worked as a nursery school teacher in Budapest. Though we did have restrictions imposed by the anti-semitic Hungarian Government, the Jews of Hungary were at that time the only ones who had not been deported. It seemed that we had escaped the fate of all the Jews of Europe. It was obvious that Germany was losing the war and we hoped that soon all would be over.

But on 19 March 1944 we found that German tanks, soldiers and machine guns lined the banks of the river Danube. When no one expected it any more, we were occupied.

First we had to buy a yellow star and sew it on our garments. Courageous Christian friends offered to hide me in Budapest. However, I decided to go home and join my parents. I had to apply for a special permit to travel. The journey was long and on arrival after the curfew for Jews of 6 p.m., I was subjected to extremely unpleasant treatment while walking home from the station. It ensured that I was never homesick again.

At home I found my 49-year-old mother had collapsed into a confused, old woman. Our flat had been searched for subversive literature and my father dragged away as a political prisoner on 22 April. My parents had intended to celebrate my twentieth birthday a day late as I arrived on the 24th.

A ghetto for Jews was created in the centre of our city. On 7 May my mother and I were moved – with one piece of luggage each – into a small room with four other women. Before that, we had to hand in our bicycles, jewels, savings bank books and cash except a few pennies. We stayed there for seven and a half weeks, with little food, until the end of June when we were marched into our first concentration camp.

Before we were allowed in, we were searched. Some people had sewn some small jewels into their clothes. If these were found on them, they were beaten and thrown into the camp already dead. The ground was polluted and filthy and we slept there. In the morning I heard a call for 50 volunteers to go to a neighbouring town. I dragged my mother to the assembly place and pushed out an older woman to enable us both to get into the group. We travelled by train for an hour and were taken to our next camp where by chance we met my father, of whom we had had no news for the past two and a half months. We did not even know if he was still alive. In pushing away that old lady, I behaved very badly, as never before or since, but it was worth it. We were now together, the three of us.

After two days, we were put into cattle-trucks – 120 of us in one truck. We sat squashed, back-to-back, knees pulled up, tightly. Although men, women, children and strangers were packed together, we had to overcome our inhibitions to use the two buckets for our human needs. The muck spilled over and we sat in it. There was little air and people became dehydrated. They became hysterical, screamed, went mad; some had heart attacks and died. We travelled for five days and five nights. On the sixth day we arrived in Auschwitz. The ramp was near the chimneys. My mother had collapsed and had to be dragged out of the truck. Hopefully she no longer understood what was happening to her. She was taken in the direction of the chimneys – from which smoke and stench poured out from the burning bodies – and this was with us day and night while we were in this extermination camp. Nearly 90 per cent of the Hungarians were killed on arrival. Men and women were separated and this was the last time I saw my father.

We younger women were taken into a very cold hall, stripped naked, and all the hair on our body was shaved by SS men. We were given one piece of clothing, no underwear, no shoes, after which they marched us away into another part of the camp called Birkenau. We were in B camp.

The part of the camp we were in consisted of very large wooden barracks with nothing in them, only powdery, yellowish-greyish soil. Wherever one looked, the same soil surrounded the numerous barracks. Around the entire complex there was electrified barbed wire, watchtowers with soldiers holding machine guns. Not a blade of grass or tree anywhere.

We were 1,200 people in the barracks, squeezed in like in the cattle-trucks. It was not easy to sleep in such a position. Though it was a very hot summer, at night the temperature dropped near to freezing. We had dysentery (severe diarrhoea) and when we had to go to the latrines – which was often – we had to climb in the pitch-dark over the sleeping bodies. Some people didn't remember where they were when they were suddenly woken by people climbing over them in the dark. When they started to scream, the soldiers shot into the barracks. The latrines were guarded by SS men and they found it very funny not to permit us to finish our business. We became filthy, stinking, disgusting as we had no access to water, either to wash or to drink. The same happened when we menstruated, although this happened only once because the body does not waste its energies uselessly.

We had to stand for hours to be counted in rows of five next to the barrack. The SS women were not very good at counting and it took a long time. Afterwards we received our so-called coffee, a brownish lukewarm liquid, vital for us because in the intense heat we needed liquid and we had none. It was given to the first in the row of five in a medium-sized pot. There was very little left when it arrived at the fourth or fifth row where I usually stood. Yet every drop was absolutely vital for us – it meant survival.

After coffee we could disperse, but there was nowhere to hide from the sun. We did not even have our hair to protect us from sunstroke and sunburn. At midday we had to stand again to get our lunch. It consisted of a tasteless soup, but it was liquid and that was important. Then a piece of bread – it should have been an eighth of a loaf, but a slice of bread meant money – one could buy cigarettes, a scarf, maybe water, maybe underwear or shoes with it. Some aggressive mates who distributed the food kept a lot for themselves and their closest family or friends, and did not worry about those whom they robbed. We sometimes received a piece of sausage and/or cheese which were salty and made us even more thirsty. This was our only meal in 24 hours.

Many collapsed from illness, dysentery, thirst, hunger and other causes, and if they were seen to be weak, they were dragged away and never heard of again.

We arrived in Auschwitz on 7 July and were put through a large 'selection' on 2 August when we were either sent to the right or the left by the camp commandant Hoess and the principal camp doctor Mengele. I was sent with others to the left. We were allowed to go on living; those sent to the right were exterminated. Then there followed a shower – it could have been gas – we did not know which until the water started to flow. We felt happy to be able to clean ourselves and drink even if the water had been poisoned. We were shaved again on our whole body in the ice-cold hall, thrown one piece of clothing and chased out.

We were told to sit down and – oh, miracle – we were given a plate of real soup and a chunk of bread. Then we were put into cattle-trucks once again. We travelled through the night and nearly the entire next day and arrived in Hessisch-Lichtenau, a small town, five and a half kilometres from Hirschagen, the second-largest munitions factory near Kassel in mid-west Germany. We had come to be slave-workers in the factory.

The camp was beautiful; there were trees and grass and flowers. The barracks were divided into rooms with 16 two-tier bunks in each. All of us received a bunk with a prickly straw-sack and a rough blanket. The sack was full of bedbugs that had a feast on me regularly. We received clothing and underwear and women with normal-size feet received shoes. I had large feet and received wooden clogs from time to time, but they broke soon and most of the time I was barefoot. Walking barefoot in pine forests and ice or snow is not to be recommended. We also received a number printed in large figures on a brick-size piece of white cloth, which we had to sew on the back of our garment. We had no names, no faces, only numbers. I was 20607.

Our commandant Willy Schaefer was not a sadist, but did everything according to the rules. We arrived in Hessisch-Lichtenau, one of the 136 out-camps of Buchenwald concentration camp, on 3 August. He made a speech: anyone trying to escape would be caught and shot. Two women escaped in September. They were brought back and given a spade each to dig their own graves. They were shot into them and we had to watch all the time, then bury them. This was according to the rules.

Schaefer always stood by when the bread was distributed to see that every piece was cut exactly the same. The bread got smaller as time went by but we always had our bread, except for two days. Our second commandant, Ernst Zorbach, was a sadistic creature with a whip in his hand when in camp, and we tried to make sure that we were nowhere near him.

In camp we also had to work occasionally. Our two SS women guards came and asked for the appropriate number of women for any job. If you volunteered, there was a chance of extra soup and you were treated decently. If no one came forward, they chose the number anyway and the people were treated badly. The job had to be done, so it made sense to volunteer. One day, they needed two people, and a campmate and I went with the guards. We were taken to a small hill. Schaefer, the commandant, stood there with his beautiful dog dead at his feet, and we had to bury him. This was at the beginning of October; it had been snowing and the soil was nearly frozen. It was hard work. When we had finished, the commandant thanked us, and from then on he greeted me when he saw me in camp. I had became a person once again, at least for this man.

A few days later, he was called back to Buchenwald to get new orders. During the two days he was away, we had no bread. On his return the bread distribution continued, though the slices became thinner and thinner.

A few days later I was standing near the two SS women guards and they were talking about how they had sold our bread and how much they earned for it. One of them said, "Don't speak, she – pointing at me – might understand." "Oh, that one is an absolute idiot, I even tried to teach her some words in German but she can't retain a single word."

Was it my facial expression that gave me away? I am a bad liar. My mother tongue was German and I understood. But I always denied it and made myself look like an idiot. I didn't want to have any dealings with the guards, men or women. A sort of personal resistance. Now they asked one of the collaborators and she gave me away. They wanted to bribe me, to make me a work-leader who had privileges. It was tempting, but work-leaders also had duties. To push around their mates, to spy on them, denounce them. I wanted to survive but not at any price – I had a choice about how to behave. I did not want to live without my integrity.

I thanked them but said no. Before they left, they said "You'll pay for this." A few days later, they returned and sent me to the assembly place. We were counted there every day, but this was not the normal counting time. I did as I was told and went. Many women came from all directions. When we were all there, our *Kapo* (supervisor) fetched the camp doctor and the commandant Schaefer. They counted us. We were 208. I was only told later that one of Schaefer's orders after going to Buchenwald was that the camp doctor had to count how many had been to her surgery during the past week. That week, there were 206. As Schaefer did everything according to the rules, he only had to deal with 206. So he took two people out. In the document I have which proves this, you can see that one of the altered numbers was 20607: my own number. The 206 were sent back to Auschwitz, never to be heard of any more. We two were to continue to survive.

We were a group of a thousand Hungarian Jewesses, sent to Hirschhagen to be slave-labourers. When we arrived, the factory foreman came to inspect us and said, "We requested workers not skeletons." So for the first couple of weeks, we were better fed and didn't have to work. We had to walk five and a half kilometres to the factory, which was in a forest on top of a steep hill. We walked about two hours, then worked a ten-hour shift, then walked home exhausted and hungry because there was no food for us at the factory.

The part of the factory where I worked produced flying bombs. They were pear-shaped, with a round rod and seven wings. They were shells which had to be filled with explosives. The people in the mixing room were mainly chemists chosen for their profession. These chemists and the workers in the filling room soon turned yellow from the materials they worked with. They were called the 'canaries'. Some of them died a terrible death through poisoning. Some of us decided that we did not want to help the German war effort and we organised a sabotage group. The bombs were soon filled with mixture that would not explode and we inflicted other damage to the bombs as we worked. We had to be very careful. It was very dangerous because if we had been found out, we would have been tortured to reveal who else was part of the group, and then killed.

My work was to screw a Bakelite (plastic-like) cap very tightly onto two of the bombs simultaneously as they passed by on the conveyor belt. When there was no supervision, I put the cap on on the slant or very loosely. The monotonous work drove me crazy. I volunteered for another job and became 'the horse'. I had to take two of the finished bombs as they came off the belt – they weighed 25 kg each – and, catching the wings, place them on a heavy flat iron trolley. Sometimes they fell and I had a toe and a nail damaged. I had to pull the trolley out of the hall, set it on rails and let it go slowly down a steep hill. In the offloading bay I tried to damage the bombs: smash the cap and bend the wings. It was quite dangerous work and depended on the person working the brakes. At the beginning a German worker operated them. He hated everything about Hitler's ideas and helped us when he could. When he was on the brake, I had no fear; I knew that he was looking after me. He also brought in tiny bits of bread or onion wrapped in newspaper when there was news of a German defeat, the advance of the Allies, anything that gave us hope. Sadly, he was transferred soon after he was discovered helping another mate. I had partial amnesia at the end of the war and could not remember his name. I have tried to find out but to no avail. I would have liked to thank him for his humanity. Any decent gesture meant a tremendous lot to us.

At the end of March 1945 there was no more material in the factory and our camp was evacuated. We were taken back east, to Leipzig. In the first camp we were bombed out and I lost a good friend. It had been an SS camp up to a few days earlier. The Americans obviously did not realize that the SS had moved out and we were now there. It was cold and snowing. I was barefoot and in a sleeveless flannel shirt. We were taken to the next camp called Tekla, where there were already many other men and women prisoners from various camps. There were approximately 15,000 of us. We arrived there on 7 April 1945. On 12 April, we were put onto the road for our death march. Someone gave me a threadbare striped jacket.

The German guards put their belongings onto wooden trolleys which we had to push and pull. We were made to walk fast in rows of five. A small American plane often accompanied us. When they saw a German uniform, they shot. The German guards put striped prisoners' jackets over their uniforms.

They marched us to the river Elbe in the direction of Dresden. The Americans were drawing near from the west, the Russians from the east. We walked in an elliptical circle, on each side of the river, nearly the same route six times. The ground was still frozen where we slept. We received no food at all. Anybody who could not get up in the morning, or who collapsed, was shot on the spot. There were fewer and fewer of us. On the tenth evening, we were on the Russian side of the river. A Russian plane flew in a circle round us in a forest clearing not far from the river. On that night, 22 April, we were given something to eat. The Germans shot a horse in front of us and we were thrown bits of raw horsemeat as if to dogs. Then we had to queue for a handful of uncooked rice which we couldn't bite. Our teeth were falling out – the gums could no longer hold them. We slept there. Very early in the morning, the guards got us up and led us to the bridge. I could hardly drag myself. It was dark. When we got there, the sun started to rise and I experienced one of the most beautiful sunrises of my life. When we got to the American side of the river, the sun was up and I collapsed. I knew that this was the end and I no longer minded. Two guards came, they shouted at me to get up, but I could not. They butted me with their guns and then one of them said, "Oh, leave her, she isn't worth a bullet any more."

And they actually left me to chase those who could still walk. It was 23 April, my 21st birthday.

Because I did not return to Hungary, I lost my nationality. I became stateless. An outcast. No papers, no residence permit, no work permit. I often worked illegally, was cold and hungry, travelled with a false passport. It took me 12 more years to obtain a nationality and become a recognised civil being again.

I dedicate this story to the future, namely to my grandson Jonathan,
my granddaughter Marina and my great-grandson Paul Ilan Fernand,
having the luck still to enjoy them.

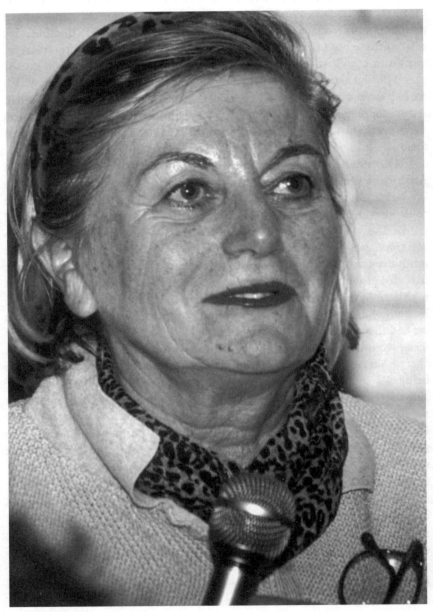

Malka Levine, 2001

MALKA LEVINE

"Look after the Children"

I was born in 1939 in a town called Vladimir-Volinsk in western Ukraine. I am one of three children and my two brothers, Chaim and Shalom, also survived the Holocaust. The rest of my wider family – 78 people in all – were all killed, including my father. My mother also survived and this is very unusual: she is the only woman I know of who managed to bring three children through the Holocaust.

When I was only three years old, in 1942, we had to go into the ghetto, leaving our home and all our possessions. The Germans gathered all the 25,000 Jews in our town and put them into one quarter. They surrounded it with fences and put notices outside, saying that the people in the ghetto were suffering from typhus. This made sure that the Christian population would have no contact with us and would not try to come in or bring help. So we were cut off from the rest of the world.

Many of the Jews in the ghetto prepared hiding places because they could see what was going to happen. But my father didn't believe that anything would happen to us. He just thought it was a terrible time that would eventually pass. Every day, he was taken out of the ghetto to work.

One Friday lunchtime, we were all sitting at the table – my grandparents on my mother's side, my other grandmother, my two brothers, myself and my mother – when the SS and Gestapo suddenly rushed into the ghetto and started shooting at random. We hadn't planned a place of shelter, but our house in the ghetto stood on stilts, about a foot off the ground, and there was a trapdoor leading to the area underneath the house. My mother grabbed a satchel, put in a bottle of water, some honey and a loaf of bread, and ushered us all down under the stilts. My mother's sister and her husband decided not to come with us and went instead up into the rafters of the house because they thought that if their newborn baby started crying, everybody would be discovered. So they went into the roof of the house and we hid under the floor on the earth.

The Germans meanwhile were looking for people in the ghetto, shouting and shooting. They came into the house, tore and broke everything and

265

looted people's possessions. For three days, we lay there under the floorboards. We had run out of food and water, so when things were quieter, my father decided to go up and search for some provisions for us. He also wanted to see if my mother's sister was safe.

He went back up into the house and when he returned, he passed another jar of honey, another loaf of bread and more water through the trapdoor to my mother. They were talking to each other very quietly at the trapdoor entrance. My mother asked what had happened to her sister, her husband and three-day-old baby. Father didn't reply at first, but then he said that they were no longer there. Suddenly, as they were talking, the trapdoor was quickly shut. That was the last time we saw my father. We heard footsteps above. Father knew that if he jumped back through the trapdoor, we would all be discovered, so he sacrificed his life for us. His last words to my mother were, "Look after the children," and this became her mission, the only thing she could cherish. I was three years old, my middle brother eight and my older brother ten.

We stayed there under the floor for 15 days. From time to time, the SS, Gestapo and Ukrainians came back to the ghetto and were still looting, screaming and shooting. But they did not even think that someone might be hiding under the stilts because it was so low, with so little room. The Germans even came with their dogs, but they never sniffed us out. We could see the hems of their coats, the bottom of the Gestapo's boots, but were not discovered.

When things had quietened down, mother crawled out surreptitiously to try and find us some food. She knew the town very well; before the war, we had owned some land that we let out to farmers, so she knew where to go at night, and she would bring back a tomato, a beet or raw potato. Every time she crawled out we were always worried that she might not come back, but she always did. In the dark at night, she couldn't see what she was picking and sometimes the fruit was unripe. To this day I can't eat red tomatoes. I only like them green because I didn't know they were supposed to be red!

When the shooting seemed to stop after we had been hiding for 15 days, mother decided it was time to come out. She hoped that the Nazis had quenched their thirst for Jewish blood. We had lost our father and many members of our family. In that first pogrom, the Nazis had shot 15,000 people.

When we crawled out of our hiding place, there were Germans everywhere, and about five miles out of town, they were making Jewish people dig holes and trenches. They were told the trenches were going to hold ammunition for the war, but they were really pits into which people were shot. Those trenches became three enormous graves: 25,000 people were taken there and shot, layer upon layer of people, machine-gunned into the pit.

After this, the Germans created two ghettos – one for the living and one for the dying. The people who were still useful to them were given work permits and they were sent to the "living" ghetto, but the older people, the children, the weak and the sick were put into the other ghetto. This meant that at any time, day or night, the Germans could come up and round them up and kill them.

My mother was a real fighter and went straight to the "living" ghetto. When she was asked what work she could do, she replied that she came from a farming family and could work in the fields. At first, they didn't want to give her a work permit – they only wanted to give them to the men. But my mother fought and fought, and eventually succeeded She was really determined to live. She was the only woman in the ghetto with a work permit.

She was taken away every morning at 5 a.m. and worked either in the fields or barracks. When she came back at night, she always brought a beet or potato from the fields, which she had hidden under her clothes for us to eat. That was how we lived for another nine months.

Then, suddenly, the shooting started again in the ghetto in the middle of one night. We children always slept with our clothes on because we never knew when we might have to flee. That was the start of the second pogrom, the second Action. While all this shooting was happening, we just tried to weather the storm. We tried to hide in one of the buildings: my grandmother and middle brother in one room; my mother, older brother and I under the bed in another.

This time, we were not so lucky. The Germans discovered us when they were looking for items of value. But they didn't find my older brother and mother begged him to stay hidden and save his life. They were rounding people up and taking them to the prison, where they lined everyone up in the yard. From there, people were taken by lorry, 33 at a time, men and women separate, to the killing pits, where they were shot. When the Germans found us, they took us to the prison – mother, my middle brother and me.

Mother thought that my older brother would perhaps be able to escape somehow. My father used to own a bicycle shop and we had a lot of contacts with Christian people in town. People bought their bicycles from our shop and also had them repaired there. So when my older brother was trying to escape, a Christian man recognised him and said, "You're Fischman's boy, aren't you?" (Fischman was our family name). This man had a business making duvets and cushions, and he offered to help my brother escape from the Germans. He took him in, gave him food and said to him, "You see, we have a room full of feathers. We'll hide you in the feathers." But my brother decided against this: he wanted to find the rest of the family. "Whatever happens to them, will also happen to me," he said.

My brother then came to the prison looking for us. We were standing there in the prison yard. It was a bitterly cold winter, blowing a gale. I had no shoes on, my coat was undone and we had had nothing to eat. There were some political prisoners in the prison who were not Jewish. One of them saw my mother, recognised her from the bicycle shop and asked her what she was doing there. Mother replied that she was doing just the same as the rest of the Jewish people – being taken to be killed. And I remember to this day how that man threw down a loaf of bread and some garlic to us. We were so grateful. We were so hungry that we ate that bread very quickly, even though we expected to be shot in an hour or two.

Men and women were separated when the Germans took people to the pits. At first, they wouldn't allow the boys to go with mother and me, but she begged them. "Please let me undress my own children and, if they die, let them die in my arms." Eventually they allowed us to stay together. Then we were lined up and they counted the next victims, one to thirty-three to a lorryload. My grandmother was number 33 and my mother 34: the groups divided between them. I was number 35 and my brother came after me. So we saw grandmother taken on the lorry to her death.

While we were waiting for the next lorry to come for us, we suddenly saw my uncle (my father's brother) arrive at the prison yard. He worked in a factory and knew a high-ranking German *Wehrmacht* army officer. His own wife and children were already dead, but he had appealed to this army officer for help, saying that his wife and children were in prison and were going to be shot. The *Wehrmacht* officer and my uncle rushed to the prison and that's how he was able to save us. Nobody could believe it. It was an absolute miracle because if my mother or I had been number 33, we would have been on the previous lorry. My uncle asked where his mother (my grandmother) was, but she had already been taken on the lorry. It was too late to save her. You could see his agony. What was happening was beyond human comprehension. In that massacre, they killed another 10,000 people in those trenches.

My uncle took us back to the ghetto. There were now only about 500-600 people left and we were among them – my mother, my two brothers and me. Again, mother had to go out to work. The ghetto itself was run by Jewish police and some of them were very vicious: they beat people up – including my brothers. So my mother took the boys out of the ghetto to a

Christian friend of hers, who kept them hidden in a cupboard for a while. But when it was quiet again, they came back to the ghetto.

After a time, the Germans started some rumours, telling all the Jewish people who were in hiding that they should come back to the ghetto; they would be repatriated and nothing would happen to them. But my mother did not believe this and sensed that something awful was going to happen. They were going to make the area *Judenrein*, free of Jews, a kind of ethnic cleansing. One of my mother's cousins, Rachel, still lived outside the ghetto because she had foreign papers stating she was a Christian. Mother appealed to her for help, asking if she knew anybody who would hide us. Rachel said it was difficult with three small children, but she would try to help: she would take my middle brother to live outside the ghetto and my older brother would go with the uncle who had saved us. At the time, a group of men, ten or twelve of them, were making plans to escape from the ghetto and hide in the marshland near Pinsk, a very harsh terrain where they thought they would be safe. My older brother was going to go with them and they suggested that mother and I would perhaps have a chance to survive there as well. Mother thought about it for a day or two, but eventually she decided that we should all stay together as a family.

So she talked again with Rachel and asked her to try and find a place where we could all be hidden together, where she could perhaps work on the land or in the house. Rachel thought of a Ukrainian acquaintance of hers called Ribke who had relatives who were farmers in a village called Biskovich. That family agreed to hide us until the war ended.

Very early one morning, mother then smuggled us out of the ghetto, through the wires, all three of us. We went to Ribke's house and waited for the farmers to come. But when they arrived and saw us, they didn't want to take us at first, especially the old man. Mother begged him. The farmer's wife was a religious woman who believed in God, and she told her husband "Listen, if you don't take them, I will. They'll be my responsibility. If they're caught, I'll tell the Germans you didn't know a thing about it." There was a lot of arguing between the farmer and his wife, but eventually the wife won and they took us to the village hidden in a wagon.

We had only been in their house for a few days when suddenly, there was a knock on the front door. We were in the back room. We heard Germans talking, the SS and the Gestapo came in and we were sure that somebody in the village had seen us. We knew that if the Germans found us, they would kill the whole village. We really thought they had come for us.

The farmer made a sign to his son to take us through the back door into the barn, and we waited there for a few hours, in terrible anxiety. Then the old man came and told us that we would have to leave. He wanted to help us, but had to think of his own family and the rest of the village. Mother started begging him and asked what had happened. It turned out that the Germans had not come looking for us, but they were going to establish a school right there in the farmhouse, to train Ukrainians to work with them.

While we were talking, the farmer's wife came in; she knelt down and made the sign of the cross. The arguments started between them again: the man kept saying that we had to go and the woman insisted she would take responsibility for us. He asked her, "What are we going to do with them? The Germans will be in the house." And she replied, "We'll dig a hole in the ground, in the barn, and cover it with twigs." The old man told his wife she was absolutely crazy, and he started screaming and shouting again. But she had the upper hand

So they dug the hole in the barn and we hid there, covered with twigs. It was freezing cold because we didn't have many warm clothes, no blankets. I was the only one small enough to stand up in the space – I was only five years old. We hid there, not knowing what was going to happen to us, for nine solid months. The Germans were all round us – we could hear them. One day, when they brought their horses to the barn where we were hiding, the old man told them, "Oh, no, no, no. You can't put your horses here. You're very important people. You must have my stables!" So the Germans put their horses in the stables and the old man put his in the barn.

Then one day, the horses started galloping right on top of us and the hole was completely demolished. We felt as if we were being buried alive. Luckily, the Germans were away on manoeuvres that day. The old man took us into the house and said they would dig the hole out again. As we ran into the house, a little village boy saw us and told his parents that the old man was hiding Jews. The boy's parents came to the farm and complained, and the farmer was afraid that the little boy would tell somebody. But they took him to the priest and made him swear before the Madonna that he would not say anything. If he did, he would be killed – and the rest of the village as well. And the boy kept it secret.

We were in the house for a few days, then we had to go back to the barn to hide because we knew the Germans were returning. We were in that living grave again. Then my mother became very ill with bad pleurisy, and for days the farmer and his wife couldn't bring us any food or water because the Germans were everywhere, preparing for the last fight. Mother crawled out at night and brought us a little basin of snow to eat, and for a few days, we ate just snow and ice. Mother had a terrible cough, but she couldn't even risk coughing because the Germans would have heard her. So we all had to sit on top of her so she couldn't cough and give away our hiding place. We all thought she was going to die.

After that, things got a bit quieter and the Germans went away for another day of manoeuvres. The farmer's daughter-in-law came and mother begged her to help. The only thing mother had left was her wedding ring, and she gave it to her, asking her to bring some medicine – hot water with dried camomile – so she could inhale and breathe better. That was how mother gradually got a bit better. But when the farmer's wife saw the ring her daughter-in-law was wearing, she asked her where it came from. She made her take it off and came to apologise to my mother. If there was an angel on earth, it was that old lady.

We had grown to recognise the footsteps of the old woman and the old man as they came towards the hole. Suddenly one day, we heard strange footsteps and our hearts stopped. Then there was a very quiet voice, calling my mother's name. It was Ribke, the man who had found the hiding place for us. He told my mother, "I know the conditions you are living in here are awful, but there are no survivors at all in the ghetto. At least you're still alive, just try and hold on." He gave us some hope that day.

We carried on hiding there for another two or three months. Then one day, we heard somebody coming and this time we recognised Ribke's footsteps. He told us, "The town has been liberated, you can come out, but I think you should stay another week or two because there might still be some Germans or hostile people about."

About a week later, after nine long months, we crawled out. My mother came out last and she was wearing a scarf. She threw it into the air and, as if she was speaking to our father, she said, "Here are the children! Here they are!" She had kept her promise to him.

This testimony is dedicated to my mother.

The Yakimchuck family who saved our lives, early 1950s

Steven aged 16, in 1942

STEVEN AND WALTER MENDELSSON

Hot Tea and Egg Sandwiches

I was born in 1926 in Breslau, Germany (now Wroclaw, Poland), a city the size of Sheffield or Liverpool, and my home was one of culture and love of music. My father played the violin and my mother the piano; they spent many evenings making music and entertaining their large circle of friends, both Jewish and Gentile. My mother also wrote beautiful poems, many of which were published. We were members of the large liberal synagogue, one of the celebrated buildings of the city.

My brother Walter was born in 1930 and we four led a happy, comfortable life until spring 1933 when Hitler came to power. This event signalled the decline of Jewish life throughout Germany.

I remember those days in the local junior school, where most of my friends were not Jewish. Together we kicked footballs around (occasionally breaking a neighbour's window), and went scrumping for apples and pears, skilfully avoiding being caught by the owners. We organised bicycle races in the side streets of the suburbs where we all lived.

Round about 1936 – just after the Olympic Games had been held in Berlin – many of my friends at school and in the neighbourhood suddenly started to avoid and ignore me. I challenged one of them to explain. Diffidently, he said, "My father forbade me to play with Jews." This was a bitter blow to my self-confidence – my hitherto happy social life had been blown to bits.

Soon after that, all Jewish children were expelled from German state schools. Fortunately, an existing small Jewish school was extended to accommodate the new pupils. There was no shortage of well qualified Jewish teachers since they had all been dismissed from German schools quite some time earlier. Soon I acquired new friends – all Jewish of course – and all seemed well for the first few weeks. But then serious problems developed at the end of the school day. Hordes of young Hitler Youth boys from a nearby German school appeared outside our school gates and as we were leaving for home, they started to lay into us. There were lots of them – we were outnumbered by about three to one – and they beat us up. In the daily fights that ensued, they often had us on the floor, hitting, beating and kicking us to their hearts' delight. It was a common daily occurrence and we ultimately reached our homes bruised, aching, bleeding, our shirts torn and satchels rifled through.

In November 1938 the Nazis unleashed a well prepared pogrom across the whole of Germany. Remaining Jewish shops were ransacked and their windows broken, which gave the name *Kristallnacht* (Night of the Broken Glass) to the operation; and synagogues were set alight and destroyed.

In addition, Jewish men over 16 years of age were rounded up and sent to concentration camps – Dachau, Buchenwald and Mauthausen. My father was deported to Buchenwald. Many detainees died there due to brutal systems of torture, humiliation and starvation. My father, thank G-d, survived – but only just. He was released after 14 weeks or so and arrived home one morning in a very sorry state. He could hardly stand up and was confined to bed for many weeks under constant medical care. We boys – Walter and I, by then aged 8 and 12 – were not allowed to see him. My mother thought that seeing him in that state would be too traumatic an experience for us. We had to tiptoe around the house all those weeks so as not to disturb him.

Early in March 1939 – a few weeks after my father's release from Buchenwald – a letter arrived offering two places on a children's transport *(Kindertransport)* to England, where we would be safe. England was the only country that was trying to save 25,000 Jewish children from ultimate extermination by the Nazis. My mother was confronted with a momentous decision. With my father recuperating slowly from his treatment at Buchenwald, she was now challenged to let go of her children, in all probability never to see them again. She had numerous sleepless nights pondering all the while what to do. With her boundless love for her children and her faith in the Almighty, she decided to let us leave the paternal home for a foreign country. She knew that at least we would be safe – whatever might happen to her and our father. Her incredible courage and sacrifice are aspects for which we, her children, are eternally grateful.

The departure soon followed – emotions were at breaking-point. For us, two young lads, it seemed like an exciting adventure, a long journey by train and boat into a land of enormous opportunities. The rest of the family – all of whom came to the station to see us off – felt quite the opposite. I remember the tears and the agony on their faces – parents, grandparents and others – waving us goodbye as the train pulled out of the station. The memory is still as vivid in my mind today as if it happened only yesterday.

The train journey took us across Germany and into Holland. From there we boarded a ferry to cross the sea to Harwich, and then we travelled again by train to London. We were in a group of 20 or so children, the youngest aged about six and the oldest, a girl of just fourteen.

The Nazis permitted us one suitcase, which we had to prove to them that we could carry. It was stuffed full of clothes. Like almost everyone else, Walter and I each wore two sets of underwear, a shirt, a sweater, a jacket and an overcoat – all items in ever-increasing sizes – for while our parents knew that we would not starve in England, they did wonder who would supply us with clothes as we grew bigger.

In Harwich we were greeted by a band of ladies who hugged us, kissed us and embraced us for what seemed an eternity. Although it was still only early spring, we were all very hot (with all those clothes on), very tired, thirsty and hungry. The good ladies distributed cups of hot tea and egg sandwiches, which struck us as very odd. In Germany, under similar circumstances, we would have been given a cold, refreshing drink and perhaps a juicy orange or two.

The train from Harwich to London Liverpool Street station, the last leg of our tiring journey, took us through the East End of London. On either side we saw rows and rows of derelict houses with caved-in roofs. Some houses, apparently still occupied, had broken or boarded-up windows. Our hearts sank; we were dismayed at the sight and started to long for our parents to comfort us. But they were no longer there to take care of us: they were left behind in Nazi Germany.

This tremendous culture shock, the absence of our beloved, caring parents, the odd "refreshments", the new, strange language, and yes, even the differing weather, presented huge obstacles at first that we would have to overcome.

Walter and I, with some other children, were ultimately accommodated in a hostel in Margate which was run by B'nai Brith, a Jewish charitable organisation. We were 60 boys there, ranging from 8 to 16 years old. My younger brother was one of the four youngest. We were taught to say "please" and "thank you" and with that extensive linguistic know-how, we were integrated into local schools. After some early weeks of mutual unease, we soon made friends with our new English peers and began to get the hang of the language. We also played a lot of football and a few of us even took a liking to cricket. Today we all drink hot tea to quench our thirst and I just love egg sandwiches.

Postscript: Our mother's courage and her faith in the Almighty were richly rewarded: our parents arrived in England 36 hours before Britain declared war on Germany, thus closing all avenues for refugees to reach these isles. We are amongst only five per cent of children saved by Britain through the

Kindertransport who were reunited with their parents. The vast majority of the *Kindertransport* children never saw their parents again – they perished in the Nazi death camps. So too did all other members of our family.

Walter aged 15, in 1945

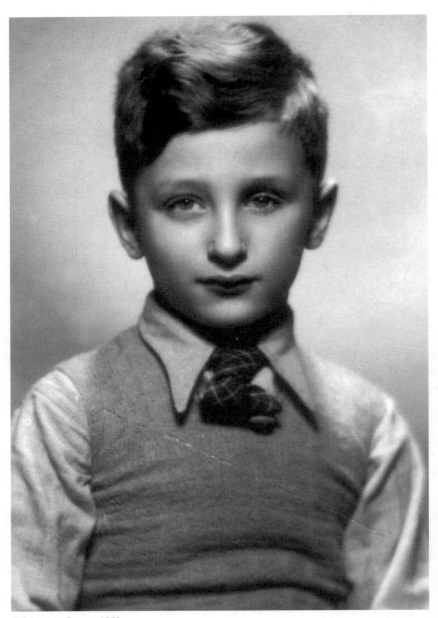

Bob Norton, Prague 1939

ROBERT NORTON

Refugees from the Nazis

I was born in 1932 in a small spa town called Teplitz Schönau, some 30 miles from the Saxon-German border in northern Czechoslovakia. It was a pretty town nestling in the foothills of the Ore Mountains with forests and lakes where we played in the summer, and skiing in the winter. The town had its theatre, opera house, coffee houses and of course its Spa House, which had the reputation of curing most ills. My family were well-to-do middle class, assimilated Jews and not very religious. Teplitz Schönau had 3,000 Jews and I think we were related in one way or another to most of them, however distantly. As a family, we observed the main Jewish holidays and were members of the synagogue which my great-grandfather or grandfather had helped to build.

My parents came from quite different backgrounds but both grew up in the central European world of the Austro-Hungarian Empire. Czechoslovakia was created after the 1914-18 war, mainly from three Slav lands and peoples, the Bohemians, the Moravians (these were the Czechs) and the Slovaks, in addition to many other ethnic people. There were at least nine different languages spoken and officially recognised. Where I grew up, the first language was German, then Czech; in parts of Slovakia, it was Slovak and then Czech.

My father was born in abject poverty in Budapest, Hungary, and migrated to northern Bohemia in search of work. He found work in the area where I was born and became apprenticed to a knitwear manufacturer. Eventually, after the First World War, he and a friend started their own knitwear company. This grew and prospered so that by 1938 it was employing some 400 people, and its merchandise was being sold both within the country and abroad.

My mother's family had lived in Northern Bohemia for at least 200 years. Her father was a GP, as well as being the non-executive director of the Spa. He was one of the first Jews to be educated as a doctor at university. In previous times, Jews were not allowed to enrol in universities unless they converted to Christianity. Two generations before him, there were also doctors in his family, but they had been apprenticed to other doctors and were really a mixture of paramedic and pharmacist. Grandmother came from a wealthy and old established family of traders in grain, horses and textiles.

My mother was one of three sisters, who after marriage each had one child. Whilst my parents and aunts and uncles were not strictly Orthodox Jews, we observed the main Jewish festivals of Hanukkah, Purim, Passover, Rosh Hashanah (New Year) and Yom Kippur. I remember very vividly going with my parents, uncles, aunts and grandparents to the service on the eve of Yom Kippur. Men in their dinner suits, ladies decked out in their best clothes. I was awed by the large, circular synagogue with its beautiful Bohemian crystal chandeliers and the choir singing the ancient liturgy. To this day, in my mind, I can see the scene every year during the Yom Kippur evening service.

On some festivals (and sometimes other) occasions, the whole family would be summoned to appear for lunch or dinner at my grandparents' large house. The table was set with white monogrammed damask table-cloth and napkins, the best silver cutlery and fine Bohemian glasses. Children had to be on their best behaviour and after the meal had to go to the kitchen to thank the cook and maids for a lovely meal. My parents and relatives had a full social life, mixing with their Jewish and Gentile neigh-bours, among whom they had lived all their lives.

I started my education when I was five and a half at the local German-speaking junior school. I remember my first day, standing with a lot of my friends with a large cornet of sweets. It was the custom for all children to receive these sweets on their first day "to sweeten the start of school". In those days, we were immediately taught the alphabet and "counting". We did not play as children do in today's primary schools. In the right seasons we went on holiday to the mountains, often as groups of friends or relatives. We often visited my aunts, uncles, grandparents and others in our extended family.

Once a year, we would go to visit my grandmother in Budapest. Since my father had become well to-do, she had no more money worries as father financed her life and that of his sister, who suffered from multiple sclerosis. Grandma spoke German well, but with the typical Hungarian sing-song accent, often interspersed with odd Hungarian words which to this day I can still remember. She would take me to the zoo, to special parks and often to lunch at well known restaurants because they were a treat for her too. My parents employed an au-pair, a girl from the Czech-speaking areas, so that I would learn the official and main language of the country.

In September 1938 this life stopped abruptly. The British Prime

Minister, Mr Chamberlain, had appeased Hitler, the dictator of neighbouring Nazi Germany. He had ceded the German-speaking part of Czechoslovakia to the German Reich on the promise that the main Czech and Slovak lands would be left in peace, and in fact that the rest of Europe would be left alone. "Peace in our time", Chamberlain proclaimed on his return to England.

I was stopped from attending school, the majority of our Gentile friends stopped speaking to us and crossed the street when they saw us. Jews were excluded from schools, public offices and jobs. Property and bank accounts were confiscated and frozen without compensation. Most Jews fled to the central Czech lands, but they had to pay a heavy price in the form of a "Jew Tax". This was levied on those wishing to leave, based on their now non-existent "wealth".

Like all the others, my father had his property, business and flat confiscated, but his bank accounts were not closed, nor was he charged a Jew Tax. By an oversight in 1918, he had not applied for Czech citizenship and as a consequence retained his Hungarian citizenship. On marriage my mother became Hungarian and on my birth I acquired my parents' citizenship. Hungary was a fascist dictatorship, friendly towards Germany, but at this time protected its citizens, even the Jews. The Germans respected the situation and whilst property was confiscated, cash was allowed to be moved.

We fled to Prague and rented a small furnished flat as most of our possessions had been confiscated. Father and all the other refugees from the north of Czechoslovakia tried to restart their lives. I was not allowed to continue schooling because no school would accept German-speaking Jews, in spite of the fact that I spoke Czech well. On 14 March 1939, Hitler decided not to honour his non-aggression agreement and invaded the rest of the country. We watched the Nazi troops, arrogant and menacing, march past our apartment into Prague. The Gestapo immediately started to arrest people, including my father's business partner.

In those first weeks, my father, uncles and most other Jews spent all day, every day, queuing at embassies for visas and entry permits to enable them to emigrate. Without a foreign visa, German exit visas were not given. A lucky few obtained visas if they had relatives in other countries or good connections.

Life for Jews became more desperate by the day as hope faded. By chance one day, I watched a man in an apartment block opposite us commit suicide by jumping off the roof. My mother's cousin committed suicide by gassing herself and her daughter, a playmate of mine. My parents whispered among themselves about this one or that one who had vanished. Finally, my parents got a visa to America because an elderly uncle in the USA was willing to vouch for us. With that entry visa, we were able to obtain a transit visa for England. And with these visas, as a Hungarian citizen, father was able to obtain a Nazi exit permit with relatively little problem, provided we went to Hungary.

Just prior to our departure, my eldest cousin, who was seventeen and a half, contracted a marriage of convenience with an English businessman and left for England. My other cousin got a place on a *Kindertransport* arranged by the Englishman, Mr. Nicholas Winton, who it later turned out had saved hundreds of children. They left their parents behind, still trying desperately to find a means of escape.

We left for Hungary with three large suitcases and stayed a week with my grandmother. After a tearful goodbye, we went by train through Austria and Germany to Holland. I remember clearly a Jewish man boarding the train in Düsseldorf and joining us in our compartment. He told father that he was on his way to Holland to start a new life. Just before the Dutch border, he unpacked his modest lunch of sandwiches and an apple. He was just peeling his apple when the Gestapo border guards appeared. His papers were not in order and he was ordered off the train, leaving behind his knife and apple. As he left, he wished us a pleasant onward journey – his own was almost certainly to death. We kept his knife for many years as a memento of a very brave man.

We stayed in Holland for a week with a Dutch friend of father's and then boarded a ship from the Hook of Holland to Harwich. During the voyage, my father took me on deck and showed me the sea, which I had never seen. We saw buoys in the sea which my father explained marked the territorial waters of Britain. So we arrived at Harwich in July 1939 with our suitcases, very little money and my mother's few words of English. We boarded a very funny little train bound for London.

In London we rented a small room with a gas ring and fire in Golders Green, the centre of the German Jewish refugee colony. My parents soon found friends from the home country who had managed to escape. They met daily, trying to arrange shipping to the USA, to exchange news from home and generally talk about conditions in Europe. On 3 September, war was declared, normal shipping to the USA was stopped and most refugees were trapped.

The news from Europe was not good. Some letters got through via neutral countries such as Sweden or Portugal. The last letter my parents received was from my aunt, who wrote that the following day they had to report to the railway station to be "re-settled in the East", i.e. Poland. After the war we discovered that sometime in the middle of 1942, they were ordered to report at the station at 6 a.m. with one small bag or case. They were loaded into cattle trucks – the young, the old like my grandparents in their 70s, children like my second cousins and playmates – and were transported for three days to Poland without food and water, and within hours of arrival gassed and burnt.

In 1940 we got permission to reside in England for the duration of the war. In that year the London blitz started and I was finally allowed to start school, but each school where I started was bombed a few days later. So I had no education, I spoke very little English and for obvious reasons had no English friends of my age. With my parents, we mixed exclusively in the refugee circle where there were some children of my age. Most nights we slept on Swiss Cottage underground station to avoid the bombs. By day I collected bomb shrapnel from the streets: you could hand it in and were paid two old pence per pound weight. By the end of 1940, father decided that we would go to live in Leicester, where he had business friends from before the war.

We arrived in Leicester and rented a small house in Wigston, a south Leicestershire village. I started school, speaking hardly any English and was something of a curiosity to my fellow pupils. Dressed in central European winter clothes (including wool tights), I was quizzed whether in my homeland people lived in houses and whether we had dogs. On hearing that German was our main language, I was immediately labelled a German spy. My father had to report to the main police station each week, the house radio was taken away and a bicycle left in the shed was also taken away in case we were spies. Some weeks later, the radio was brought back by a detective, who, unknown to us, lived just across the road. He told us that if we found it less embarrassing, he would pop round once a week rather than father having to report to the police station. So every week Sergeant Honey came round for a cup of tea and chat, and remained a friend of father until he died twenty years later.

My parents were not allowed to work according to their temporary permit to stay. They were running out of money, so they worked illegally until the end of 1943 when they were given permission to work and earn some money. In the meantime, I played with children in my street, went to school, learned perfect Midland-dialect English and ceased to be a curiosity. The war brought many German-speaking Jewish refugees to Leicester and they formed an inclusive social circle, from which they and my parents never broke out until their deaths in the 1980s.

The war came to an end in 1945 with the terrible revelation of what had happened to our relatives in particular, and to our people in general. At a family conference we decided we had nothing to go back to except horror:

as we had lived in England for five years and become settled, we would continue to live here rather than move again to America. In 1949 my parents applied for British citizenship and proudly signed their oaths of allegiance to the Crown. So as a minor, I too became a British subject.

At the age of 54, father started a tiny clothing factory with the help of friends, in which the whole family worked. After school I helped for a few hours, then went home for supper and homework. I finished my secondary education and carried on at the local Technical College with a three-year diploma course in Textiles. Father retired some years later and sold the company, which had grown to employ some 50 people. I grew up in Leicester, made many lifetime friends and eventually married a local Jewish girl, to whom I have been happily married for some 43 years. We have two married sons and three wonderful grandchildren.

For many years I worked as an export sales manager for large clothing companies such as Courtaulds, Coates Viyella and a number of other companies, covering the whole of Europe, the Middle East and occasionally North America. In the mid 1970s, my wife and I started our own company, acting as export agents and supplying corporate clothing to companies in Britain. Over the years we built our business into a sizeable distribution company and we were 50 per cent owners of two small factories, employing some 60 people. In 1997 we sold our business to a competitor and retired. Like many similar survivor-refugees, I have contributed to Britain and repaid in a small way the enormous debt we owe to our adoptive country for the sanctuary we received, for our lives and those of our children and grandchildren.

In memory of the millions who died,
and to all of our children and their children, may they live in peace.

The family's safe arrival, London, 1940

Eve, Paul and Rudi at Beth Shalom, 1999

EVE, RUDI AND PAUL OPPENHEIMER

The Last Train From Belsen

Every Holocaust survivor has a different story. This is certainly true for the story of the three Oppenheimer children, Eve, Rudi and Paul, who were fortunate to survive for five years under the Nazis in Holland, and in the camps of Westerbork and Bergen-Belsen, and who finished up on 'The Last Train from Belsen'.

Our parents, Hans and Rita Oppenheimer, lived in Berlin. We were a typical middle-class family of assimilated Jews, who rarely ventured into a synagogue. Paul and Rudi were born in Berlin in 1928 and 1931, respectively.

With the advent of Hitler and the Nazis, life became progressively more difficult for all Jewish people living in Germany. Many Jewish families wanted to leave Germany, but most other countries would not accept these refugees. Our father, Hans, worked at the Mendelssohn Bank in Berlin which had a branch office in Amsterdam in Holland. He had managed to obtain a transfer to the Amsterdam branch in 1936 and the family went to live in Holland, near the seaside in Heemstede. These were happy days for the Oppenheimer children, but they only lasted for four years.

In May 1940, the Germans invaded Holland and within five days, the Dutch army surrendered. The Germans occupied the whole country, took over its government, and soon started to persecute the Jews who lived there. Anti-Jewish laws were introduced in an insidious step-by-step manner to restrict the life of all Jewish people in Holland. We were not allowed into public places like parks, zoos, restaurants, hotels, museums, libraries and swimming pools. We had to attend Jewish schools. We had to live in Amsterdam. We had to wear the yellow star. We had a curfew. We had to hand in our bicycles. We were not allowed on the bus or tram.

Then the deportations started for "re-settlement in the East" and gradually all the Jews in Holland were transferred from Amsterdam to Westerbork, the transit camp in the north-east of Holland near the German border. From Westerbork there were regular weekly transports to the extermination camps of Auschwitz and Sobibor. Out of 100,000 deportees, less than 1,000 survived – 1 in a 100 survived, but 99 out of 100 never came back...

Our family was rounded up in Amsterdam in June 1943 and sent to Westerbork, but we were exempt from deportation to Auschwitz or Sobibor because our sister, Eve, was British. She had been born in London in 1936 during a six-months spell when we were living with an uncle and aunt in London, on our journey from Germany to Holland. This fortunate event eventually saved our lives. In Westerbork, Eve and our family were classified as "Exchange Jews", people the Nazis wanted to exchange against Germans held by the Allies. After seven months in Westerbork, in February 1944, all five of us were deported to Bergen-Belsen in Germany. By this time, Paul was 15 years old, Rudi 12 and Eve was only 7.

Bergen-Belsen

We travelled by train in third-class passenger coaches and arrived early in the morning at another camp, called Bergen-Belsen, or Belsen for short. We had never heard this name before and had no idea what it was like. But as soon as we marched into the camp, we could see that it was even larger than Westerbork – and much worse. In addition to the barbed wire and guard towers, there were electrified fences and lots of SS soldiers with bloodhounds, machine guns and searchlights. It was a real concentration camp.

We had certain privileges in the Exchange Camp in Belsen. We were allowed to wear our civilian clothes with the yellow star and our camp became known as the Star Camp. We did not have to wear the usual black-and-white striped pyjama outfits. We did not have our hair shaved off. We were allowed to keep our luggage, a suitcase full of clothes and books and games.

But like other concentration camp inmates, we lived in barracks, male and female, and we slept in three-tier bunk beds. Every morning, we lined up in rows of five to be counted on the assembly yard. We received three "meals" each day – a mug of warm brown liquid in the morning (substitute coffee), a bowl of turnip soup for lunch and about one and a half inches of bread in the evening.

Although Paul was 15 years old in Belsen, he did not have to work – and Rudi and Eve were also too young. We were confined to the Star Camp, surrounded by barbed wire. We had a broom to sweep our barracks, and were not allowed any schooling, or games or sports. We messed around in groups of kids, looking for scraps of food, and wasted our time. We did nothing all day; every day was the same, it was extremely boring.

We arrived at Belsen in February 1944 when it was cold, but we were in reasonably good condition and could cope. Then it was summer and not too bad. But it was the last winter of the war, 1944-1945, when it all went wrong. We had been in Belsen for more than six months and were very hungry, under-nourished, starving, exhausted skeletons. The daily roll-calls became more and more traumatic. We had to stand in line for hours, even in the rain, sleet and snow, when it was freezing cold and the icy winds blew across the heathland area around Belsen.

This was when many people fell ill with diarrhoea, pneumonia, tuber-culosis and various other illnesses, and they were unable to resist or recover. In January 1945 our mother fell ill; she went into the hospital barracks and we visited her every evening. We never knew what precise illness she had because there were no doctors, no nurses and no medicines. And there was no extra food. We could see that she was getting worse, but there was nothing we could do to help her. And one evening when we came, she was no longer there. She had died and her body had been taken away to make room for someone else in the hospital barracks. Our mother was not yet 43 years old and we realize now that we never really got to know her very well.

It was particularly bad for our sister Eve because she was only eight years old at that time and all alone in one of the female barracks. Fortunately, an Orthodox family called Birnbaum, who had six children of their own, offered to look after her during the last few weeks in Belsen.

Early in 1945, a typhus epidemic broke out in the camp, transmitted by lice. There were lice everywhere – in the barracks, in the bunk beds, on our bodies, in our clothes. We were always itching and scratching and we spent hours "hunting" the lice. They used to breed in the warm parts of our bodies and we were never able to get rid of them. Most people who died in Belsen, died of typhus – along with other diseases, starvation and exhaustion.

In March 1945 our father fell ill and he went into the hospital barracks. We went to see him every evening, but after a few days, he was no longer there. He had also died, almost certainly of typhus. He was 43 years old; he had survived for almost two years in the camps and died within one month of Liberation. It was very sad.

At this time, 600 people were dying in Belsen every day, including Anne Frank and her sister Margot in another section of the camp. But we realized that the Allies were winning the war. Eventually we could hear the Allied guns approaching Belsen and we looked forward to our liberation and freedom. But there was another ordeal in store for us because the Germans wanted to keep the "Exchange Jews" as hostages and the Star Camp was evacuated. All the inmates were marched to the nearby railway loading ramp and we boarded the third of three trains. The other two trains departed; the first one was liberated by the American army within just a few days, the second one may have reached Theresienstadt, the perceived destination of all three trains.

The Last Train

The third train – the one we were on – was the last to leave Belsen, on 10 April 1945, composed of passenger coaches and cattle trucks. It travelled in a northerly direction, taking the remnants of the so-called privileged prisoners from the Star Camp: some 2,500 people out of the original 4,000; the others had died. Another 500 unfortunate "Exchange Jews" would not survive the train journey and the Liberation.

On the day we left, the British army was just 20 miles from Belsen. We missed being liberated by this short distance. Five days later, on 15 April 1945, the British army liberated the camp, but our train had travelled some 25 miles north towards a town called Lüneburg. And this became the pattern of our train journey; we slowly moved forward ahead of the British army. We had SS guards on the train, but no food at all.

Our train was attacked by Allied planes on several occasions because the Germans had attached military equipment to the back of our train. Whenever we had an air attack, the train would stop and we were allowed off. We would lie in the fields and watch the Allied planes swoop down and attack the train. It was very exciting, but we did not feel in danger. On the contrary, whilst experiencing the air attacks, we would look for food because we had absolutely nothing to eat on the train. We collected anything that looked edible, such as grass, leaves and raw potatoes. After the air attacks, we carried our "food" onto the train. We lit fires on the train platforms and cooked our grass, leaves and potatoes for our meals. That is how we lived on the train as we slowly moved across Germany in an easterly direction.

We passed through Berlin on 19 April 1945, just before the Russian army got there and just before Hitler committed suicide in his bunker. We remembered that we used to live in Berlin ten years before, but it was not a happy home-coming. We saw Berlin in ruins, bombed, flattened, destroyed, and in flames, but we felt no pity for the German population. We saw schoolboys dressed in military uniforms, ready to defend the German capital. We fancied our chances of survival better than theirs.

As the Russian army approached from the east, our train turned in a southerly direction, and we continued our nomadic life: whenever the train stopped, we collected food. Unfortunately, the typhus epidemic never left us and many dear colleagues died during the journey. There were regular burial ceremonies every day by the side of the railway track.

Eventually, on 23 April 1945, after we had been on the train for two weeks – but travelled only about 500 miles – we woke up in the morning and noticed that the SS guards had disappeared. And when we looked out into the distance, we could see soldiers on horses. They were Russian Cossacks from the Red Army and we were liberated; we were free...

Liberation

Liberation was a massive anti-climax. There was no hugging, no kissing, no laughing or singing, not even hand-shaking or dancing. Most of us had not been "free" for five years, since the German occupation of Holland in May 1940. We were in no mood and in no condition to celebrate. Perhaps surprise, relief and excitement best describe our feelings when we realized that we had finally been liberated.

The Russians wanted to know who we were. This was quite difficult to explain because we could not speak Russian and the Russians could not speak Dutch, the language we spoke on the train. And we did not dare to speak German in case they thought we were Germans and might shoot us. Eventually the Russians understood that we were on their side and against the Germans, and they let us loose.

Not surprisingly, we were obsessed with food – or rather the lack of food – after more than a year in Belsen. We all went hunting for food. Paul collected loads of grass, leaves and potatoes, as usual, for everyone on the train, because many people were ill and could not forage for themselves. But Rudi and his friends were much more enterprising: they went into a nearby German village called Tröbitz, entered the shops and helped themselves. If they encountered any trouble, they got a Russian soldier to sort it out. They came back to the train with bread, butter, milk and honey. They were not impressed with Paul's grass and told him to do better next day!

On the next morning, we all went off hunting for food again and Paul found an abandoned factory where they made tubes of cheese paste, and he also found a wheelbarrow. He came back to the train with this great, big wheelbarrow, full of tubes of cheese paste for everyone on the train. He thought he had done well this time. But Rudi and his friends went back to the German village and this time they went into the German homes, into their cellars where they kept their goodies, and they came back with preserves of meat, vegetables, fruit and gateaux. They were not impressed with Paul's cheese paste! They had also acquired watches and radios and Rudi had a motorbike; "organising" we called it.

Rudi and his friends had appreciated the new situation much quicker than Paul, who blames his poor performance on his poor state of health. His body, and especially his legs, were very bloated and swollen and he had some difficulty moving around. Apparently this condition, called oedema, is caused by an excess of fluids in the tissues, in his case due to severe malnutrition. It often precedes death.... Paul's condition actually got worse because the next day he and Rudi had spots all over their bodies. It was typhus and we were both taken to a Russian army hospital in a nearby town called Riesa with high temperatures, fever, delirium and all the other symptoms of typhus. But we must have received very good treatment from the Russian doctors and nurses because we both survived, and a few weeks later were ready to leave the Russian army hospital.

We then found out that the war was over: Germany had been divided up into four parts: British, French, American and Russian, and we were in the Russian zone. We explained to the Russians that we wanted to return to Holland, and as a first step we were transported to Leipzig, which was in the American zone. We had to explain to the Americans who we were, where we came from and where we wanted to go. It was all quite difficult; we did not have much paperwork or documentation, but eventually the Americans agreed to repatriate us back to Holland. We were put onto an open truck which would take us to a railway station, and from there a train would take us to Holland (and Belgium and France for other survivors). Just as we went out of this camp in Leipzig, another open truck came into the camp with lots of little children on board, including our sister Eve.

This is a very embarrassing part of our story, because somehow we seem to have forgotten our sister Eve and had actually lost her. We cannot explain how this happened, except that life was very confused at the end of the war and we had plenty of problems ourselves. We know that during the last weeks in Belsen, Eve was looked after by the Birnbaum family in their "orphanage". And we also know that they were evacuated from Belsen on the same last train as us, but they were in a different carriage. And they were liberated near Tröbitz, just like us. But we seem to have spent all our time looking for food and we never looked for Eve and never made contact with her. Then we got typhus and were taken away to Riesa and eventually finished up in Leipzig. By that time, we seemed to have forgotten about her. There was nothing we could do about it anyway.

Thus it was a miracle when we suddenly saw our little sister Eve in Leipzig. If our truck had left five minutes earlier, or Eve's truck had arrived five minutes later, we might never have seen our sister again. This would have been very bad in itself, but also we had only survived because of Eve's British nationality and we owed it all to her. We now know that without Eve, we would have been deported from Westerbork to Auschwitz or Sobibor, and our chances of survival there would have been slim. It was very bad of us to have forgotten about our sister.

We stopped the other truck, Eve joined ours and we drove to the railway station. The train took us to Holland and we arrived in Maastricht in June 1945. From there we contacted our uncle and aunt in London. Our uncle was in the British army and he came to Holland in September 1945 and took Eve straight back to England. As she was British, she could get in. Paul and Rudi were refugees once more, "Displaced Persons" they called us, and we had to apply for visas to enter England.

We lived in a Jewish orphanage in Laren, went back to school, but six months later, in November 1945, we got our visas and came to England. We lived with our uncle and aunt in London for some time. We were very lonely; we had lost both our parents in Belsen and our four grandparents had been killed in Sobibor. We made a new life in England and for the next 40 years, we never talked about our wartime experiences. No one asked us about those terrible times, no one seemed to be interested and we did not particularly want to talk about our misfortunes. Gradually, we forgot those childhood experiences, as we adjusted to a normal life in England.

It is probably fair to say that Eve was the most affected by her ordeals. She was only a child during her years of captivity, bewildered by the ominous circumstances, terrified by the uniforms of the authorities, unable to understand what was happening and totally devastated by the deaths of her parents. She was lonely in every sense of the word; she had no friends for many years and her childhood had been denied.

Eve experienced great difficulties in adjusting to normality in England. She was sent to a boarding school in Hove and hated the school environment. The other children had families and a normal existence, but nobody made the effort to understand her unusual and tragic life. Soon after, Eve was accepted into the Lingfield House children's home. This was a most remarkable home for 24 children who came to England in 1945-46. Most of them had been rescued from the concentration camps. The home was run by Alice Goldberger, a wonderful lady, loved and admired by all who knew her. The children were encouraged to lead normal lives and they received lots of love and care to help them gain the strength to cope with future years. Fellow survivors, such as Rabbi Hugo Gryn and Ben Helfgott, paid regular vists to Lingfield House during that time. Eventually, Eve started work in her uncle's gloves business and she moved into her own flat in Highgate. Eve enjoys her close relationship to the expanding Oppenheimer family. Indeed, she is the favourite aunt amongst the younger generation. She keeps in touch with her Lingfield colleagues and is happy among other child survivors.

Rudi was always the adventurer. Alert, quick-witted and intelligent, he sensed danger and used his natural abilities to avoid it. He was also tremendously inventive, finding ways of helping the whole family from an early age. In Westerbork, when he was just 12 years old, he watched what was going on and learned the art of survival. In Belsen, he was in charge of dishing out the food in our barracks – a job of the utmost importance. Rudi undoubtedly remembers the war years much better than Eve and Paul.

On our arrival in England, Rudi lived with our uncle and aunt in north-west London and with their friends from the refugee community. Rudi became an engineer, studying at Imperial College, London, from where he graduated with a degree in electrical engineering in 1953. After serving a two-year apprenticeship with BTH (British Thomson Houston) in Rugby, he worked for Shell for 34 years and spent time on overseas assignments, including several years in Venezuela. He completed his career with Shell at their head office in The Hague, Holland, living in his own house in nearby Wassenaar. Rudi is now retired and has returned to England. He has integrated within the UK survivor community and is a great supporter of Beth Shalom, the Holocaust Education Centre in Newark, Nottinghamshire.

He regularly relates his wartime experiences to students from schools all over the country – for Beth Shalom, for the Holocaust Educational Trust, for the London Jewish Cultural Centre, and he is also associated with the Anne Frank touring exhibition. His speaking engagements have become the major preoccupation in his life and he really enjoys his conversations with students and teachers.

Paul also stayed with our uncle and aunt in north-west London for the first year of his return to 'normality'. He wanted to become an engineer and went to live in Birmingham, in a hostel with pre-war refugees. He completed a five-year apprenticeship and worked nine years for the BSA group of companies, followed by 34 years with Lucas-Girling. Paul studied in the evenings to obtain an engineering degree and became a professional engineer in the motor industry. He wanted to become British and applied for naturalisation at the first opportunity in 1951. His only contact with the Jewish community was via sports: he played football, tennis and table-tennis.

In 1964 Paul married Corinne Orme, who was not Jewish. After the birth of their three children – Nick (1965), Simon (1967) and Judith (1970) – Corinne converted to Judaism and became closely associated with the Birmingham Progressive Synagogue. The three children attended Sunday school and became Bar and Bat Mitzvah, and Corinne and Paul also attend weekly services – a major change for Paul, compared with his pre-war secular lifestyle. Paul and Corinne have been blessed with four grandchildren: Alex (1996), Beth (1997), Josh (2002) and Yoni (2002).

In 1990 Paul was awarded an MBE by HM The Queen at Buckingham Palace. One month later, in April 1990, he returned to Belsen with Rudi and Judith for a commemoration ceremony. That was the beginning of a whole new episode in his life, when he started to remember and talk about his former life, his childhood and the Holocaust. The talking has never stopped: in schools, colleges and universities, at Beth Shalom and to adult groups, beyond 500 talks in total, including more than 100 at Beth Shalom. Despite increasing transportation difficulties, the full attention and positive reaction from students and teachers, in their questions and subsequent letters, makes it all worthwhile and enables Paul to make a constructive contribution to society, even in his later years. Many students tell him they will remember his lecture for the rest of their lives, and hopefully this will help to prevent such persecutions of 'different' people in the future. Everyone should be equal, no one should be afraid. And doing nothing may not be enough.

Dedicated to our grandchildren, Alex, Beth, Josh and Yoni and their generation.

A more comprehensive version of our story was published by Beth Shalom Ltd. in 1996, *From Belsen to Buckingham Palace* by Paul Oppenheimer.

Before the war in Heemstede, Holland – Paul, Eve, Rudi and our mother Rita, 1937

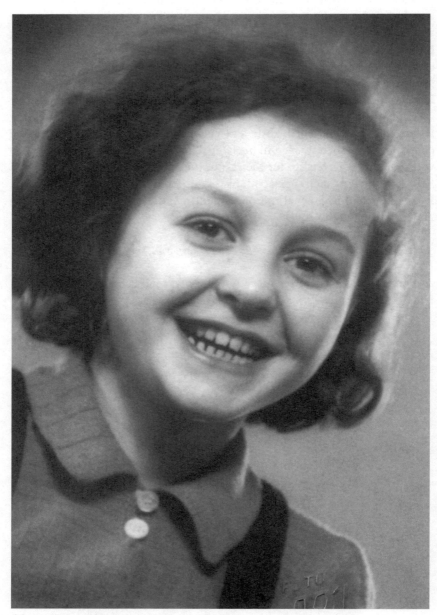

A happy 10-year-old in Prague, 1938

SUSANNE PEARSON

I Would Never See My Parents Again

I was born Susanne Ehrmann on 11 April 1928 in a town called Moravska Ostrava in what was then Czechoslovakia. My father, Paul, was born in Brno in 1900 and studied engineering at university. His father was a lawyer. My mother was born in Moravia in 1904; her father was a stationmaster. My parents met and married in Ostrava where I was born. We moved to Prague when I was four years old for my father's job.

We lived in a flat in Vinohrady, where I continued to live the indulged life of an only child of a middle-class family. I had many friends and as well as school, spent my time reading books, going swimming and doing gymnastics, having piano lessons and ice-skating in the winter when the river froze over. We went to concerts and the opera, and in my last summer at home, father took me walking in the Tatra Mountains.

My mother had many friends, loved parties and nice clothes. We were both members of the *Rote Falcons*, an international youth movement which had links with the Woodcraft Folk in this country, mother as a helper. I have happy memories of the camps we went to. At that time, we little knew that it was probably the membership of this organization that would save my life.

In 1938 we moved to a larger flat and so were able to accommodate families from Germany and Austria who had fled from Hitler. Their arrival brought the reality of what it meant to be a Jew in the occupied countries. I also began to realize that changes were taking place in our daily life. My parents listened anxiously to the radio and looked worried at what they heard. They had always had lots of friends who called at our flat, coming for a meal, talking and laughing. Now, if anyone came, the curtains would be drawn before they sat down and talked together in hushed, anxious voices. It seemed that because we were Jews, and even though we were not observant Jews, we were in great danger. I found this very difficult to understand, because I did not think I was any different from my friends, most of whom were not Jewish.

I have a vivid memory of the panic when we heard about the occupation of the Sudetenland, and the total desolation we felt on 15 March 1939 when the rest of Czechoslovakia was occupied.

That was a day I shall always remember. My parents had listened nearly all night to the radio which was giving out continuous news about the invasion, and they were looking more and more worried, until in the end I started to cry, wondering what was going to happen to us. My mother tried to comfort me, but must have found it very difficult because she knew how great the danger was for us. I did not want to go to school, but father said I must – our lives must carry on as normal for as long as possible, and so I went to school as usual. As an eleven-year-old, it was my last year in primary school; I had already secured a place at a Czech *Gymnasium* (grammar school), and my parents had high hopes for my future education.

At school the teachers also looked anxious, particularly it seemed to me, when they looked at me and the other Jewish children. They tried to carry on school as normal, but then, in the afternoon, an order came that all the children were to be taken out of school to line the route where the Nazi troops would be coming. Nobody wanted to go, and many of us cried, but the teachers said we must, otherwise they would get into trouble. It was a cold March day, and we put on our hats, coats and gloves in silence. We then walked to the main road which ran alongside the river and were told where to stand, lining the pavements, and were given flags to wave. We knew they were not the flags of our country, but belonged to the invading army we were now being made to greet. The flags, which bore the hated swastika emblem, were made of paper and many of the children tore them and threw them on the ground. This again made the teachers look very worried, and they urged us to pick them up. They were clearly afraid of the men in the menacing-looking uniforms who were now passing in front of us, riding on tanks, in armoured cars and on horseback. It was a very sad day for us, for our town and country.

My parents and most of our Jewish friends were now seeking ways to leave the country. This was proving impossible as the world had closed its doors to Jewish refugees. However, there were efforts made to bring out children, particularly by a British stockbroker called Nicholas Winton who was on holiday in Prague. He realized the plight of the Jews and resolved to do something. He gained permission from the British government to bring out children, providing he could find families to care for them and a guarantee of £50 per child for re-immigration. In this way he made it possible for 1,000 children to come to Britain. However, the start of the Second World War prevented the last transport leaving, but nevertheless he was able to rescue about 680 children.

The demand for places was very high, but I was probably given one because the Woodcraft Folk in England were able to offer 20 homes for *Rote Falcons*. They were prompted to do so having met up with some of us at a camp in Brighton in 1938. It is difficult to know how my parents felt when they learned that they had been successful in their application for me to be one of these children. I have often wondered, particularly when my own daughters were the age I was then. The decision my parents made to send me must have been a very brave and difficult one, because they knew they could not come with me. Nor did they know whether they would ever be able to join me.

My transport left Prague on 29 June 1939 with about 241 children aged 2-15. I find it difficult to remember how I felt on that day when my parents took me to the railway station, and I became one of the children on one of the last trains to safety before the war started. Perhaps it seemed an adventure, and I certainly did not realize that I would never see my parents again. I understand that the few adults who accompanied us had to return when we reached the Dutch border. Our journey through Germany was uneventful. The train stopped in Holland where people from the Red Cross brought us cocoa and cake. We boarded a boat in Rotterdam, a new experience for most of us, and arrived in Harwich the following morning.

Our group remained together and we were taken to a Woodcraft Folk camp in Epping Forest. We stayed there for an acclimatisation week and were then collected by our carers. Just one other girl and myself came to Sheffield, the others mainly stayed in the London area. I stayed with the same family for the next five years. They were keen members of the Woodcraft Folk, so there were many camps and hikes to go on, and young people to mix with, activities I was used to. They were of course difficult years. I missed my parents constantly and worried about what was happening to them.

After my arrival, I received nearly daily letters from my parents, always expressing the hope that they would be able to join me soon. Mother, who was a good cook, was taking lessons in English cookery, and Father, being a qualified engineer, would surely be needed somewhere. These hopes and letters came to a sudden end when war was declared. In fact I only ever received two or three letters after that, and part of the reason for this – which I discovered many years later – was that they were deported to Poland in October 1941, on the first deportation of Jews by the Nazis from Prague. On the day before his deportation to Lodz, my father wrote to me, "Despite all the difficulties, life here has been good with the love and goodness of the people around us. In the office and at home, I have been surrounded with love and friendship and I remain convinced that man is good and that all the badness arises from the bad organisation of society. I do think that after the horrors of this war, people in all countries will demand more fairness and more mutual understanding, so that the next generation will be spared this tragedy."

In Sheffield I started school, apparently learnt English quickly and left at 14 after a rather patchy education. I went to work in an office, and then at 16 as a nursemaid in a small children's hospital. I liked the work, and so went on to train as a nurse at a hospital in London. Then the war ended, and eventually I got the news of my parents' deportation to the ghetto in Lodz. This news was sent to me by my father's secretary: my father had left with her a letter for me and some belongings. I knew my father to be a resourceful man who would have tried to contact me if he were still alive, and so I realized that he and mother were not likely to be returning.

At first I thought of going to Europe to look for them, but soon began to recognise the impossibility of this. When my boyfriend (who was then in the forces) suggested I go back to Sheffield to stay with his mother, I rather grasped at the idea. I continually tried to get information about the fate of my parents, but it was only in the 1970s that I learnt that my father's death is recorded in Lodz in October 1942. My mother was still alive there in 1943, but after that there are no records and I do not know how either of them died.

The past 50 odd years have certainly given me the opportunity to catch up and recreate. I married, and initially trained and worked as a Nursery Nurse. After the birth of our first two daughters, 1 became involved in the Pre-school Playgroup Movement and my husband and I also became foster parents for the Local Authority. We fostered young babies and the fifteenth of these eventually became our third daughter.

When she started school, I recommenced my studies at the age of 37, first getting the necessary academic qualifications to enable me to do a three-year teacher training course. I then had a 22-year career as an infant teacher, the head of an inner city nursery school and lecturer in early years' education.

In my later years I still have many interests. I have a long-standing involvement with volunteer groups who support parents and children and have been a Samaritan volunteer for many years. In 1985 I was involved in the setting up of the Anne Frank Exhibition in Sheffield. This resulted in my being invited into schools to talk about my own experience. Initially I found this a very difficult thing to do, for like many others in similar circumstances, I had divulged very little of my past. I am now persuaded that this is a worthwhile thing to do, and continue to visit schools and other groups, as well as being invited to give talks at, and on behalf of, the Beth Shalom Centre in Nottinghamshire.

I have been well rewarded; a long marriage, three successful daughters and seven lovely grandchildren. I have also been honored with two awards: an MBE for services to Education and an Honorary Doctorate from Sheffield Hallam University. Lastly, I think myself fortunate still to have the energy for my family and several voluntary organizations, as well as continuing to give talks on Holocaust Education. My own beliefs remain intact. My Jewishness is a positive part of myself, although I am not obser-vant. I am on the left of politics, and like to think of myself as tolerant and anti-racist. My hope is that by telling my story, it will help young people to begin to understand what can happen to ordinary people when they become the victims of racism, discrimination and prejudice.

For my parents, who in our short life together gave me so much love and taught me how to enjoy the good things in life.

Grateful to have reached 75 and to be able to enjoy my seven grandchildren, 2003

*Josef about three months after Liberation, still wearing
striped camp uniform.*

At Beth Shalom, 2002

JOSEF PERL

Faces in the Smoke

My name is Josef Perl and I was born on 27 April 1930 in the town of Veliky Bochkov, which was then part of Czechoslovakia. My parents, Frieda and Lazar, had nine children. I was the eighth child, the only son. My father ran a sawmill and dealt in wood and we lived in a smallholding with many animals.

We were an Orthodox family, not fanatically religious, but we took our religion seriously. Like all the Jewish children, I went to *Cheder* (classes for religious studies) twice a day. Each day, I would go from 6 a.m. until 7.30 a.m. and then go to state school from 8 a.m. until 4 p.m. Then it was back to *Cheder* from 4.30 p.m. until 7 p.m., followed by synagogue service until 7.30 p.m. There was not a lot of free time, but I remember my early childhood as being happy. I was part of a warm, loving family and for these memories I am grateful.

In my part of the world there was very little antisemitism. At school, where about one quarter of the children were Jewish, we all played happily and harmoniously together, Jews and Christians. But the carefree days were not to last. In 1938, our teachers were dismissed and replaced by Hungarian teachers who were specifically trained in Nazi ideology. When we arrived at school, instead of sitting in our usual places, we were told where to sit. We were all, Jews and Christians alike, confused and bewildered. Suddenly we were told that we were different, that we were to be segregated: Jews on one side of the classroom and Christians on the other.

It soon became evident that these new teachers were indoctrinating the non-Jewish children to hate us. Our happy, peaceful world was shattered. Within two or three days, children who had been my friends would no longer talk to me. When I approached one of them, he spat, "Don't come near me, you dirty Jew!" Older children began to harass Jewish children and to make our lives miserable, waiting for us outside school and beating us up as we left.

After almost a year of this bullying at school, I was walking home one day when I saw scores of Hungarian soldiers sitting at the roadside. They immediately knew I was Jewish because I had the traditional *peyes* (side-locks worn by Orthodox Jewish males) and wore a skullcap. One of them came over to me. Pulling out his bayonet, he cut off my curls, which they all found highly amusing. I was mortified and humiliated. After that I only attended *Cheder* which was then being run clandestinely. My formal education ended when I was eight and a half years old.

One day, in the spring of 1940, at Passover-time, an uneasy tension descended on our town. Something was going to happen. We had no idea what it might be, and no one in civilised humanity would ever have pictured what was to come. We lived in the heart of our town, on the main road. On that dreadful day, Hungarian militia working under the command of the Germans suddenly surrounded all the Jewish homes in the town centre. Everyone was told to report to the synagogue, where a census would be carried out.

Although we had been told not to be afraid, we left our homes apprehensively, and made our way to the synagogue. The old, the sick, toddlers, even the new-born, no one was exempt. When we got there, it was full to bursting and many people had to stay outside. Meanwhile there was no sign of anyone taking a census. In fact, no list was ever made of our group. As it turned out, this was unusual for the Germans, who were nor-mally so meticulous at record-keeping.

Suddenly at 4 a.m., after hours of waiting, there was a great commotion. The doors crashed open and Hungarian soldiers and a German SS officer came rushing into the synagogue with dogs and carrying batons and guns. All hell let loose. There was shouting and screaming as everyone was ordered out.

Everyone was pushed and shoved, kicked and beaten in the direction of the railway station where a train of cattle wagons was waiting for us. Once I was in the train, I peered through a gap in the planks, trying vainly to comprehend the horrors I was witnessing. After what seemed like an eternity, silence descended. Even the children and babies stopped crying as we waited in fear to see what would happen next. Packed into the wagons like sardines, we looked at each other in silence. What could anyone say? There was no water and no sanitation. The doors were closed and locked. The only air was through a small opening in the side of the wagon, stuffed with barbed wire.

Eventually the train started to move slowly forward. After a while the tension relaxed a little and some began to cry. In the wagon, I was with my mother, father, my youngest sister, Priva, and my three oldest sisters, Frimid, Rivka and Leah, and their five children. You can't imagine what it was like – unable to move, we had to perform all of our bodily functions where we were. Some people fainted, a few suffered heart attacks, others died, but they had to remain in the wagon with us for the next two days and nights. The air was foul.

The train eventually stopped, deep inside a forest, somewhere in Poland. We were forced off the train and found ourselves in a clearing in which a huge, circus-like tent had been erected, surrounded by barbed wire. The first people to go inside the tent were so exhausted that they simply collapsed by the entrance. As more and more of us were pushed in, those following had to try and climb over them in order to find a place. People tripped and fell and scores of people were crushed to death. Bodies lay where they fell for two days, while our captors organised themselves.

They partitioned off a small area inside the tent in order to search us. We were made to undress and, 50 at a time, we had to pick up our bundles of clothing and go in front of the German commandant and guards. Anything of value was handed to the SS.

One day during the first week in the tent, my father and I witnessed an event that was to have a profound effect on us. A boy of about my own age had got into trouble and one of the Polish guards was beating him to a pulp. When his father tried to protect him, they were both summarily killed. I clutched my father in horror. We talked about it and he reluctantly agreed that if one of us fell into trouble, the other would not come and help. That way, one of us might survive.

One night when I was preparing to sneak out to find food, my father called me to him. "Yossel," he said, "before you go out tonight, I want to bestow on you the blessing the Rabbi would normally give when you become a man at age 13. You are already carrying out the duties and responsibilities of a man, and G-d only knows when we will see each other again." So saying, he placed his hands on my head and blessed me. I didn't understand what he meant: I was going under the wire with some other boys but would be back before morning. Later that night, we were picking our way back to the camp in the dark when we heard a great commotion. It was too dark to see much at first, but the terrible noises of screaming, crying, gun shots and barking dogs carried clearly and stopped us in our tracks. We hid behind some trees, near enough to watch aghast as everyone was being forced into lorries and driven away.

When everything had gone quiet, we crept out of hiding and went down to the camp. Those who had been too old, too young or too weak to jump on the lorries were strewn on the ground like so much rubbish. They had shot those left behind, but some were not quite dead.

For the next year, I wandered around Poland on my own, picking up a trail or a rumour here and there, always hoping to find my family. It was a hard, dangerous life, living rough, eating any food I could obtain. In the late summer of 1941, I found myself outside a ghetto. There was a Jewish policeman on duty at the gates and I told him I was Jewish and wanted to get in to find my family. Inside, I was sickened to see the squalid conditions and dilapidated state of the place; the people were walking around like zombies, all skin and bone, their eyes dull and lifeless. How could people be dehumanised in this way? Could my family possibly be amongst these people? Then an old man advised me to get out of there while I could. He took me through the sewers, and I made my way out into the countryside again.

After about six weeks of wandering, I came near to a prison camp. I was wondering how to get in when suddenly I heard a click behind me. I didn't turn around as I knew there was a gun to my head, and an SS officer marched me towards the camp. We had only gone a short way when I saw a column of naked men, women and children being marched out, hundreds of them, five abreast. The guard ordered me to strip, then pushed me in among them and we were marching deep into the forest. We were stopped alongside a huge pit which had been dug out. I heard the ratatat of machine gunfire and as I neared the front of the column, I could clearly see what was happening to each row of five. They were brought to the edge of the trench, then with their backs to the soldiers, they were shot and fell into the pit, and the next group was brought forward.

As I neared the pit, I began to distinguish the features of those who were dying in front of me. Then, when I was about seven rows from the front, to my horror I recognised the whole row. It was my mother and four of my sisters. I wanted to call out, to say goodbye, but it was too late, they were gone. Then my five nephews and nieces, aged between three and seven years old, were pushed forward and told to 'hold hands' by their murderers. The bullets hit them so hard that they were lifted off the ground before falling into the pit. At that moment I felt the world had unhinged itself.

Soon it would be my turn to step forward and die. Suddenly an air raid siren sounded and we were all ordered to lie face-down on the ground. Instead, everyone began to run all over the place. I ran straight into the forest. I ran and ran, naked and alone, knowing I would never see half of my family again... Then I found an old potato sack on the ground, picked it up and ripped three holes in it for my head and arms. I emerged from the forest and made my way to a farm nearby.

I spent 6-8 weeks working there, but very early one morning the farmer came rushing into the barn where I was asleep, shouting, "Josef, you must leave. The Germans are making a sweep of the area... Be quick!" He pointed me towards the nearest railway station and when I got there, a train was about to depart. I hid between two carriages and was so exhausted that I fell asleep. I don't know how long I slept or how far we travelled, but I was awoken when the train suddenly jerked to a halt. A railway guard grabbed me by the shoulder and handed me over to an SS officer. We were in Cracow station and the officer took me to a nearby ghetto, where I was used as a slave labourer. One day, I decided to try my luck and see if I could escape, but I was caught and marched into Cracow-Plaszow concentration camp.

The Camp commandant, Amon Göth, was an overweight, ugly-looking brute. Every morning he would go out onto his balcony and shoot at anyone he could see. One day as I was kneeling down working in the camp, I saw a pair of hooves near me. Without thinking, I looked up. There was Göth astride his beautiful white horse. He leaned down and slashed me across the face with his riding crop. "No one looks at me!" he snarled and rode on. I was lucky. Others had been shot for much less.

In late 1942, a 'selection' was made in the camp and we were again tightly packed into cattle wagons. Again we had no food, no water, no sanitation and insufficient air. After four days of waiting, another train, already filled with prisoners, was hooked onto ours and we started our journey. It was not long before the train stopped and the front wagons pulled up at a platform. The people inside, who had clearly come directly from their homes, were marched away and disappeared down some steps – straight to the gas chambers. We were in Auschwitz.

The doors of our wagons were unlocked and we had to jump down. There was a smartly dressed commandant deciding who would live and who would die. Waving his riding crop, he indicated *"links oder rechts"* (left or right) with a casual flick of the wrist. Those he sent to the left (over 70 per cent) went immediately to the gas chambers, those to the right had been selected, either for work or experimentation. It was Dr Mengele.

Dr Mengele sent me to the right and I lived. We were marched off to a block where we had to undress and our hair was cut off. Then we were ordered to walk to the concrete building to 'shower', so they said. We were crowded into the room and, overcome by cold and fear, some broke down and cried. Then, to our utter relief, cold water rained down on us. Afterwards we were given striped uniforms and marched back to our blocks.

There were a thousand people to a block and we were counted every morning and evening. After a roll-call one day, a section of us on the parade ground were ordered to fill waiting lorries. We were then taken to a railway station and loaded onto open train wagons. From Poland, we travelled through Czechoslovakia into Germany. Passing under one bridge in

Czechoslovakia, we were showered with pieces of bread thrown down by the locals. It gave us a wonderful feeling to realize that some people out there were still willing to put themselves at risk for us.

We arrived at Dachau, and here, as in most places, the camp was divided into different sections – work groups, kitchen groups, those dealing with disposal of the dead. Initially I worked in the kitchen, but I never stood still, always volunteering, believing that as long as I worked, I would stay alive. One day, people were being rounded up, and I joined the others filing onto the transport. It took us on a long journey to Bergen-Belsen in north Germany.

Belsen was huge and covered a vast area. There was no work there and people just walked about aimlessly. Because of this, the Germans invented 'jobs' and luckily I found myself working in the kitchen again. I was peeling potatoes and carrots and generally helping out. In this way, I had enough to eat while I was there and managed to remain at that job until I left Belsen.

That winter, 1943, I was put on a transport to Gross Rosen camp in Lower Silesia. When my transport arrived there, overcrowding was so severe that we were given canvas tents to sleep in. Even in the tents there was insufficient space and we slept leaning on one another as a litter of puppies might snuggle up to their mother. There were numerous satellite camps in the vicinity and shortly after our arrival, I was sent to one of them, Bolkenhain, to work. I worked at a factory called VDM (*Vereinigte Deutsche Metalwerke*) which manufactured aircraft parts and explosives.

In late 1944, after I had been in Bolkenhain for about a year, someone in the factory sidled up to me and said, "Slow down Joe, not a lot of work is coming in and we don't know what's going to happen. If we run out, the Germans might kill us all." He was part of the underground movement who were trying to sabotage the factory and he later asked me to send a hand grenade down the chute.

It caused a loud explosion. The guards came in firing their guns and screaming. They were shooting randomly and I was sure we would all be killed. So I ran forward and shouted, "Stop! I did it!" I told them I had done it alone, but they didn't believe me; they wanted to know who had put me up to it.

As I wouldn't tell, the torture started, with constant questions and beatings. They put needles under my fingernails and gave me electric shocks. My feet were whipped till they were raw and bleeding. Eventually I decided that instead of screaming with pain, I would laugh, and so the more they hurt me, the more I laughed, until they concluded that I had gone completely mad. They decided it was a waste of time beating me any more and left me alone. They were going to send me back to Gross Rosen where I would be hung as an example to anyone else who was thinking of causing trouble.

At Gross Rosen I was put into a tiny cell and informed that the following morning I would be publicly hung. By that time my mental and physical state was such that all I could think of was sleep. I dreamt vividly of my mother, who told me how to escape from there. When I woke up, I felt rested; miraculously I felt strength surging through my body and the pain seemed to disappear. I could hear my mother's voice echoing in my mind and following her instructions, I climbed out of the cell, wriggled beneath the electric wire and ran into the snow-covered forest.

An SS officer saw me and fired: one shot went straight through my left leg and the other lodged in my left knee. He left me for dead. Some time passed and in the still of the night, I heard voices in the distance and saw a group of prisoners being marched along a nearby road. I hobbled over and when I saw an opportunity, stepped into the line. One man died soon after I joined them and in the darkness I exchanged my bloodstained clothes for his.

We were marched back into Bolkenhain! When we arrived, it was clear that the camp was being emptied and the Germans were preparing to evacuate it. The old and the weak had been shot and were being buried in mass graves. It was the end of 1944 and things were going badly for the Germans. Although they were coming to realize that they could not win the war, they were determined to continue slaughtering as many of us as they could before it ended. So they kept marching us from camp to camp, on death march after death march.

When we left Bolkenhain, no one knew where we were going; there seemed to be no plan and we were just marched deeper into Germany. About 5,000 of us started out on the march, but those who slowed down or collapsed from weariness were shot or clubbed to death. Conditions were so horrendous that some people deliberately fell behind so they would be killed in order to end it all.

We walked for days and days, sleeping in barns, sawmills or open fields. One night, after two weeks of marching, we stopped at a farm and were directed into the barns. I stumbled in. I felt I couldn't go on any longer. I was so weak: my hands and feet were still raw from my torture at Bolkenhain and my leg was throbbing with pain. I decided to make a run for it. I hid until nightfall and after the prisoners had been marched away, I stayed hidden, stealing food under cover of darkness, regaining my strength.

After a week, another worn-out, pitiful group of prisoners arrived to stay overnight at the farm and I decided to slip in amongst them, wherever they were going. After another week of marching, we arrived in the camp at Hirschberg. By this time Hirschberg was seriously overcrowded and the Germans did not know what to do with us. We were marched up and down like soldiers, ordered to do exercises, called for roll-calls at any time of the day or night and kept there for hours on end.

As the Russians advanced from the East, the Germans decided to evacuate Hirschberg, taking as many of us with them as they could. They selected those they would take by making us dig a very long ditch, four feet wide and seven feet deep. When it was finished, we had to run and jump over it. Those who managed the jump successfully lived; those who didn't, fell into the ditch and were shot. When my turn came, I started to run, forcing the pain in my leg to the back of my mind. I jumped with all my strength. I was still alive and determined to remain so despite my wounds.

So we set off again and after a few days of marching and sleeping in the open, we stopped at a sawmill overnight. The next morning, we were marched to a nearby railway station and put into open cattle trucks. It was bitterly cold and we were shunted backwards and forwards for days as no one in authority could decide what to do with us. As people succumbed to exhaustion and starvation, the guards threw the bodies over the sides of the trucks. After many days had passed, there were only four of us alive in my wagon.

When our train journey finally came to an end and we were lined up and counted, there were only 178 of us left. We stumbled into Buchenwald camp and were taken to the showers and given other uniforms. By that time, overcrowding in Buchenwald had reached catastrophic proportions, as had the death rate. People were arriving in vast numbers as the Germans moved prisoners further into Germany, away from the oncoming Allied forces. We had no work there; we just had to lie on our bunks, immobile, in a state of limbo lasting several weeks. Towards the end, the bodies of the dead weren't even disposed of; they were either just left in piles around the camp, or simply where they had fallen.

Rumours began to circulate that the underground movement within Buchenwald was arming itself and planning to liberate the camp from within. When the Americans finally entered the camp late in the afternoon of 11 April 1945, they found that the prisoners had liberated themselves. Most of the German guards had fled and the only SS still there were those who had been taken prisoner. It was sixteen days before my fifteenth birthday.

Our liberators had arrived at the camp unprepared. The only food they had was their own rations. Shocked by what they saw, and in their eagerness to try and alleviate the suffering around them, they plied the inmates with their supplies. Army rations – pork, beans and chocolate – were totally unsuitable and tragically, many more lives were lost. Of the 21,000 people who were liberated, only about 700 were alive a few weeks later, and I was one of them.

I gradually became a little stronger and resolved to leave Buchenwald and make my journey homeward. I had fortified myself with the blind belief that everything would be all right when I arrived home: everyone would be there waiting for me, and we could resume our lives. I never doubted for a minute that my father would be there. But when I got home, the door of our house was closed in my face and like countless other survivors, I realized that I had no one in the world with whom to share my name. I was the last of my line. I learned much later that of the 300 families totalling about 1,700 Jews living in Veliky Bochkov in 1938, only about 50 people survived.

I continued my search for my family at Refugee Centres and through all the people I met. After five months in a TB sanatorium in Prague, I managed to reach England in June 1946 with the help of the Jewish Committee for Relief Abroad. I was welcomed and cared for, and spent four years in Morland Hall Hospital, Hampshire, for treatment on my knee. Amazingly, I discovered through a visitor to another patient that my sisters Sara and Rachel were both alive and living in Israel. Sara had gone to Budapest to be a nurse and had somehow avoided being rounded up. Rachel had survived Auschwitz, but during her time there had been experimented on by Mengele. Much later, I learned that another sister, Devorah, had also survived.

In 1952, I went to live in Brighton and worked in a dress factory. There, I met my wife, Sylvia, at a dance and nine months later we were married. We have been blessed with two wonderful children, a daughter, Frances, and a son, Mark. Frances is married to Albert and they have two adorable children, Benjamin and Ella. They are my pride and joy.

In the summer of 1959, I received a letter from my father. I don't know how he managed to trace me, but he had eventually returned home and was still living there. In those days, however, it was impossible to travel from the West since the area was now behind the Iron Curtain. We finally met again in Budapest in May 1966.

My experiences have not destroyed my belief in humanity's goodness. What they have done is make me feel peripheral, always on the outside. After all these years, I still feel as if I'm in transit. I have watched the world unhinge itself and sometimes when I wake up from my nightmares, I wonder, was I really that little boy who saw all that?

This story is dedicated to our two grandchildren, Benjamin and Ella.

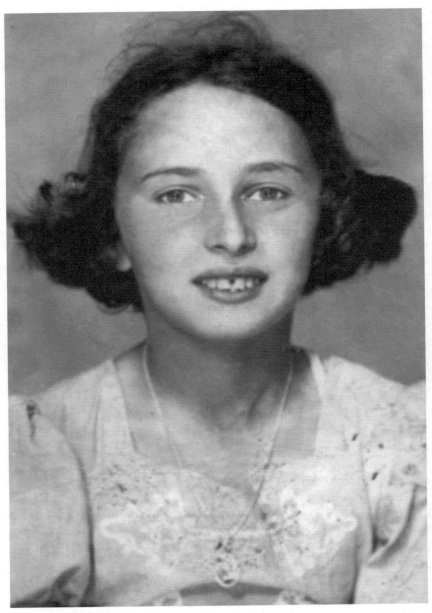

Susan, aged eight, 1938

SUSAN POLLACK

A Holocaust Survivor's Life in Miniature

As my early childhood recedes in an amorphous warm and pleasant recall, I welcome the opportunity to give those few happy years the dignity they deserve.

I was born Zsuzsanna Blau in Felsögöd, Hungary, on 9 September 1930. My father, Ernö Blau, moved to Felsögöd after marriage and established a small coal and wood trading centre. My brother Laci and I knew all about the trade as we became his helpers from early on. We helped to stack the wood in the yard and kept the yard clean.

My father was a progressive, self-educated man. He was the treasurer of our small local synagogue and served for a while on the local council. I think he was born in 1885. He served in the First World War, was decorated and nearly lost his life when captured by the Russian army. He kept us amused by retelling his escape from Omsk, Tomsk, Irkutsk and Vladivostok. He often said how gratefully he kissed the Hungarian soil on his arrival back home.

My mother, Gisella, was a good partner, a loving mother. Both parents hoped that the future would offer an easier existence for us and were very encouraging in wanting a good education for their children.

As children, my brother and I spent our summer holidays at my grand-parents' establishment in Nógrád, not far from the market town of Vác. Nógrád was a small village, nestled by mountains and farms. The rutted roads leading to the next village were often travelled by some of us children – all cousins who were made welcome by the Kohn family (my grandparents on my mother's side). On average, we were ten years old. My grandfather, the patriarch of the family, was a strict Orthodox Jew. Each morning, all the children were assembled in front of him to recite the Benediction of our faith. We were further questioned about Hebrew studies, and solemnly promised to do more.

I think my grandfather built the pub and the distillery in the centre of the village. The many sheds and outhouses were ideal for playing hide and seek. One of my uncles, dear uncle Dezsó, an unhurried, affectionate soul, always had time for us, and I don't remember a cross word, though we often deserved it. Each year, there was a new baby in his family. Together we all shared the few beds in very few rooms.

Sometimes we slept on the wide rafter holding up the roof, inside the pub. On days of festivities and weddings, the gypsy band played well into the small hours, and we were all mesmerised by the many-skirted, colourful peasant dancers moving to the rhythmic tunes of *csárdás* (Hungarian dances).

The six or ten of us used to help with bottling the locally-found spring water. We were entrusted with putting the gas into the bottles, and were told to pay close attention to the gauge on the gas cylinder. But mostly we did it by counting, and never had a mishap. Our uncle knew our capabilities, he said.

But the highlight for me was when my father visited us. I could tell he was coming from afar. He had one of those early motorcycles – a really noisy contraption which needed constant revving. I jumped on the back seat, held him tight, and we zoomed around the villages feeling like royalty. My mother arrived later by train, with other aunts, and in no time cleaned up the entire household, washed the clothes in a large wooden trough, and cooked and baked enough food for a week.

Once I had had my satisfaction on the bike, all the others got a ride as well. This was important – to give everyone a share, treat all equally. We did value the large family we were part of. It was a blessing, we were reminded constantly. To this day, a belief in family values is an essential part of myself.

In that small village, other close members of my family lived. Some families had eight children. My handsome uncle, the last married, had a seven-year-old boy who showed a special aptitude with figures and reading. His mother tutored him, and on visiting days there, we free-spirited cousins were more closely supervised.

All the summer holidays came to an abrupt end. In late 1938, my handsome uncle was murdered in Nógrád. A fascist attacked him from the back when he was on a horse-driven wagon going up the mountain, splitting his head with a hatchet. His attacker was sentenced to two years' imprisonment, but only served a short time, and then continued to live across the road from my widowed aunt.

Late 1938 was more visibly difficult for my family. My brother, Laci, was affected by one of the social exclusion laws – the *Numerus Clausus*. This decree was an all-pervasive academic limit on Jewish students aiming to be accepted in higher education. In most faculties, the limit was set to two per cent Jewish intake. We could not afford to send him abroad to study, although some neighbouring countries – those with less close cooperation with Nazi Germany than Hungary – still had a modicum of relative equality. But Hungary became part of the Axis Alliance, and all the Nuremberg laws affected us in the same measure as in Germany. We heard about Jews converting to Christianity in order to remain in employment and retain their civil rights. But it was to no avail: conversion could only help if it reached back to generations before.

After the outbreak of the war in September 1939, we were desperate for news from the west, as only Nazi propaganda was broadcast on our radio. Everywhere, including on the cinema newsreel (an important source of information then), we heard about the success of the annexation (*Anschluss*) of Austria, and the speedy conquest in Poland and elsewhere filled us with uncertainty and fear. There were rumours that we would eventually be resettled somewhere in the East. But that was all we knew.

In our desperation, we set up a seance table at night, with upside-down glasses resting on paper messages asking, "Will the Allied forces be victorious soon? Are we going to survive – *all of us?*" The BBC World Service news that we listened to at great risk to our lives was soon jammed. The Nazi propaganda machinery – Hungarian-style – was evident everywhere. There were graffiti on walls – "Jews get out!" and the radio boomed with economic, social and racial accusations against us. There were wide-scale physical abuses; my brother, for instance, was seriously beaten up at Boy Scouts meetings, and the leader shrugged his shoulders in resignation. The Church remained silent.

Where could we find rescue? We had no passports, no offers of help and no knowledge of the fate of other Jews who had by then been murdered or sent to concentration camps. We were totally isolated. So when the fathers – the few living in Felsögöd – received a notice from the local council to attend a meeting about the welfare of their families, they attended bravely, but distrustfully, on that fateful morning. All the families were there to see our dear fathers being herded onto the waiting lorries, but not before blows from heavy sticks bent them in agony.

We heard which camp they had been taken to. Though we diligently sewed the yellow star on the sleeves of all our coats, we were no longer permitted to use public transport. We asked a Christian woman from our village to visit father, taking a basket of bread and food. When she came back, she conveyed her own alarm at seeing him, telling us, "He was unrecognisable." Whether he died in Hungary, or was taken to the many extermination camps in Germany or Poland, and under what circumstances, I don't know. May his soul rest in peace.

My school years ended when I was 13 years old. I spent the last year at Logat utca secondary school in Budapest. We had to wear the yellow star and we Jews were segregated from the mainstream in the classrooms and in the playground. But wearing the star identity was no safeguard from open brutality: some of us children were arrested and never seen again.

The sound of explosives over Budapest gave us some hope of the imminence of a Russian conquest. But that proved to be a desperate hope. That early rumour of resettlement to the east now loomed ever closer. On 15 April 1944 the notorious Adolf Eichmann, the planner of the extermination camps, took charge of deportation. Within six weeks all Hungarian Jews, except some in Budapest, had been sent to concentration camps, mainly to Auschwitz.

A Hungarian local policeman came to our door, and ordered us to get ready to leave, taking only belongings that we could carry on our backs. Still clinging to the illusion of resettlement, I took our portable sewing machine with some food and clothes, and carried them in a sheet on my back.

At first, the three of us – my mother, brother and I – were taken to a ghetto in Vác, then from there to another internment camp, an open clay mine for a brick factory where we slept outdoors – on that clay soil – and got stuck in the clay when it rained. We ate the food we had brought from home and listened to rumours, waiting for the bread distribution which did not reach us. Then we lined up hoping for exemptions from deportation, but they did not affect us. All the time we surreptitiously looked at the armed guards up high, pointing their guns down on us – on defenceless women, children and the elderly.

I think that was in late May 1944. It was a hot summer – too hot for carrying my load with the sewing machine on my back all the way to the cattle trains. It was a very long walk. A long column of people hardly resembling their former selves.

Now the speed, the haste, the inhumanity of this march alerted us to the darkness of the future. The cattle trains were awaiting us and in the midst of shouting and pushing, we were forced into the trucks, more and more people, all standing up on the straw floor with one bucket of water and another for the excrement. There was no air to breathe, no light to see. Only the desperate sounds on the subliminal level reached us in our semi-conscious state as the train shuttled frequently back and forth.

When the train finally came to a stop after 5-7 days of this journey, and the doors opened, we were glad to breathe some fresh air and stretch our legs, but it was not for long. It was evening and the strong beams of light on the platform shone in our faces. I couldn't open my eyes at first. The shouting, the dogs barking, and the immediate separation of the young from the elderly filled us with terror. These were the Nazis in their pressed uniforms with sticks in their hands. We were in Auschwitz.

My brother disappeared from before my eyes, my mother was pushed to the group of the elderly. She was 42 years old, but had aged through the sufferings inflicted. I cried out to follow her, but someone brutally pulled me away from her. That large group of dear people – including my mother – were sent to the gas chamber. May her soul rest in peace and may they all be granted eternal life.

Then we young girls were stripped of our clothes, showered with disinfectant, our hair was shaved off, and we were thrown a pair of shoes and any-size striped pyjama clothes, and quickly marched into a large wooden barrack. I was on the top bunk with six other girls, one blanket between us. In a whispering voice, I learned about the gassing, the crematorium, the fear of selections that determined whether we were to live.

Each morning we stood for roll-call while the SS counted us and made us stand until they were satisfied. Our daily ration consisted of a small piece of hard bread in the morning and some soup slop in the evening. How did we fare under this regime of malnutrition? That was for Dr Mengele to decide. We were frequently inspected stark naked, with our cheeks pinched until some colour appeared, and our chests lifted when we passed in front of that doctor, who held our lives in his hand.

To escape physically was all but impossible – there were electrified fences and high lookouts, and the several attempts we witnessed negated that hope. But to escape mentally, we created a world of make-believe. In hardly audible voices, we asked each other, "And what will you have for breakfast this morning?" The starvation gnawed at our bones, but those moments of sweet memories from home came flooding back. "I'll have jam and bread, and perhaps an egg." We played these games for a while, but not long. The stark reality of daily terror was all-pervasive and mostly we just lay in a stupor.

I was in Auschwitz Lager C Block D for about 8-10 weeks, but then, discovering some flesh on my body, Dr Mengele sent me to Gubben, Germany, to do some slave labour. I was used for armament production and walked every day to the factory, in bright daylight, visible to all the local inhabitants. Then, as the Allied forces were advancing, we were made to trudge through the snow and sleet and frozen fields to Bergen-Belsen, on one of the notorious death marches. On good days, some boiled potatoes were cooked by the farmers in whose barns we slept. Mostly we scraped for beet roots in the fields and listened to the many gun shots fired at those who could no longer keep up. It was winter 1944-45, bitterly cold.

Belsen was a resting place for the dying. Infectious diseases were raging; corpses were hauled into large piles, but most were left in the huts – alongside the barely living. Food was rarely distributed and few of us could walk any more.

With so many dead around me, I managed to crawl to the next hut, where I found our neighbour, Mrs Schwartz, whose two little ones had been transported from Felsögöd. She recognized me, after almost a year since Auschwitz: my hair had grown back and so had hers. She was bloated and I could hardly hear her voice when she asked me, "Zsuzsi, do you think we will survive and live a free life?" I tried to reassure her. She was the first person whom I knew from home. When I crawled back to see her the following day, the lice from her scalp had covered her forehead, an indication that there was nothing more to feed on.

The following day, 15 April 1945, we were liberated by the British army.

The huge clean-up operation began immediately, but not before the volunteer medics had collected us from the ditches. I was hospitalized and later sent to Sweden for treatment. I suffered from tuberculosis, typhoid and severe malnutrition.

No one from Nógrád survived. Not one relative. More than 50 members of my family were murdered. My brother, Laci, was in the *Sonderkommando* unit where the victims were forced to remove the gassed bodies into the ovens. He was grossly disturbed for most of his life, and continued to live in our parents' home. It was 20 years before I could visit him in Hungary. I lived in Sweden until 1948 and then in Canada. We were almost strangers when we first met again.

Laci died in 1995. I went on a long journey on the road of recovery. Physical recovery was easier to achieve – I received valuable help in Sweden. Mental stamina, and most importantly, a secure belief in a world of tolerance and acceptance, were an uphill struggle.

Living in Sweden together with other survivors was immensely satisfying as we all shared a common past. We had all lost most of our families and we all knew that going back to our homes, which were now desolate and empty, would not provide us with a safe and loving place to live. So we each set out to different destinations.

I was the only one from Stockholm to be sent to Toronto in Canada. It was there that I met my husband who had a similar background. We had a family of three loving daughters, Sandra, Joan and Diane, and now I have my own family with six grandchildren – my two grandsons, Anthony and David, and four granddaughters, Abigail, Lydia, Emily and Lucy.

I have educated myself – and contributed to the social fabric of community life. I volunteered for the Samaritans and am now involved in talking to groups of students about my experiences. I believe firmly that Holocaust studies will forever remain as a warning sign for all generations and will hopefully mediate our behaviour towards each other with tolerance and goodwill.

Remembering the loss of the children

Who would have thought that the straggling group of children
Barely able to walk across the frozen fields
Scraping for buried turnips, risking the ire of their guards
Could reach their ultimate destination?

Who would dare to think that some might survive
The cruel months in Belsen until the British liberation?

Who could imagine that the child within me
All alone then would reach an age
When tolerance and goodwill, friendship and acceptance
Would triumph due to all our determination?

We are humbly standing together today, to feel the loss
Of a million and a half innocent children
Whose lives were brutally ended.

Together we stand in dedication
To safeguard the future of all our
children
So that we may all enter
Into a family of humanity.

January 27 2003:
British National Holocaust Day

In memory of all my lost family and in
dedication to my loving daughters and
grandchildren, and to my husband:
"You keep the sunshine glowing when
dark clouds threaten my sight."

My father Ernö Blau with two locals in Felsögöd

Bela at Bulldogs Bank aged three. "What is this on my plate?"

Else Rosenthal, my mother, aged 16

BELA ROSENTHAL

Bela's Story

My mother, Else Schallmach, was born on 24 December 1902 in Posen, which was then part of Germany. Her father hired out carriages for special occasions like weddings. She had an older sister called Selma who married a non-Jew and went to live in Lübeck in the north of Germany. In around 1920 my grandparents and my mother moved to Berlin because the area, which included Posen, had been granted to Poland after the First World War and many Jews did not want to live under Polish rule. This was because the Polish people were known to be very antisemitic.

My mother married her first husband, Martin Fischer, in Berlin. Unfortunately he became ill and he died in 1941. I do not know whether they had any children together. Not long after Martin died, my mother married my father, Siegfried Rosenthal. By then, both my father's parents and my mother's father had died and were buried in the Weissensee Jewish Cemetery in Berlin.

After the Nuremberg Laws were passed in 1935, my mother was forced to work in the Siemens factory in Gartenfeld, which is a suburb of Berlin. There she had to work separated from the non-Jewish workers and was given the most menial of jobs for very little pay. None of the Jewish workers were allowed to socialise and work with non-Jewish workers, and in fact Siemens built a screen dividing them. The factory was responsible for making equipment to help the Nazis in their fight against the Allies. My father meanwhile was forced to give up his work as a businessman and was made to clean the streets of Berlin and clear up any rubbish, also for very little pay.

The passing of the Nuremberg Laws made life very difficult for Jews and for my parents. Not only were they forced to report for work to a local government office, but other severe restrictions were imposed on them. Jews were declared to be non-German; their German documents were taken away and they were given special Jewish papers – they became non-citizens; they were not allowed to use public transport or visit public places of entertainment; they were not allowed to mix, either in business or socially, with non-Jews; Jewish children could only go to Jewish schools; Jews were not allowed access to the law i.e. could not sign any contracts, or to law enforcement, which meant that if they were assaulted or their property was stolen, they could not call on the police to protect them. There were many other restrictions which made life extremely difficult for Jews.

My parents and my maternal grandmother, Auguste Schallmach, were unable to leave Germany as all the international borders were closed – no country was prepared to accept Jewish refugees despite urgent appeals to the Heads of State and religious leaders. A very few were able to escape – those with money, those with business and family connections in other countries and some unaccompanied children. My family were trapped in Germany and at the mercy of the Nazis.

My grandmother was the first person in my family to be deported in September 1942. This was because she was too old to work and the Nazis had no use for her. She was deported first of all to Theresienstadt in Czechoslovakia and then on to Auschwitz in Poland. She was deported with other elderly Jews in one of the infamous cattle truck trains. She arrived in Auschwitz where all her clothes were taken from her and she was herded into a large shed. This shed had shower heads fixed onto the ceiling and Jews thought that they were going to be cleaned, given new clothes and put to work. However, it was gas – not water – that came out, and many thousands of Jews at a time were killed in this way. My grandmother was one of these.

Meanwhile we continued to live in Berlin. My father was the next member of my family to be deported. In March 1943 the Nazis decided to rid Berlin of Jews and my father was picked up with many other Jews and deported to Auschwitz. He died there in much the same way as my grandmother.

My mother and I were still living in Berlin until June 1943 when the Nazis came for us. They broke the locks of our apartment, forced their way in and took us away to the Jewish Hospital, which was being used as a holding camp until they decided where to send us. My mother had to pay all the outstanding bills on the apartment, pay to repair the broken lock and for the cleaning of the apartment so that a Nazi sympathiser could move into it. She also had to sign a document listing all the contents of the apartment. There was a nominal value placed on each item. I believe that the Nazis reasoned that if someone were to claim compensation, then our possessions would be recorded as virtually worthless. When all these papers were completed, we were deported together to Theresienstadt.

Theresienstadt was a camp not far from Prague in Czechoslovakia in a farming area. It had been used as a military camp and there was a wall all around with barbed wire and watch towers and a river running around. The buildings were barracks which had been used by soldiers and this made Theresienstadt an ideal place for a concentration camp. At times there were seven times the number of people accommodated there than it was originally designed for, so that the overcrowding was terrible. This made living conditions even more unbearable. Nearly 141,000 Jews were deported to Theresienstadt and a quarter of the people died there. 15,000 children were deported to Theresienstadt and less than 150 children survived – I was one of those lucky ones. There was a crematorium there and they burned 190 bodies each day in the ovens. The bodies were so thin that they cremated four bodies at a time in each oven, although they were designed for only one.

On arrival at Theresienstadt, my mother went to a women-only house and I was taken with other very young children to another house. My mother lived in a room where there were bunk beds all around the walls. These were in three tiers and were deeper than the bunk beds that are in use today, so that Jews were made to sleep across the bunks side by side on each of the three layers. This was so that far more people were accommodated in each room. There were no cupboards so there was nowhere to keep any change of clothing. My mother was made to work very long hours in the camp and she came to visit me when she could. There was very little food and hardly any washing facilities. The food consisted of a watery soup and a small piece of bread each day. Many Jews died of starvation, overwork, disease and execution. There were many diseases due to the living conditions, very little medical care and no medicines. Diseases such as polio, typhoid, scarlet fever and hepatitis were widespread. My mother died of tuberculosis after a few months of living and working there.

I continued to live in the camp for a further year with five other very young orphans. Women from the camp brought us a little food and, as each one in turn was deported to Auschwitz, another woman took her place. We were kept in a room without toys; we only had each other for company and we learned to rely on each other. I caught scarlet fever and hepatitis but managed to recover. I was fortunate that I was a strong child and survived without permanent physical damage – some other children were not so lucky.

The International Red Cross heard rumours about the conditions in Theresienstadt and came to visit. When the Nazis were informed that they were coming, they got people to quickly paint the buildings, clean up the streets, print some camp money, build shower facilities, open coffee bars etc. They also built a cemetery! The Nazis reasoned that in a real town people died – so they put up grave stones with names on, but there were no bodies in the graves and the names bore no relation to anyone who died there. The Nazis also deported all the Jews who were thin, diseased and who could tell the Red Cross what had been going on, and they brought in new Jews who looked healthy. The ashes that had accumulated in the crematorium were thrown into the river so that they did not have to account for them. My mother's ashes were thrown into the river along with others at that time. All the preparations to influence the Red Cross were successful in diverting attention away from the atrocities that were happening there. As soon as the Red Cross left, everything went back to the way it was before, and none of the new facilities was ever used.

In May 1945 the Russian army liberated Theresienstadt and they brought with them doctors and nurses to help treat the Jews in the camp. I was too ill to be moved until June 1945 when I joined the other children at Olesovickych Castle just outside Prague. There we were looked after while the international community checked to see whether we had relatives who had survived the Holocaust, and to see whether any of us had homes to go back to. No one was found to claim me and it was unthinkable to send me back to Berlin. In August 1945 the British Government allowed up to 1,000 children into the UK on temporary visas and I was one of the 301 children who went on the transport to Crosby on Eden in Westmorland. The six of us who were in Theresienstadt together were kept there until October while the Jewish community decided what to do with us. Eventually they found two refugee German nurses to look after us at a house called Bulldogs Bank in Sussex.

The six of us spent a year at Bulldogs Bank learning to use a knife and fork, learning to play with toys, learning to be children, learning to speak English and learning to socialise with others. It was a difficult time trying to adjust to a completely different way of life and we were forbidden to speak about the past or to speak German. We kept very close to each other and often gave our carers a hard time.

After a year we joined the older children at Weir Courtney in Lingfield. We had again to adjust to a different environment and to interact with other children. This was not always easy as the older children had already made friends, were going to school and resented us younger ones joining in their games.

After a while the Jewish community decided that the six of us were still young enough to be adopted into families. We started to visit families on a trial basis for weekends. We were regularly returned. However, one day I did not come back. An older Jewish couple decided to adopt me. They did not have children of their own so I became an only child. On the way to London to their apartment, I was told that my name was to be changed from Bela to Joanna, as they considered my name to be too German. I was told that I must not talk about my past and that from now on I was their child and the past was to be forgotten. I felt totally confused.

I started to go to school in London but found school life difficult. What did I have in common with the other children? I had no background or experience in common with any of them. There was a certain amount of antisemitism in the UK at that time so it was not good to be Jewish; Germans were not popular just after the war, as could be expected, and the fact that I was adopted singled me out from others. I was good at all sports which was the only thing that made my school years bearable. Though I am intelligent, I did not do very well at school as I found the emotional stress extremely difficult to handle. I continued my studies as an adult. The stress resulted in me putting on weight and developing a stammer. The weight continues to be a problem, but with a lot of hard work I have managed to conquer the stammer except in moments of extreme stress.

I was married and have three children who are now all married with children of their own. It gives me great satisfaction that they are all happy and getting on with their lives. I told them about my story when they were teenagers. They understand, but have not let it interfere with their lives too much, for which I am grateful. The most lasting effect all this has had on me is my lack of trust in people and a determination to be as self-sufficient as possible. I dislike being reliant on anyone for any favour – I even find it hard to rely in any way on my children.

The reason why I talk to people about my experiences and that of my family is to help prevent any repetition of these awful events. It is so important to stress that each one of us can make a difference and that to say or do nothing is not an option if we wish to make our world a better place. It is also important to underline the fact that the Holocaust did happen. There are many archives in Berlin with actual documents and films from this period. The Nazis were proud of what they did – there was no attempt to hide their antisemitic activities. It is also important to realize that Germans knew what was going on and did nothing because it didn't matter – it only affected Jews.

This testimony is dedicated to my parents, Else and Siegfried Rosenthal,
and my grandmother, Auguste Schallmach,
who all perished in concentration camps.

Renee at Beth Shalom, 2003

My sister aged about 6, around 1937

RENEE SALT

Through The Eyes of a Child

I was born Rywka Ruchla Berkowitz in Zdunska-Vola, Poland, in 1929 and lived with my parents and younger sister. My father was an accountant and my mother a housewife. We had a very comfortable lifestyle. Ours was a very large, well-known family, as my father was one of eight children and my mother one of four, so I had lots of aunts and uncles, many cousins, two sets of grandparents and a large extended family. My parents were elegant, cultured people, much respected by a wide circle of family and friends. We, the children, went to a Jewish school and generally we did the same things as children all over the world. After school we did our homework, played with friends, went to parties, the pictures; weekends were spent visiting families. When the weather was good, we visited a beautiful park with a lake where we had picnics and boat rides, and we thought that this was how it was always going to be.

Our grandparents lived in different towns from us, and holidays and Jewish festivals were spent with either one set or the other. We spent the summer vacation before the war with my mother's parents and everyone was talking about a war breaking out. Everyone was nervous, and of course it rubbed off on us children. We returned from holiday at the end of August 1939 and immediately my mother started buying in lots of groceries and coal, so that we would have enough for as long as the war might last. We had no idea, or course, that it would last for six years. Also, the same night we came home from holiday, a large lorry arrived with materials, because my grandfather had a factory and did not want to keep all the stock in one place. So he sent out lorries to different members of the family, which were unloaded during the night, so that no one should see. We could hardly get into our flat.

On 1 September war was declared and the German army marched into Poland. It only took them about two weeks to overrun the whole country. When they came to our town, the officers liked our flat, so we were thrown out and left standing in the street with just what we had on. They soon brought machines, installed them in the quadrangle of our block of flats, brought in Poles and from all the material available in our flat they worked for three days making blankets for the German army. We were told that all our clothes and valuables from the flat had been put on lorries and sent to Germany. Since we had nowhere to live, our family had to split up, with each member going to a different aunt or uncle. I was ten years old then, and was sent to my mother's parents in Kalisz. While I was away, my mother found a room and scrounged a few bits and pieces from family and friends, because at that time it was impossible to buy anything even if you had the money, and she set up a little home.

As soon as the Germans entered Poland, they began to persecute the Jews. Jews were not permitted to practise their professions, they were not allowed to keep their shops open or walk on the pavement. They soon made us wear a yellow Star of David, pinned on the front and back of our clothes; without it you were not allowed to go out. Jews were beaten up all the time. The queues for bread were miles long and when it came to your turn, they were usually sold out, so you had to queue again the next day. Right from the beginning, there was a great shortage of food.

After I had been only a short time in Kalisz with my grandparents, the Germans decided to make it *Judenrein* – free of Jews. Since Kalisz was a beautiful town near the German border, they didn't want any Jews there. One morning they called us all into a large market hall. We were only allowed to take a small parcel with us and leave everything else behind. From there they started sending people to different parts of Poland. When my mother heard what was going on in Kalisz, she somehow managed to obtain a special pass and came and took me back home to Zdunska-Vola. My grandparents and my mother's two younger brothers were sent away, but they managed to get back to us in Zdunska-Vola, and we all lived together in one room.

At the end of 1939, the Germans decided to make a ghetto in Zdunska-Vola. All the Jews had to leave the better parts of town and move into the slum area, which was then cordoned off – no one was allowed in or out. My mother found a room in the ghetto – there were eight of us living in one room without sanitation. Every drop of water had to be fetched from a well at the back of the block, and the toilets were even further away, half a mile in fact. Needless to say, it was very difficult – the overcrowding, the cold, the starvation. From other small towns they sent the Jews into our ghetto, so we were even more overcrowded.

The Germans installed factories in the ghetto. Everyone who wanted a ration card had to work in the factories. We had to work very hard and were often beaten up going or coming from work. I worked in a factory making socks for the army. I didn't know anything about how to make socks. Someone had to teach me for two weeks, then I had to show someone else for two weeks, and then straight on to production – while the guards stood over us so that we didn't waste a minute. There was no medication at all; many died from starvation or illness. One day, the Germans brought in some Polish workers who erected ten gallows in a row in a square in the centre of the ghetto. They brought ten Jewish men and hanged them all together, having gathered hundreds of people to stand by and watch. Afterwards they left the poor bodies hanging for days on end, so everyone should see. These gallows were never dismantled, but every few months the procedure was repeated – and we actually thought this was bad, not knowing the terrible things that were yet to come.

Early one morning, in the summer of 1942, we were woken up with screams of *"Alle Juden 'raus!"*– all Jews out! We had already heard rumours by then – but they were only rumours because we had no communication with the outside world – no letters, newspapers, radios, nothing – yet rumours were circulating that children and old people were being exterminated up and down the country. We hid my grandparents and my four-year-old cousin in the attic, fully expecting to return soon to our room in the ghetto. In fact it was the last time we saw them and we later learnt that they had all been shot.

The rest of us, having dressed in a hurry, went out into the street, which was by then crammed with people, and like sheep we followed one another until we came to a large field, which was surrounded with Gestapo and SS men, all armed and with large guard dogs. It took a long time for everyone to gather there and then the Gestapo and SS started giving orders over the loudspeakers. First they ordered us all to sit down so that they could watch us better. Then they ordered parents to hand over all children up to 18 years of age. The cries of the children and the mothers' screams of "Almighty God help us, where are you?" still ring in my ears today. You could soon see the children running towards the officers – little ones, bigger ones, some of the bigger ones carrying their younger siblings. They were all placed in enclosed lorries. It was indescribable.

During all this my mother was trying to hide me on one side of her and my sister, who was ten years old, on the other, covering us over with a coat. Of course it was not long before they found my sister and my mother received a beating. It was sheer luck that they did not find me as well. The little girl turned round to the SS man and said, "Please don't hurt her, this is not my mother." Before they took her away, she asked my mother, "Mummy, are they going to kill us?" and my mother replied, "No darling, they are going to take you to your grandma in the Lodz ghetto." My sister ran away with tears running down her face, and we never saw her again.

When all the children had been rounded up, we were lined up and taken to the Jewish cemetery outside town. At the entrance I witnessed the first of the many 'selections' that I endured. With their usual 'one to the right', 'one to the left', they took all the old people, invalids, pregnant women, people who were not fit to work, all were directed to one side; the rest to the other. But when it grew dark, there was no more selection; everyone else was directed to the unlucky side. We sat on the gravestones for two days and two nights, and throughout that time they continued selecting people from our side to move to the unlucky side. I was together with my parents and one of my aunts; the rest of the family were on the unlucky side. They installed electric lights all round the cemetery so no one should escape.

A young woman sitting near us was rambling on about how happy she was and how lucky she was, because her little boy had died a few weeks earlier. No one, she said, could take him away because he was buried there. Some people tried to make me look older, someone found a lipstick, someone else found a powder compact; they made up my face, put a scarf on my head. One woman even swapped her high-heeled shoes for mine. Even so, just before we left the cemetery, I was spotted by an SS man who came running over and, pointing at me, said, "You, stand up, how old are you?" I was paralysed with fright and could not answer. My father, who was sitting nearby, answered, "She's 18 years old, I know her." In fact I was twelve years old and looked eight! The SS man could see clearly that I was not 18; he looked hard at me for what seemed an eternity, and then said, "She may sit down!" Everyone around me was so relieved – I still believe that God was protecting me and would not let them take me away. Soon after, we were taken out of the cemetery. There were only 1,200 people left, including only three children, of whom I was one. In the ghetto there had originally been 28,000 people.

We were taken to the railway sidings where guards carrying sacks were collecting our money and valuables. We gave everything away, but my father wore a ring which was so deeply embedded that he could not take it off, so he left it on, hoping for the best. Then they called out the president of the ghetto, shot him in front of us and kicked his body into a corner. We were packed into the waiting cattle trucks without any food or water. We had had nothing to eat or drink since we left our homes. They closed the big doors of the trucks, bolted them and off we went to what we later learned was the Lodz ghetto, a journey of 45 kilometres which normally took one hour, but which lasted 24 hours. The stench in the trucks was overpowering as people had to relieve themselves wherever they stood – over a hundred people suffocated on that journey as the trucks had no windows.

When we arrived in Lodz, my father's mother, who lived in the ghetto there, took us in, but after two weeks another 'selection' took place in our block. We had to go down to the quadrangle where the Gestapo and SS came with their closed-in lorries and once again took invalids, old people, children, pregnant women, people who looked too ill to work – and put them all on the lorries. Once again, I slipped through the net, but this time they took my grandmother away. One of the SS guards noticed the ring on my father's finger and said, "Hand over the ring." My father explained that he couldn't get it off, so the SS man tried and couldn't move it, and he said to the guards, "Fetch an axe and chop the finger off." Like a miracle, after he had said these words, the ring slipped off onto the ground and the SS man took it. My father received a few kicks and that was the end of the ring. We were then allowed to go back to our room.

We all found work in the ghetto factories where the conditions of over-crowding, sickness and starvation were appalling. There was no medication and so many people were dying, even of simple illnesses, and from starvation. One day after I came home from work with a high fever and the doctor diagnosed typhus – which was rife in the ghetto – I was taken straight into the hospital. On the first night, I was told afterwards, I nearly died, but somehow they found an injection for me, which was a very rare commodity, most probably because I was a child. On the second night I heard a great commotion, a lot of screaming and shouting. I learned the next morning that the Gestapo and SS had come with their lorries and emptied the whole hospital, but once again I was saved because they kept away from the contagious ward I was in. My parents took me out of the hospital, and I lay alone locked in our room when my parents had to go to work, terribly frightened. Every time I heard a knock or someone walking, I thought the SS had come to take me away. As soon as I was able to, I went back to work rather than stay on my own.

This is how we lived until the summer of 1944, when the Germans began evacuating all the ghettos. The SS would come to our workplaces, assemble everyone in the quadrangles, and make soothing speeches – they told us that the ghetto was going to be closed down and we would be sent away to working camps, where we would get good food and excellent conditions, with good medical care; they promised us everything. The only thing they asked of us was that we should go to the railway stations voluntarily. At first, people didn't want to leave the ghetto, but gradually conditions worsened to such an extent that we were driven to leave, and people started going to the stations. However, when the cattle trucks returned empty to take a new batch of people, station cleaners found little notes left in the trucks, saying that the people had been taken to concentration camps where mass killings were taking place. We didn't and couldn't believe it, although of course we should have done! And so people continued to leave voluntarily.

One day, when there seemed no option, my parents and I arrived at the station. We were packed tightly onto the cattle trucks, the doors were slammed shut and bolted and we were left without any food, water or air. The journey took some 24 hours. Again the stench was overpowering. Dawn was just breaking when the train stopped. Immediately you could hear dogs barking. They opened the doors and there was a screaming and bellowing – "Everybody off the train, get a move on, be quick."

We looked out and it seemed that an army of Gestapo and SS men were waiting, all heavily armed and with large guard dogs. We were dazed, unable to get our bearings. My father jumped first and after I jumped, I never saw him again. Without a kiss or goodbye, he disappeared. Men went to one side, women to the other. All around us was illuminated electrified fencing and above stood a rank of high watchtowers. Guards moved in, shoving us into columns, some whispering, "You are in Auschwitz-Birkenau, this is the place where people are being taken straight to the gas chambers." We had heard nothing about this bewildering place. We were still there when they came with lorries to take away our luggage for sorting. We were pushed into a queue and at the head a 'selection' was being made by the infamous Dr Mengele – the "butcher of Auschwitz" – as we later learned.

Again they sent all the old people, invalids, children and pregnant women to the right. Only the movement of Dr Mengele's hand determined whether you lived or died. Once again I slipped through the net and went to the left, together with my mother, which was a great relief. All those who went to the right were taken straight to what I later learnt were the gas chambers. Those of us on the left side were also lined up in rows of five, and taken through the camp to a large hall. On the way, we heard a most beautiful orchestra which you could hear all over the camp; after all, they had the best musicians from all over Europe.

We were told to strip and leave our clothes on the benches. Then everyone had their heads shaved. Mine wasn't touched because I only had short curls growing back from when my head had been shaved in the hospital. Guards were walking up and down collecting whatever valuables anybody had, and while all this was going on, the young officers were walking up and down, laughing and joking, having the time of their lives. Then we were pushed through some heavy doors to what looked like a shower room without windows. We were all saying prayers, hugging and kissing one another as we thought this was our last hour. However, instead of gas, water came through. We were the lucky ones – they still needed us for hard labour. After that we were pushed through another set of doors to another room where we were given clothing. They gave me a large skirt that would not stay up and a man's pyjama jacket, and that was all. Then we were registered and given a number on a white piece of oblong linen with black lettering, which we had to pin onto whatever we wore. When we walked out of there, we could not recognise one another; we looked as though we had just come out of a lunatic asylum. We were taken to a small open space and left sitting there overnight without food or water, and the cold that night nearly killed me.

The following day we were allocated to an empty hut, and we had to sit against the wall, five in a column, squashed between each other's legs. In this position we had to sit day and night. Roll-calls were taking place twice a day, early morning and late afternoon. Meals were served once a day – just a saucepan of soup which had to be shared between the five people in each column, without a spoon.

Although we did not expect to leave Auschwitz alive, my mother and I were sent to Hamburg for demolition work caused by Allied bombing, and then to a small camp, Poppenbittel, also in the Hamburg area. We suffered terribly from cold and starvation, and the work was very hard and dangerous. On one occasion, we were working near a slaughterhouse in Hamburg Altona when a bull escaped and wounded my mother very seriously, cutting her face open. From that day on she could never work again.

We somehow carried on until sometime in March 1945 when all the small camps were closed down and we were sent to Bergen-Belsen. My mother was taken on a stretcher and was in a different cattle truck from me. Soon after arrival at Belsen, we found ourselves covered from head to foot with lice. The camp was completely infested. No food was coming into the camp and the water supply had been cut off. Like leaves that fall from a tree, people were falling down and dying. There was sheer chaos in the camp. After a few days of frantic searching, I finally found my mother in one of the huts, still alive – but only just.

By then we realized that the war was coming to an end, as the SS men and women were walking around with white armbands, to show that they were surrendering, hoping to save themselves. However, we also knew that we couldn't last much longer and had given up all hope of surviving. The British 2nd army liberated Belsen on 15 April 1945. As soon as possible, we were transferred to the tank-training school six kilometres away for delousing and then to makeshift hospitals, where German doctors and nurses were made to look after us. I was unconscious for ten days after we were liberated. Two days after I regained consciousness, on 27 April, my mother died aged

42 and was buried in a mass grave, together with the thousands of others who died from starvation and disease after the liberation.

I remained in hospital for several weeks until I was fit to come out, when I was given some clothes and allocated a room with several other survivors – refugees from every country in Europe. We picked up a little of each other's languages and, by mixing in a little German, managed to communicate. But we were not really interested in each other or in the fact that the war was over. Everyone had two preoccupations – staying alive and being reunited with any surviving relatives. After a few weeks, my aunt Miriam, who was in a nearby camp at Braunschweig, came to Belsen to look up the register of survivors, and found my name on it. I was so grateful that someone from my family had found me, and she took me back with her to Braunschweig.

After a few months, we made our way back to Lodz in Poland and I realized that I had lost my home, my possessions, my entire family, my health and my education. The journey was very difficult since we had no money and the trains did not run properly, so it took three weeks to get back to Lodz. We walked part of the way, hitched lifts and travelled on the roofs of trains. We lived on potatoes or whatever scraps we could scrounge from local farmers. One day, we were sitting in a goods train on the Polish border. I was holding a parcel containing my shoes – on my feet was a pair of new shoes, two sizes too small, which my aunt had obtained for her son, whom she hoped to find alive. The idea was that if we were robbed, the new shoes would not be taken. Of course we were robbed – by Russian soldiers who swept through the train and left us with nothing. So I had a lovely pair of tight shoes to start a new life with!

In Lodz I found one of my mother's sisters, Gitl, who had also come back from one of the camps. She took me in and shared what little she had with me. I was very ill with a festering skin disease. Because we had no money to buy ointment, I was told to rub salt into the itchy, open wounds. The skin disease eventually cleared up – but I don't recommend the salt treatment! At the end of 1945, Gitl remarried and together we made our way back to Germany, via Czechoslovakia and Austria, since Poland was very antisemitic. From Germany, we made our way to Paris. In the beginning, life in Paris was very difficult for us – we had no official papers, no money, and we could not speak French.

In 1949 I met my husband, Charles, in Paris. He is British and, coincidentally, was one of the Military Police who were among the first to enter Belsen. He arrested the woman commandant, Irma Grese, who was later hanged. He brought me back to London and we were married the same year. We have a son and a daughter and five grandchildren.

My parents in Zdunska-Vola in 1938

This testimony is dedicated to my darling grandchildren,
Rebecca, Daniela and Susanna, Adrian and Benjamin,
and to the memory of my family who perished in the Holocaust.

Freddie (Avram) aged three, 1929

AVRAM SCHAUFELD
A Journey – Chorzów to Wembley

I was 13 years old in 1939 when the Germans invaded Poland. I had had
my bar mitzvah about two months before, and among my presents was a
wristwatch of which I was very proud. Almost immediately after the
Germans arrived, my father was taken away and we never saw him again. A
few weeks later, some officials came to our house. They made an inventory
of everything that was valuable and put seals on it, telling us that we were
not allowed to sell any of the listed articles. Our part of Upper Silesia was
swiftly incorporated into the Third Reich and in the spring of 1940 was
made *Judenrein* (free of Jews). We were simply given a date by which we had
to leave and were left to make our own arrangements. My mother hired a
horse and cart and we loaded onto it all that remained of our belongings.
Then our sad little group trekked over the border to Sosnowitz in Poland,
20 miles away from home, where Jews were still permitted to live.

The *Judenrat* (Jewish Council) in Sosnowitz allocated us one room in
the flat of a Miss Borenstein. It was a four-roomed flat and there was a family
in every room, including the kitchen! Later that year the Germans started
taking Jews to forced labour camps. At first people who got ill were sent
back home and were able to tell us about the hard work and brutality they
had had to endure, so naturally everybody who could tried to avoid being
taken away for forced labour.

The Germans instituted a system of different colour identity cards
which they called *Kennkarte*. There were different colours for the unemployed,
self-employed, people employed by the *Judenrat* and so on. The most
prized one was the yellow card, which meant that you worked for the
Germans and, we thought, offered maximum security. People paid a lot of
money to get such employment. My mother had no money, but she had
good connections with some important people and so in due course we were
all employed in the big Hans Held concern which manufactured uniforms
for the German army. My brother worked in the office, mother was sewing
on buttons and I packed the finished uniforms for delivery.

I liked the nightshift best; there were very few Germans about and in the room next to us were lots of young girls using sewing machines and they sang songs and told stories while they worked.

Alas, things were getting worse: the Germans now had their sights on us and started taking people from the firms which worked for them. One fine spring day in 1942 they descended on our factory and took part of the workforce away. It was not my lucky day. I remember one minute I was packing khaki shirts for General Rommel's Africa army and the next thing I knew I was being marched off by guards with dogs and whips in their hands. We were taken to the transit place in a heavily-guarded former Jewish secondary school. Here we received a foretaste of what was to come. Constant *appells* (roll-calls), beatings, kicks and so called *gymnastik*, after which some people had to be carried away on stretchers.

Sometimes, the guards allowed people to stand on the pavement opposite the building where we were being held. On the day before we left for Germany, my older brother came and we were able to shout to each other. As I was on the third floor and everyone else was calling to their relatives as well, we really couldn't hear anything at all. It didn't matter, as we were all saying more or less the same things. On a sudden impulse I took off my wristwatch, wrapped it in a handkerchief and threw it down to my brother. He did not catch it and it probably broke as it fell to the ground, but I felt I had established contact with him. Where I was going I had no need of a watch.

I was taken to the forced labour camp, Gräditz, in Lower Silesia, Germany, where I arrived in autumn 1942. The place had once been a factory and was three storeys high. It had huge rooms with small windows and a narrow stone staircase. It looked grim. The guard room was near the exit gates, the *Appellplatz* (assembly place) was a small patch of concreted ground at the back of the building and the kitchen was in a wooden shed nearby. The food usually consisted of unpeeled potatoes and big green leaves of unknown origin, cooked with all the dirt still on. Some bread and sugarbeet jam completed our provisions. I still remember the jubilation when some friends and I were detailed to bring in a horse that had dropped dead in the nearby small town. Meat for a few days!

The work consisted of converting a big redundant brick factory into a *Wehrmacht* (German army) store. One day when we arrived, the German engineer in charge, an absolute sadist, shouted, "Carpenters step forward!" As I have no ambition in that direction and woodwork at school was a nightmare, I thought that I didn't qualify. But being short of the number of carpenters needed, the Nazi just pointed at me and some others and said, *"Du bist ein Zimmermann"* (You're a carpenter). When I protested, I was rewarded with a slap and kicks. The woodwork involved wasn't difficult and all the others could do it, but I am ashamed to say that I just could not. I tried hard and my friends showed me repeatedly, but all was in vain. The engineer quickly found out that I had two left hands and twice daily came directly to me shouting *"Saboteur"* and beating me up. The German foreman, who was quite decent, tried to intercede, pointing out that I definitely was no carpenter, but it was to no avail.

And then a miracle happened! The engineer was away for a few days and a request came for carpenters to be sent to Laurahütte in Upper Silesia, just a few miles down the road from where I once lived. The foreman quickly sent me away and on arrival in Laurahütte, we carpenters were employed in carrying planks of wood round the workplace. That level of carpentry was just up my street! Then fate intervened again and I was sent every day from Laurahütte to work in Königshütte, five minutes by tram from my former home.

Königshütte was also a huge steelworks, part of the Herrman Göring Werke, and we were helping to build new iron-smelting ovens. The old foundations had to be blown up first and here I could show where my skills lay! As I was a local boy and spoke the local patois (swear-words included), I had a certain advantage, and was chosen to work with two former miners in demolishing the old parts. We drilled holes in the bricks and concrete and stuffed dynamite into them, and the fuses led to a plunger just like you see in Western films. I was given a red peaked cap and a loud hooter and carried a red flag. *On my orders* everybody had to leave the danger area and then the charges were detonated. I have never been so important, before or since!

My downfall was unexpected and sudden. On Saturdays my bosses finished work at midday, but we had to continue till five o'clock. I was allowed to stay in our little shed till then and afterwards joined the rest of the workers. It was a hot day and I dozed off, and at five o'clock when everybody assembled to go back to the camp, I was missing. The search started and when I finally emerged from the hut, I was accused of trying to escape. On our return to the camp, I was publicly flogged and put into the *Straffkollonne* (penal gang) which was not allowed to leave the camp and worked under a brutal and sadistic German foreman.

Then in 1943, I was sent from Laurahütte to work on construction in a camp called Blechhammer. Prisoners of war from half a dozen countries were working there, as well as civilians dragged away from their homelands, and Jews like me. Conditions in the camp were bad. We worked and slept in the same clothes and the place was full of lice and bedbugs. There was only cold water and the food was meagre. The paper mattresses on our bunks only contained a little dirty straw which was never changed. We were occasionally taken to a delousing place, but five minutes later, we were full of vermin again.

At first our guards were a motley assortment of people, but in early 1944 a whole lot of SS men descended on us, and things changed. They started with a 'selection', and all the sick and unfit were sent to their death at Auschwitz. Then we were photographed, tattooed and had new camp clothes with our numbers on them. We were drilled to exhaustion, and *Mützen auf* and *Mützen ab* (cap on and cap off) had to be in unison – no easy task with 5,000 people!

On the positive side, everything was deloused. There was hot water in the showers and washrooms. Everything had to be spotless and the food got better with an SS cook in the kitchen. Unfortunately, there was also an SS medic in the sick bay so it was better not to go there – those thought to be too ill were sent to Auschwitz.

Two rather unusual things happened at Blechhammer. Firstly, the SS set us to work on beautifying the place: everything was painted, the floors oiled and so on. Rumours were circulating that the SS intended to make us a model camp which would be inspected by the International Red Cross. Postcards were handed out and we were told to write home, this in a camp that was 100 per cent Jewish and in late 1944. I often wondered what happened to those postcards and what was the purpose of it all? Maybe they intended to make us docile and pretended all was well with the world.

Then something even stranger occurred: one Sunday afternoon all the young people were summoned and an SS officer made a speech, saying they wanted to teach us different trades, and asking us what we wanted to be – painters, mechanics, bricklayers etc. From then on, when the factory hooter went at 12 noon, we started school, learning about different bricks and their weight, mortar and so on. I am ashamed to say that I became the star pupil because I could speak German and had been working with bricks and mortar for the last three years! Then, as the Soviet army approached, our schooling stopped. I often wonder today what was behind the whole idea. Did the SS really think our skills would be needed to rebuild the Reich, or were they trying to give themselves an alibi?

It was obvious to us that the Germans were losing the war, and we witnessed our factory being bombed. January 1945 came; the weather was terribly cold and it snowed a lot. On sunny days we could see different planes circling around – usually single planes, flying very high for a short time. The ex-servicemen among us said they were Soviet reconnaissance planes, and so the Red Army could not be that far away. Suddenly we were told that the SS had decided to give us a couple of days' holiday and we stayed in the camp.

On 21 January, the SS started to evacuate the camp and there was complete chaos. I only discovered after the war that the Red Army had broken through near Warsaw on 16 January 1945. The Germans opened the food stores and some people grabbed a lot of provisions; the majority (including me) got nothing. We started on our march, not knowing where we were going or how long it would last. Even on the first day, older and weaker people fell behind and we heard shots as they were being murdered by the SS. Each night we rested in a farm or abandoned factory and, if we were lucky, we received a few potatoes.

We were soon starving. I vividly remember that when we were passing a house, a woman threw out some potato and onion peelings and a mass of prisoners fought for the scraps. The guards waded in with rifle butts and in the end some people lay dying by the roadside. Another time, we were given a loaf to be shared between ten of us. While we were trying to share it out, an air raid started and the lights went out. A desperate struggle ensued and I felt somebody grabbing my bread. I knew that I had to have it back and in the pitch dark, I took somebody else's ration away. The loss of bread was like a death sentence. To this day I feel deeply ashamed of this, but by then we were reduced to the level of savages.

We trudged on. There were fewer of us each day and we were getting weaker. One day, as we went into a barn, there was very little space left and I climbed onto some farm machinery, where to my surprise I found a quantity of unmilled wheat. I filled my little bag with it and chewed it as I walked, sharing it with friends or exchanging it for sugar beet. After two days a German guard saw me eating. He took my bag, emptied the corn on the ground and ground it with his boots. Other guards kicked over churns of milk or water that farmers put out for us.

By now I had an ulcer on my foot and walked with a limp. One morning, as I was staggering out of the barn, two SS officers stopped me and asked, *"Kannst Du nicht laufen?"* (Can't you walk?). As this was said with a smile on their faces, it lulled me into a stupor; after all those years at their mercy I should have known better. I replied, *"Nein"* and was directed to a row of horse-drawn carriages standing nearby. The minute I climbed on one, I recognised my mistake as it was full of *Muselmen*, camp inmates who had lost the will to live. Alas, it was too late: we were guarded and there was no going back. Although I could hardly walk and was crawling with lice, I still didn't consider myself a *Muselman* and when the carriages started to move, I started to think of some way of escape. But it was not feasible: in winter it gets dark very early and when we arrived at our destination, it was already dusk. I could see that we were outside a cemetery, bordered by a brick wall.

The SS now started shoving us towards the wall and total bedlam followed as people realized what was at stake. They started shouting and praying. I walked towards the wall, climbed over and lay down in the snow among the gravestones. There was no thinking or planning involved, adrenaline and self preservation took over. I heard the shooting and screaming, and then single shots as they finished off those who were still alive. Then I heard German voices and an SS man entered the cemetery and, not far from me, undid his greatcoat and passed water. By the light of the moon I could clearly see his belt buckle and pressed myself hard into the snow and hoped. Luck was on my side and he didn't see me. When he left and joined the rest of the SS, I could hear them leaving and then all was silent.

I got up, cold, hungry, not knowing where I was, and left the cemetery. In the distance I saw the lights of a village and started walking towards it. I lost my wooden shoes and was now barefoot. It took me some time to reach the village; it straddled a road and I didn't walk down it, but went through the back of the houses. I tried lots of gates and eventually one was open. I walked in, found a shed with some hay and being utterly tired, covered myself and fell instantly asleep.

I was shaken and woken up to female shouts of "Jesus Maria" and could make out the farmer's wife holding a lantern, her husband pointing a pitchfork at me and a German policeman holding a rifle – and a dog barking and jumping at me. There was the inevitable *"Hände Hoch"* (Hands up) and then the policeman handcuffed me and I was led out of the farm. He took me to the small village police station and hearing the commotion, two of the wives came to see me. To my surprise, they showed more compassion than the farmer's wife and I could hear them saying *"Armer Kerl, so jung"* (Poor lad, so young) and they brought me bread and coffee. It was obvious to the two policemen where I came from and so I was handcuffed again and a quite elderly *Shupo* (*Schutzpolizei*, ordinary German policeman) with a rifle took me back to the SS, who by then were in a small neighbouring town. All the way the policeman tried to be nice, saying that he would let me go but *"Befehl ist Befehl"* (Orders are orders), that the SS would probably shoot me and he had a son missing in Russia. I am afraid that he didn't succeed in cheering me up; too much had happened that night and now that dawn was breaking, I was completely exhausted and shocked.

On reaching the SS, he went in to report, and again luck intervened in the shape of women who gathered on the landing of the house where they were staying that night. I started hearing some more "Jesus Marias" and when the SS man came out with a greatcoat over his pyjamas, he looked at the woman and asked me, "What's your number?" He wrote it down and shouted to a guard, "Take the *Schweinhund* to the barn, I'll deal with him in Buchenwald." There I rejoined my transport and after a short time we were on the march again. Soon afterwards, as we reached the river Neisse, we could see burning villages and hear gunfire in the distance. The bridge was guarded by the *Volksturm* (Home Guard) and was wired for demolition, but the Nazis still got us across. The next day we reached Gross Rosen concentration camp.

In the dark we could see searchlights sweeping over Gross Rosen. We were directed to a field outside where an extension to the camp was being built. Even in January 1945 the Nazis were still extending camps and even building new ones. We were cramped into an unfinished barrack where most of the time we had to sit with our knees bent so we could all fit into the place. The *Kapos* (prisoners in charge) cordoned off a big comfortable place for themselves and as most of them were "green triangle" prisoners (common criminals), and carried huge cudgels, we were completely at their mercy. We had to stand for hours in the bitter weather for the *Zählappell* (head count) and as new transports arrived constantly from the east, the numbers never tallied anyway. There I finally lost track of people I knew and did not even possess a tin plate, spoon or mug. Luckily I found a rusty old tin from which I could drink the watery soup.

After a few days we were loaded onto an open train. The wagons had previously been used for coal, and we were soon covered in coal dust. Because of air raids and troop transports, we travelled very slowly and made frequent stops. We tried to relieve ourselves by sitting precariously over the edge of the wagon and the stops were convenient for throwing out the corpses.

After a few days we arrived at Weimar where we were bombed by the Americans. Luckily their aim wasn't too good, but it was fun to see the SS escort running for shelter. From Weimar it is only a short distance to Buchenwald, where we were greeted by SS men with dogs, and escorted to the quarantine camp. There we were deprived of everything we had and went through a delousing procedure, after which we were issued with clothing and shoes. My trousers once belonged to a Dutchman: they had no fly but the whole front unbuttoned. Unfortunately, they had no buttons or belt, and so I had to keep the flap closed with my hand. Later, I was very lucky indeed to find a piece of string.

Then we were admitted to the camp which was terribly overcrowded and apart from being counted, we were able to rest. I don't remember how long this lasted, but one day we were inspected by an SS doctor who tried to transfer as many people as possible to other camps.

Once again I found myself on a train, but this time the journey was short and we stopped at a station called Langenstein in the Harz Mountains. We got off and were marched through the village to the partly finished camp of Langenstein-Zwieberge. It was located among beautiful scenery, but was the worst place I experienced.

On arrival we stood on the *Appellplatz* and the camp commander gave us a lecture, the gist of which was that any transgression was punishable by death. After that, we were allocated an unfinished barrack with no glass in the windows or sleeping bunks. We slept in our working clothes on the floor and fought like animals over our food. During air raids we quickly had to put out the solitary light bulb or the sentries from the watchtower would shoot at it. All the people from our transport were so emaciated that going to work was an achievement, never mind the back-breaking task of digging tunnels in the mountains for Hitler's war factories. None of the good *Kommandos* (work-crews) wanted *Muselmen* in their ranks and so every morning we had to run from group to group, and the weakest people always ended up with the worst work allocation. The food was minimal and the mortality rate very high. The dead were stacked like cordwood outside the *Krankenbau* (sick bay) awaiting disposal and the living helped themselves to any of their clothing so some of the corpses lay completely naked.

One day my turn came and it happened very suddenly. My legs gave way and however hard I tried, I couldn't get up. I was left lying by the side of the railway track till the end of the shift and then my workmates had to carry me back to camp. There I was dropped in the mud and snow of the *Appellplatz* till the counting was over and everybody had left. I lay in the dark, more and more frozen, would probably not have survived very much longer without the help of two young Russians, who asked me what was wrong. My Russian was fairly good then and they decided to carry me to my barrack. So I lay in the block but nobody took any notice of me, and for good measure I was also incontinent.

In the morning everybody left for work and the *Stubendienst* (prisoner in charge of the barrack) came round, warning me that the SS made searches every morning; if they found an "unofficial" sick prisoner, my chances wouldn't be too bright. Alas, I had no choice and so awaited my fate with resignation. Soon enough two SS with an Alsatian came round. I shut my eyes, held my breath and thought that after all my experiences this was a silly way to die. I could feel the dog's wet nose sniffing me and the SS men poking me with the tips of their jackboots. Then they left me. The *Stubendienst* couldn't get over this very unusual behaviour for the SS.

Later in the day, two orderlies came with a stretcher and carried me to the sick bay, saying they were bringing a dysentery case. The dysentery room was small, had no windows and the stench was nightmarish. I spent a night there and in the morning the orderly said, "You didn't shit yourself, so you don't have dysentery, you have pneumonia" and he had me transferred to a biggish room, this time with windows.

I was brushed with some disinfectant and given a short shirt reaching only to my navel. We lay two to a bunk and had one blanket between us, the mattress was made from paper and very dirty, and in spite of the disinfectant, the lice and bedbugs had a feast. The Nazis in their wisdom gave reduced rations to the sick and so every morning the orderly had the task of removing the dead – which he did by dragging them by their feet across the floor, their heads bumping up and down to the accompaniment of choice Russian swear-words. Whilst I was there, I shared my bunk with three people who died.

One day the Germans started to evacuate the camp. An SS man with an automatic gun entered and said, "*Alle 'raus* (All out), we're going to burn the place down." People crawled on all fours out of the barrack and after the war we heard that very few people survived the evacuation. Those of us who could not even crawl stayed behind, and again luck was with us – they did not burn the camp down. Suddenly all was quiet and only a few guards were left, along with a few decent doctors and orderlies who stayed. During the night we heard distant gunfire and then in the morning stillness. Our guards had disappeared, and one brave fellow went to the gate and came back with American soldiers in a jeep. The strange thing is we didn't cheer or wave: apathy reigned.

The American soldiers quickly alerted the medical corps and soon the place was swarming with people. The local Germans had to come and see what their Führer had achieved. They then had to bury the dead and start cleaning and cooking. Unfortunately the food was too rich and after quite a few of us died, the rest were transferred to a US Army Hospital.

From the US army hospital in Halberstadt, Germany, I was later transferred to a foreigners' hospital in Braunschweig which was in the British zone of Germany. Afterwards, I spent over two and a half years in a Displaced Persons Camp.

I came to the UK in 1948 as a European Voluntary Worker and trained as a miner in Cowdenbeath, Scotland. In 1949, I went to Israel where I worked on a kibbutz and in 1952 married Vera. After we lost our first baby, we left and came to London in 1954. While Vera worked as a teacher, I trained to become a Chartered Physiotherapist and later was Head Physiotherapist of a large department of a London hospital. In 1991, at the age of 65, I retired.

Trainee coalminer, Cowdenbeath, Scotland, 1948

Avram and Vera in Kibbutz Nitzanim, Israel, in 1953

I dedicate my story to our four grandchildren, Ben, Ellie, Jackie and Helen.

On the way to England with a Dutch friend of my parents, Mine Stapensea, Hook of Holland, 1 June 1939

VERA SCHAUFELD

Saved by the Kindertransport

I will begin by telling you a little about my family. My father was born in a small town in south-west Bohemia called Klatovy. I believe that my grandfather's brother went there as a Hebrew teacher some time in the 19th century, and the rest of the family followed. My father and his brother and two sisters began life in the synagogue courtyard, living in rooms above the religious school next to the synagogue, but later my grandfather prospered and owned a brick factory and a match factory, and the children were educated in Czech schools.

My father studied law and greatly admired one of his teachers, Professor Masaryk, who later became President of Czechoslovakia. My father was very proud of being a Czech citizen. Though he practised law in Klatovy, he also represented Czechoslovakia at international law conferences, as well as being the leader of the local Jewish community.

My mother was born in Iserlohn, a town in Westphalia, Germany, and from an early age, she was determined to be a doctor. In fact she became the first girl in her town to attend the boys' grammar school so that she could study science and go to the university of Heidelberg.

My parents met on a sight-seeing bus tour of Frankfurt am Main in Germany when my father offered my mother his window seat. They began talking and found that they were both Jewish. He kept returning to Germany until she agreed to marry him, but only on condition that she could continue her studies in Prague. They married in 1929 and I was born ten months later.

I grew up in Klatovy, where in 1930 the town had a population of about 8,000, of whom about 350 were Jews. The community was a progressive one, the synagogue housed an organ and had a choir, but the nearest kosher butcher was in Pilsen, which was about 30 miles away.

My grandmother left Germany in 1934 and came to live with us, and then our household became more observant. We started to keep kosher and my grandmother lit candles on Friday nights. My mother finished her studies in Prague and went to Paris to specialise in paediatrics. In 1936 my nurse became her receptionist, and she set up her medical practice in the same building in the town square where my father had his offices.

I remember my life in Klatovy as being very happy. I was an only child and felt very loved by parents and relatives and had lots of friends. I was one of the few Jewish children in the local primary school, but was hardly aware of this until 15 March 1938 when the Germans invaded Czechoslovakia. We all sat around the radio and my nurse said, "England has betrayed us," as we listened to the broadcast. Within a few days, my father was arrested and suddenly an atmosphere of fear grew. German soldiers took away our radio and we saw soldiers everywhere.

My father was soon released but everything started to change. My nurse and our cook were not allowed to work for us any more, and my friends told me that my teacher, whom I had always liked, had made anti-semitic remarks when my mother kept me away from school until my father was home again. Until this time, I had very little understanding of what was happening in Germany. I suppose my parents wanted to shelter me, but now this was no longer possible.

One day in early May 1939, my mother surprised me by meeting me outside the school and taking me to the little park opposite. We sat down on a bench and she told me that I was to go alone to England. She promised that as soon as they could, she and my father would either join me or send for me to join them, but in the meantime I was to go on a train with other children to safety. I was only nine years old.

The next few days were very busy. I visited my nurse, who gave me a small rosary which I still have, and all my friends wrote in my new auto-graph album. I felt a mixture of excitement and some anxiety as we packed.

On arriving at Prague station, I found that my parents were not allowed onto the platform and my last sight of them was as they stood behind the barrier, waving white handkerchiefs, while I looked at them out of the train window.

As we travelled through Germany, my Uncle Rudolf and Aunt Elsa joined the train and stood with me in the corridor until they had to leave at the Dutch border. I never saw either of them again. In Holland, Dutch friends of my parents came to see me onto the boat.

My next memory is of sitting on Liverpool Street station in London, hearing announcements in a strange language, seeing children all round me being collected and fearing that I would be left there alone. At last a lady called Miss Leigh came and took me and two other children in her car. During the journey I had to keep asking her to stop the car so that I could get out and be sick. Luckily, she spoke German.

The Christian family who had agreed to take in a refugee child had a daughter who was three years older than me, and who was very kind. Yet I was desperately homesick. Everything was strange: the bread was white, the table manners were different and I could only communicate with signs. One great comfort was the letters and cards from home which arrived nearly every day. My parents could also send parcels with presents for my guardians' daughter and Czech books for me; best of all they could even speak to me on the telephone.

Then came 3 September and war broke out. Suddenly all those letters which had spoken of possible visas for my parents in Mexico, Shanghai and South America, stopped arriving. I felt terribly lonely and unhappy. My guardians treated me very well, but I was not their child. I knew that they had only expected to keep me for a few months and now they had to look after me for the duration of the war. I kept thinking, against all reason, that perhaps somehow it was my fault that I had had to leave home, and if I had been a better child, I could have stayed with my family.

Time passed and I quickly forgot Czech and German, though I had been literate in both, and English became my sole language. I went to a Methodist boarding school with my guardians' daughter and settled down to wartime conditions like everyone else.

When our English lesson was interrupted on 7 May 1945 by the news that the war in Europe was over, I shouted, "Hooray!" and was sent out of the classroom for causing a disturbance. I remember thinking, "This is wonderful. I shall see all my family and friends soon, but how will I pass my School Certificate Exams now that I have forgotten all my Czech?" Then I decided not to worry if I had to stay down a class for a year or two, because what mattered was to be back home again.

I don't know how I heard the news that no one in my family had survived. I only remember those terrible pictures of the camps we saw in the cinema, and not being able to believe that this was what had become of my parents.

After the war, the friends of my parents who had met me in Holland, who were not Jewish, invited me to visit them. They gave me some things my mother and father had sent to them for safe-keeping, and among these were their wedding rings. I now wear my mother's ring, and I often wonder what they felt and what they were thinking when they took the rings off their fingers and sent them to Holland for me to have.

I was lucky to be able to go to college and become independent as a teacher and in charge of my own future. Because I had had almost no contact with Jewish people, I decided to go to Israel and spend a year working on a kibbutz. My first night in Israel happened to be the first evening of Passover and I sat next to a young kibbutz member who was a shepherd. His name was Avram and he had survived slave labour in Auschwitz and Buchenwald and finally arrived in Kibbutz Nitzanim. It was here that we later married.

After some years, we decided to return to England and brought up our two daughters while I continued to work as a teacher. I was lucky enough to be able to work first with children, and then with teachers in teaching English as a second language to immigrant children. My own experience helped me to empathise with their difficulties and try to support them in gaining a new language and finding themselves in a strange culture.

It was only when I was invited to Esther Rantzen's television programme that I became aware of the role that Nicholas Winton had played in my rescue. I suddenly found other people who had also come on the *Kindertransports* and felt that I was not alone in this experience. For the first time in 50 years, I could face having my parents' letters translated and be able to read them and find they were not full of reproaches to me for not writing enough and forgetting so much. Instead I found how full of love they were and how my parents tried so hard to find good news to share with me.

I dedicate my story to my guardians, Leonard and Nancy Faires
of Bury St. Edmunds, Suffolk, and to my parents who saved my life.

Vera in Klatovy aged eight, 1938

My parents Frieda and Samuel Koenig with their three children, Helen aged seven, Renée aged four and Joé aged two and a half, about 1937

HELEN STEIN

The Courage of Marianne

I was a little girl like many others in 1936. I lived in Strasbourg in France, near the German border, with my parents and sister and brother. We had a pleasant family life, but we were aware of what was happening over the border in Germany. We had relations who lived just across the river Rhine; they were living under a Nazi government, and were oppressed and persecuted. The German radio broadcast terrible, threatening propaganda speeches. My parents were demoralised and depressed, and feared for the future.

In 1939 war broke out in Europe, and the whole population of Alsace was evacuated. We had to leave our possessions behind. My father was in the French army, and my mother settled with the three children in a little town near Limoges.

In 1940, the German army occupied part of France, and the armistice was signed. Then a pro-German government was established in Vichy, which was in the non-occupied zone. Limoges was in this part of France.

The life of Jewish citizens was becoming very difficult as new laws were passed. Jews had to register with the police and were not allowed to move to another address. Identity cards were stamped with the word "Jew" in red, and even ration cards. Most professions were prohibited for Jews, and later no work was allowed. We were not allowed to travel. There was very little to eat as the Germans confiscated much of the food available to send to their own country. There were long queues outside the bakeries and grocers. We tried to live as best we could, to retain a semblance of normal life.

In the occupied zone, Jews had even more restrictions. They had to wear a yellow star on their clothes to be easily recognised. People complied with these different demands, wishing to remain in order with the authorities. Some people arranged to get false papers, but my parents were terrified of the repercussions if they were found out. I envied other little girls who had a more normal life, but I had a few friends and loved going to the cinema which was a treat at the time. I was then 11 years old.

At the end of 1942, the Allies landed in North Africa and the Germans occupied the whole of France. The French government abandoned its Jewish citizens to the Nazis and French collaborators helped them. We were being hounded, and groups of people were taken away. Some friends of ours were taken at five o'clock in the morning with a brutal knock at the door. We never heard of them again. Some of the police force – those who were patriotic and felt sorry for us – managed to forewarn their Jewish friends of an imminent raid. I remember once we hid for a couple of days in a convent. Another time, my parents were hidden by a kind lady on a farm. But an SS regiment was stationed in the town for a few days and she saw them marching along the road. She must have been very frightened because she told my parents, "I can't keep you any more, it's my life or yours." The penalty for hiding Jews was death.

My parents had good friends and they supported each other, but we lived in fear. Informers were lurking everywhere, waiting to denounce Jews to the Gestapo for a money reward. In my mind, I imagined our arrest: the dreaded doorbell ringing. I visualised myself escaping through the gardens, but then I realized that I could not leave my parents and sister and brother. How would I survive?

One day, a Jewish holiday, when all the men were in a hall of worship, my mother saw a lorry full of German soldiers passing by. She immediately thought they had come to arrest us. She was frantic because the Nazis often rounded up Jews in synagogues. She sent me to warn the men to disperse and hide. But it was a false alarm.

We were deprived of our basic human rights. A few bishops and some clergy protested by sending letters and preaching that people should help to hide Jews. It was forbidden to listen to foreign radio stations, but at night we listened secretly to the BBC from London, which gave us real news about the war. Sometimes it was a real morale booster, for example when we heard about the battle of Stalingrad in Russia, the first great defeat of the German army.

The Nazis reacted with brutal repression to the increasing activity and acts of sabotage by the Resistance. Even when they caught boy partisans of only 16 or 17, they shot them and showed no mercy. In retaliation for any sabotage, they took innocent civilian hostages. Many young boys helped the Resistance by distributing leaflets and carrying clandestine information.

People simply vanished. At school, if you had a good friend who was Jewish, one morning he wouldn't turn up, and you would never see him again. Children might go home for dinner one day to find that their father or mother had disappeared; the children had to be put in an orphanage and were often later deported.

By the end of 1943, Jewish organisations were working secretly to set up networks for saving babies and children. Their task was to find Christian families, convents, colleges who would help to hide children. The children were placed in a totally different environment and had to assume a new identity and act accordingly. They had to deny their origins. Young women from the organisations had to take on the role of social worker and visit the children once a month to pay for their upkeep and to bring them things they needed, like a pair of shoes or soap, and to comfort them. Some children could not adapt and the organisation arranged a new scheme to arrange illegal passages into Switzerland and Spain. Some children had to walk five hours over the high Pyrenees mountains into Spain. Lots of people tried to escape to Switzerland, but often the Swiss guards sent them back to their death.

The situation was getting worse all the time and my parents took the agonising decision to send us to Switzerland. I was thirteen, my sister was ten and my brother nine. We were provided with false papers and taken to the city of Limoges, where we waited a few days for a convoy of children to be formed. We were very sad to be separated from our parents. My mother went back home with a heavy heart, crying, with our little two-year-old sister, and my father went to hide in a forest.

We went to Limoges station where the enormous hall was full of German soldiers in uniform, with their black jackboots. They looked frightening and I was shaking. I was glad to get into the train carriage and sit in a corner; I would have liked to be invisible. From there, we travelled to Lyon and stayed in a convent with some very nice nuns who looked after us and comforted us. During the night, there was an air raid and we had to go to the shelters. I remember saying, "I'm not scared of bombs, there's no comparison with fear of Germans."

After a few days in Lyon, we left for Annecy near the Swiss border. Our organisation told their Swiss contact that 30 children would be crossing the border. But in Geneva the Jewish official warned our minders, "Don't pass so many children at once. It's too great a risk. The Gestapo and Customs officers are everywhere." Unfortunately, our convoy had already left.

The border on the French side was patrolled and illuminated by flashing lights; it could only be passed at certain times of night between patrols. We were waiting on the lakeside for our guide, in cheerful mood. Freedom was near. Our guide was late, but at last she arrived. She was called Marianne; she was 21 years old and had a lovely smile. She talked to us and explained that the Swiss guards wore a similar uniform to the Germans, saying we should not be frightened. We got into a van and travelled to the border.

From where the van stopped, it was only one minute's walk across a meadow to Switzerland.

But before we had time to get out, I saw a black car appear and four men with dogs stepped out. *Les Allemands* (The Germans). Marianne had to show our false papers and explained that we were going to a children's home. Meanwhile, one of the boys tried to run away and was grabbed by a dog just like a parcel. He was very traumatised and kept shouting, "I'm not Jewish." The other children told him to be quiet. There was panic in the van. We tried to destroy some identity papers and a little Swiss money that we had. I told my sister and brother that we were going to die.

Marianne told them that we were from Lyon, that the city had been bombarded and we were on our way to a children's home. Somehow it worked, and we were allowed to travel to the children's home. The Matron there realized that we were not the children she had been expecting, but she said nothing. Perhaps she phoned the Germans later. I will never know. We went to bed.

At three o'clock in the morning, the Germans came back. They came into the dormitories and held torches near our faces to select the older children for questioning. They started questioning Marianne, slapping her furiously and beating up the boys. At dawn, we were taken away in a van and I asked a guard, "Where are we going?" He didn't answer me.

They took us to Annemasse, their regional headquarters, to the "Prison du Pax", the prison for partisans and political prisoners. They also kept people there who had been captured trying to escape to Switzerland before sending them to be deported. Partisans were tortured there and we heard their screams. We were put in cells; we sat and slept on straw mattresses, and had only one cold water tap above a hole which functioned as a toilet. Marianne gave us warmth and tried to cheer us up. The youngest child was a little girl of three years old and we all tried to mother her.

The mayor of Annemasse, Mr Deffaught, had good contact with the Nazis. They trusted him, but in fact he was a true patriot and was helping the Resistance. Exceptionally, he was allowed to come into the prison and visit. He arranged for us to be brought soup every day by a charity. He was very kind, we felt that he was on our side and he saved some people.

Marianne was taken away every day for questioning and was tortured. She would come back with a red face and swollen eyes. I was always waiting for her and felt better when she was there. She told me that she was subjected to hot and cold baths. But she was very courageous and never let the Germans know the truth: that she was Jewish. They thought she was a French Resistance fighter, but she was from Germany. Her surname was

"Cohn" and a forger had cleverly changed it to "Colin" on her papers. They questioned her regularly: they wanted to know who and where the organisers were; who provided the false papers. But she did not betray her contacts. She told them she had saved 200 children and would do it again.

Our French driver was freed after a few days because Marianne stuck to her story: we had missed the train and were hitch-hiking; the driver had picked us up and didn't know anything. We children were told that we were going to be interrogated by the Gestapo, each of us separately. It was an agonising thought. When my turn came, I went into their office, my heart pounding. I saw two Nazis, one sitting on a desk with a revolver pointed towards me and the other in front of a typewriter. There was a whip on the desk. The one at the desk asked my name and address and questioned me intensely. "Who organised your journey? Where did you get your false papers? What is the name of the organisation?" To each question, I replied, "I don't know." He then asked me if I was Jewish, and I said yes. "Do you speak German?" I answered "No," but he didn't believe me and said to his colleague in German, "She's lying." I was in such turmoil, I didn't know whether to say yes or no. But I had not given my real address. When the interview was finished, I was drained and a sense of helplessness came over me.

Marianne had asked the Mayor to plead with the Nazis to free us, and he persuaded them at least to liberate the younger children, those under 14. They agreed to send us to a nearby children's home under strict German supervision. They could not send us yet to Lyon because the railway lines in the region had been damaged by sabotage and bombardments. But there was a condition: the Mayor stressed to all of us that we must not try to escape. He had had to sign a guarantee that he would be a hostage and would be shot if any of us tried to run away. We were well looked after in a Catholic children's home, but I lived with great anxiety as I knew the Germans would come sooner or later to take us back.

One morning, 6 June 1944, we were told the news that the Allies had landed on the beaches of Normandy. It was a great joy.

The older children had to stay in prison with Marianne, and they had to work, cleaning cells and peeling vegetables for the Nazis. They heard the screams of prisoners being tortured. Marianne knew that her fate was sealed and she asked the mayor to bring her books. She read classics, she wrote poetry, she asked for prayer books, but did not get any. She was offered a chance to escape by pretending to have appendicitis, and another when two of her friends outside concocted an escape plan with the help of the local Resistance. But after a day of deliberating, she refused. The children were her responsibility and she could not leave them. The Mayor's wife had sewn a secret pocket into his trousers and he used to smuggle in letters and postcards for her. Her father's birthday was 1 July and at the end of June, she wrote him a card saying, "Another 1 July that you'll be without me. Don't despair, this time it's the last. I would like you to know that in spite of all I've done to make you unhappy, my greatest wish is to live with you again and try to make you forget a little all you have suffered this last year. I embrace you and think of you." She had been arrested by the Gestapo at the end of 1943, then released, so I imagine her parents must have begged her to stop this very dangerous mission.

Marianne was woken on the night of 7 July 1944, along with five of the partisans, and told to get dressed. She asked the prison chief, "Can I take my toothbrush?" He answered, "You won't be needing it." They were taken outside the town to a clearing. Marianne was beaten and hit with a shovel, and they were all shot.

The children in prison missed Marianne and asked where she was. They didn't know that she had been killed. Two weeks later, the Gestapo chief told the Mayor, "These children must disappear. I need the space." The mayor pleaded that they were innocent children. He appealed to him as a father himself and offered to find a place for the children to stay. Mr Deffaught was desperate to say something that could trigger a gesture of mercy or leniency. Marianne's two underground partisan friends were in Annemasse trying to find a way of rescuing the children. They asked Mr Deffaught to negotiate with the Gestapo and pass on a message to the chief. The message ran like this: "The German occupation is coming to an end in the region, and liberation is imminent. If you kill the children, you'll pay with your life. But if you don't touch them, we'll let you escape to Switzerland."

Mr Deffaught had to keep his word and he let the two main Gestapo officials escape to Geneva. At the same time, fierce battles were raging between the German army and the Resistance which was very strong in that part of France, and the American army advancing from the south. The German army capitulated in Annemasse on 18 August 1944. That day two Resistance fighters came and took us quickly to Geneva because they were frightened that the Germans could recapture the town. A few weeks later, Paris was liberated, but the war carried on in the East and on German soil until 8 May 1945.

I was very ill by this time and recuperated in Geneva in a big hotel which had been converted into a refugee centre. The Jewish organisation there wanted to send us to families in the country to recuperate, but I refused vehemently. All I wanted was to go back to my parents. Our parents did not even know about our arrest, but they missed us terribly.

They used to go and hug our clothes in the wardrobe, and cry. I don't know what they would have done if they had known the truth.

My parents were very happy to be reunited with us, but shocked and amazed when they heard what had happened. When the war was over, they wanted to return to their home town of Strasbourg and start a normal life again. They were grieving for the loss of their parents, sisters, brothers and family. But for various reasons it was not possible: my father started work again for an insurance company; and my mother – whose health was affected by her suffering in the war – was very busy bringing up five children, including a little girl of three and a new arrival, a little brother born in 1947.

Marianne had sacrificed her life. She was awarded the Croix de Guerre and Resistance Medal posthumously. There are various monuments to her memory and her story is told in several Holocaust museums. Her name is a symbol of courage and we owe our lives to her.

Marianne Cohn's work for the French Resistance is further described in *Organisation Juive de Combat*, by Georges Loinger and in *Chemins de Passage* by Jean-Claude Croquet.

Four generations of my family: Helen, her daughter Linda, granddaughter Natalie and great-grandson Michael

Triumph over adversity, Three generations of the Stimler family: grandparents, children and grandchildren

BARBARA STIMLER

Destined to Survive

I was born Barbara Krakowski in Alexandrow Kujawski, Poland, on 5 February 1927, the only child of Jacob and Sarah Krakowski. My parents derived our income from my father's small textile shop in Alexandrow, and being the only child, I was showered with love and affection by my parents. No expense was spared to give me a good education and everything I desired. I attended a nursery and private elementary school supervised by Christian nuns, where I was the only Jewish child. I had a large circle of friends, and am still in touch with the few of them who attended my school.

The gathering storm of an imminent war between Poland and Germany brought fear to the Jewish population of Poland. Two hours after hostilities started, the Luftwaffe was bombing our town, sowing panic among the defenceless population. After Poland's defeat, the Germans forcibly despatched the Jewish population of our town to unknown destinations. My parents realized that we had to leave quickly before this forced evacuation. They acquired a horse and cart and we set off with a few belongings to a town called Lubraniec, where my father's brother lived, hoping to take respite there. But newcomers to the town soon had to leave by order of the Gestapo.

We set off again, this time by sledge, towards Warsaw, stopping on the way in Kutno where we found shelter with a Christian family called Lebiedzinski, our previous neighbours from our home town. To avoid endangering our hosts, we left their apartment and found shelter with a Jewish family by the name of Kronsilber, who were still running a grocery shop near the railway. In the middle of the night in January 1940, two drunken German soldiers raided our house and the shop. Hearing the commotion outside, we all ran away into waist-deep snow – all except my mother who was caught. Dressed only in a nightdress, I first ran in the direction of the home of our friends, the Lebiedzinskis. My mother, having been severely beaten, was forced by the Nazis to call me back. I returned to our room, my nightdress was torn off me and I was ordered to bed with the purpose of being raped. I was 13 years old. My mother, realising what was going to happen, ran outside screaming to attract the attention of passers-by, then grabbed a kitchen knife and came to my defence. Meanwhile the Nazis' attention was diverted by German voices outside and they speedily left the room.

We stayed with our hosts until May 1940. Suddenly, we and all the Jews of the town were arrested. Taking only personal belongings, we were marched off to another area of the town and locked into a disused tobacco factory. On the following day, my father was chosen for Nazi 'entertainment'. He was made to undress, put on *teffilin* (small boxes containing biblical passages worn during prayer) and dance. The Nazis then formed two columns facing inwards; they fired a pistol near his ear and made him walk between the lines – while they kicked and spat at him all the way. Exhausted, he was thrown onto a heap of straw. I had to witness this bestiality with all the other prisoners.

A few weeks later, we were woken in the middle of the night and marched off some distance to an abandoned sugar beet factory. We were locked in there, along with some 11,000 inhabitants of Kutno. The conditions in the camp there were indescribable, with hunger and disease rampant. An occasional loaf of bread was thrown over the gates, and during a rainstorm, the water was several inches deep because the roof was damaged; we had to stand on the tables and chairs. We were incarcerated there for six to eight weeks. Watching me starving, my father exchanged the only thing he possessed – his wedding ring – for a bread roll and a glass of milk for me.

Suddenly one day, we heard our names called out by a policeman who had a pass issued by the Germans to transport us to Lubraniec. My father's brother had some influence in the *Judenrat* (Jewish council) and with some bribery had managed to get us freed from Kutno death camp. In Lubraniec we were forced to do manual labour for the Germans.

A week later, the Germans raided Jewish homes and houses of worship. They ordered the Jews to load the holy books and scriptures onto a cart pulled by the local rabbi. He had to start a bonfire and throw all the Torahs and prayer books to feed the flame.

Sometime at the end of 1941, they called all Jewish men, including my father, to the town square, and from there they were transported to Fort Radziwil near Poznan. We received a card from my father telling us that the elderly and young would be returned to Lubraniec. Regrettably, that was the last we heard of him.

About three months later, the Jewish women were all collected in the square and transported to Lodz Ghetto. The first thing we saw there was people lying dead on the streets from starvation. Going further into the ghetto, my mother and I noticed two women in white uniforms who were enquiring if anyone had nursing experience with children. Although I was only 14, I volunteered, and was accepted with a bit of persuasion. The work was in a children's hospital which was for orphan children. Since my father had been taken from us, my mother could not look after herself. I had to be the breadwinner and take responsibility for her, which weighed heavily on me. I found a room which we shared with a widow and her young son, where I slept on two chairs. I also found a job for my mother in a soup kitchen, which at least alleviated the hunger. I started working in the hospital, but a month later my mother was taken to hospital in severe pain, but as they had very little medication, she came home completely paralysed.

Some days later, we heard on the grapevine that the Germans were going to raid our street. The following morning and every day after that, I concealed my mother in the garden before I left for work, hoping she would be still there when I got home. Several months later, two gas lorries with SS men appeared at the hospital entrance and forced the children into the lorries. The vision of those frightened little faces will haunt me for the rest of my days. Those lorries were equipped to gas them instantaneously.

Having lost my job in the hospital, I found a new occupation knitting tablecloths for German women. Everyone had to be employed in the ghetto to earn their plate of soup. Then we were once again forcibly transferred to another area of the town where we were employed packing components for the German army. At midday, when food was distributed, I had to make a daily run across open country in mid-winter to take some soup for my mother. I never fell over carrying the soup, but I quite often did on my return journey through the frozen fields.

One fateful Sunday, the SS raided unexpectedly. I was trying to mix some flour with water to feed us and suddenly the SS appeared in the doorway to take me away. In that desperate moment, my parting words to my mother were, "Mum, may God be with us from now on." I cannot describe how I felt leaving my mother behind like that.

I was taken directly by cattle train to Auschwitz. The journey was indescribable. When we got off the train, the SS separated the men, women and children, and the different columns were marched in through individual gates. Our group of women was led into a large room where we had to undress in front of the SS guard, then parade around while another 'selection' took place. The old, weak, and infirm were taken away to be disposed of in the gas chambers. The remainder, including myself, were beaten with horsewhips on our naked bodies. We were then shaved, tattooed and allocated to barracks, where we were given one dress each and nothing else.

The sleeping facilities consisted of two-tier wooden bunks of bare wood. Early in the morning, we were woken by the Block *Altester* (overseer), ordered out regardless of the weather and lined up in rows of five. After a few hours, the SS began counting the columns again, and this was often repeated and only finished by 10-11 a.m. Some inmates fainted, unable to withstand the agony of the roll-call. Then we were fed with a piece of so-called bread and green water. The camp toilets consisted of a barrack with a large hole, and time was limited by guards with whips. We tore off pieces of our dresses to use as toilet paper.

When all hope seemed lost, I heard from someone in our block that two brothers from my home town were working in a neighbouring barrack, so I sneaked out to meet them. One of them, Henek Klusky, came to speak to me. Seeing me in those distressed circumstances, he helped by bringing me some clothing – a pair of shoes, a scarf, an apron and some bread. He introduced me to the block supervisor, telling her I had a beautiful voice and could sing. From then on, I was popular and my conditions improved considerably, which enabled me to go to other barracks in my section. Henek also brought me some pieces of bread because those who were working had certain privileges.

Visiting other blocks, I met a girl called Bela Krout from Lodz and we became very close friends. When I could, I helped her with extra food and cigarettes which I received as payment for my singing. On another occasion, I was walking with Bela when I saw that Dr Mengele was visiting my block. We quickly moved to another one where there were no sleeping facilities, only solid earth, and we stayed there with a few hundred other women. At night, we were almost lying on top of each other, and when someone woke up in discomfort and reacted violently, the whole block jumped to its feet. I was sleeping near the centre corridor and the block supervisor grabbed a wooden clog and started beating me up. This was the last straw and I decided to face life or death 'selection' by Dr. Mengele, who later came to our barrack. We lined up naked on one side of the barrack and when the selection finished, those who were lined up, including me, were marched out. Then we found ourselves in a large place with showers on the ceiling. The thought of gas coming through instead of water was devastating. We held our breath and squeezed each other's hands, then suddenly the miracle of seeing water was overwhelming. We were each issued with one dress, Dutch clogs, a coat with a red cross on the back and one loaf of bread. We were then loaded onto a passenger train which took us to Pirshkow in the region of the Polish/German border. We got off and walked to a large farm where we found shelter in one of the many barns. In our group, there were about 200 Polish and 800 Hungarian women.

The next day, the Germans made up groups of 100 women under the supervision of the SS. We were led into an open field on the old Polish/German border line, and ordered to dig anti-tank trenches with picks and spades – which made us think that the Russian advance was near. During the day we were fed with a plate of soup – very little to sustain us in our hard labour. As winter approached, it was almost impossible to dig into the frozen ground. In the end they used dynamite to blow up holes, and we had to shovel the earth away.

After Christmas 1944, we were woken in the middle of the night and lined up for inspection. We were issued with one blanket to every four people – to be used as a stretcher to carry those who could not continue – and then marched off. Any girl who was unable to go on and fell into the ditch was executed on the spot. After a while, the Germans gave us a few handcarts which we loaded with those who could not go on and pushed ourselves. When we passed through a forest, we had to unload the handcarts and the people were all shot. This was the famous death march.

After a few days living only on snow, I fell into a ditch and passed out from sheer exhaustion. I don't know how the SS didn't see this happen. The next thing I remember is a lorry with *Wehrmacht* (German army) soldiers passing by. They stopped, picked me up and put me on the lorry. I explained how I had been separated from a group of girls, but seeing the cross on the back of my coat, they threw me off the lorry. I eventually managed to rejoin my group.

Further on we walked through a forest and were allowed to stop for a rest. Beside the road, there was a farm with barns and high stacks of straw. I dug a deep hole in one of the straw stacks and crawled far into it. When the SS probed the straw with their bayonets, I was deep enough not to be reached. While I was hidden there, I heard a woman pleading with a German to leave her there as she could not walk any further. She said, "What difference does it make whether you kill me now or on the march?" She was lucky because he left her there.

As soon as the Germans left, I went over and spoke to her for a while. Her name was Irma Weiss. For ten days, we lived on raw potatoes and snow, and our stomachs swelled up after a few days. We then left our hiding place and started walking towards a nearby village. In the distance we heard explosions – which gave us hope that the Russian army was advancing and we would be liberated. On entering the village, we encountered a German woman bending over a fence. We asked her in German for some water, but she turned away and walked off, so we went further and then heard Polish spoken. Poles who were working on the farm gave us cooked potatoes which we packed everywhere on our bodies. But before we could leave, two German policemen appeared and arrested us, intending to take us to the nearest town. Suddenly we saw planes bombing the town and the German gendarmes ran away. We went back to our old hiding place in the straw.

After a few days, the farmer came with an Alsatian dog that kept barking and we were arrested again. We were then taken to another farm where Poles were working. One of them told us to hide in the loft, saying he would look after us until the Russians freed us. That same night, two German soldiers came and raped us in the loft, then ordered us out of the hiding place.

For a while after this, we mixed with the other people working there – it appeared to be an army camp. When the Germans formed marching columns, we joined them, but in the darkness before we got to the next town, we secretly separated from the column and reached a house nearby. There, we cut the red crosses off our coats, as this would betray us as Jewish. The following day, we left this house to find some means of sustenance and finished up finding employment and food in a small boarding house. I remember that three SS officers came for dinner and I overheard one of them say that Roosevelt was dead.

Two weeks later, an order was issued that all foreign workers were to be sent to a different place. We were on the march again, but this time not as Jews. In the last town we passed through, the Germans were running away from the advancing Russian army. The remaining guard didn't really know who we were or what to do with us, and so he ran away with the Germans. The town was empty, so we went inside a house, and found food, clothing and some money. Then we went to the nearest railway station and took a train to a town called Lieben, where we reported to a local labour exchange. We told them we were Polish and were looking for work, and that we had lost our personal documents as we fled from the Russians.

We were sent to work on a nearby farm where we were employed as labourers. About three weeks later, we were finally freed by the Russian army. We then obtained a horse and cart, loaded it with food and clothing from abandoned German homes and proceeded towards Poland. But when my friend and I reached Lignica, the Russians confiscated everything.

We established ourselves in the empty town in a new flat which had all home comforts. I got employment as a secretary in the town hall, but Irma was ill. I managed to obtain medical help from two Russian Jewish doctors, and after she improved, I left Lignica in search of survivors from my family and friends.

I stayed overnight in a town called Lodz. The offices where survivors registered were not yet open, but people were gathering outside the building. I noticed a girl who once worked with me in Pirshkow. She was talking to three men I didn't know and introduced me to them. One of them introduced himself as Mr Weiss, but in the excitement his first name didn't register. I asked him if he had a brother called Ignatz, and the answer came like a thunderbolt: "I am Ignatz!" I had found my friend's husband and could not believe this million-to-one chance. When I told him his wife was alive, he was speechless and could not stop crying. We sent a telegram to Irma to share this miraculous news.

From there I went to my home town, Alexandrow Kujawski, and to Lubraniec, but no one from my immediate family had survived. I returned to Lignica to my secretarial job and some days later, when my friend and I were out at work, our luxurious flat was cleared of everything, and a large note was left on the door in Russian, "Everything is gone."

After some effort, we managed to find another smaller place and soon Irma was reunited with her husband. We became a family and I was treated like their sister. I continued to work in the town hall and on several occasions we were visited by foreign newspaper correspondents, among them an English journalist. I had remembered that my father had a brother, sister and parents in England, and I approached the journalist for an interview and explained my predicament. He placed an advertisement in the English newspapers and I also sent a letter to London via a young American representative.

Some time later, I received an invitation from my family to come to England and arrived in London in 1946, full of hopes for a happy future. Regrettably, it did not immediately work out like that. Being under age, I was dependent on my aunt and uncle for protection and shelter, but after staying with them for one year, I decided to go and live with my grandmother who was 94 at the time. I devoted myself to her for one year, and then decided to return to Europe to rejoin my old and trusted friends, Irma and Ignatz Weiss.

However, before I did this, some work friends introduced me to Leonard, a young ex-serviceman from the Polish army. After only three meetings, he proposed to me and I accepted. After a short engagement, we were married in Alie Street Synagogue in the East End of London, and our first son Harvey was born in October 1949. My husband worked in a tailor's factory, and after a while, he opened his own business and I started to work with him. After five years of hard work and careful management, we succeeded in putting a deposit on a little house in Neesden, North London. It was the proudest day of my life that my child could have the comforts I had missed during the Holocaust.

My second son Stuart was born in 1955, and with the added responsibility and my war experiences, I suffered a nervous breakdown. As Stuart was only a few months old, my husband could not look after him and run the business. He had to place him in council care and this had a lasting effect on Stuart, although he is now a mature married man of 39. My husband and I derive a lot of pleasure from our children and our grandchildren, Marcus who is 23 and Tamara, who is 21. This is our greatest reward, yet the scars of my past experiences can never leave my subconscious mind. Evil will not prevail if we are determined to destroy it before it destroys us.

I dedicate my story to my children and grandchildren, who are my pride and joy:
to my grandson, Marcus, now 23 years old,
who graduated from Leeds Metropolitan University with First Class Honours,
and my granddaughter, Tamara, now in her second year at Birmingham University.
May this also be a constant reminder to future generations that you cannot be a bystander while evil is perpetrated before your eyes.

Moments of my youth sheltered by my parents, Jacob and Sarah Krakowski

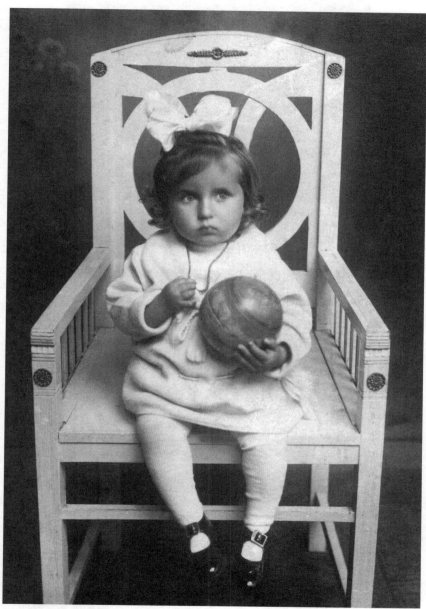

My childhood lost in time

Back row, left to right: Aunt Rosa Hildesheim, my mother Sara, Aunt Frania Klein (who died in Ravensbrück) Aunt Dora holding Idzia, Uncle Marcus Klein. Middle row: my cousin, my brother Ben. Bottom row: me, my cousins Samuel Hildesheim and Gienek Klein.

With friends post-war in Bergen-Belsen. Mala is second from the left and Sister Luba, who looked after them in the children's barrack, is the lady on the right.

MALA TRIBICH

A Child in the Holocaust

I was born Mala Helfgott on 24 September 1930 in Piotrkow Trybunalski, Poland. After the outbreak of the Second World War on 1 September 1939, life changed drastically for us. Although we were full of hope that hostilities would soon be over, five and a half years later I emerged alive – but only just – having gone through the experience of being hidden with a Catholic family, the ordeal of the ghettos, a slave labour camp, concentration camps and finally being liberated in Bergen-Belsen on 15 April 1945.

The Nazi invasion started with the bombing of Polish towns. When my home town was bombed on Saturday 2 September 1939, people in panic gathered their families and some belongings together and by evening were fleeing east. My family and I were among them. By early morning we had reached Sulejow, a small town some 15 kilometres away. My parents decided to stop there, especially as my father had met his younger brother Fishel, his wife Irene and their two-year-old daughter Hania. But later that day, the bombing started there too and within minutes much of the town was in flames.

Together with other families, we were in one of the few brick buildings in the town and it was only my mother's presence of mind that saved us. She stood at the door and prevented us from fleeing the safety of the house. When the bombing seemed to have stopped, she opened the door and we all ran to the nearby woods. We were lucky to survive that short but perilous run as German planes were strafing over our heads.

For the next few days, in order to avoid the bombing, we travelled by night and hid by day in the forests until the advancing armies caught up with us. It was futile to continue eastwards and my parents decided to return to Piotrkow, but on the way there we were told that our town was on fire. This was dreadful news, but we nevertheless continued. From a distance it looked as if the whole town was alight, but we found that the railway carrying coal wagons had received a direct hit and was burning furiously, but elsewhere the bomb damage was minimal.

By October 1939 the new, brutal Nazi regime issued orders that all

Jews in our town were to move to a ghetto by 1 November. This was the first ghetto in Poland, located in an old part of town with houses in poor condition. My father managed to find two rooms and a kitchen, with toilet but no bathroom. We were lucky to have this accommodation for our family of five and at some point we even shared it with my mother's sister, Gucia, who came to join us from Sieradz.

As the ghetto became more and more crowded, we had to give up one room to another family, but we were still lucky to have such a large room and a kitchen to ourselves. In some instances there were two or three families to a room. Many Jews from the surrounding areas had joined us, particularly from western Poland which was now incorporated into Germany's Third Reich. Altogether there were 28,000 people in that small enclosure.

Although there was an official checkpoint, the ghetto was not yet surrounded by a barbed wire fence. Those over the age of 12 were ordered to wear armbands with the Star of David and we were not allowed out of the ghetto at any time. Anyone found outside was severely punished and often shot. Within the ghetto, there were curfews and we were not allowed on the streets after 8 p.m.

At the beginning life somehow continued, we had some cultural and social activities and I had lessons with other children. This was, of course, strictly illegal as formal schooling for Jewish children had stopped, but some education continued despite the dangers.

Although conditions seemed reasonably tolerable at first, they began to deteriorate almost daily. There were frequent raids and searches, and the streets were patrolled by the SS with ferocious dogs. Able-bodied men were never safe as there were frequent round-ups for special assignments and many never came back. New laws were constantly being issued – to hand in valuables, jewellery, fur coats, etc.

My father, who was a very enterprising man, continued to have dealings with merchants outside the ghetto and managed to obtain provisions for us and also for other families. I remember one day he needed to send a message outside the ghetto to one of the dealers and I volunteered – much against my mother's protestations. My father pacified her by explaining that since I did not look Jewish there was not much chance of being caught, and in any case the message was verbal, he would not risk me carrying a note.

At that time, there were many places where one could just walk out of the ghetto, if that point was not being patrolled at the time. In the event I got out easily and proceeded on a long walk to the farmhouse. On arrival I was greeted warmly and given a glass of milk. I delivered the message and the men said they were leaving with the flour and sugar on a horse-drawn cart, so I rode back with them. On the way we were stopped and the men were searched and questioned. When the policemen turned to me, I just said that I had hitched a lift and knew nothing about the men or their merchandise. I then got off the cart, my heart pounding, and walked back to the ghetto, trying to avoid any police or SS on duty. The men were taken to the police station and later released; the goods were confiscated.

As time progressed, things got worse; overcrowding and insanitary conditions caused an outbreak of typhoid. By the time the deportations to the concentration camp Treblinka took place, this epidemic had reduced the ghetto population to 24,000.

In 1942 rumours began to circulate that the ghetto was to be reduced to just the Jewish administration and those with work permits. The majority of the inhabitants were to be rounded up, selections would take place and people would be deported to labour and concentration camps, and in the majority of cases to their deaths. The atmosphere became very tense and people were in a state of panic trying to think of ways to save themselves.

Those who could made arrangements to go into hiding outside the ghetto. This required not only the means to pay for the "privilege", but also connections and trusted friends outside, for if you were caught or betrayed the penalty was certain death.

My father knew a lot of people outside the ghetto and managed to secure the services of a Christian family in the town of Czestochowa. This arrangement concerned myself and my cousin, Idzia Klein, who was almost 11, one year younger than me. We were both to be taken to Czestochowa to pass as Christian children and stay there for the duration of the deportations.

The day arrived when a man and woman, named Maciejewski, both aged about 30, turned up at our flat to collect payment in advance. We all sat down at the table and the adults started discussing terms and conditions. I cannot recall the details but I remember the man saying he would come back next week to collect me, then the following week for Idzia. It would be too dangerous to take us both on the train journey at the same time. My aunt pleaded with them to take Idzia first as she was their only child, whereas I was one of three children. But they insisted on their original plan.

The arrangements went according to plan and we found ourselves in a house on the outskirts of Czestochowa with the man's parents-in-law. Life there was very precarious and we were extremely vulnerable. We were frightened and homesick and exposed to many dangers. To make our identity more anonymous, we were supposed to be relatives from Warsaw. However, we were not very well briefed and when asked questions by visitors – like the actual relationship or our exact address – we were often stumped for answers and had to do some quick thinking. Whenever there was a knock on the door, we were quickly bundled into a wardrobe and had to stay there till the visitors left. On other occasions it was safe to mix.

I remember going with the family to visit some relatives and feeling quite comfortable in their company – even though one of them was engaged to a German soldier who was present that day.

I recall another evening when a very weird-looking old lady arrived. She wore a cloak and a scarf on her head, and we all sat round the iron stove in the middle of the room. She seemed to be particularly interested in the two of us but we didn't know why. I learned much later that she was a messenger sent by our parents to find out how we were. There was, of course, no other means of communication.

Life somehow continued under these conditions. We both missed our parents but Idzia was so homesick that she asked to go back home. She was told that it was not yet safe as the deportations were still happening. But when she told them that she could go to very good friends, the Mackowiaks in Piotrkow, who were looking after valuables for her parents, they agreed.

I thought that Idzia was lucky because she was back with her parents and I still had to wait. When I was eventually taken back and handed over to my father, Idzia's father was present too and asked where his daughter was. He was told that they had brought her back and left her with the Mackowiaks some time previously. "What do you mean?" he said. He looked horrified, turned pale and started pacing up and down, repeating, "What have you done with my child?" I was shocked beyond words and we just looked on helplessly. Many years later, I learned that the couple had gone to the Mackowiaks, collected a suitcase full of valuables and then departed with Idzia and the suitcase. Idzia was never seen again and the circumstances of her disappearance remain a mystery to this day.

My father smuggled me back into the ghetto when returning with his working party, and I was relieved to find my mother, sister Lusia and brother Ben there. I could feel my mother's delight at having her children home safely. Home was now a corner of a room in the small ghetto, two half-streets housing 2,400 people. My mother and Lusia had also been hidden outside the ghetto, as was my father. I was the last one of my family to return. Our immediate family was still intact, but alas not for long.

Soon afterwards, when people thought it was safe, they started returning to the ghetto and the authorities turned a blind eye. Anybody in the ghetto without a work permit was "illegal", but nevertheless it was formally declared that the "illegals" were safe. This prompted those still in hiding to surface, but they were walking into a trap. Over the next few days, they rounded up most of the "illegals" and gathered them in the Great Synagogue, once a beautiful and imposing building. They were kept there under dreadful conditions: without sanitation, light, food or water. To amuse themselves, the Ukrainian guards would shoot into the synagogue through the windows, killing and wounding people.

Among the victims incarcerated in that hell were my mother and Lusia. The only reason I was spared was that when our room was raided, I was in bed and my mother said to the Jewish policeman in charge, Tadek Glogowski, that I was not well. His response was to let me stay while he rounded up everybody else in that room. Why this young policeman should have wanted to save my life I cannot imagine, because he did not know me and I did not know him. After the war he was tracked down, arrested and tried in Piotrkow for his role in the deportations. Aunt Dora, Idzia's mother, was a witness at the trial. She told the court that he was responsible for the deaths of my mother and sister, but that he saved me. She felt that out of all his wrongdoings, he performed one kind and compassionate act.

During that fateful week in the synagogue, a lot of bartering took place; some people were exchanged for others and a bribe could sometimes secure a release. My father used all his influence to get my mother and Lusia released. But they were not letting children out under any circumstances and since my mother would not leave without Lusia, her fate was sealed.

On the morning of 20 December 1942 they were taken out in groups of 50 and marched to Rakow forest, where newly dug mass graves awaited them. They were told to undress and stand at the edge of the graves where they were shot. The wounded were buried with the dead. My mother was 37 and Lusia was 8 years old.

The SS were always rounding people up and sending them to various labour and concentration camps. During one of these raids, my aunt Irene was torn from her five-year-old daughter, Hania, (her husband Fishel having been shot about two weeks earlier) and sent to a labour camp shouting, "Who will look after my child?" We were the only relatives left: my brother Ben who worked in the glass factory, my father and myself. As the only female relative, it fell to me to take care of Hania. I was 12 years old.

At the end of July 1943, the ghetto was liquidated and only two groups of workers remained who were to be allocated to the local glass factory, Hortensia, and the big woodworking concern, Dietrich und Fischer. As children, Hania and I were useless for these factories, and during this liquidation, we were lined up outside the barbed wire fence of the ghetto, ready to board the lorries. These would take us to the railway station or some other destination for onward transmission to concentration camps.

The column was four deep and very long and we were surrounded by guards with machine guns. The woman in front of us, with a baby in her arms, was hit over the head with a rifle. I don't know what she had done to warrant this blow, but she was in a terrible state, bleeding profusely, and it was very frightening. When we were close to boarding the lorry, I suddenly left the line, went to the SS officer in charge and asked if he would allow me to go back to my father and brother, from whom I had been separated. The SS officer looked very surprised, but he smiled and said "Yes". He instructed a policeman to take me back and on the way I said, "Just a minute, I have to collect my cousin." The policeman told me that permission was only for me, that my cousin would not be allowed to return. It was an impossible situation; I was terrified at the prospect of leaving Hania or losing the chance of being reunited with my father and Ben. I begged and pleaded, saying that I could not go back to the ghetto without her. He eventually relented and Hania went with me.

My father managed to arrange for all of us to go to the woodworking concern, even though my little cousin was far too young to work. Life there was hard: long working shifts, cramped and primitive living conditions. There were separate barracks for men and women, except for a few privileged families who enjoyed the privacy of one room per family. The women's barracks had two-tier bunks and the men's four tiers. There were usually two people to a bunk. I shared mine with Hania and there were two other women in the upper tier. There was an iron stove at one end of the barrack which was kept burning with smuggled firewood from the factory.

Even at this stage my father still supplemented our meagre rations through his connections outside the compound, and we managed to go on, keeping our spirits up with the occasional concert (there was so much talent) and whatever hopeful news filtered through from the outside. My own little cultural sustenance was in the form of meeting my friend, Pema Blachman, whose mother had the book *Gone With The Wind*. Pema used to read it secretly when her mother was out and relate the story to me on our walks. For me, meeting a friend outside working hours was no simple matter because Hania would not let me out of her sight, she was so afraid of losing me. On the few occasions when I met Pema, Hania either came with me or I made arrangements for someone in the barrack to keep an eye on her. She did, of course, have to allow me to go to work; this was not optional.

It was nearing the end of 1944 and although we now know that the war was drawing to a close, for us the worst was yet to come. At the end of November 1944, we were all marched to the railway station and various groups were sent to different places. My father and Ben, I learned later, were sent to Buchenwald, Hania and I ended up in Ravensbrück concentration camp. We travelled in cattle trucks without food or water, we did not know where we were going. I have no idea how long the journey took, but we eventually reached our destination.

On arrival in Ravensbrück, we queued at a reception centre where all personal details were recorded. Our few possessions were taken from us, we were told to strip, our heads were shaved and we had communal showers under cold water. We were then given the typical concentration camp pyjama-like garb and clogs.

Now we were really stripped of our personality as well; we could not even recognize one another. The years of suffering, deprivation and the deteriorating conditions were taking their toll; depression and despair were setting in. My aunt Frania Klein died soon after arrival and a few days later so did my friend Pema. Hania was getting thinner and my main worry was how to keep her alive.

We had daily roll-calls which meant that we had to rise at 6 a.m. and stand outside the barracks to be counted. Sometimes they counted us again and again, and we had to stand for hours. It was in the depths of a European winter, and we were wearing thin clothing with no underwear, no tights and no outer garments; people used to faint or die.

Our rations were a slice of black bread and soup. Although the soup resembled dishwater, we were glad to have it. Sometimes we would also get imitation coffee which was really brown water. We were in the women's camp where some of the women worked outside in the fields, but neither Hania nor I worked. Occasionally one of the women would smuggle in a potato, turnip or radish, but if anyone was caught, the punishment was very severe, mostly death. On one occasion aunt Dora brought us a potato.

After about two and a half months there, we were again put into cattle trucks to travel to another concentration camp, Bergen-Belsen, where we found total chaos. There was terrible overcrowding, sanitation in the form of open pits and hardly any food. People walked around like zombies and looked like skeletons; there were piles of corpses and dead bodies lying around everywhere. Typhus was rife and there was an air of utter hopelessness. The degradation, humiliation and despair were clearly visible on people's faces. You could be speaking to someone and she would literally drop dead in front of you.

There was no room for us in the barracks at Belsen so we were put up in a large tent on bare ground, along with hundreds of other people of all ages and nationalities. There was only space to sit, lying down was not an option. My worldly possessions – a comb, a piece of bread and a hankie – were in a little bundle, which was very important to me. Somehow during the night, even in this sitting position on freezing ground, I managed to fall asleep. When I awoke, my bundle was gone.

Fortunately, the war was nearing its end as no one could survive in Belsen for long. Anne Frank was there at that time and we know her fate. But luck was once again on my side. I had heard that there was a children's barrack somewhere in the camp, so I set out with Hania to search for it.

We found a little hut with Dr Bimko and Sister Luba who were in charge of the children's barrack. They interviewed us and among other details asked our age. I knew that it would be expedient to make myself younger, but in my confusion in giving the year of my birth, I made myself a year older! At first they said I was too old, but I pleaded with them to take Hania because she was so young, thin and frail that she would not survive in the main camp. They agreed. But Hania absolutely refused to leave me. I tried everything I could to persuade her to stay, but to no avail. I told them that we would return next day. We did so – and this time, when Hania again would not hear of leaving me, they agreed to take us both.

The children's barrack was run by Sister Luba and a team of Jewish "nurses", themselves inmates, who were very kind and devoted. I know that they used to beg, steal and do everything in their power to obtain a little extra food for the children. And they also gave us loving care. The barrack was situated opposite a large hut with a pile of corpses. I recall a procession of women dragging bodies in blankets or by a limb along the ground, adding to this pile all day long.

A typhus epidemic was raging throughout the camp and many children caught it, including me. There was no medication and no treatment of any kind. I just lay there semi-conscious, quite oblivious of what was happening around me. My bunk was near the window and one day I suddenly became aware of people outside running. My only thought was one of amazement that they could run when I could not even move a muscle. I think I realized that the war was over, but don't have any clear memories of that period of liberation.

The British army, who subsequently liberated the camp, sent ambulances and medical teams to transfer us to a hospital/children's home. I remember wanting to walk to the ambulance and actually trying, but after one step I collapsed and had to be carried on a stretcher. It was many weeks before I could walk again. Hania was going through the same experience, but I was not aware of it at the time. A few months after liberation, we were sent to Sweden with a group of other children and spent the following two years there.

I was in Sweden, not really expecting anyone from my family to be alive, when one day I received a letter from England. It was from my brother Ben. He was always very resourceful, like our father, and started making inquiries immediately after the war and even returned to Piotrkow to see if anyone had survived. But of our immediate family, we were the only ones still alive. I only have a vague memory of my sister Lusia as she was so young. I don't even have a photograph of her, but Ben obtained a copy of her birth certificate and so there is some proof of her having existed.

I do have a photograph of each of my parents retrieved from relatives abroad which I treasure. Ben learned from a witness that my father was shot when trying to escape from one of the death marches. Tragically, this was only a few days before the end of the war.

Hania's mother survived the war and they were eventually reunited, but her father was killed in February 1943, along with my uncle, Joseph Klein, Idzia's father. Hania now lives in Australia with her husband and children, as does her mother.

Idzia's mother, aunt Dora, survived and settled in Israel but she never got over the tragedy of losing her only child.

I came to England in March 1947 to be reunited with Ben. In 1949 I met Maurice Tribich whom I married in 1950, and was embraced by his very warm and loving family. Subsequently, we had two children, Shannon and Jeffrey. I settled down to family life, became active in the community and when the children were in their teens, I embarked on a full-time course of study encouraged by Maurice and gained a BSc Honours degree in Sociology from London University.

In the intervening years I did not talk about my childhood experiences during the war, and although my family and friends knew that I had lived through the Holocaust, they did not ask any questions. They felt that it was too sensitive and that it would be too painful for me. Nevertheless, over the years they gradually learned a little of that period of my life.

In recent years, however, there has been a lot of interest in the subject and when I am invited to talk to schoolchildren or other groups, I accept whenever possible. I feel that it is my duty to speak for all those who have not survived to speak for themselves and tell what happened in those dark days in Europe. By speaking out, it is my greatest hope that something positive will be handed to the future generation.

Dedicated to my children, my grandchildren Miriam, Samuel and Declan
and in memory of my husband Maurice
and my family who perished in the Holocaust.

Still optimistic in old age!

LISA VINCENT

Goodbye to Nuremberg

My name is Lisa Vincent and I was 11 years old when Hitler came to power in Germany in 1933. We lived in a little village 20 miles outside Nuremberg, a beautiful little village with cherry blossoms. I was very happy growing up there. My mother was Jewish but my father was not. He was an architect and I didn't see a lot of him because he was always travelling. After the Nuremberg laws came out, he divorced my mother and turned his back on us.

When Hitler came to power, the first thing I knew about antisemitism was the burning of the books. The Nazis came along to all the libraries and took all the books by Communist or Jewish authors; they put them in a big pile and just burnt them. We didn't have elections until 1934 and the only candidate was Adolf Hitler. My mother, being Jewish, did not vote for him and the next day the Lord Mayor told her she should have voted for Hitler, our new Führer, our new leader, our new Germany. So that was already a black mark.

So in 1934 when Hitler actually came to power, we still lived in the village quite comfortably. I went to a very good girls' grammar school in Nuremberg and travelled every day to school by a little steam train. I can remember not wanting to go to school on Thursdays and the teacher asking me, "Now Beck (they always used your surname), why don't you like school on Thursdays?" I told her, "Well, there's a restaurant attached to the station and they slaughter a pig on the platform every Thursday morning. It's horrible with all the blood flowing." But my teacher told me it was only a pig, that Germans were not interested in questions of animal rights or cruelty to animals. As you can see later on, they were cruel to people as well. It was a good school and there were some other Jewish girls there. In Hitler's early days, I was regarded as half-Jewish because I was from a mixed marriage. We had a kind of school uniform – a velvet peaked cap with a gold and blue ribbon on it.

Everything changed in 1935 when the Nuremberg laws came out, and since we lived in Nuremberg, we were the first to be affected. If you were a child from a mixed marriage and your mother was Jewish, you were automatically classified as full Jews, whether you kept the religion or not. The first thing that happened when I was made Jewish in 1935 was that I wasn't allowed to sit next to my German girl friends at school any more. I had to sit on my own at the back of the classroom. When I asked why, I was told it was because I was Jewish. From then on, the other girls said they couldn't really speak to me any more at break time. This made a great impression on me and my schoolwork suffered tremendously.

Some of the girls came to school in Nazi uniforms, gorgeous little bomber jackets, nice short skirts and I thought how nice it would be to wear the same uniform, but I couldn't because I was Jewish. Then I was told I couldn't go on trips or go swimming any more.

Later in 1935, the Lord Mayor sent for my mother and said, "I'm sorry Mrs Beck, but this village has got to be *Judenfrei*, free of Jews. It's got to be cleansed, so you've got to move." We had to move to Nuremberg and that was the first feeling of a kind of ghetto existence because all the Jews from the various villages and smaller communities were gathering in the big towns. Later on, it made it very easy for the Germans to deport them. Signs went up banning Jews from restaurants and swimming pools, and the Nazi newspaper, *Der Stürmer*, incited more antisemitic feeling amongst the population.

After 1935 Germans were basically not allowed to speak or associate with Jews, so later on when the deportations started, the Germans already looked on us as separate and not part of the nation. You couldn't keep your friends any more. I remember one family shaking hands with my mother, saying, "If we see you in the street, don't mind if we look away because we aren't allowed to say hello to you." I was really sad to leave my village because I was really happy there, and people we knew shook hands with us and said, "Well, that's the law. You see you're Jewish and that's the way it is." I didn't feel particularly Jewish because we weren't Orthodox and we didn't speak Hebrew. I felt more German than Jewish.

Things changed dramatically in school too. Biology lessons became race theory lessons and the few Jewish girls in the class were fetched out to the front and the rest of the class was told, "Look, they've got long noses, swarthy complexions, black, curly hair. They are the scourge, the vermin. They have the money, they are evil." I was lucky because I didn't look particularly Jewish, so I didn't suffer to that degree. Our race theory teacher was rather nice to me and let me sit in the park and come back after the lesson. He didn't want me to go through the degradation of his lesson, although he knew he had to teach it.

One day the music teacher stopped me in the corridor and said, "Come here, I want to talk to you, Beck." I went over and said, "Good morning Dr..." He told me that was not the correct German greeting, whacked me on the head and told me I must say, *"Heil Hitler"*. We had to say *Heil Hitler* eight times a day, at the beginning and end of each lesson.

I had a very blonde girl called Suzy sitting in front of me. She had lovely, long blonde curls and somehow I imagined that she looked very German, very Aryan, very blue-eyed – and I didn't. So I dipped her plaits into the inkwell to make her dark-haired! I liked her and wanted her to look like me.

Some of the teachers came in Nazi uniforms to give lessons. Geography got extremely interesting because they printed new atlases before any invasions took place. When Austria and Czechoslovakia were invaded later on in 1937 and 1938, we already had the atlases showing just Greater Germany.

Hitler loved Nuremberg and held all the Nazi rallies there, and at first I was made to go and watch them. They mainly took place at night with torchlight processions: all the children, wearing Nazi uniforms, were given these huge torches and sang Nazi songs. It was really powerful and incited the youngsters to believe in all that Hitler said. The adoration for Hitler had to be seen to be believed. I can remember the streets being full of roses, and carnations being strewn in the street for Hitler's car to drive over. The 1936 Olympic games were real propaganda for all the world to see. When Hitler spoke on the radio (there was no TV then), if you were in a public place in a restaurant, you had to put down your knife and fork. I would try and finish my dinner and some German would say, "Don't do that. Listen to the Führer; listen to what he's got say."

I remember that in 1937 I needed a hernia operation and the Jewish hospitals were already closed. German hospitals were not allowed to operate on Jews and my mother went all around Nuremberg to try and find a private clinic, or someone who would do the operation. Eventually, she did find someone, but he said, "Yes I'll do the operation, but she can't stay here. There must be no records, nobody must know."

In late 1937, early 1938, a new girl called Ruth Muller came to school. There was nowhere for her to sit in class so she sat down next to me. I was really pleased, we got on well and I thought I had a new friend, although I didn't tell her I was Jewish. She invited me to tea the next day at her house and I was very happy. She gave me the address and I went to the flat. The door opened and inside in the living room were paintings, portraits of Hitler, Goering, Goebbels, Himmler, and all the Nazis. I asked Ruth what her father did for a living and she told me he was the new minister of works for Bavaria. I thought I'd better tell her I was Jewish, and she just told me not to touch anything, to go away as quickly as possible. At school, another desk was found for Ruth and I was at the back on my own again.

Because I had mixed parentage, I had actually been christened: my father had insisted on that. This meant that on Palm Sunday 1938, I had to be confirmed in the Lutheran church with my class. But confirmation was different under the Nazis: we had to go to the altar all dressed in black and swear allegiance to Hitler. By that time he had become a pseudo-Christ to many German youngsters. But I didn't actually swear the oath because I thought it was wrong in a house of God.

The real tragic beginning of the Holocaust was *Kristallnacht*, 9 November 1938. People had been attacked in the streets before this and if you looked particularly Jewish, you had stones thrown at you, but nothing dramatic had happened until 9 November after a young Jew murdered a German diplomat in Paris. This was a marvellous opportunity for Goebbels, the German propaganda minister, to make all the Jews in Germany suffer. We listened to it all on the radio and didn't really think very much of it, but that same night, we were all dragged out of our beds, a lot of crystal glass got smashed and our piano was hacked in two. The SS came in with guns and ordered us out onto the square in Nuremberg. Synagogues were already burning, shops smashed and I witnessed a few people thrown out of first floor windows. We stood in our nighties and watched the men being loaded on lorries for Dachau, and then to concentration camp. My mother was taken away, but came back two days later. I found that our flat was completely smashed and my uncle had his arm broken.

When I went to school next day, the Head told me that I had to leave for my own safety. "I'm sorry," he said, "but we're not allowed to keep Jewish children any more." He actually shook hands with me, but asked me to pack all my things and leave straight away.

When my mother came back, we realized the seriousness of the situation, but it wasn't easy to leave Germany. England didn't take too many people in, and for America you might wait years and years. It wasn't a simple thing for Jews to get out. But Jewish parents wanted to get their children out. They thought things were not going to get any better, but nobody knew that the exterminations and deportations would take place the way they did.

After 1938 when I was thrown out of school, my mother didn't know what to do and she told me about a school that was partly Jewish, on the Danube near the little town of Ulm. She decided to send me there for a month until we could leave the country. It was in a lovely white house built on the hillside on the edge of the Black Forest, and was run by a Jewish woman who had adopted ten German children. After *Kristallnacht*, those ten German children weren't allowed to be in their mother's house, but had to move into the village below, boarded out with different families. She was already closing the house and trying to emigrate, but she did give us a few lessons. One day, the SS came and said, "A white house? A Jewish house? Paint that house brown by tomorrow so that it looks like the earth, like dirt." And we all had to paint the outside of the house brown. The degradations happened on a daily basis.

Word got around that the Cadbury and Sainsbury families in England were kind people, and were helping Jewish children in Germany to get out of the country to Holland. So, at the end of August 1939, three days before the Second World War, I remember being pushed onto a train in Nuremberg, with loads of crying parents and little children with labels round their necks. I was nearly seventeen and was put in charge of some three and four-year-olds. We got to the German side of the Dutch border and the army and SS people who were on the train with us made us get out onto the platform, bend down and lick the floor and paving stones, humiliating us. Suddenly, one boy who was with me noticed that the train was going to leave without us. He gave me a push and we got back on, with the Dutch people pulling us in. The rest of the children stood on the platform and were sent back. I never heard of them again.

We landed in Holland first and then left for England just before the Germans invaded – otherwise I would have been transported back to Germany and to a concentration camp. In the Nuremberg area, we had thousands of Jews, but only six returned from the camps.

I found England very difficult at first, I couldn't understand why people laughed here. I wondered what there was to laugh about. I had left my mother behind and didn't know when I would see her again. Fortunately, we did meet up again in 1940 when she came out with the help of the Red Cross. When she arrived, I wouldn't let her out of my sight, I was scared stiff I might lose her again.

Some 50 years later, in 1993, I had a letter from the mayor of Nuremberg inviting me as a former Jewish citizen to go back for a fortnight's free stay at a five-star hotel. In the end my daughter and I decided to go and we had an absolutely fantastic time. The Lord Mayor was then 60, so he had only been ten years old at the time of the Nazis, and the very first thing he said on the first night was, "This is your town, you belonged here, you spent your youth here, you were thrown out cruelly, you survived the Holocaust and I want to make you welcome. Perhaps at the end of the fortnight, you might forgive us the terrible crimes committed against you. Perhaps we might shake hands and say we are friends."

On the Thursday night of this visit, the programme included "meeting old friends". I wasn't really all that keen to go, but felt I ought to. And there to my amazement I discovered Ruth Muller and other girls from my grammar school. They had read my name in the newspaper and come specially to meet me again. So then the questions started and we caught up on all that had happened. They wanted to know what had happened to me and I asked them why they had watched it all, why they hadn't said or done something about the Jews.

Those eight schoolfriends saw me off at the airport and one gave me a little book as I left. When I opened it, there in the middle was over 1,000 Marks (almost £1,000) with a note saying, "Please come back every year and stay with us." I wasn't sure then how I felt about Nuremberg and my friends, but I have gone back every year and stayed with them. But I'm still not certain if it's really friendship or trying to make up for the past. I feel I'll never know for sure.

To Sophie and Craig, my grandchildren, who have shown an interest in my story since studying the subject in History and Religious Education.

Returning to our house in Cadolzburg in 1993, which we had to leave in 1935.

Being given the freedom of Cadolzburg in 2002 by the Lord Mayor

At Beth Shalom before a talk to schoolchildren, May 2003

FREDA WINEMAN

The Red-Coated Survivor

Early Years

I was born Freda Silberberg on 6 September 1923 in Metz, Lorraine, in north-eastern France. Eight years later, together with my parents, elder brother David and younger brothers, Armand and Marcel, I moved to Sarreguemines, situated on France's eastern border with Germany. My father was a jeweller, my mother stayed at home and my brothers and I went to the local *lycée* (grammar school). As a family, we were Orthodox Jews.

In August 1939, with war imminent, our town was evacuated to the south-west of France. The Maginot Line of defence was no protection in the face of the German army. My father decided to move 200 km south, hoping that if war happened, it would not last. World War II was declared on 3 September 1939, the eve of my 16th birthday.

At first, life carried on with some normality. My father went about his work, my brothers went to the local school and I worked in a local office. Food was still available.

Things changed dramatically in June 1940. The German army invaded Belgium and were on their way towards Paris. Suddenly, everyone was on the run. The Germans overtook us in Vichy, so we moved south to St. Etienne. By now, we were homeless and almost penniless, having left most of our valuables behind as we sought to escape from the advancing Germans. France had capitulated.

With the collaboration of the French government under Marshal Pétain and Prime Minister Pierre Laval, France was divided into 'Occupied' and 'Free' France. But the Vichy government in the southern part of France passed new anti-Jewish laws and in 1942, the whole of France was occupied by the German forces. We were in danger of arrest at any time and were living in constant fear.

Arrest

In May 1944, my mother found a convent willing to give us shelter, but before we could go there, we were arrested. It happened on 17 May 1944.

By chance the *Milice* (Vichy police) stopped my mother and found she was carrying all our ration books, which identified us as Jews and told the Gestapo that there were six of us in the family. My mother was arrested immediately.

I was on my way home from work when a neighbour told me what had happened to my mother, and warned me not to go home. But I felt I had to go in order to try and protect my youngest brothers, Armand and Marcel. Soon, the *Milice* arrived and I tried to help my brothers to escape. They were caught; Armand in the flat, and Marcel, who left at the rear of the house, but whose curiosity impelled him to come and see what was happening to the rest of us.

Armand, Marcel and I were taken to the Gestapo offices for interrogation. There, I was beaten repeatedly and thrown into jail as I refused to give them any information concerning the whereabouts of the other members of my family. From there, I was taken to barracks in St. Etienne where hundreds of arrested Jews were already being held.

Marcel was murdered, together with my mother and father, in Auschwitz.

Drancy

A few days later, our entire family had been rounded up and arrested, and we were all put on a train to Drancy, near Paris. There, we were placed in what looked like a crowded housing estate, packed with French gendarmes and German soldiers. There seemed to be thousands of people of all ages – women with children, babies, the old and the infirm. After a few days, we were put on a lorry and taken to Drancy station.

This time, we were herded into a cattle truck with our few remaining possessions. There were 120 of us squeezed into the truck with a bucket in the corner serving as the toilet for all of us. There was no food, no water, no room to move, barely space to breathe. It was a hot summer day and the atmosphere soon became unbearable. We did not know where our journey would end.

Arrival in Auschwitz

After three days and three nights, the train stopped. It was dawn. The doors to the cattle truck were unlocked and all we could hear was dogs barking and guards shouting at us. This was Auschwitz. We had to leave our luggage. I remember the smell of ashes and we saw flakes in the air, but could not understand what they were.

Men in striped clothing whispered to us to give the babies to older women. My mother took a baby from a young Dutchwoman. Everything happened so quickly. My father and my brothers, David and Armand, were separated from us. I never saw my father again. My mother, my youngest brother Marcel and I were standing in lines. A German officer, whom I now know to have been the infamous Dr Mengele, was holding a stick and was moving people to the left and to the right. I went with my mother and Marcel, but was called back. Could it have been the red coat that my mother insisted I wore on that unbearably hot journey that made me stand out? The officer told me to go with the young people as my mother would be looking after the small children. I was heartbroken at being separated from my mother and Marcel, but had no choice but to join a group of about 80 people. It was the last time I saw my mother, who went with that little Dutch baby in her arms, and Marcel. Having also been separated from my two other brothers, I only saw one of them, David, much later when by chance I spotted him going in the opposite direction to me on his way to work. He and Armand, like me, survived the ordeal of the camps.

Initially, we were taken to a room, told to take our clothes off and forced to hand over any jewellery we possessed. Young inmates tattooed a number on our arms. Mine was A.7181, a reference to the convoy from France dated 2 June 1944. We were then moved to a room with showers. Later, we realized that we could have been gassed there and then. We showered without soap and without a towel. We were left in an adjoining room for what seemed like an endless time. At last, a young woman who spoke many languages came to us and we questioned her about what had happened to our loved ones. She was Belgian and her name was Mallah; she worked in the camp offices because of her linguistic skills. She tried to make us understand the fate that had befallen many of them, including my parents and Marcel.

We were then taken into another hall where there were boxes of odd shoes and a variety of old clothes. Our heads were shaved. We were suddenly unrecognisable and had completely lost the identity we had brought with us into the camp. We were dehumanised and dejected.

We were taken to a block where there were already many girls from a number of countries. My first priority in Auschwitz, beyond surviving, was to keep myself as clean as I could. I gave up my first slice of bread for a toothbrush. Nevertheless, all the camp inmates soon succumbed to infections and boils as malnutrition and the general conditions undermined our basic health.

Each morning, there was a selection made of who was to work. Some of our friends worked in terrible *Kommandos* (work crews). Each day, they returned half-dead, beaten up. Often, one or two didn't make it back to the hut alive.

During those days in 1944, around 10,000 a day arrived at Auschwitz –

Hungarians, Poles, Czechs, Greeks and North Africans. Precious few of them ever entered the camp. They were directed straight to the gas chambers and then taken to the crematorium.

We all became deeply depressed as the dark smoke, the smell and the visible night fires made it obvious what was happening. We were helpless, lost and forgotten. Keeping going from day to day became the hardest thing of all.

Surviving Auschwitz

I will never forget 17 August 1944. The whole camp was gathered and stood on the *Appellplatz* (assembly place). We didn't know why.

An SS woman came over to our group. I was in the front row of five. I was one of those asked to stand aside. The group that was selected, *Kommando Kanada*, was sent to a place where we saw a mountain of clothes, suitcases, shoes, baby shoes and spectacles. We were told to sort them out and make parcels. It was a tearful, heart-rending task as we recognised some of the clothes and names on the suitcases.

After work, and before re-entering the camp, we were permitted to shower. This was in the open air and the German guards mocked us, often throwing buckets of water on us. Yet more humiliation for us, all young girls.

We tried to bring shoes or underwear back for our unfortunate friends working in the trenches – even though it was strictly forbidden. One day we were stopped. Three of our group were brought to the Camp commandant, told to strip and found to have the extra clothes on them. It could have been any of us. We were all assembled to witness our three friends being publicly hanged.

After this event, we were taken off *Kommando Kanada* (which the Germans regarded as a privilege) and put on a *Kommando* working in front of the crematorium, digging trenches, with guards and their dogs snapping at us all the time. There was now no food. It was barbaric. Lots of people died. They just couldn't take any more.

Hungarian convoys were arriving in thousands at that time. The Germans couldn't cope with the influx. As a result, many of those people still had their hair and no tattoo. This meant they would not work, but would be exterminated.

One day, three sisters, witnessing our hardship, offered us one ration of their bread to share. This was a godsend as we were all starving. Many years later, at the first reunion of survivors in Israel, I met one of these sisters again. All three had survived and were alive and well.

The Revolt

Some men tried to escape on 14 October 1944 in order to tell the world what was happening in Auschwitz. Whilst working in front of the crematorium, our group of inmates witnessed these men, tied together, and being dragged away. Alas, they all suffered a cruel death.

Working at several *Straff Kommandos* (punishment work) meant we were very harshly treated. It was completely exhausting and demoralising, especially since we had lost so many friends.

30 October 1944

A selection was made on 30 October 1944 for 1,200 women to be sent to Bergen-Belsen. By now our health had greatly deteriorated. The journey took several days in a cattle truck. On arrival in Bergen-Belsen, we were put into tents, sleeping on straw. During the night a storm blew away our tent and all of us were left standing in the rain.

The SS guards were very cruel. They screamed at us and hit us for no reason. Eventually, we were put into barracks and left there. We all suffered from boils and were infested with skin lice that bothered us terribly. Sometimes we got food, a watery sort of soup, but mostly there was nothing to eat. We were left to wait for death.

On 3 February 1945, some 750 of us were taken by cattle truck to Raguhn, a satellite camp of Ravensbrück, to work in an aeroplane factory. I worked as a welder. By then we were all very weak. We worked long, exhausting hours. None of the Germans showed us any compassion. The only respite was when the factory was under attack from the Allies. When this happened, we were put into shelters.

With the advance of the Allies, some of us were again put on cattle trucks to another destination. The German plan was for us to be exterminated so that none of us would survive to tell what had happened. On the journey, the train was bombed. Frightened by this attack, the guard in our truck opened the doors to save himself. I tried to escape twice, but both times to no avail. The guard threatened to shoot me in the act of trying to escape. But he didn't and I survived.

At that time, thousands of inmates were taken, often in open trucks, to other extermination camps. Each time it was to take them further and further from the Allies. Again, the Nazis wanted to leave no trace.

On 20 April 1945 we arrived eventually in Theresienstadt. We were a pitiful sight, sick and weak, like corpses. Out of 720, 250 had died on the journey. By comparison to us, the inmates of Theresienstadt looked well. Some of these people took pity on us and found us shelter and doctors. I was very ill, but I was lucky that a Czech gentleman found a doctor who came to help me and gave me some medication to try and save me. The Allies were now not far away, but most of the German guards made their escape. We had to wait until 9 May 1945, the day the war ended in Europe, to be liberated by the Russian army. Typhus was rampant amongst us, but the Russian soldiers tried very hard to save as many of us as possible.

On 31 May 1945, some of us, mostly French people, left for Pilsen where the American army took responsibility for our care.

We were repatriated by plane to Lyons on 4 June and taken immediately to the hospital, the Croix Rousse, where we were given medical care and lovely food. But we couldn't eat as our stomachs had shrunk to nothing. From there, we departed for a period of convalescence in Le Chambon sur Lignon on 17 June 1945. It is now well known that some 5,000 Jews were saved there during the occupation, having been hidden and protected by Huguenot (French Protestant) families. Tragically for us, we had no idea this was happening as we were trying to avoid arrest in 1944.

During my convalescence, the social worker and medical staff were trying to bring us back again to some kind of normal life. But we couldn't speak about the hell we had been through – in any case nobody really wanted to hear it, as they tried to put back together their own lives after the war. After three months, we had to face reality. This was a very bleak prospect. David, Armand and I were now orphans. We had nowhere to live as our house in St. Etienne had been destroyed by bombs in 1944.

We found another flat and lived there together. David got married and Armand went to Paris to study. David and I started a jewellery business together, building on our father's contacts. It was very difficult as we had no experience.

Most of my family perished in the Holocaust. Only a few cousins of my late father survived, having been in England since before the war started. I visited them several times. On one of these visits, I met my future husband, David. We married in 1950. We had two children, Sandra and Irene. Irene was born six weeks before David died at the tragically young age of 42. Sandra and Irene are now married and I have six grandchildren, aged from 15 to 24.

Like so many other survivors, it took me over 50 years to be able to confront what had happened to me and to share it with others. I do so now because if people like me do not proclaim their experiences for others to hear and to reflect upon, then future generations will not learn the lessons of these, perhaps the darkest, moments of our history.

My brother Marcel

My father

My mother.

Photos found after the Liberation in the rubble of our flat
in St. Etienne after the bombardment of the town, 1944.

To my beloved daughters,
Sandra and Irene, and their husbands Arnold and Paul,
and my grandchildren, Rachel, Avital, Michal, David, Raphael and Gabriela.
May G-d shield them from any future 'Kingdom of Night'.

Simon today aged 65, 2003

*Simon with his older brother Joseph, shortly
after the war, aged seven and nine*

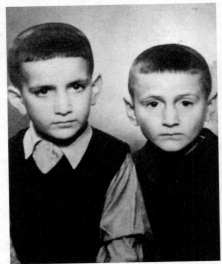

SIMON WINSTON

I was Born in Radzivillov

I was born in 1938 in a small town called Radzivillov, then part of Poland, now in the independent state of the Ukraine. In 1939 Germany invaded Poland and in 1941 the Nazis entered our town. The first thing they did was to build a ghetto there, holding some 15,000 Jews. The ghetto was surrounded by tall brick walls and barbed wire and we were not allowed out, except for those who were occasionally sent out for forced labour duties.

For the next two years we experienced and witnessed brutality and murder of an unequalled scale. I remember very little of my plight. This may be because I was very young then, or it may be that my mind has deliberately repressed such horrible experiences. I remember some incidents vividly, but I will also rely heavily on what my father told me, particularly in a testimony he wrote in 1948.

Before the war, Jews in Radzivillov worked mainly in the grain industry, as small shopkeepers, and supplied the surrounding farmsteads. Some owned their own mills, as did my grandfather. Being such a large community, Jews naturally had their own synagogues, schools and study centres. Life was quite good until 1936. Then there was an anti-Jewish "putsch" in Poland which may well have come from Nazi Germany – many ethnic Germans were then living in Poland. There was a boycott of Jewish shops, excessive taxes for Jews – all this to drive Jews from their previously sound economic situation.

At the outbreak of war on 1 September 1939, a terrible panic gripped Poland. Polish Resistance was soon smashed and large numbers of refugees fled eastwards, including many Jews. Having made a deal with Hitler, the Russian army quickly occupied the eastern part of Poland, including our town. The Jews breathed a sigh of relief because they thus avoided falling into Nazi hands.

Life in the town gradually returned to normal, but with one important difference. The Russians brought with them Stalinist Communism. This meant that all Jewish enterprises and bursaries were dissolved. Jewish schools were closed down and large comprehensive schools set up.

Together with a central library and public halls, they served to indoctrinate everyone towards Communism. Some Jews joined the Russian army and most others were involved in military work and building roads.

On 22 June 1941, Germany invaded Russia. This involved bitter battles in the Ukraine and Volhyn area where we lived. The Russian army retreated and many battalions passed through Radzivillov. Some Jews, fearing for their lives, joined the Russian army. Others tried to flee by car, horse and on foot, but only a few succeeded. Many Jews fleeing from other towns finished up in Radzivillov and by then the Jewish population increased to more than 20,000.

On 29 June 1941, German boots were heard on the stone pathways of our town. The Ukrainian population, grateful to be liberated from the Russians and hoping to become independent, cheered the oncoming German army, shouting, "Our saviours have arrived." The Ukrainians started looting the old co-operatives and soon took delight in looting Jewish homes and pointing them out to the Germans.

In early July 1941, a German commandant was appointed for our town, and along with him came some SS men. Soon after they arrived, antisemitic regulations were issued:

1) Jews must wear white armbands with a blue Star of David.

2) Jews must hand in all radios.

3) Jews must not leave the town.

The death penalty was threatened for not carrying out these regulations. We immediately felt helpless and cut off from the rest of the world.

Gestapo men arrived on 15 July 1941 and demanded a list of names and addresses of "especially dangerous Jews". The Ukrainians quickly put together a list of 200 Jews and a separate list of well-to-do Jews. On the lists, for the most part, were Jews with whom the Ukrainians had personal scores to settle.

That day Gestapo thugs chased out a group of Jews towards the Brody Forest, near the Radzivillov-Brody railroad, handed them shovels and ordered them to dig a large ditch. When the ditch was finished, the frightened Jews were told to run home quickly. Halfway home they heard shooting and wretched outcries from the unfortunate victims. This was reported by one of the Jews who dug the ditch.

The next day, a band of Ukrainians went to the large synagogue, threw all the Torah scrolls out onto the street and set fire to them. A second group took the rabbi and forced him to dance around the fire. After this shameful deed, Jews were further humiliated by being forced to do all the dirty work – sweeping the streets and digging trenches – whilst German soldiers supervised their labour.

On 15 August 1941, a Jewish committee was formed, called the *Judenraat*. Although its members tried to help ease the pain and poor conditions of their fellow Jews, they were in fact selected and supervised by the Nazis, thus concealing the real intent: to subjugate and kill off all the Jews as smoothly as possible.

Later that month there was a visit to Radzivillov by high-ranking Gestapo. An order was issued that all Jews, young and old, healthy and sick, must present themselves within two hours at the market square, on pain of death. They were then force-marched to Waldman's Yard, and by the same order had to leave their homes unlocked. Waldman's Yard was then locked up. Suddenly, as if from nowhere, a battalion of Gestapo men carrying machine guns appeared. A terrible panic broke out amongst us. We started to cry and were bidding a last farewell to each other.

We were squeezed together like herrings in a barrel, but then suddenly our situation took a turn for the better. A high-ranking officer came and spoke to the leader of the Gestapo unit. The doors were opened; we were let out in rows and lined up in the market square. The machine guns were removed and the Ukrainian militia was charged with sending us to work.

Thus, as it turned out, we only suffered fright that day. But when the Jews went home from work, they found that their homes had been ransacked. Anything of the slightest value had been carted away. A few days later, posters announced that within two days, Jews must turn in all gold, silver and other valuables to the local authority.

On 20 December 1941, an order from the Nazi Commissioner decreed that round, yellow patches were to replace the white armbands, to be worn on the left side of the chest and on the back.

By this time Jewish morale was as low as possible and this was compounded by Nazi soldiers who plundered the last vestiges of our previous existence, such as wedding rings and semi-precious keepsakes. Any still reasonably healthy Jews were commissioned to labour camps in the district. They were away for weeks and some never came back.

There was further distress on 5 March 1942. Eighty local peasants, headed by a Ukrainian police chief and his men, entered the town and ordered all Jews out of their houses. The Ukrainians then entered the houses and took away anything of value, including all our furniture. We now had nothing left. News soon filtered through about the mass slaughter of Jews in other towns and this weighed heavily on our weary and tortured minds. Would we be next?

On 9 April 1942, the few completely Jewish streets were surrounded with barbed wire. All Jews had to move into those streets and this became the ghetto. For an entire day, Jews dragged themselves and their various bundles of torn rags and broken kitchenware. The *Judenraat* was empowered to allocate the housing and settle everyone in the ghetto. Every Jew was supposed to get just two square metres of housing. But because the committee set aside some buildings for itself, each person could only receive 1.8 sq. metres of space. Living conditions were terribly cramped and there was no room for broken pieces of furniture.

The quarter set aside for the ghetto was the poorest in the town with low houses. Essential furnishings such as ovens were often shared and made up part of each person's 1.8 sq. metres. Living and sleeping conditions were very cramped. Bunk beds were arranged, but because the rooms were so low, there was very little air to breathe.

The large synagogue, which was within the ghetto, was turned into a German military warehouse which Jews themselves had to guard. The ghetto itself was divided into three sections which could only be entered through two gates, one directly opposite the other.

At first, with *Judenraat* consent, Jews could live wherever they wished in the ghetto. A week later, however, an order was issued that only useful workers, the so-called "useful Jews", should live together on one side of the ghetto. The "useful Jews" were issued special passes. People began to check why these passes were being issued and soon found out that those murdered in Rovno and other towns had not had passes. In fact, the only ones left alive were those with passes. Thus a desperate rush for passes started.

At 4 a.m. on 30 June 1942, we realized that our fate had come. Heavy military steps could be heard from the direction of the station. About 30 SS men were approaching one of the gates. They surrounded the ghetto and then shooting and yelling was heard. In panic, some Jews ran for cover or to escape. They were soon shot down and their wailing death cries could be heard all around. Meanwhile, the murderers were mercilessly beating up whoever they came across. The SS men ran from house to house shouting, *"Raus! 'Raus!"* (Out! Out!), chasing everybody onto the streets. Anyone who tried to hide and was discovered was shot dead.

Everyone was brutally herded from the streets to the synagogue court-yard. Here the men were separated from the women and children. The old and the helplessly sick were shot on the spot and tossed onto wagons. The fit men were marched out of the ghetto towards a train standing nearby.

At first we thought the Jews were being taken to the train. There was hope. But at the intersection, it was clear that they were being driven in another direction, towards the Radzivillov Plain – the killing fields. Two large, deep ditches had already been prepared there, approximately 50 x 20 metres, on the north side of the plain. To this "Gala event", all the notables of the town had come.

Then the murderers began their bloody work. In a bestial manner, whips flaying and with wild shouts, they forced the Jews to take off all their clothes, move to the edge of the lime-covered ditch and throw themselves in. All around stood SS men with automatic weapons, shooting the unfortunates into the ditch. Not all were killed by the bullets and even more were not hit at all. Still alive, and splashed with the blood of other victims, they also fell into the ditch. Soon all were covered with earth and vanished forever from the world. That was the fate of the men of our unfortunate town in this first "Action".

The women and children from this section of the ghetto (Ghetto 1) remained all this time in the synagogue courtyard which was surrounded by Ukrainian police. Their convulsive wails and cries could be heard all around. They knew what had happened. They awaited the return of the murderers of their menfolk, wondering when they themselves would be led to the slaughter.

At 8.00 a.m. the women and children were marched away in the same direction. They were to suffer the same fate as their husbands, fathers and brothers. When the women and children finally arrived at the plain, two large ditches confronted them – one recently filled with earth, the other empty, newly dug and lime-covered.

With their last breaths, the women wailed and cried in anguish at what was about to happen. A few went mad on the spot. They followed their menfolk and a freshly made hill covered these poor souls too. Their murderers left the killing field and wrote a report which eventually found its way to Adolf Hitler. It confirmed that in a corner of some open countryside, near a small wood, on the road between Radzivillov and the Radzivillov Plain, 2,540 Jews were killed and buried.

The guard at Ghetto 1 was re-established, even though there were no longer any residents there. As early as 11.00 a.m. that day, many frightened Jews were driven from Ghetto 2 to Ghetto 1. Their task was to cover up all traces of the bloodshed and extermination, and to restore order in the streets and courtyards.

My father was one of those sent out to restore order. At the first opportunity he ran to the house where his parents had last lived. He searched for them in various hiding places he had prepared in anticipation of such a calamitous event. One hiding place was a woodshed which he had camouflaged with wood chippings – but they weren't there. All his searching was in vain. They had perished with the others whose bodies were to be found in two mass graves.

The situation of those who remained in Ghetto 2 got worse from day to day and they could only live one day at a time. Huddled in close ranks, they continued to go out to work in the town, escorted by Ukrainian and

Jewish police. To add to their humiliation, these Jews would be led down the middle of the streets, like cattle, because they were not allowed to walk on the pavements.

The whole ghetto then went through a terrifying time because news filtered through that a children's "Action" was being prepared. Everybody began hiding children wherever they possibly could. My mother and father would split us up – my brother, aged six, and myself, four years old – and take us to their separate places of work. My father found a hiding place for my brother in the sawmill. My mother would try to hide me where she worked. My father was close to being discovered on a number of occasions, but his sixth sense enabled him to perceive danger and he managed always to be one step ahead.

On 5 June 1942, the Labour leader came to the ghetto to recruit workers for the Rovno labour camps. About 40 people were sent away but almost none of them returned. They met their deaths where they worked. One person who escaped reported that they had worked for the entire time in a closed camp. When the work was finished, they were surrounded by Ukrainians and SS men who led them off and shot them.

At that time, different diseases spread through the ghetto. This was mainly due to the very cramped living conditions. There was a scarcity of water, and in what remained of the ghetto, there was only one well. The pump was often out of order and deep mud puddles made it very difficult to access the well.

Elsewhere, the extermination of Jews in the region of Volhynia drew ever nearer. We were hearing reports of full-scale liquidation. Volhynian towns, one after the other, were becoming *Judenrein* (Jew-free).

On about 14 July 1942, an SS squad came to our ghetto, accompanied by the local SS and Ukrainian police. Their first act was to enter the houses of the Jews and take out everything, including food. These items were placed on wagons and carted away. From what we had heard from other towns, this was the signal that our own town was about to become *Judenrein*. A desperate urge to flee and hide ensued.

Some hiding places had been planned and negotiated a long time ago, but these were very scarce and often unreliable. These "places" were usually promises from local peasants who had been entrusted with Jewish possessions and promised remuneration.

A chase for places began. In those terrible days, dealing in "places" became commonplace. Anyone who knew a peasant who "had a good name" and was "reliable", became a power in the ghetto. Secretive talks were held between people who still had some hidden reserves and those who had "places". The first concern had to be the possibility to get food, at least for the initial stage of any attempted escape. The ghetto was now completely without food. Previously reliable sources came to the rescue and these were often the same Christians who would later provide "places".

The next most important items were falsified Aryan papers. My mother and father were lucky to be able to acquire such papers, and on them gave their names as Ivan and Maria Ivanyuk. But not all who had these papers survived. Some did not leave the ghetto early enough. Others perished because they could not fit properly into the surroundings. A few were caught because they were recognized by their former Ukrainian neighbours, who then turned them in to the Gestapo. Yet some did manage to survive by using Aryan papers.

By far the majority neither possessed nor knew about the existence of Aryan papers, nor "places". Tragically their fate was sealed because there was no escape for them. The young among them talked bravely about putting up some resistance. They had nothing left to lose and refused to allow themselves to be slaughtered like sheep.

At the end of September 1942, we learned that Russian prisoners of war were being detailed to dig more trenches on the plain. The uncertainty in the ghetto reached a climax. People saw no way out for themselves but suicide – rather than endure the horrors that others had suffered before them. There was a mad rush for poison – arsenic, cyanide, some other lethal brew – to rid oneself of the suffering.

This was also the time when some Jews started to escape. When the authorities found out, they added extra guards and completely surrounded the ghetto. A few hours earlier, my father and brother left the main ghetto, went into the destroyed section of Ghetto I, and hid in the attic of a little house. As previously planned, my mother and I soon joined them. Meanwhile we could hear the search that was going on for escaped Jews. Ukrainian police brutally beat anyone outside the main ghetto and threw their bodies back inside.

A few Jews managed to escape to Brody, a town where some Jews still lived. A month earlier, a mass "Action" had taken place there, in which more than 3,000 Jews had been taken away, in closed, tightly packed freight wagons to Belzec in Galicia, where they were exterminated in gas chambers. My mother's parents and brother were included in this convoy.

Those who had escaped from the Radzivillov ghetto made their way through the Brody Forest, mostly by night, and reached Brody in the morning. Many, less fortunate, were shot and killed by the Ukrainian guards whilst trying to escape. When we left the attic to make our way there, my father first went to a peasant he knew. His name was Feishulia, a carpenter's son. He refused to let us into his house but was kind enough to show us how to get to Brody more safely. We would have to cross the river and avoid the main roads, because they were manned by ruthless Ukrainian police.

At the river we met about 15 Jews. We warned them not to stay there because they would be caught, but they stubbornly refused to move. Taking his life in his hands, my father entered the river to see how deep it was. The water reached his neck. He came back and carried each one of us – hands in the air – until we were all across. We had to stop because our clothes were wet and there was the danger of arousing suspicion when passing through the next village. At that moment a Ukrainian woman came over to us. Seeing our plight, she kindly let us into her house and gave us temporary shelter.

We eventually arrived in Brody where we found some Jews still living in their original homes, together with other families who had lost theirs. My father had the foresight to split us up so that we lived in two different places. That way it would be more difficult to be recognized by the Radzivillov police who often came over to Brody looking for escaped Jews. There was one occasion when they spotted an escaped Radzivillov Jew, took him back and led him through the streets with a placard tied around his neck containing shameful, anti-Jewish slogans.

The small network of Jews who escaped from the Radzivillov ghetto then searched for willing and trustworthy Ukrainians who would be prepared to hide Jews – at a price. This required some form of practical exchange currency. To this end my father and others had earlier prepared small gold bars, hidden in the false bottoms of shoes, in brushes and in other places. This was the currency of survival, and I am alive today as proof that it worked.

We were in hiding for more than two years. When my father found an agreeable protector, he would give details of how he wanted the survival bunker to be made, and how large. Some bunkers were larger when more than one family was to be hidden. Usually the bunker would be well disguised, such as under a pig sty.

I remember on one occasion, we were outside a farmhouse when an alert was sounded to warn us that a group of soldiers was approaching. We were rushed into our bunker under a pig sty and the trap door was closed and covered over. We soon heard the voices of German soldiers above us and at one stage, there was a profusion of warm liquid cascading down upon us. We were later told that the Germans had urinated on us!

Our protectors were mostly farmers and we sometimes made friends with the children of the farm. One day, we were playing hide-and-seek in a cornfield. I took up a hiding place in the corn and waited. To my dismay, the other children had fled and I was discovered by a group of Ukrainian police. They asked me what I was doing. I said that I was playing hide-and-seek and that my friends were coming to get me. They accepted my explanation and left. The miracle was that I was able to speak to those men at all in fluent Ukrainian, which was not my native tongue.

Most of the time we were not allowed out of our bunker in daylight. Our protectors were afraid – our detection would mean their death too. There were frequent visits by German soldiers or Ukrainian police and we would have to stay absolutely silent for hours.

Just before the war finally ended, the Russians liberated the Volhyn-Galicia area and we were free. But we hadn't anywhere to go. Radzivillov and Brody were hostile places for us. The Russians didn't know what to do with us. We eventually finished up in a refugee camp in Rovno where other Jewish survivors had gathered. For another two years we moved from one Displaced Persons (DP) Camp to another. We asked to go to Palestine, but this was rejected. Our last DP Camp was Hoffgeismar in Germany.

Fortunately I had an uncle, my mother's older brother, who wisely had had the foresight to escape Nazi Europe before the war started. He made great efforts to take us out of an embattled and embittered Germany. In November 1947 we were eventually allowed into Britain on Displaced Persons' passports. My father found regular work in a flour mill in Nottingham and five years later we became naturalised Britons.

Our ordeal had a lasting effect on our health and our state of mind. My mother suffered continually from chronic asthma and bronchitis and died in 1954. My brother lost the sight in one eye. My father had the strongest will of all of us. He was ever pragmatic, showed great foresight and had a strong sense of survival. We owed our lives to him. He died in Israel, aged 84.

We survived the Holocaust, but we lost nearly all our relatives and friends. We lost our health, our sanity and our dignity – and I lost my childhood.

After arriving in Britain, my family didn't talk much about their plight during the war – only with relatives and close friends. I myself never brought up the subject publicly for over 40 years. It was a distasteful and humiliating experience. The bitterness was always there, but we had to integrate into a new country and a new way of life. I had to get on with my own life and not dwell on the murky past. I studied and eventually became a secondary school teacher of Maths and Special Needs.

Then, a few years ago, I heard about Beth Shalom, the newly opened Holocaust Centre. It was not far from where I lived, so I decided to visit the place and I met the Smith family. I recognized immediately the sincerity with which they had undertaken the task of telling the world what had happened, and what can still happen if we don't learn from the past.

I handed over to Stephen Smith my father's manuscript and he was very moved. More than that, he made me feel that our story was worth telling, and then I took on a more active role at Beth Shalom. I have spoken there occasionally, including to students from local schools, and my story was published in the local newspaper, *The Nottingham Evening Post*. I feel more fulfilled and I am no longer inhibited by the past. The genie has come out of the bottle!

I applaud everything the Smith family have done and are still doing. They have treated the matter of genocide with reverence and have placed it on an international platform for everyone to take note, examine and learn from. They have done this with dignity, professionalism and courage and, in these troubled times, if nobody else can save this crazy world, perhaps the Smiths can!

Happier times. Simon, third right, with Jewish friends in Nottingham, circa 1956-8

Stanley Bullard's sculpture, 'Hidden Childhood', in the garden of Beth Shalom, inspired by Simon Winston's story.

NOTES FOR TEACHERS

This collection of survivor testimonies provides an invaluable resource for both teachers and students studying the Holocaust. The testimonies contain personal accounts and reflections on a heinous episode in history. They provide stimulus not only for the study of history but also for citizenship and literacy. By looking at individual and collective testimonies, teachers and pupils can also focus upon particular aspects of the Holocaust, for example, *Kristallnacht*, life under Nazi rule, antisemitism, the *Kindertransports*, the experiences of hidden children, life in the ghettoes and concentration camps, and liberation experiences. Themes of this kind can be explored across several testimonies using the Index as a guide.

We recommmend that teachers provide some further explanation of context to increase accessibility and depth of understanding for students.

The following suggestions for using the testimonies are by no means exhaustive, but intended to stimulate further activities and discussion.

History

1. Pupils could construct timelines of individual lives to look in detail at some personal experiences.
2. Stages of discrimination and types of persecution could be identified and discussed.
3. Pupils could identify acts of resistance, discussing and explaining the difficulties of these acts.
4. Two or more accounts could be compared to look at similarities and differences of survivors from the same or different countries.
5. Pupils could discuss the idea of a "Jewish experience" or if such a thing exists.
6. Post war issues could be discussed: eg how to punish those involved and what decisions were made by the Allies.
7. Biographies could be researched of those who played a role in rescuing some survivors.

8. Use the Westerbork alphabet to determine what was important to children in the camp, and why?

Citizenship

1. Pupils could identify examples of what they feel were the acts of a good citizen.
2. Pupils could discuss what the Nazis viewed as acts of a good citizen, and then discuss why they think the two examples are so different.
3. Acts of resistance could be identified and why there were not more of them.
4. The role of the international community and their responsibility in the Holocaust could be discussed.
5. The lives of the survivors post-Holocaust can be discussed, particularly with reference to the debate surrounding present day asylum seekers.
6. Pupils can explore the issues of blame and responsibility for the Holocaust. Who should be punished for the crimes and how?

Literacy

1. Pupils could write empathetic accounts based on other people identified in the survivor testimonies, e.g. the account of someone who helped a survivor.
2. Pupils could dramatise scenes from the testimonies.
3. Responses, either in prose or poem form, could be written by pupils.
4. Pupils could also write ghetto diaries which describe the experiences of those survivors who were in the ghetto.
5. Newspapers could be created by pupils for those in the camps and the ghettos, like the ones produced in the Warsaw ghetto and Theresienstadt.

These are just some suggestions for teaching activities. Above all, it is important to emphasise that each survivor's testimony and experience was unique and personal. The testimonies should be used to reinforce the fact that the Holocaust was not just about numbers but about people – people who for the benefit of future generations have had the courage to tell their individual stories.

Welcome to The Holocaust Centre, Beth Shalom

Memorial Gardens, Beth Shalom

"Abandoned", a sculpture by survivor Naomi Blake

The Gateway of the Righteous, set in the Memorial Gardens

The Children's Memorial, where visitors can place a stone in remembrance of the 1,500,000 children who lost their lives at the hands of the Nazis and their collaborators.

INDEX